Angels
Lies

The inspirational story of
how lies and neglect can
destroy an entire family. Of
triumph over evil, and
the resilience and
determination of damaged
children

sandy brown

I wish to dedicate this book to my husband Gordon for believing in me, and providing me with endless cups of coffee, and toast. To my granddaughter for the inspiration I received every time I looked into her big brown eyes.

My parents who are now true Angels!

Acknowledgements.
Author's Note.
Prologue.
Poem.
Chapter One – The Perfect Childhood.
Chapter Two – Sudden Adulthood.
Chapter Three – A Country Girl with a City Life.
Chapter Four – Motherhood.
Chapter Five – Rescue and Reprieve.
Chapter Six – The Phoenix Rises.
Chapter Seven – Faith, Belief and Conversion.
Chapter Eight – Loss Takes Many Forms.
Chapter Nine – Moving On.
Chapter Ten – Bitter Sweet.
Chapter Eleven – A Merciless Angel.
Chapter Twelve – A New Generation.
Chapter Thirteen – Mixed Blessings
Chapter Fourteen - Empty Nest Refilled
Chapter Fifteen – Venomous Repercussions
Chapter Sixteen – Monumental Changes
Chapter Seventeen – Death Life and Trauma
Chapter Eighteen – What a Tangled Web
Chapter Nineteen – Hell's Not Full Yet
Chapter Twenty - Fragmentation
Chapter Twenty One – Forget Retirement
Chapter Twenty Two – A professional Approach
Chapter Twenty Three – Old Friends – New Beginnings
Chapter Twenty Four – A New Life – Or The Final Solution

Chapter Twenty Five – The Icing On The Cake
Ten Top Tips for Successful Parenting
Epilogue
Poem Conclusion

The writing of this book has been quite literally many years, and much heartache in the making. It has taken a lifetime for these events to take place, and many times along the way I have often said, "I could write a book!" until one day, someone actually replied "Why don't you?" My deepest thanks therefore, goes to Jane, of The Agency's Sheffield Office, for constantly encouraging me to put pen to paper, and telling me, I *could* do it. This made me stop and take stock of life's bumpy journey.

I would like to thank my long-suffering husband, Gordon, for the endless cups of coffee and refreshment which gave me sustenance. For the tedious copying and printing, and sorting out my laptop each time it freaked out on me. For believing in me when I didn't believe in my own abilities, and encouraging me to keep going.

Thanks to Chelsea, for guiding me around the complexities of the computer and educating me on how to correct errors, for there were many along the way.

To Andrea for inspiration, and the many 'nail' repairs frequently required, following the ravages of the keyboard.

To Xanthe, for her unconditional love, and to all the other children for being mindful of the days when I needed quiet time to concentrate. But to all of them for their love and support, not to mention all the children whose memories are immortalised herein.

A great deal of thanks and appreciation goes also to The Agency in Yorkshire and Lincolnshire for their support, and endless training, in *everything* needed to carry out our task professionally.

Strangely, last but not least, thanks to my dysfunctional family for making me appreciate life more, and in the process, 'providing' the material for this book.
I knew there had to be some purpose to all this. They have been the source of so much grief over the years, and yet without their unique makeup, I would not have been inspired to analyse the awful truth. I would, however prefer them *not* to provide material for a sequel. Here it must end! However, watch this space.

I truly hope the words contained herein will be helpful to others, for there are many lessons to be learned. Most of all, thanks to you, the reader for taking the time to listen.

AUTHOR'S NOTE

Some of the names, places, and time scales in this book have been changed in order to protect the innocent, and in doing so, have also protected the guilty.

This book is a work of non-fiction based on the life, experiences and recollections of the author, the contents of which are true events.

As I stand in this awful place, I watch with fascination as the colony of snails creeps up and down, devouring the egg which has festooned itself down Dora's kitchen window. A myriad kamikaze flies have taken up occupancy and are buzzing around my head as they home in on the sugar and jam, which are sitting, vulnerable and naked on the worktop. Their little feet are struggling to manoeuvre in the gelatinous covering of grease, nestling in solidified pools on the cooker, despite these also being coated with a fine carpet of clinging dust. I struggle to breathe through the stench arising from the commode, which is sitting next to the sink.

In the midst of despair, I can't help thinking what an excellent job the snails would have done of cleaning this now opaque window, had it not been for the trail of silvery ribbons they have left behind them, though at least these have some pleasant decorative value in these grim surroundings, as the sun plays on their rainbow of colours. There I go again, turning the negative into positive.

My mind clicks back to reality as Dora's fourteen year old grandson, Leo, volunteers to 'clean' the window. Had he noticed my despair? Had he in his teenage wisdom *known* how I felt at that precise moment? I had dealt with many traumas in my life which had led me to where I am now, but I was getting older, and not so wiser, as to working out solutions to the continuing concerns I now felt for Dora. She had struggled all her life, one way or another. There have been times when I have cried for her, protected her, been angry with her, but now I just despaired. This lifestyle could not continue, her health, even her life, could be in danger.

This was a different kitchen, in a different house, yet I could not forget earlier, similar traumas, when Dora's kitchen had caught fire. The chip pan sat, as always, atop the cooker. The cat had leapt up, using the cooker top as a 'stepping stone' to reach his favourite spot on the top of the freezer, to curl up out of everyone's way, but alas had caught the knob with his paw and unwittingly lit the gas ring under the resting chip pan. The hot oil had ignited, the ensuing conflagration gutting the entire kitchen, which then burnt itself out, but not before *melting* the freezer top and the cooker itself, blackening the walls and everything in it's path. Sophie, the black and white cat, had perished where she lay in her bed. Prince, the white guy, had sensibly and instinctively put his nose to the bottom of the door to draw in what little air made itself available through the gap beneath, this is how he survived. His little pink nose and tongue were now black, and he rasped as he struggled to breathe in my arms.

The closed kitchen door, to keep in the cats overnight, was what had saved the lives of Dora, Tina and Leo as they slept away their Sunday morning in the next room, totally unaware of the destruction that had raged around them. This time I had to enlist the help of others. I was all out of ideas; my days of rescue and reprieve were spent and worn out. I would now need to draw on past experience for a solution to this, perhaps the final solution.

What happened? I ask myself as I often sit and reflect on the past. My early life was wonderful, I felt loved, and I loved in return. My family were the best, and my childhood was filled with happy and amusing memories. I try so hard to remember when events took a turn for the worst, but I'm still at a loss to decide which of the tragedies strikes at the core of my happiness the most.

There were many ups and downs in my past and as I deal with today's traumas with mundane regularity, I look forward to sitting quietly when evening comes, with a glass of wine, and remembering those I loved who are now gone, and I wonder what they would make of my present life.

Where do I begin? And how far back should I go? I think I'll go right back to the beginning and start with happier times. After all, it is those memories that keep me going, that inspire me to this day to realise from where my strengths originate and how that and life's experiences should serve me. I know only too well how important it is to search for the positive within the most negative.

I'll go to bed now, and tomorrow another day of the traumas and incidents which have now become so ordinary, will unfold.

ANGELS DO TELL LIES!

Beware, when you listen to secretive things,

For Devils have horns, and Angels have wings.

They'll tell you a tale, they'll tell you it's true,

But mayhem and chaos is *bound* to ensue.

For truth must be proved, the facts must come out,

The result mustn't leave you with one ounce of doubt.

You *must* know by now, that Angels tell Lies!

Or are they just Devils, in disguise?

Chapter One

The Perfect Childhood

It was an idyllic childhood for my sister Dora and me. Nothing it seemed could be more perfect than growing up in this small village in the Derbyshire countryside. It was a lush green valley surrounded by hills which took on a new perspective with each season of the year. Throughout all the seasons, their mystic shapes were enhanced with the variegated green hues of the ferns, interspersed with primroses or bluebells, and as a child I marvelled at the dozens of different varieties of grasses. In autumn, the ferns would turn to bracken and the hillsides would be covered in a mixture of gold with the purple of the heather breaking through in spring. However, my favourite season, but only out of the window from inside, was winter. The never ending fields would be protected by a blanket of pure virgin snow, almost like a white fleece thrown over it all.

Looking out from within, and the warmth of a log fire, my window frame transformed the scene into the most beautiful picture out there. It was great fun to venture outside after a heavy snowfall, to check out the fresh footprints of birds, foxes and rabbits, plus the occasional cat. When my feet pressed down to break through the crisp, ice topped blanket it reminded me of meringue, and how it feels, biting into it for the first time.

Our family came to be in this beautiful place, long before I did, as my maternal grandparents settled here from the Welsh valleys at the turn of the century. Work was scarce in those days, and a huge project was beginning here which brought work to many families. Reservoirs were being created in the valley and my grandfather was a Blacksmith by trade, therefore there would be plenty of work here for him, and a living to be made, for his ever growing family. The work began in the Derwent Valley and several villages were going to be demolished and flooded to form the reservoirs. Viaducts were needed, roads, sophisticated filtration systems, for this would provide drinking water for a very large area.

Of course all of this was going to take many years to complete, therefore these men and their family's would need homes, and so they set about building a temporary village called Birchinlee. The entire village was constructed of pre-fabricated huts, yet they would house entire families. Quite a little community soon sprang up amongst the workers and their wives and children. There was a village hall, a sweet shop, even an isolation hospital, for there were, in those days before vaccination, such contagious diseases as polio, diphtheria and smallpox.

The work must have been heavy and labour intensive for my grandfather, yet despite this he and my grandmother managed to produce nine children during those hard years, but sadly not all survived. One child at least, died here in Birchinlee, her name was Emily and she would have been the first of three girls, the rest were boys.

When the reservoirs of Derwent, Howden and Ladybower were almost complete the growing family moved home with their surviving children to the nearby village of Bradwell in the Hope Valley, and settled in a tiny cottage high on the hill. It was in
this village that their youngest child was born – my mother.

Grandfather took up his role as village Blacksmith, and as my mother grew, she would help him as a child, working the huge leather bellows which made his fire white hot! This enabled him to create brassware, gates etc., and shoes for the horses which led the milk and coal carts. Eventually, there was the need to find a larger home. The little cottage's thick stone walls were bulging with children, so they moved to 'Brook Buildings', which was a larger 'proper' house, much more able to accommodate this expanding family.

Now there were times unbelievably, when my grandparents didn't speak to each other, and would communicate via the children. At the supper table the children would pass a message from mum to dad, to pass the salt/sugar/sauce etc., and vice versa. Apparently, my mother much later told me, that her parents didn't speak to each other directly for *two whole years*! This was obviously *after* they had produced and completed their brood!

As the years passed, the children grew into adults, then married and left home one by one, until my mother, being the youngest, was the only sibling left. However, she eventually met and married my father, Tim, who had moved from Hull, in Yorkshire to work at the local cement factory. He was a handsome man, slim with wavy red hair and a ready wit. They lived together with my grandparents, until they, Catherine and William died, after which my parents continued to live in the 'proper' house, alone. It was large, and so damp that the wallpaper would peel away from the walls, but there was little choice then, and one didn't complain to the landlord for fear of being evicted. Even my early memories were of dim little gas mantles that glimmered on the walls, for electricity was a rare commodity. The toilet was situated in a little hut at the top of the garden, nothing more than a wooden board with a hole in the middle. Being economical meant unceremoniously using cut-up pieces of the

Beano or Dandy to be used as toilet paper. It was cut into neat squares and pierced at the corner with a piece of string pulled through, which meant we could hang it on the 6" rusty nail by the door, but in fact, it was no worse that the Izal variety, which was an occasional luxury.

It was around now that my parents had their first daughter. Dora was an exceptionally beautiful child, slender, with strawberry blonde hair, bluey green eyes and freckles. She was the first of my parent's children, the apple of their eye! Life was as good as it could be, despite these being the war years with rationing etc. The family had a roof over their heads, dad had a good job and although it would be a struggle at times, the daily grind continued. On Friday nights, the tin bath would be taken down from yet another useful nail on which it hung, outside on the wall, and brought into the kitchen, to be placed in front of the roaring log fire. The gas boiler would be lit to heat up the water for the bath. Everyone would take turns to bathe in the *same* water, topped up now and then from the ever bubbling boiler, until they were all squeaky clean. The house was pleasantly situated opposite the village church, by a babbling brook. On the corner of the bridge stood Hancock's grocery store, where we could buy sugar and flour, which would be weighed out into blue paper bags, and butter and cheese would be cut with a wire, from a huge block,

freshly churned and 'patted' into shape and size with wooden paddles, and a criss-cross or wonderful 'thistle' pattern would emerge.
I would visit the shop with my mother and watch with fascination as bacon was sliced so thinly on the big circular machine. Two ounces of sweets could be weighed out from the rows of tantalising jars on the shelf, and put into a little cone shaped bag, folded at the top so neatly, in exchange for a three-penny bit. The choice was at times impossible to make. Dolly Mixtures, Floral Gums, Satin Cushions, and the beautiful rainbow coloured sherbet, that dissolved on your tongue, so sharp, it caused involuntary contortions of the facial muscles. On the opposite corner of the bridge, in complete contrast was Bradwell's Ice Cream Shop! This was the humble beginning of the now famous country-wide brand. Mr. Bradwell would create his secret recipe in a shed by the brook, and produce it in milk churns, roll them across to the little shop and in no time at all, the churn would be emptied. The yellow, buttery, creamy delight was so irresistible it would have been scooped and sold before it could even thaw.

This was a very right-knit community, the way small villages are, and everyone was very well aware of the skeletons in each other's cupboards, but as far as I can now recall, there were *no* skeletons in our cupboards. It was a very hardworking and well respected family. It was in the years and months that followed that my mother conceived and lost three more children, including a set of twins, but seven years after Dora, along came another, surviving child, chubbier than Dora but with the same big blue eyes and freckles, the strawberry blonde hair which soon turned to snow-white tight curls. This child was me! So here we were my mother and father, Dora and me, living in the 'proper' although damp house, together.

Now the Welsh are known for their beautiful singing voices and my family were no exception. My mother had the most ethereal soprano voice and her sister Gwyneth could play any tune on the piano without a single sheet of music, she was what you would call truly gifted. Together they would perform at various venues and always gathered around the piano along with the rest of the family at such times as Christmas or important family occasions. The local community would always encourage them to perform wherever they went, and so in 1947 they were accepted for audition to appear on the 'Carol Levis Show' in Manchester at the BBC studios, a sort of earlier 'Opportunity Knocks' or 'X Factor'. They prepared to travel the next morning but when they arose, although it was day, the windows were darkened by snow! This was the notorious winter of 1947, and no-one could get out of the house, and even if they had, their route over the Derbyshire moors would have been impassable.

The snow had drifted above the windows and doors. Their opportunity for fame was gone!

Those early years were placid and happy, and as I grew I would sit with my dad and make rugs from pieces of fabric cut from old coats etc, which would no longer fit. These 'memory' rugs would never wear out, just like our love. Dad would make toys carved from wood whenever he wasn't working as a laboratory technician at the cement factory in the next village. He had grown up in a very poor family. The youngest of thirteen children meant food was often short. The children would therefore take a trip to the docks in Hull where they lived and the sailors on the incoming cargo ships would allow them to eat the bananas etc. so long as they didn't take them on shore, they were breaking no laws. As he grew older his mother made sure he could cook and sew to perfection. When I wasn't making rugs with dad, I would love to help mum with the dusting on the condition that she would sing my favourite song, Ave Maria, as we worked. I loved to hear her perfect voice, and she
would have a secret stash of chocolate flakes in her makeup drawer, which was my reward if I had done a good job. Life couldn't be better.

Although Dora and I would now be the only siblings, we did have cousins, and a very large extended family which were close, so there were many loving aunts and uncles dotted around and so our numbers were great. There was Jayne, who was the eldest cousin in the village, and then Dora was the next one down in age, then Julie, Carla and little me. Jayne was the cousin I adored, and in my childhood years would respect and try to emulate her the most. I would stay over at her house, and we would read together before going to sleep. Julie and I would play together now and then, and Carla – well now, Carla, therein lies another story. However, clothes were passed from one to the other as they were outgrown. The hems would be taken up, and then down, seams taken in then let out again, and guess who had the dubious privilege of wearing them the last?

At the age of five I started school. I didn't have far to go, right across the road, next to the church. In fact the school was run by the Church of England. Each day, we would be taken to pray and made to look upon the effigies displayed on the cross beams high up in the wooden rafters of the church. The centre figure was that of Jesus, portrayed with blood pouring from his head hands and feet, stretched out on a 'cross', this instrument of torture and death. His face looked so desolate and forlorn. Beside him was Mary, his mother, and Mary Magdalene, on their knees weeping and desperate. The vicar's thunderous voice would announce; "Jesus died for *you*, and we must give thanks!" I couldn't understand, and no-one seemed able or willing to explain to me *just* why Jesus died for *me*, because *I* certainly didn't wish anyone to have suffered such pain on my account, and I didn't even know Jesus! If we had forgotten our bonnets, we would be made to tie a knot into each corner of our hanky, and put it on our head. Why? No-one explained. Now, as if this was not confusing enough for me as a child, my mother was a practising Methodist and would also take us to Chapel. However, I couldn't join the choir at chapel, because I went to the church school etc., etc. This was to affect my beliefs later on, but my mother would exercise her God-given soprano voice in the chapel choir, on a Sunday and my enjoyment of this was enough to encourage me to conform to each religion as it pleased everyone else. Another part of daily school routine was having our milk delivered by the local farmer, who would load up the churns on his horse and cart, then roll them down into the school yard. We would all line up with our little beakers. Mine was pink, and had a little piece of red wool on the handle to be easily recognised. Dora was 'milk monitor' and would take our beakers in turn, and scoop up a measure of the sickly tasting milk which was still warm from the cow. I was very proud that it was my sister who had this honour; it was a very important job. We didn't have exercise books to begin with; we had little slates with wooden frames, and pieces of chalk which would sit in grooves along the top of the wooden desk. During our cold valley winters, there was a large iron stove in the corner of the classroom, encircled by a wire cage which enabled the heat to reach us, but our freezing little fingers could not be injured by the flying sparks as the teacher fed the huge iron monster with coal and logs which were piled up in the corner. However, comes summer, we would often have our lessons out in the schoolyard, or take a nature walk and sit in the field.

Schooldays were otherwise reasonably enjoyable, but one morning as I prepared for

the daily routine, washing my face in the china bowl, on the marble washstand which stood in the corner of the damp bedroom, I felt familiar pains in my legs. I had had twinges now and then, but my mother would assure me that these were 'growing pains' and were quite normal. Mum called to me to hurry or I would be late for school but as I stood at the top of the steep stairs that day, the pains in my legs getting worse, I felt my knees give way beneath me. The next memory I have is of lying at the bottom of the stairs feeling very poorly and my mother in complete panic. The village doctor was called and I was diagnosed with rheumatic fever, a condition very rare these days, but it would appear the large damp house had taken it's toll. The weeks that followed passed in a blur of pain and nausea, and being unable to get out of bed left me feeling weak and depressed. I was six years old. My lovely cousin Jayne would make cakes and deserts and bring them to tempt me to eat. I remember one such cake she made which resembled an iced basket, half open and filled with fruit and cream. She must have been very fond of me to make such an effort, yet still I couldn't eat. I was also given a dishful of desiccated coconut every day as the doctor considered it to be beneficial for rheumatic conditions. My father used to buy me the pink and white variety in a vain effort to tempt my taste buds. This was to ensure my lifelong dislike of coconut.

Over the following weeks however, I slowly recovered and gained strength. This was a miracle achieved by being administered with penicillin, the only antibiotic available back then, and the village doctor made sure I was given and ample supply and therefore prescribed '2 tablets – 3 times daily.' He would dip his hand into the recycled sweet jar which stood on his desk and deposit an unspecified number into an equally recycled envelope, and once he had adequately licked the lead tip of the pencil he held, to make sure it wrote very clearly, he carefully scribed my name on the crinkled paper. I was privileged I suppose, as most were given a brown pungent mixture poured into a glass bottle with measurements on the side, and a cork jammed into the top. This was administered whether one had a broken arm or pneumonia. However, these wonderful little white miracles *I* had been given were to be my constant companions for the next *ten* years!

Recovery was slow, but my mother was very attentive towards me and we enjoyed long walks together through the fields, gathering wild primroses and bluebells, dad wouldn't allow me out to play without a jacket or cardigan and I was *always* made to wear a 'Liberty Bodice'. For those of you too young to know, and are asking what this garment could possibly be, well – it was a strange little 'vest' with small rubber buttons down the front, which would occasionally pop off as the garment went through the mangle on wash day. All in all though, life returned to normal, and I returned to school dutifully taken by Dora.

If I had learned nothing else in my life that would be relevant to my present situation, one thing I did learn quite young was this: - *Never* lie to children!! The little tale that taught me this, was the story of Snowy the cat. My dad had chosen him as kitten from amongst the feral cats which roamed around the cement works. The men there would often take scraps from home with which to feed them. Snowy was, as you might imagine white with ginger patches and paws. We all thought Snowy was quite clever, as dad would put 'Nibbits' on the seat of the rocking chair, and as it rocked backwards and forwards Snowy would grab a Nibbit with his paw. However, my house-proud mother always was a very particular housekeeper and didn't feel that animals had a place in the home. Therefore, one day my father explained to Dora and me that Snowy would not be coming home. Apparently he had 'slipped' into the babbling brook and drowned. Had Snowy died for me like Jesus? Imagine my surprise and relief, and my parent's horror when one week later Snowy walked in the door. Had he been resurrected? My father wouldn't hurt a fly, and Snowy had obviously found his way home from wherever he had been taken.

Now, if you stood in the middle of our village, in the valley, it was *just* that – a valley, and all you could see wherever you turned were lush green hills. To me as such a small child, at the point where the rolling green hills touched the blue of the sky, that was where the world ended! In my mind there was nothing beyond. Until one day, my earliest memory of an adventure, we were taken by the *only* charabanc in the village to the next village of Hope, and to the train station. We obtained our tickets and boarded the train. As the Station Master blew his whistle, this long iron monster chugged into action. It was so exciting, the clickety-click of the wheels, the steam, the way in which the windows could be raised and lowered by a leather strap. After what seemed an age, we arrived at the nearest large city – Sheffield. It was quite scary, noisy and busy, cars and trams steaming up and down the streets. However, dad took us to a restaurant and we sat at a huge round table, but I was to see the most fascinating sight of my *entire* life – all six years of it! Sitting at the next table was a family, mum, dad, and a little girl about my age –*but* – their skin was as black as the coal in our coal shed, and they had the biggest, most beautiful brown eyes I had ever seen. The little girl had a floppy red bow around her curly hair, but *her* curls were as black as mine were snow white. She had lashes to die for and was the most beautiful person I had ever set eyes upon. My father had to prevent me from staring but from that moment on, all I wanted was a sister with black skin and brown eyes. So guess what I got for Christmas that year? A black pot dolly, with a big red bow in her pot hair, with eyes that opened and closed and long feathery lashes. Her name was Boko

In 1955 we received great news. We had the opportunity of moving to a brand new house. It was situated near the outskirts of the village, and the babbling brook would now run along the bottom of our garden and open out into a marshy pond, before gushing on it's way and tumbling down the waterfall. Every year a pair of swans would grace us with their presence before leaving again with their young cygnets. At night we could hear moorhens and curlews, in the daytime, summer was heralded by the call of the cuckoo. The house was stone built, Dora and I had our own bedrooms and the toilet was indoors for goodness sake!! As was the bath, and a washbasin with *hot* running water. This was heaven. We also had an enormous garden which happily enabled dad to pursue his love of horticulture. He was a hard worker and providing for his family was paramount to him. But his love of gardening served a dual purpose. He grew prize roses, chrysanthemums, even passion flowers, for his own and our pleasure. The house was always filled with flowers, and the garden was a plethora of colour all year round, but the happiest aspect of this large garden was the greenhouse where tomatoes, cucumbers, and aubergines filled the whole place with a beautiful aroma. Peas, beans, lettuce, and onions – you name it – my dad grew it, and thrilled us all with the prizes he won in the local horticultural shows. Everything we ate was freshly picked each day. Combined with the sheep carcass the farmer would pop over the hedge from the adjacent field which dad would cut into joints and salt, then hang

on the back of the bedroom door. Nothing of the carcass would be wasted, even the head was used to make brawn but I'm afraid *I* had to draw the line somewhere! Dad would occasionally go shooting and arrive home proudly carrying a brace of dead rabbits, but as soon as mum started to skin and prepare them for the stew pot the smell would ensure that I didn't eat dinner that day. Gladly (for me not the rabbits) the onset of mixematosis would put an end to the rabbit stews.

It was about this time, in this ideal life, that I began to notice that Dora thought and behaved differently from others. We were two very different people, Dora and I, in some ways we were close but in others we were worlds apart. Where I would watch and learn from my parents, Dora would seemingly ignore anything they said, and when my father became completely exasperated, he would send Dora to sit on the doorstep, weather permitting of course. By no stretch of the imagination was my father a violent man, and rightly or wrongly I suppose this was an alternative way for him to distance himself from her at the time. I however, felt so sorry for Dora sitting out there on the doorstep, crying, that I would wait until my parents were otherwise engaged, and sneak out with a handkerchief for her. I was seven years old and didn't know what else I could do to comfort her. She would always fail to get up in the morning despite my parent's pleas for her not to be late for school, not just to drop her clothing around and leave it. Was this just normal teenage behaviour? Even the budgie, copying dad, would swear at Dora.

Eventually dad joined the village Fire Brigade part-time, and I would often sit in fascination of the stories he would tell after he had attended a fire. A local barn full of hay had burned down, or a cow had got wedged down a shaft on the hillside, much worse a child slipped into a cave, and died. This was, I think, the saddest story he had to tell. Dora didn't find this interesting at all, and would wonder off and do other things. My dad being a fireman wasn't always so exciting though. Sometimes it was a downright nuisance. The bell- to alert him- was situated at the bottom of the stairs and would suddenly and without warning force its shrill, ear-splitting sound throughout the whole house at the most inappropriate times. I have watched my dad on many occasions, after a night's shift; just settle into a warm bed at 6 am to be woken from his sleep. I would worry about him as I watched him through the window, cycling up the road on Dora's pushbike, donning his uniform as he went.

By the time Dora left school at fifteen, my dad had secured a job for her at the local hardware store. This was owned by Rob, a mate of dad's and a Fire Service colleague. Dora seemed to enjoy her new found independence and having money of her own. Sweets were the main things she would buy, and I would often sit with her amongst a group of her friends and peers. She would hand round the sweets, but tell me I couldn't have one. Such a small thing really, but a memory which has always remained with me.

Meanwhile mum and Auntie Gwyneth – aka- 'The Williams Sisters' would travel around performing their art. Carla – remember Carla? Was Gwyneth's daughter, and she and I would often have to sit in her dad's care in the car park, whilst both our parents were in the pub or club singing, one of them would periodically nip out with crisps and pop. A practice which would nowadays be frowned upon. It was a nightmare sitting in that car, in the dark with Carla. She also displayed strange

thoughts and behaviour, but in a *much* more destructive way than Dora. She would crate arguments where there were none. She would tell me the utmost lies about *anything* she knew would upset me, but there was no escape from these onslaughts, in a small car. She had a captive audience!

This singing career was to continue for many years. My mother hoped to improve her role in the duo, and began piano lessons, taught by the local undertaker. I used to sit in a big old armchair, all the time thinking about the coffins stashed up next door, and wait, and listen, for a whole hour to the discordant sounds my mother made. Eventually she gave up and realised that *her* gift, was her voice. Gwyneth just had a natural gift for the piano.

By now I was attending the junior school, but being in the new house meant further to walk each day. I was a small child for my age and was therefore occasionally bullied to some extent by my peers who were bigger and taller. One in particular, Susan, would taunt me mercilessly, but being my father's daughter, I was patient and slow to anger, but one day Susan went too far. She grabbed my favourite blue and brown bonnet, with the tassel at the back, as I balanced along the top of the dry-stone wall causing me to fall over into the field full of sheep. Now my father's nickname for me was 'Squib' (dictionary definition; a small explosive firework) this name was not afforded me for nothing. As I picked myself up, and clambered back over the wall, I ran after Susan as fast as my short little legs would carry me, even the sheep in the field could sense my anger. As I snatched my bonnet, bereft of tassel, from Susan's grip, her little finger was bent right back, causing her obvious, and loud pain. She never bullied me again, and word soon passed around school; 'Don't mess with Sandy!' I have never been violent to another child again from that day to this, and never wish to be; my father taught me how to settle issues without violence,

Of course not all of my friends were bullies, one in particular, Brian had a very kind and thoughtful nature, albeit towards animals rather than human beings. You may remember earlier that I said the rabbit stews came to an end with the onset of mixematosis? Well, of course I was happy there would be no more rabbit stew, but it was rather hurtful to see the poor animals suffer. It was a slow and painful death for them. Their eyes would bulge and eventually they would just lay there gasping for breath for a long time. Now Brian was not prepared to sit back and let his furry friends suffer in this way! He already had a Barn Owl which used to sit on his shoulder, and a fox that would walk beside him wherever he went, so most days after school, Brian would pick up his gun and go off towards the World's End. Whenever he came across a suffering and dying animal, he would carefully place his foot on it and shoot it clean in the head to put it out of its misery. Brian was a good shot-normally – however, there was just the one occasion he missed and shot off his toe! This did not deter him, and once his foot was treated and bandaged he continued his mission of mercy. Poor Brian, his intentions were good, and he saved a good many fluffy creatures from a lingering death.

Once again the years passed by in childhood bliss. We had 'Wakes Week' in the summer, when Bible scenes would be created in wet clay with flower petals, moss leaves etc., they were called Well Dressings. It was a pagan festival, and I'm sure there will be many a reader who will not thank me for that, for it was intended to

Thank God for the rain. However, if it rained during the ceremony of the Blessing of the

Wells, we villagers would become very disgruntled at getting wet! The Fair would also roll into the village at this time. That was so exciting, and the Swing Boats were my favourite. On those hot lazy days, I would take the little wooden boat dad had made for me, with a piece of sheet for a sail, and a 6" nail serving as a mast, and I would float it down the river attached to a piece of string. What dad didn't know was that when I reached the bridge, I would let go the string, run and catch it at the other side before it reached the little whirl pool further down-stream and be gone forever.

My most depressing memory of village life was the church bells. The church clock would boom as its heavy hands struck the hour – *every* – hour. The bells would toll to call all Christians to service on a Sunday; they would toll for funerals, for weddings, etc. It seemed any excuse could be given to toll the bells!

At the age of nine I unfortunately succumbed to rheumatic fever yet again. Apparently it's unusual for someone to be affected twice but, I have, and always will, prefer to be different. And so once again many weeks of suffering lay ahead. When Dora came home in an evening, my parents would request that she sit with me and read stories. I always felt that she did this with great resentment, and I couldn't blame her I suppose, she was after all only sixteen. Her efforts however, fell quite literally upon deaf ears. The fever took its toll in many forms and one of them was complete loss of hearing for a while, although no-one would yet again believe me until the doctor confirmed this. Far into the future I was to discover that many people would not listen to this small person, to their regret. However once again the doctor was called. This one was relatively new in the village. He was a tall, well-built Irish man, with no bedside manner whatsoever, or any other pleasant manner in fact. It was winter, and no central heating in those days meant the house was heated only by a big coal fire in the living room. As ice formed on the outside of the windows, it would also encrust itself upon the inside. This bullish Irish man took out his stethoscope and seemed to take great delight in pressing it to my chest. After what felt like a gravely silent hour, but in fact was mere seconds, he stood back, pulled the instrument from his ears and announced to my mother, who was holding my hand, that "As this ailment affects the heart, and she has now contracted it twice, she will not live to be thirty!" Those words fixed my mother to the spot, she was speechless! I can now, looking back only imagine what the main topic of conversation must have been in our household for a long time, Sandy's going to die. I on the other hand, I was quite unconcerned, anyway, who wants to be *thirty*! It's wonderful and amazing what a bottle of Lucozade and a quarter of Cherry Balsams could do for a sick child, and that was exactly what my lovely dad would obtain for me. The medicinal qualities of these commodities were truly phenomenal.

As I slowly recovered, the snow outside my window was crisp and virgin, yet again. Untrodden, bearing only the spiky little footprints of birds. I begged my mother to allow me to go outside to build a snowman. Although this was risky, I felt my mother wished me to enjoy myself whilst I could, and gave in. She wrapped me in so many jumpers, socks and boots that I could barely move. As I waded through the deep snow with shovel in gloved hand, I dug and moulded until the snow took on human form. I took a carrot for his nose and two pieces of coal from the coal shed for his eyes. Mum gave me an old scarf 'to keep him warm.' I was then returned to my room, to watch

my snowman slowly melt to nothing, over the next couple of weeks. In the meantime, the only adventure for me, out of my room, was to be wrapped in a blanket and carried downstairs to watch Popeye on our black and white T.V. and then back up again. During this time Carla was doing her worst and Dora just plodded on, being late for work etc.

Once more, life returned to its peaceful 'norm.' Some things progressed however. Now instead of sitting in the car park whilst The Williams Sisters sang Carla and I were permitted to stay at *her* house, since we were a little older. On one such occasion, all the adults were preparing for such a 'gig'. It was Christmas time, and Carla and I were given sweets and pop. The T.V. Times was handy to tell us what was on T.V. so off they went. No sooner had our favourite adults left the door, than Carla shot upstairs like a bullet out of a gun. Five minutes later she was back down again, her face 'decorated' like the Christmas tree in makeup so thick and colourful, it put me in mind of a parrot. She promptly warned me to stay put, watch the T.V. she would be back soon. In seconds there was a blast on a horn outside, and Carla climbed into a car with two young men and was gone! She was thirteen years old, I was ten.

Shortly before midnight Carla came bursting through the door. Up the stairs she went at lightning speed, and on her return to the living room, totally bereft of makeup and wearing pyjamas and slippers, she flounced onto the settee, poured herself a drink and grilled me as to the content of the programmes I had watched, as I had sat alone, and afraid in that cottage on the hill, then told me malevolently to keep my mouth shut! Within minutes our parents were home, and Carla, relaxed and calm, relayed to them how great or amusing the T.V. had been that 'we' had been watching all evening. She had quintessential timing, surely only Angels can be so perfect, and Carla *was* an Angel in everyone else's eyes.

Life became more and more exciting as I grew older. You may remember all those Aunts and uncles I had, well, dad would take me to the train station in the next village of Hope, and after purchasing a ticket he would seat me comfortably on a train bound for Hull. It was so exciting and I felt so grown up travelling all that way on my own, it was quite safe to do so in those days. As the train steamed in to its final destination at the end of the line, my auntie Sarah would be standing there on the platform waiting to meet me. On these stays with auntie Sarah I would enjoy spending time with the friends I had made there, Hannah and Marion. We would be taken to East Park, in Hull and our favourite pastime was feeding the ducks on the boating lake, Marion always appeared envious of her sister Hannah for no reason that I could comprehend. On one such visit to the boating lake, Hannah and I were enjoying the congregation of ducks as we crumbled the stale bread auntie Sarah had given us. Marion joined us as we became more and more excited at the different variations of birds clamouring for the food we had on offer. In an instant – Hannah was gone! I felt sure I had seen Marion push her. After many hours of searching, the divers finally pulled Hannah from the tangled weed on the bed of the lake. Her lifeless body was taken away. Once again, no-one believed the murmurings of a distraught small child, and Marion was satisfied. Now she had all the attention at home.

On another later occasion, I was staying with my cousin Bernice who was twenty years my senior. She and her husband Jack had split up. Jack had moved in with a

sixteen year old girl, the daughter of one of their friends. One evening Bernice and I were tackling a piece of needlework, when Jack knocked at the door wanting to collect some of his things. It was a while before he emerged from the tool shed and strolled into the living room – and hurled a hatchet at poor Bernice, who instantly ducked allowing the hatchet to land with a dull thud when it became deeply embedded in the sideboard door. I ran furiously out of the house and over the garden fence to the neighbours, to call the police. Life, it seemed however short it would be, would certainly be filled with the most unthinkable of situations, and there would be many more to come. Why couldn't people be peaceable and kind toward one another? Life
really *was* too short – literally, for such battles, and nobody ever won the war.

However, I would remain there for the whole six weeks of the summer holidays, and flit from one auntie to another. They all seemed to love me so much; I could feel the love and warmth they gave me in so many ways. However, I did feel a little homesick now and then, and missed my parents; I even missed Dora and her quaint ways.

In the autumn of 1959 I started attending Hope Valley College. It was very new and very modern, unlike the old Victorian buildings we were used to in the countryside. Interestingly, my cousin Colin, had by now graduated university, and became a teacher at the College. It was often a strange situation for me, being taught by one's own cousin. He was considered at the time, to be quite a handsome young man, quite a catch, and all the girls in the senior classes would constantly badger me for information about him, whether or not he had a girlfriend. Could I arrange a date with him, that sort of thing? Of course this had its advantages due to the fact that all the senior girls were friendly and protective towards me, as they wished to stay in my favour for obvious reasons. Now as the College was situated in the next village, it was essential that we were not late for the one and only school bus which took us there every morning and brought us home each evening. If we missed it we had to walk the distance, there was no excuse. My education had suffered greatly due to my long illnesses, but I was determined that I would catch up with my peers. For whatever reason, Dora had not taken the route of further education, perhaps it was the effort required, but whatever it took, and however hard it would be, I would make sure my education served me well.

By this time my mother was working, and so I would come home from school, and prepare everyone a meal. You see I was now learning to cook, and my parent's hearts must have sunk when they came home from a hard day, to face my huge bowl of mashed potato and cheese, followed by my effort at apple crumble, but they never said anything other than encouraging words. Meanwhile I would still visit Auntie Gwyneth and Carla. Auntie Gwyneth also worked in the daytime, so there were occasions when Carla and I would have the house to ourselves, during the long school holidays. No sooner had her mother left the house than almost the entire contents of that cottage were out on the lawn. If Carla could carry it – out it went! There were dining chairs, occasional tables, rugs even the crockery did not escape. She wanted to play house. She would then run down to the corner shop with Gwyneth's credit book, and buy sweets, biscuits, pop, cake and have it added to the bill, all of which her mum would have to pay for at the end of the week. Then would come the words I had grown accustomed to – 'keep your mouth shut.' If it rained, God help Gwyneth's lovely polished furniture and rugs, for Carla would curse at the inconvenience of it all, run for cover and leave it out there.

However, Dora now aged eighteen or so was having a night out. A friend had given me a beautiful white skirt embellished with blue Swiss embroidery. I was so pleased with this skirt because it had only been worn by one other person before me, rather that four. Dora asked if she could borrow the skirt and I readily said yes, happy that *she* wanted to wear something of *mine*. As she prepared for her evening, I watched her put on her makeup, and back-comb her Hiltoned hair to perfection, she was a very slim and attractive girl, and looked a million dollars. The next morning however, as I entered the kitchen for breakfast, I saw my lovely blue and white skirt draped over a bucket. As Dora appeared I asked her if she had had an accident with the skirt and she confidently told me that she had spilled coffee on it but "not to worry," she had put it to soak the minute she got in! What she didn't tell me was that she had carefully placed, just the stained part, into a bucket of bleach! Odd behaviour indeed for someone of her age, even I knew that was ridiculous. The skirt was ruined. Why was Dora so different? Or rather was it *me* who was different, because Carla also had these strange but more destructive ways. I used to joke with mum and dad and ask them if Dora had been dropped on her head, or fallen out of her pram as a baby. Then, the most horrible thought crossed my mind, what if *I* was adopted? I was smaller, chubbier, chattier that all the others. What if all those lovely aunts and uncles and cousins didn't really belong to me? Perhaps they adopted me because they felt sorry for me because I was going to die. At that moment nothing made sense, I seemed unable to put my life into any chronological order which would enable me to detect the truth! I quickly put these thoughts aside as, had I uttered one word, the whole family – maybe the whole village would have been thrown into chaos if this were true! Anyway, no-one would take any notice of *me.*

It was around now that Dora met Vince. He came from a neighbouring village and was a very handsome young man. With black curly hair combed into a 'D.A.' at the back (if you don't know what a D.A. is, ask your mother.) In fact Vince was what was known back then as a Teddy boy. With his pale blue three quarter length jacket, tight drainpipe white jeans and white sneakers, added to his smouldering 'gypsy' features he really looked the part. There was however one draw back to all this, my dad was not a happy man having his eldest daughter seen out with someone of this nature. Teddy Boys had a reputation for violence and nuisance, but Vince was not like that at all. In fact he was a lovely young man, and he and I hit it off from the start, he was like my own brother. Eventually my parents grew fond of him, and so their courtship continued. He bought a little M.G. sports car, it was bright red but Vince had it resprayed Peacock Blue and he would roar up to the house and proudly jump out, jump over the garden gate, whistling as he went.

Meanwhile, I was also growing up, and now was receiving five shillings a week pocket money. This gave me new found responsibility because I had to make choices. Every fortnight there was a dance at the clubhouse where my dad worked, and there would be a band, usually Enzo and the Fiestas, where we had a great time. However I would also need a decent pair of stockings to wear. SO! On the week there was no dance I would walk into the village and for five shillings purchase a pair of American Tan stockings from Middleton's drapery, they made your legs look brown and tanned.

So then the week of the dance I could buy the five shilling ticket. This plan worked perfectly. It usually worked out that the dance would fall on dad's afternoon shift at work so I would walk to the dance, over the fields, struggling in my high heels, but by ten p.m. *prompt*, dad would appear at the door and whistle me from across the room. I had to go instantly, and he would walk me back home across the fields.

I frequently had a battle with my dad over such stuff as makeup. He would examine my face before I went out, and eyeliner was an absolute *no-no*! However, I have always been a resourceful little devil, and in my makeup purse, was a very dark grey eye shadow. I found that if I drew this eye shadow, *just* above my lashes it would serve very well as eyeliner. My dad had to agree – it was *not* eyeliner! My mother was obviously a little more understanding of girly things and helped me with what to wear. Her favourite hobby was dressmaking, and this was extremely useful given that I could never buy any adult clothing that actually fitted, so on her trusty treadle machine, she would whip out wonderful creations which were like no others, so any garments that I had which were not handed down, were usually created by mum, but I always looked different. This was to be a skill that mum taught me which would prove to be one of the most useful skills I have. However I never considered that I could ever be as beautiful as Dora though I tried to emulate her, and found her quite helpful when teaching me how to be a grown-up.

Remember those little white miracle pills, now known as the Magic Bullets? Well I was still taking them, six a day, still wearing cardis and jackets and even our school uniform required us to wear bottle green knickers with long elasticated legs. However, one day whilst shopping with Dora, she was buying some sexy little 'briefs' which were black with red lace all over the front. I wanted so much to be like

Dora, so I bought a pair with my pocket money. By now of course, I was about half way to the '30' mark, only another sixteen years or so to live. As this thought crossed my mind I made a bold decision. When my mother reminded me to go for another fistful of '2 tablets – 3 times daily' I informed her emphatically, that I was taking no more! The next day I cast off my cardigan, I also wore the red and black knickers to school, but I forgot it was P.E. day and when these offending articles were revealed whilst undressing for the P.E. lesson I was unceremoniously hauled off to the headmistress's office. 'Flash' we called her because we were always catching glimpses of her long bloomers when she sat on the stage during assembly, so I was fully aware that she was not going to approve of my new miracle garment. Also, through a freak of nature I had rather 'perky' boobs and whilst she was at it she pointed out to me that in her opinion, my bra was too tight. I therefore very politely pointed out to her, that as she was so flat chested, she couldn't possibly know how difficult it was to keep them restrained. I was promptly labelled a hussy and told never to wear them again! Was I bothered? Not at all, I just found more discreet methods of changing for P.E. it had felt delightfully wicked, wearing those pants, I wasn't going to stop now, I had always wanted an opportunity to be naughty at school, it was just something else I needed to achieve before I died, and telling 'Flash' what I thought was absolutely *the* best! My classmates thought I was so brave, however when my dad found out, he had other opinions.

I was by now, without realising why, beginning to attract the attention of boys! I know what you're thinking but it wasn't the red lacy knickers, they never saw them, (at this point anyway.) Would you believe that the Head Boy was quite drawn to me? I couldn't understand why because all the other girls in school were much more elegant and attractive than I was, with my unruly curly hair, fair lashes and chubby little shape. My mother, of course was highly delighted at the prospect of the most important pupil in the school paying attention to *her* daughter. He would have a well known flower service, deliver a dozen red roses to the door, then just when we were settled in front of the telly, the postmaster would knock on the window:- "Greetings Telegram for your Sandra." He would exclaim, as though it had been a great imposition to have had to make this effort for such a small insignificant young person. Although I was important to my mother, as she would have no-one shorten my name in her hearing. Pete's attentions however, were not my cup of tea, lovely young man though he was, (he would give me a delicate little peck on the forehead after delivering me to the garden gate from night school) I was not your Jane Austen type, I was more your rough, Catherine Cookson type, as you will discover later on, therefore I gently made my exit. No doubt one day some lucky young lady will snap him up.

The Dora/Vince relationship had other advantages for the family, as Vince's mother churned her own cheese and butter, so dad would trade tomatoes and cabbages for such creamy spoils. Now Dora and Vince had been courting for quite a while and had a steady relationship. Carla however had quite a few boyfriends – frequently. *I* was still young and naïve. However, a bombshell was dropped one day in our perfectly respectable world. Dora announced that she was pregnant! We are recalling here, the early sixties, and being pregnant out of wedlock was the biggest skeleton, anyone could have in their cupboard, but one that couldn't remain in the cupboard very long for obvious reasons. My parents were devastated. My father was so angry he reached the trusty old brown suitcase down from the loft and told Dora – 'Fill it, and get out!' Of course, he didn't mean it, he loved his eldest daughter despite her differences, and once he calmed down, we all sat and made decisions for the future. Dad had a heart-to heart with Vince and told him he didn't *have* to marry Dora, but they had been together for a year or two by now, and Vince was in no doubt that he wanted the marriage to go ahead, and so the wedding was planned. I was bridesmaid once I had stamped my feet literally; about the shoes I would wear (heels of course.) The wedding ceremony was held at the Methodist Chapel; not Church for some reason, perhaps the Chapel Vicar was a little more liberal minded than the Church one. Dora wore pink, not being allowed to wear white which apparently was for 'virgins' (What was a virgin?) If Dora wasn't one then I hoped I wasn't either! I had been a bridesmaid eight times before this, I suppose being blonde, curly and chubby, I was the perfect 'cutesy pie' dressed in organza with flowers in my hair. However, once they were wed, Vince moved in with us all. He acquired a new job as a lorry driver and life settled down once more. As time went by Dora grew larger and larger in her pregnancy until her time was due. Then one day in mid-August, she gave birth to a beautiful little girl, with big blue eyes and a little downy blonde head. I was an auntie at the tender age of fourteen, I was so proud. Vince was, as he so delicately put it, "chuffed to bits!"

This child was from now on, to be completely adored by me and everyone else around her, but the birth of this child – this 'Angel' was to herald the beginning of the end of this idyllic childhood.

Chapter Two

Sudden Adulthood

Despite the initial shock at Dora being pregnant, everyone was now in raptures over this new addition to the family. Vince went to work early each morning and mum and dad also. I went to school, and Dora would sleep most of the morning, and watch T.V. for the rest of the day. And yet again I would return home from a day at school and cook a meal for five of us. I would love to clean the house before mum and dad came home. I wanted them to relax after a busy day at work and I would feel such juvenile pride as they walked in and the cushions were plumped and the sideboard was polished.

This new life form, this little 'Angel' was very demanding the way infants are. She was so beautiful with a cheeky grin, adorable just like her mother had been as a young child, and *I* adored her. However, life was very difficult for us all living together, despite our spacious house, but fortunately a cottage, half way up the hill, hear Gwyneth and Len, became available for Dora and Vince. It was right opposite the chapel where they were married, and so they moved out of the family home. Strangely, I missed them. I missed Vince's humour and even Dora's odd little ways, but most of all, I missed the presence of my much loved little niece, who was named Dana. I missed being woken in the night for feeds, watching her little cupid lips latching onto the bottle and the comforting sound of sucking, as her big blue eyes opened and closed as she relaxed, cycle complete –feed, change nappy, sleep, happy!

However, they settled into life as a separate little unit in the small cottage on the hill. My mother would call on her way to work, to find no reply to her knocks, and call on her way home again in the afternoon and then knock and knock until Dora answered bleary eyed in her nightgown, Dana ecstatic to be out of her cot despite her nappy so soggy it was down to her knees. The cottage was not always kept what you might call clean and Dana seemed to spend most of her life in the soggy nappies. This was very upsetting for my parents and me. The cottage was set next to a vast field and therefore the field mice were enticed by the flour and sugar, jam and biscuits etc., in the pantry. You *could* say they had a 'field day!' However, each morning I would walk up the hill to Dora's cottage in order to empty the traps of dead mice. *I* found this quite upsetting, as these cute little creatures were doing what came naturally to them, and here was a prolific food source which they could comfortably harvest and we were slaughtering them one by one.

Now, life in the cottage was not easy, Dana, the little 'Angel' was growing and demanding and Dora needed help, and so it was decided that

they should move back in with us. As for me, I was getting older too. I had decided to stay at school for an extra year after my leaving age. I was still very determined to make sure I got those all important qualifications. I had wanted to go to art school, as art and design were my first loves, but alas, the nearest Art College was in Manchester, many miles away and it would have meant boarding out. My beloved dad would not let me go, being the ever protective parent that he was. The only other option left to us in this 'basin' this valley was a career in commerce. Dad bought me a portable typewriter, and would pay for any exams I was prepared to sit, as in those days they were not free. With a lot of hard work I would certainly make up for lost time in my earlier life. As a result of
my hard work and determination, I would eventually achieve:- Royal Society of Arts Art and Craft, English Language. College of Preceptors, English Language and History. U.L.C.I. English Language, Typewriting stage one, Pitman Shorthand 60/70/80/90 words per minute. Oh, and Housecraft – cakes! Nowadays I can't even make a decent sandwich, but at last I felt I was on my way to being 'normal.'

My remaining fifteen years were now down to fourteen, and my life was filled with helping to care for Dana. As I was now gaining confidence and experience, I was offered a job in Chapel-en-le-Frith. This would mean leaving school and travelling each morning and evening over the moors. However, I decided against all advice that this was for me. My new employer also agreed that I could take day classes once a week for half a day and would travel by bus each a.m. to work, then take the train back to college one afternoon per week, and walk home two miles in the evening, all in the name of learning and education. My boss Reg, was a nice man, he was very kind to me. The factory produced brake-linings, and I worked in the science section, typing up laboratory reports which had been scribbled down by professors from various parts of the world that I had never heard of. They would occasionally use me as a 'lightweight' for testing the pressure on the brakes as I was still only 4'11" and weighed only six and a half stone, but, I was still alive – and well! Each a.m. I had to go from one office to the next, and then down into the testing bays to collect reports to be typed that day. On one such morning all the men had gone to the canteen for their coffee break, except one. As I walked up to the desk, he grabbed me, and was pulling me to a corner of the office. I screamed at him to let me go, and instinctively slapped his face in self-preservation. The shock was enough to ensure I could make a getaway. I ran down the corridor, back to my office, the girls, and Reg, in distress. When questioned as to what had happened, I really wasn't quite sure, my parents had protected me so well, that they had omitted to mention these types to me. However, Reg immediately marched me down to the testing bays and in front of all his colleagues explained very graphically what had just happened. I was shocked at Reg's forthrightness, but the man was completely floored at his little game being out in the open.

Reg grew very fond of me and even used to visit our house, and invite me home to tea with his wife and daughter. Vince however was also very protective of me and didn't like Reg at all, he wondered what his motives might be but it appeared there were none. Reg even gave me his lucky silver dollar which he had kept since the war. I still have it to this day.

In my spare time I would take Dana, who was by now a toddler, to the playing field. We would swing on the swings, and take a wild adventure riding astride the big iron rocking horse, as fast as we could make him go. It was on one of these adventures that I would meet the second most important man in my life. Dana had taken off at great speed down the path and ran straight into the arms of the young man who caught her. He was very slim, skinny in fact with a *lot* of wavy fair hair. He scooped Dana up in his arms, held her high and then handed her back to me. His name was Gordon. He was over for the day from Sheffield with a group of lads. Here to visit the countryside to sample our peace and tranquillity, they had all travelled together in a mate's Mini. It's amazing how many young fellas you can fit into a Mini. The year was 1964, ironic as I look back; to think that it was due to my little 'Angel' that Gordon and I met.

This group of friends made frequent visits to the village subsequently, and I decided not to mention my meetings with 'the lads' to my parents but as anyone who lives within a small village will tell you, that is impossible! Carla for one soon found out there were boys available, so it was inevitable. She knew how my parents had always kept boys away. For example one boy had been on his way to the door, but before he was half way up the garden path, the window opened and my father was standing there with shoe in hand. His words will haunt me to this day:-"If he takes one more step, he gets my shoe toe up his arse!" My embarrassment was plain for all to see. It was for this reason that I tried to keep it a secret. Carla, however, saw this as another opportunity to control me, and in her usual subversive manner, made sure my parents found out. She then informed me of what a dreadful person Gordon was, as he had pinned a cat to a board and skinned it alive! (Totally untrue) but she knew this would appal me. Despite Carla's obvious lies, I continued to see Gordon. To save the hassle of much explanation we would meet in the village. The lads would turn up in Keith's little blue Mini and pile out, we would all trek up Bradwell Dale and climb the rocks. One of us, over 18, would call at the local pub and collect a crate of beer, someone else would bring a 'tranny' (transistor radio) and it was my job to sneak out some potatoes freshly dug from dad's garden to bake on the open fire we would make. It was great on a Sunday evening, eating hot potatoes, swigging beer and dancing to Top of the Pops. However on one such evening as the embers of the fire were reduced to a glow, and the batteries had run down on the tranny, we were enjoying the quiet of the 'Dale' when we heard it for the first time. It was the most haunting sound we had ever heard. It was coming from a crevice high up in the rock face, it was very eerie indeed. I was not afraid that it was a ghost, for as I no longer acknowledged the existence of a god, meant there was no afterlife or living dead, or whatever anyone wished to call it. So the question remained, what *was* this unearthly sound? Gordon and his friend John decided to find out. The next night they arrived equipped with ropes, and together scaled the rock face to reach the mysterious crevice to discover the source of the sound. All they found on the ledge were a few owl pellets, but decided to bring them down anyway, and collected them up. It was in the local 'paper a few days later, after investigation of the pellets was complete and the eerie sound had been described, experts informed us that the Dale had been occupied by a Snowy Owl. As one would expect, these are large white owls found only in the Scottish Highlands, they have a wingspan of about eight feet, and make the eerie heavy breathing sound we had heard. The bird had a long journey to reach our tiny village. On another of our Sunday jaunts to Top of the Pops, a goat had broken loose, and took exception to other 'animals' belting our "The House of the Rising Sun" plus our jiving antics, and head butted and chased us until we were scrambling down the rocks, and clinging on for dear life. That night my American Tan, five shilling stockings were ripped to shreds!

However, eventually I confided my fears regarding Carla's lies to Dora, and we would have sisterly chats, all the while she was plodding on – watching T.V. and 'being' there. On one occasion I came home to find the now crawling Dana sitting in the kitchen and eating the contents of the day's supply of nappies, which had been slung in the corner.

Since the wedding and birth of Dana, Vince had to give up his beloved M.G. but as life was progressing he bought an old motorbike, took it to bits, and started to rebuild it piece by piece on the patio at the back of the house. Now, Gordon similarly had a

motorbike, which gave them something in common. My parents by now had heard all the gory details about the fella I was seeing, and so my mother decided that they should meet him.

A Sunday tea was arranged and Gordon was invited to our house. I was ecstatic, I had a boyfriend and he was coming to be introduced to my family! The best crockery was brought out of the cupboard, the dust blown off, the polished oak folding leaves of the dining table opened like the wings of a butterfly emerging from its cocoon, and the beautiful cloth, hand-embroidered by my mother's own fair hands was wafted high and floated back down to settle perfectly in place, as it rippled over the highly polished surface. As I assisted in this procedure, I couldn't help wondering what my 'Catherine Cookson' type would make of all this. As teatime grew ever nearer, my mother drifted upstairs to make herself presentable. I caught sight of her as I passed the bathroom door, with lipstick in hand, pursing her lips to seal the full colour newly applied from the tube she held, smiling at her reflection to test its effectiveness. As we waited I heard a familiar roar outside the window, Gordon was here on his motorbike, the thing my dad hated the most. He was not wearing a helmet; his jeans were so tight he could barely dismount his trusty steed. I helped him settle comfortably on the sofa, and hung up his fringed leather jacket which was encrusted with studs, his feet were shod with the latest 'Winkle Pickers'. My mother floated down the stairs with the smile she had practiced, fixed firmly on her face, and entered the living room with such presence. However, as she set eyes upon the figure lounging on her new chintz sofa, the smile visibly and rapidly dissolved into astonishment. Gordon had landed! He *was* my 'Catherine Cookson' rough type, definitely *not* the Jane Austen, Mr. Darcy hero my mother had hoped for. He had not ridden up to my front door on a dazzling white charger; it was actually a reconstituted Norton Dominator. To add insult to injury, he was a 'Townie' a Sheffielder. How could I do this to her?! Tea progressed in stony silence; the only dialogue was when mum produced her piéste-resistance, her very own handcrafted sherry trifle, nestling beautifully in Grandma's cut-glass bowl. As she courteously asked Gordon if he would like some, he surveyed Grandma's heirloom meticulously before announcing "No thanks, it's got soggy sponge int' bottom!" This utterance, this lone statement, was to stain his character for a very long time.

As he left the door and roared off into the sunset on his trusty, or was it rusty, machine, my mother turned to me and said "Don't *EVER* let the neighbours see *THAT* walk up my garden path again!"

As I waited for Gordon in the village one night, he didn't arrive, unusual as he was and always has been so reliable. As I later discovered, he had ditched his motorbike on a bend, ripped his jeans and cut his leg top to bottom. Vince was helping to remove the broken key in the ignition with a screwdriver. A couple more incidents happened with the motorbike until it was eventually written off. Gordon decided it was time for a change, and as I had always refused flatly to ride pillion for fear of my dad finding out, для rest assured he would have, and so Gordon took his driving test and bought a cheap second hand car. This meant that I could go out comfortably with him in his vehicle. What he omitted to tell me was that he had *not* passed the test he took because he knew that I would refuse this mode of transport also. I was *not* impressed. However, he was given an ultimatum, ditch the car or pass your test – properly! He took a second test and this time passed with flying colours.

The next few months followed in a very busy haze. I continued work, day release and night school almost every day and night. Gordon would travel from Sheffield, pick me up from night school, and see me for about an hour before I had to be indoors and then travel back home again. By this time he had bought an old 'banger' and one night as he collected me to take me home, he stopped as we passed over the little stone bridge. I thought he was getting a little romantic, but instead, in true 'Cookson' style he jumped out and picked up the rear mudguard which he had ripped off on the turret of the bridge on his way over, but didn't want to be late. My parents disliked this town lout but tolerated his presence. Carla was quite bemused, I think. Why have one boyfriend when you could have a few? And she had plenty. I always thought this may be because she was lovely and slender with dark hair, whilst I was a bit on the curvy side, with boobs that arrived before the rest of me, but perhaps there were other reasons that I was not yet aware of!

By this time I had changed my job, and had secured a secretarial post nearer home. The office was walking distance for me, about a mile and a half, a few hundred yards along a narrow country lane, in the middle of nowhere. Apart from the boss, an accountant and his assistant, in their offices, there were only two of us in the main office, Mary, and myself. Although I call it a main office, it had just one long desk under the window, and behind us, an open fire which was wonderful in winter, and we would take crumpets for our lunch (no shops around here) and toast them on the end of a very long toasting fork, for fear of sparks from the logs catching our arms. I would watch for Gordon to come speeding down the lane to see me for about half an hour during his lunch break, then whiz back to Sheffield for the afternoon, this must be true love. Mary lived on her parent's farm and would milk the herd of cows before she came to work in the morning and milk them all again in the evening, after a day's hard work at the office. Her boyfriend Bill was employed as mole catcher and gamekeeper on nearby Chatsworth Estate. He would occasionally collect Mary after work if her car was out of action, and give me a lift too, in his Morris Traveller – with a few brace if ripening pheasant reclining on the back seat, after a shoot on the estate. It was on these occasions that the walk home in the fresh air would have been most welcome, but I wouldn't offend by declining their offer.

It was one of these mundane days, that I had done a morning's typing, answered a dozen 'phone calls, and toasted my crumpets, that I received a call from dad, urgently asking if I could go home – in the middle of the afternoon, to look after Dana. His reason for this was that "Vince wasn't well." I knew by my father's voice, that something wasn't right. He was a very calm man who took everything in his stride, and yet there was a hint of panic in his voice that day. Someone, I don't remember who, gave me a lift home. As I walked into the house the first sight to greet me, was my mum sitting bolt upright on a dining chair sobbing and shaking her head. I couldn't get a word from her. My attentions were drawn from my mother, to the far corner of the room where Dora was on the floor, staring into space and screaming at the top of her voice. I was sixteen years old, I couldn't make sense of what was happening I had *never* seen my family behave this way before, my head was pounding. I had to stop this screaming. I was repeatedly shaking

Dora by the shoulders and appealing to her to tell me *what* was wrong, the only way I could stop the screaming was to slap her face, I'd seen it somewhere in the movies, and thankfully, it really did work. The noise stopped immediately and the only sound was the soft sobbing of my mother who was still sitting upright on the chair. My head was in a whirl as I noticed dad through the window. I rushed out to meet him halfway down the road, he had been to the 'phone box by the fire station in the village, we had no house 'phone in those days. "Is Vince alright? Is he alright?" I asked. My dad couldn't look at me and brushed me aside with the words "No, he's dead!" as he continued towards the house. At this point, the only thing I remember doing was running to my favourite cousin Jayne, she owned a newsagents shop at the top end of the village, she would comfort me when I told her the news. Beyond that I remember nothing else until I was back home. My whole world fell apart, at the age of twenty four my best friend was gone, no-one I loved, so close to me had ever died before, not to mention Dora losing her husband and Dana, her daddy. I didn't know how to handle this, and neither did anyone else in the household for that matter. My poor dad knew of no other way to handle his grief other than silence.

In the dark days that followed it became clearer and clearer what had happened. Apparently Vince had been driving his lorry down a steep hill in Conisborough. The lorry in front of him was carrying steel girders, when a car sped across the road at the bottom of the hill. The lorry in front had to brake suddenly and the impetus created by the steep hill meant that Vince's brakes needed a few seconds more to kick in than he had obviously anticipated, which meant he had gone further than intended by the time the brakes did their job, the steel girders went straight through the cab, and into Vince. The large steering wheel had also fractured his pelvis, and pinned him to the seat, but he was still alive. Over the next few hours, the rescue squad cut him free with acetylene burners, talking to him all the while as he slipped in and out of consciousness. It was later the same day, in hospital that he died from his injuries, internal bleeding and shock. This was Vince, who used to jump out of his M.G. without opening the door, who used to jump over the garden gate rather than open that too, whistling as he did so – *GONE*! The police came to the house with 'photos of the aftermath of the accident. Dad and I had to be strong for mum Dora and Dana. He and I looked at the wreckage in the pictures and tried to figure out how anyone could have escaped at all – dead *or* alive.

Now it was at this point in my life that I decided how I felt about Jesus *and* God, for they have to be two separate beings, otherwise how could the voice from Heaven (God's) speak, as Jesus was rising from the Jordan River after being baptised and say: - "This is my beloved son in whom I am well pleased." and the Holy Spirit descended in the form of a dove, if they were 'one' or a Trinity? Not possible. I decided however, that I could not 'give thanks' any more. I *knew* instinctively that Vince did *not* die for me or anyone else. He loved life, loved his wife and daughter and would have wanted to live forever if he could. Therefore it was now, much to the disgrace of my family that I became an atheist, I even mocked God. The vicar came to visit us all, I think to give his condolences, although he sat and said absolutely nothing after I fired at him the fact that, the loving God for whom he advocated was in fact cruel and sadistic, much to my mother's horror. I don't even know whether he was a 'church' vicar or a 'Methodist' one, didn't care either!

So Dora was a widow at the age of twenty three, and at the age of two, Dana had no daddy but *I* still adored my little angel, and so did my parents. She was enveloped with love and affection, there would be no attachment issues with *this* child, she was afforded every ounce of attention any of us could give her. My dad plodded on in his usual quiet, reliable manner, arranging the funeral. Vince's parents and sisters were obviously equally shocked too.

The funeral was arranged in the chapel opposite the cottage they lived in. Three years after they married there, this was where Vince would be buried, how ironic. His body was brought from the hospital, and laid in the chapel-of-rest. The doctor had been to visit Dora, who appeared still to be in a catatonic state. He decided that she should see the body in order to believe that Vince was dead. A visit was arranged to the undertaker's to see Vince, but despite him having two sisters, neither they, nor his parents wanted to go, they each had their own reasons and I respected that, but how could I allow Dora to make this visit on her own? However, I volunteered to accompany her on this final meeting with Vince. We were shown into a tiny room, with the coffin laid on a bench. Vince looked as though he was sleeping peacefully. The undertaker had done an excellent job considering his injuries. His black curly hair was quaffed at the front and he had a huge sort of sticking plaster covering almost half of his face. His hands were hidden from view, concealed within the white satin shroud. I guessed this must have been because he had further injuries. We had earlier received his signet ring amongst his personal effects, and it was squashed beyond all recognition. As I gazed down at my dead best friend, I couldn't help thinking that in a few short years, this would be me, and hoped that Dora would visit *me* for *my* last time on earth. I had about thirteen years left to go, if I was lucky!

I had thoroughly enjoyed my childhood, and made the most of what I had, but from now on, I knew I would have to grow up pretty quickly. Dana needed lots of care, but then so did Dora. She found it so hard to come to terms with the loss of Vince. She had been prescribed tranquilisers to help her sleep, but they were completely ineffective. We were woken so many nights by her cries that I decided it would be kinder for everyone if I moved into her room at night so that she didn't feel quite so alone. She would sit and talk throughout most of the night about Vince, and the things they did, places they went. During the daytime, everyone would avoid the subject, not talk about it for fear of upsetting her. They were oblivious to mine and Dora's chats at night, but I couldn't help feeling it was the right thing to do. It seemed to somehow be therapeutic for her to get it all out. However these sleepless nights were proving very stressful, as I was going to work the next day feeling exhausted before I even began. Things also started to take a much more sinister turn. Dora woke one night, just as we had finally drifted off to sleep, and shook me to complete consciousness. "Wake up, wake up, can you hear it? But she wouldn't tell me *what* I was supposed to hear. This continued night after night until, one such early morning, I sat in bed trying to hear something, *anything*, when chillingly I heard Vince's familiar whistle coming from the patio below. I was an atheist and didn't believe in life after death, and yet there was no mistaking what I heard. We kept this from the family because I knew they wouldn't believe *me* as always. This couldn't be Vince, could it? Surely this God I now mocked would not be cruel enough to take him away from us, only to taunt us with his intangible presence. The next day I had a little walk round to the patio, thoughts jangling in my head. The motorbike that Vince was renovating was here,

covered with a large tarpaulin secured at each corner with some very large boulders to hold it down. However, today, the tarpaulin was thrown back, but the boulders were still in place! No-one knew how. I spoke to Gordon about this as I knew he would understand, and knowing a bit about bikes (he was a mechanic) also having one himself he decided that the sooner the bike was completed and sold, the better, he, therefore, did just that. The proceeds were very welcome to the newly widowed Dora.

Following this I began to have dreams of Vince standing in the living room, in full Naval Officer's uniform, with a huge smile on his face, not speaking a word. In my dream I was imploring him to tell me how he was, what had happened, but he stood silent. Dora would later confide in me that she was also having dreams, but chillingly she described in identical detail, the same dream. I found this both distressing and confusing. There were also several occasions when Dana would wake up screaming. My dad would carry her downstairs wrapped in a blanket, just as he had done with me years before when I was ill. We would comfort her; cuddle her, as she explained how a man with dark hair was trying to take her out of her cot. Could this be the cruel God trying to make her believe it was her daddy? If so, he was not succeeding with *me*!

Not too long afterwards, the vicious God made his presence known once more. Vince's youngest sister had two small sons. Their grandfather (Vince's dad) worked at the local corn mill, situated as one would expect, beside a waterfall. It was winter, and the snow had thawed, causing the river to be in full flood, a torrent of white water, as the snow slowly melted down from the surrounding hills. During the Christmas holiday, the mill was closed and the boys, aged about seven and three had gone to feed the ducks, walking along the little wooden bridge, right above the waterfall. The wood was wet and slippery and sadly, the younger boy lost his footing and plunged into the swirling waters. His older brother, very bravely jumped in to try and save him but to no avail. He was found much further downstream, caught on an overhanging tree. Once more, the ducks were fed at the expense of human life. However, I attended this child's funeral, and the vicar giving the service, explained to the congregation, that "God had seen this little child as a beautiful flower, and picked him for His garden in Heaven!!" I had to leave the church! How cruel could anyone be, to 'give' someone a little child, and then take him away, like a carrot being dangled before a donkey? I went home that day and gave Dana extra hugs. I didn't want to lose *her*! However, once more I wondered if *I* would be a flower in His garden! And if I was I decided I would give off the most pungent of odours in revenge, and anyway I was sure I would be a weed!

Dana was now growing, she had her daddy's cheeky little grin. Gordon would help out when he could, my parents now tolerating him a little more. Dora began slowly to come back down to earth, so I decided a holiday might be good for her. I arranged some time off work, and organised a week in Blackpool. Carla wanted to come too. We had a room at the very top of a small, but clean boarding house, right on the sea front. The room had a double and single bed so it was great for the three of us.

It was July, and it was to be my seventeenth birthday whilst we were there so we thought it would be fun to celebrate. I booked tickets at the local Locano Ballroom in the town, there would be Susan Maughan, Freddy and the Dreamers, and Jerry and the Pacemakers – and dancing! We had to walk a fair distance, over the bridge away from the sea front. Dora wasn't feeling too well, her throat was sore, but she so much wanted and needed to go. The landlady had given us a 'late' key, for they locked the doors at midnight. The evening started off very well, we danced and the bands were great. As the evening wore on, Dora began to feel worse, and so I thought we should go back to the 'digs.' I called to Carla to explain, but she waved me off and said she would follow us in a few minutes. She was dancing with a young man, and was wrapped around him like a python around its prey. Dora and I walked back over the bridge, through the town and let ourselves in with the 'late' key, whereupon the resident dog escaped through the open door. I encouraged Dora to go up to bed and I would wait for Carla who should have been following us by now. It was just after midnight, I sat on the garden bench, and waited, and the black dog sat with me. When I reached the Locano, it was in darkness, completely deserted, and so were the streets. No sign of Carla. I walked back yet again to the boarding house and climbed the stairs wearily to check on Dora. I sat on the bed and wept silently so as not to disturb her. I was sixteen years old. Where was Carla? She could be lying in a ditch somewhere – dead, my vivid imagination ran riot. I sat and cried until 4 a.m. when I heard the door bang, three floors below, the dog bark and Carla call it a "fucking mutt!" She then burst into the room, waking Dora, and proceeded to give us a barrage of abuse when we queried where she had been. For the whole of the next day she refused to even speak to us. Dora and I went to the joke shop and bought a spoon with a hole in the bottom and settled it into the sugar bowl on the table at breakfast. She didn't find it funny. We put a fake spider in the bed, that didn't bring her round either, or tap into the sense of humour that didn't appear to be there. As it turned out, Carla's parents were also spending a few days in a hotel at the other end of the town and we had arranged to meet them the next day. Carla would not leave my side, and once more, threatened me to 'keep my mouth shut!' I *so* wanted to tell my lovely auntie Gwyneth, how Carla had behaved but I knew how much it would hurt her, so once more I dutifully kept my mouth well and truly shut!

Gordon and I had been together a while now. It was the early sixties, the era of bouffant hairdos, Mary Quant, the Beatles – and mini skirts! This was the first time round for the mini skirt and it caused quite a sensation. As you might imagine, dad didn't want his little girl wearing such provocative garments, but they were the 'in' thing, so once again, I had to find a way of keeping dad happy, but being trendy also. This was an easy one. I could wear skirts of a very modest length, but once out of sight, I rolled the waistband over and over as close as my stocking tops would allow, and hey presto! I was wearing a mini. However as if this was not bad enough, Gordon would appear to pick me up and announce that he was not taking me out wearing *that*! My reply of course was, "So don't take me!" I was controlled by my father in a healthy way because I had so much respect for him and knew his concern grew out of love, but I was not about to embark on a life of being controlled by a partner. Remember, Eve was taken from Adam's rib, from his side to be equal to him, not from his feet to be beneath him! It was also an era of Mods and Rockers. Mods had scooters, Rockers had proper bikes. Gordon of course, had always been a Rocker, although now he had passed his driving test, he had moved on and now owned a car. He then decided that I should learn to drive. So, I obtained a provisional driving license, and he took me to a huge car park to practice. Unfortunately the car he

then had, an Austen A40 Devon, could only be started by placing a starting handle into the front, and turning it quickly. Here endeth the first lesson, as it was necessary for him to get out and turn the handle so many times, he was totally exhausted. I lost interest, he lost the energy

Meanwhile I started a new job in the big city and travelled every day by train, and back home again at night. At weekends, I would now occasionally be allowed to stay over at Gordon's. His mother was a widow, as his dad

had died of cancer when Gordon was thirteen years old, and she was a woman who was very set in her ways. Occasionally Gordon would work nights, and despite my age, his mother and I were in bed with a cup of Ovaltine by 9 p.m sharp. I would have little sleep as I shared a room with her, and she snored very loudly indeed, a trait which Gordon has sadly inherited,
but all in the name of love.

As I was settling into an organised way of life, working by day, seeing Gordon at night, and caring for Dana whenever I could, Dora had met a new man. His name was Joe. Now Joe had a prosthetic leg due to a motorcycle accident when in the Navy. He was a handsome young man, but alas a townie, like Gordon. Dora and Dana however, were still trying to adjust to life without Vince. To give them a break, I decided that we should visit auntie Maggie in Hull, who had said we could stay any time. We packed our suitcases and explained to Dana that she was going on a holiday with mummy and me. Gordon had stepped in and offered to drive us there, which would be preferable to taking the train. The night before we were due to travel, Dora and Joe went out for a drink, a mile or two away in a neighbouring village. Dora had her own key, and so at around 10 p.m. my parents and I went up to bed, we had a busy day tomorrow. Dana was already fast asleep in her cot, and by now, I was back sleeping in my own room. At 2 a.m. I was woken by a knocking on the front door. My parents were sleeping deeply and were oblivious to the knocking. Who could this be, disturbing us at this hour? I ventured quietly downstairs and answered the door to two uniformed police officers. They proceeded to ask me if Dora lived at this address, my heart skipped a beat, this was so familiar, and memories of losing Vince came flooding back. However, they confirmed that Dora and Joe had been involved in a accident on the way home. Once more my faulty heart flipped. Apparently the hand controls on Joe's specially adapted car, had jammed on a bend, and they had crashed into a large oak tree. At this point the police were unclear regarding Dora's condition, although Joe had been discharged from hospital. I woke my parents and they were also understandably shocked at this devastating news.

There was no way of getting to the hospital in Sheffield that night, and a 'phone call had to suffice to establish Dora's condition, which thankfully was stable. However, my father agreed that mum and I should go to the hospital the next day. When we arrived, they refused to let us see her, declaring that her mother was already at her bedside. I was now tiring of the shock, the lack of information and the concern for Dora's condition. Unfortunately, I informed the nurse, not so calmly, that *we* were her family and if we didn't set eyes on Dora in the next five minutes, I would call the police! She complied. When we entered the ward, Dora looked dreadful. Her face was peppered with tiny shards of glass from the windscreen, her legs were cut and bruised where they had connected with the dashboard of the car, but otherwise she

had had a narrow escape. No seatbelts in those days, her face had collided with the windscreen, and her legs had come into sharp contact with the low dashboard of the car. However, sitting beside the bed was Joe – and *his* mother! They had lied and told
the nurses they were her family in order to see her, hence our ordeal at reception.

Once we were satisfied that Dora was going to be o.k., we decided that I would still take Dana on her holiday to Hull as planned. So the next day Gordon drove Dana and me there and deposited us with Auntie Maggie. I enjoyed the next few days as I was able to give Dana my full attention 24/7 and loved her company, her chatty cheery little ways. I bought her toys and clothes and pushed her for miles in her little buggy. On our return home to Derbyshire Dora was out of hospital with her face and legs now bereft of glass shards. She now needed recovery time yet again. My dad also needed some recovery time too. He had been having trouble focusing, and a visit to the optician proved he had cataracts on both eyes. He spent a couple of weeks in hospital having the cataracts removed, and his eyelids were stitched down until they healed. He came out wearing very thick spectacles. This was a sad time for dad, not only due to now needing glasses permanently, but it also meant that he would have to leave the Fire Service, which he loved. It was the only time I remember dad ever being ill or being away from work in the forty years he was there.

Now Gordon had asked me to marry him a couple of times but I knew what reaction we would have from my parents, so he bought me a little friendship ring and we settled for that temporarily. I decided that perhaps now was a good time to tell him, that he may not have a wife for many years, due to my lovely G.P.'s prediction. He told me it didn't make any difference to the way he felt and he would ask me again to marry him later.

Speaking of marriage, Dora and Joe decided to tie the knot eventually, and so plans were made. This time Dora wore pale yellow. I was so very pleased that she had found what I thought was happiness again. My only concern was whether Joe would take to Dana and be a good stepfather to her, for I realised it could not be easy caring for a child who was not your own. Either way, I was going to make damn sure my little angel would be o.k. Woe betides *anyone* who wronged her. They married and moved to the big city and I missed them both terribly, but as I was travelling to and from work, and staying with Gordon and his mum now and then, it was relatively easy for me to visit them quite frequently. It was around now that Gordon asked me yet again to marry him, and so we approached my father for permission to become engaged. The age of consent was twenty one back then, and my dad couldn't understand why we didn't wait until I was older and tried to reason with us that this would be more beneficial, but Gordon was very persuasive and put it to my dad that it wouldn't make any difference, he wanted to marry me anyway. Dad eventually gave in; he could see that we were adamant, and perhaps it was better to agree than face the alternative, e.g. going down the same road as Dora, getting pregnant with nowhere to live etc., not that we would have of course. There was no big party however, no celebration, we didn't want to rub salt in dad's wounds so Gordon bought me a ring with a deep blue sapphire in the centre, surrounded by diamonds. I was over the moon.

I didn't know how long our marriage might last. Marriages, apart from my parent's didn't appear to be very enduring for whatever reason, but it seemed like a good idea at the time, we may get two or three years of togetherness, who knows?

My attitude was, if it didn't work, well we could just get a divorce like everyone else – if I lived long enough!

Chapter Three
A Country Girl With A City Life

The wedding preparations were exciting. Mum decided to make the bridesmaid dresses, I wouldn't have it any other way, and it made her so proud to use her skills. We did have a little disagreement however, me being quite wilful, and *always* wanting to be that little bit different, a rebel in fact. You see I wanted my bridesmaids dressed in bright red velvet and white fur – unheard of in this era – but mum finally compromised, only *after* I told her I wanted a black organza wedding gown, at which point she hit the roof! Remember, this was 1967, in a tiny backwater. One *had* to wear white, and one *had* to be married in church – or chapel, against my better judgement, but I had been informed that otherwise it aint happening. I chose the church, simply because it had a lovely long aisle to walk up and a prettier setting, I thought, despite the tombstones.

We had the opportunity of a two-up-two-down, back to back terraced house in Sheffield, this was one reason my father had agreed to our wedding. He had realised that, although young, we were being sensible and doing things the right way. Now we had the house secured, and the rent was reasonable, about nineteen shillings and sixpence, (95p) per week, we had to decide on an actual date for the wedding. In those days, if you were married before the end of the tax year, the government gave you a tax rebate, so to give us as long as possible (six weeks in fact) we decided on the nearest Saturday to the tax year end. This was 1st of April 1967. April Fool's Day!

So now, mum got busy on her trusty treadle, with yards of soft bright red velvet. However, she was *not* going to compromise on the black organza wedding gown, and at the first opportunity, whisked me off to town in search of a fluffy *white* organza creation, which I was going to have if it killed her! So long as I didn't look like one of those toilet roll holders, I had no choice but to comply. I was eighteen years old, still not an adult, what could I do? At the end of a very tiring day treading the streets and pavements of Sheffield, we *still* had not found anything that would fit me! Wedding gowns were for glamorous grown-ups, with painted faces and quaffed hairdos, like the ones I had seen in magazines. I, on the other hand, was 4'11", weighing six and a half stone, and in my opinion very plain, with this most unruly curly hair. What did it really matter? I would have been happy, nipping to the register office in my lunch hour, the goal would have been achieved and dad would still have money in the bank.

Anyhow, as we made our way back to the bus station that day, we had one more bridal shop to see. It was, perhaps, the biggest and boldest, and the most expensive, which was possibly why it had been avoided to begin with, but as I glanced at the window, by now flagging and wishing I had chosen to 'live over the brush,' as they say, I spotted the gown for me! It was *very* straight with a pleated shiny satin train extended from the back, *not* the full flouncy balloon which I was trying so hard to avoid. My mother was also very tired by now and readily agreed to go inside. I would guess she was thinking 'at least it's white.' By this time I had become miraculously revived, as though someone had thrown a jug of water in my face, whilst the assistant disappeared to find me the smallest size they had. I was so excited as I stood in the fitting room and she and my mother helped me into this beautiful creation. The feel and the smell was wonderful to my senses, a rare experience for me, worlds apart from the fifth-hand garments I had been used to as a child. As I stepped into the dress, I could feel the zipper being carefully raised up my spine as I gazed at the unfamiliar reflection in the full length mirror, trying to imagine what I would look like with makeup and hairdo, and a pair of petite size two sandals. To my horror, the hem of the dress piled in a heap at my feet which could not even be seen, I resembled a stubby candle with the wax melted around my toes. The beautiful pointed cuffs of the sleeves were hanging way beyond my fingertips, I was devastated. The very courteous shop assistant could see my obvious disappointment and desperation. She patted my arm in comfort and said "Don't worry dear; I just need to make a 'phone call." Five minutes later she returned with a huge smile on her face. She had rung the designer, who had agreed to make up a dress for me to my exact measurements. Mum and I sat on the bus all the way back to Derbyshire, feeling that we had made great progress. However, I couldn't help the nagging doubt that with so little time to go, the dress may not be ready in time, and I would be the biggest April Fool ever, but things turned out o.k. It was ready the *day before* the wedding!

Meanwhile, back in Sheffield, Gordon had persuaded his mum to allow *him* to marry; he was not yet twenty one. She had also taken him to buy a suit as he had never owned one, and he could hardly walk down the aisle in his beloved leather jacket and Jeans. They never fitted tight enough when new, so Gordon would put them on and lay in the bath to make them shrink to a perfect fit. 'Drainpipes' had to fit perfectly, as the name suggests, but a suit was found, and he was even persuaded to have his shoulder length hair, cut, and shave off his beard. Wow!

The day arrived, Dora was my Matron of Honour (whatever that was all about) Dana, and Gordon's young niece Irene were bridesmaids, and my little nephew Nathan was page boy. Early morning on the 1st April, 1967, I had an appointment with the hairdresser. My wayward curls were to be 'quiffed and quaffed' into an actual style. My pearl tiara was carefully placed between the back-combed strands, the little wisps which usually floated somewhere around my ears were obediently sitting where they had been lacquered to create a framework for this face, which today, *was* wearing eyeliner! My nails had been painted – a delicate pearly shade of course, and I had been eased into my circle stitched, long-line bra which apparently would 'give me a better shape' for the dress! This was later to be stuffed, by a friend, with handfuls of confetti. By now the fog was descending rapidly and I was glad I was not superstitious as this could have been an eerie and gloomy omen for the future.

The church bells tolled, much to my dismay, to announce our forthcoming nuptials as we pulled up at the bottom of the drive. I knew that there would be a very large crowd of villagers gathered outside the gates, watching with hawk-like eyes as I placed my size two sandaled foot out of the car door. This was not because I was an important or

popular person, or bride of the year, for I had gone largely unnoticed by everyone until now. It was as though they had gathered for a public stoning as I stepped out onto the gravel path, and all eyes were on *me*! This you see, was a great pastime, waiting to see if the bride wore white, to see how well the dress fitted, and most importantly, whether there was a 'bump' appearing. *I* proudly had no bump, and my very straight and slim fitting white satin and lace dress, clung to my 4'11" frame perfectly.

As the church organ spewed out the Wedding March, my dad took me by the arm and proudly led me down the aisle, towards Gordon, whom I could see swaying by the alter. I later discovered he had downed twelve straight vodkas in the Bath Hotel, and another six in the Shoulder of Mutton, although he felt stone cold sober. As he giggled his way through the ceremony, this happy feeling was infectious, and as we kneeled to pray at the alter, a strange vision entered my head. I was wearing false nails due to the rough work we had been doing in our new house, and all I could imagine, was one of them coming off in the vicar's hand as he offered mine to Gordon! This caused me to convulse into silent hysterics, and as my shoulders shook, many in the congregation that day had thought I was overcome with emotion. Why disillusion them?

Despite my reluctance to have all this fuss, the day went well. Gordon didn't look at all like a townie, to my mother's approval, and we actually enjoyed the whole experience, with all of our large families, coming from all over, to be with us that day.

As the day, and evening wore on and friends and family drifted home, Gordon and I made our way back to my house to change. A few close family and friends also drifted back for a final drink. As I took care of the ;pleasantries of chatting to everyone, and making sure Gordon's mother and neighbours had managed to secure a lift home, I noticed that Gordon was, one by one, removing all the wedding presents, which had been put on display at one end of the living room. This was the custom, way back then in our part of the world. However, I excused myself in order to investigate what he was doing. His reply was simple: - "We're not going home without them." By the time he had pushed various items, pots, pans, frying pans (we had no less than five) toasters etc., into every nook and cranny, he then carefully piled bedding and towels on the passenger seat, for me to sit on. The only place for my feet was the dashboard and so we drove back to our little two-up-two-down for our wedding night. No honeymoon for us, as my mother-in-law's friend was over from London for the wedding and we were expected to take her out and entertain her the next day.

However, when we arrived at the house that night, I felt completely exhausted *and* hungry. There was a fish and chip shop on the corner of the next street, a complete novelty for me, and I really fancied some after the exhausting day. I asked Gordon if we could have a little walk in the fresh air for some chips. His reply was very authoritative. "This is our wedding night, now let's go upstairs!" Well!! Now my Mother's favourite saying was 'start as you mean to go on' so I decided to exercise this sound education, and promptly informed Gordon, politely, that if I didn't get my fish and chips, he didn't get his 'oats'! As he stomped his way up the steep wooden stairs, I settled down on the kitchen floor in front of the gas fire. I was starting as I meant to go on. Remember my previous quotation: - "Eve was taken from Adam's rib, from his side to be equal to him, not from his feet to be beneath him." This was to be my favourite phrase, one which Gordon would be frequently reminded of in the

future. I was going to be beneath *no* man or woman for that matter. It would appear that Gordon had decided that now we were married I belonged to him in some way, like a possession. How wrong could he be? He would soon find out that this little 'squib' had a mind and a will of her own.

So now, the excitement and anticipation, the planning and the day, were all over. It was Monday morning and back to work at the office. I hadn't been able to have time off for a honeymoon. I did however, enjoy living in the big city and soon found my way around. A bus stop on every corner, shops everywhere, easier to get to work every day, it took minutes instead of an hour and a half. Working so hard to catch up on my education had also paid off. With my qualifications I could get a job almost anywhere with little effort. City life was so exciting for a bumpkin like me, although the view from my window left a lot to be desired. Instead of rolling hills and trees, the babbling brook, the swans and my dad's beautiful garden, we had someone else's back yard, dirty red brick replaced the green fields and across the street someone else's front door, and traffic! I was so used to walking along the street saying hello to everyone I passed, but when I greeted anyone approaching me here, it was met with a puzzled look or an angry glare, so many people, and yet they were so insular and isolated in the midst of a crowd, in their own little worlds, strange! But this was something which later in life would give me great understanding of how children would feel who were taken out of their familiar environment, and into a strange new world, needing to adjust.

It was around this time that our friends across the street decided to take over the tenancy of a local pub, and asked us if we would like to work for them. Both of us were working full time but we thought it might be interesting and bring in some extra cash. So we began working there each evening. Gordon worked sorting the barrels in the cellar, and Jeff put *me* in charge of the small cocktail bar. I felt quite important on that first night behind the bar. I was also being paid half a crown (12.1/2p) per hour. As the customers started rolling in, I put on my best smile. Now, bearing in mind I had rarely been in a pub at all much less worked in one, and considering my sheltered upbringing, one may think this was quite brave. Well actually it was downright stupid! I tried to stick at it for quite a while (not being one to quit easily) but one night when a sleazy looking guy in a beige pac-a-mac, demanded a mop, as he had spilled his drink, I felt I could take no more of these loutish townies, with no manners. I therefore decided to fetch him the mop he so desperately desired, but this time my tiny frame served me well. 'Unfortunately' – as I pushed the mop across the bar, I didn't quite reach too well and the stringy decaying mop head which reeked of Dettol became firmly attached to his face, rather like an unruly beard. That's my version – take it or leave it! Therefore on that high note I walked out. No more bolshy, belligerent men, no more fights amongst the female drinkers in the Tap Room. This new experience I could well do without.

However, Dora was also settling down to life in the big city. Now that we were both city dwellers, we lived within easy reach of one another. Her life with Joe however, was not as settled as we had all hoped. Dora still had her odd ways, no advice seemed to register, and Joe and Dana did not have a father/daughter relationship. They had, by now moved into a first floor maisonette on a housing estate, but the house was rarely clean, and Dora didn't seem too inclined to rectify this. By now though, she was pregnant with her second child, Joe's first. I couldn't help feeling however, that Dana would be pushed out a little when the new baby arrived, which it did a few months later. A baby girl, Tina, she was beautiful, with big eyes and dark curly hair, but something did not seem right with Tina. Dora was told that she had been briefly starved of oxygen during birth and appeared slightly blue. But as she developed over the next few months, she appeared to be o.k. Of course with two children in the family, Dora now found it more difficult than ever to cope. Therefore, Gordon and I would take great pleasure in bringing Dana home at the weekends. We still had no children of our own yet, so we doted on this Angel

It was 1969 and Gordon and I had still had no honeymoon, or any holiday for that matter, so I decided it was time for a break from work, and Dora's problems etc. I therefore booked a holiday for two weeks in Spain, the Costa Brava. It was rare for many people to travel abroad back then, so it was quite exciting. It cost me £39.00 for two weeks full board. It was fantastic, neither of us had ever been abroad before, and everything about it was exquisite. The sea was so blue, the sky was even bluer, the sun shone and the food was great, we didn't want to come home. For the first time in ages we had time to ourselves.

Anyway, a couple of years after this, Dora gave birth to her third daughter, Sally. Sally was a robust bouncing baby, unlike Tina, who was still rather thin and not so mobile, but they were a family unit. However as time passed, I could see cracks in their relationship. Joe was inclined to lose his temper easily, and would often take his anger out on Dora. I could understand why he would be so unhappy, given the state of the house, but there was no excuse for violence and I couldn't condone this, therefore I started to make my feeling known. How long before Joe might lose his temper with my Dana?

Things went from bad to worse. By now Dana had started nursery but was hardly ever there. Dora seemed unable to raise herself out of bed much before midday; the little ones would creep downstairs and salvage what they could for breakfast from the half empty cups left from the night before. They would take handfuls of dry cereal from the packets in the kitchen cupboards, or flour or sugar as an alternative when there was nothing else. Sally would linger in the same nappy she had worn at bedtime.

Dora was always ringing to tell me the latest row she and Joe had had, or the injuries she had sustained from the violence, but the call I received one day was quite different. Dora had been admitted to hospital via emergency. It appeared she had appendicitis and had to spend a couple of weeks in there. Obviously, when she was sent home, she would need time to recover, so I would visit after work or whenever I could, and look after Dana at the weekend. I decided one day that I should help Dora with some washing. She had a cupboard in the kitchen into which she would throw all dirty laundry, until washday. As I opened the cupboard that day, the odour was overpowering, but we filled up the twin tub washing machine and pretty soon had a system going, whereby Dora would load the machine whilst I ran up and down the public staircase to the wash lines below. By the time I was back up the stairs, the next load would be ready for hanging out to dry. After three or four loads, I breathlessly climbed the stairs once more to find Dora also completely exhausted by now, and told her to rest. Not wanting to waste time, I decided to load up the machine which would have been for the last time, when Dora asked me what I was doing, as she said she had washed the nappies and here was I industriously working away at the job in hand and therefore put in the final load of clothing. This was no big deal except that I hadn't realised that the nappies were not pre-sterilised, and still held their contents of faeces and urine! This final wash load was therefore slightly *less* clean than before it entered the machine, and certainly not white! And so life would continue once more, Dora sleeping 'till noon, kids not going to school, Joe working, for if nothing else he was a hard worker, and in the pub drinking most evenings. In between, the calls would continue from Dora with her tales of woe.

Let's not forget our other 'Angel' Carla. She had by now married her latest boyfriend, Keith, mainly because she was pregnant. However she was given a beautiful wedding in the village church. The usual crowd had gathered to see her in her pale blue lace, as she smiled all the way down the aisle. My mum, and hers, had spent hours in another little two-up-two-down, painting, papering and scrubbing. Carla was also soon to become a city dweller like Dora and I. However, she and Keith hadn't long moved into this little house and settled down when it was revealed that the baby Carla was carrying wasn't Keith's, the father was in fact his best friend! Chaos and mayhem ensued here. Wow! This was yet again a skeleton we could not keep in the cupboard. This was an occasion when Carla couldn't tell me to keep my mouth shut. She had to take full responsibility for this one. Forthwith, Keith and Carla were promptly divorced, and Carla discreetly married the father of her child, but to the family, she was still an Angel, she was *so* credible you see, when she wanted you to believe what she was telling you that is, unless you knew her inside out as I did, you could be so easily deceived.

One of the saddest outcomes of Carla's machinations was shortly after my uncle Jack died. I used to love going to stay with uncle Jack and auntie Cass in Knutsford. There were many members of my very large extended family whom I loved dearly, and these were two of them. Knutsford is one of the prettiest little towns in Cheshire. Auntie and uncle owned a small dairy on a tiny cobbled street, which last time I visited had been turned into a fancy lingerie shop, its old charm completely destroyed. Anyway apart from my dad, uncle Jack was one of the most patient men I have ever known, and also the most wonderful artist. He would sit with me by the lake near their home, puffing out a soothing aroma from his pipe, which appeared to be a permanent attachment as we rarely saw him without it. He and auntie Cass had never had children of their own, they were actually cousins, so whenever I went to stay, they doted on me and of course I loved the attention. Auntie Cass was a busy, enthusiastic lady, and would chat with the customers who came into the dairy to buy custard pies and vanilla slices, and those lovely cream horns filled with jam and of course swirly fresh cream. She would lovingly create for me, a fishing net from some wire, threaded through one of her very strong stocking tops chopped off and tied in a knot underneath so that I could go down to the stream and catch minoes. I was strangely disappointed when they died, as I hadn't realised they needed food, if only someone had enlightened me!

Uncle Jack, as I said was a fine artist, but not just on canvas, or modelling clay, oh no! He could turn *anything* into an art form. He would mould clay, paint for hours with me and show me how to form the lake, the swans, the shade and the light. He would take a small sharp knife and carve someone's face out of wood. It fascinated me and I loved being with him, and I loved art. Their best friends owned a pub at the top of the street and they would often take me to see them and one Saturday afternoon, auntie Cass took me through to the dairy to choose my sweets as always, but as an extra treat had bought me some Babychams from the pub. As we sat watching T.V. that evening they lovingly poured the Babycham into a long stemmed glass with the Babycham logo on the side. It felt so grown up and it tasted wonderful. It was 'pear juice' you see, and would be good for me. They poured me more and more, and as I later discovered, I had downed no less that six bottles of this 'harmless' pear juice. Apparently, as I sipped the last drop, I went out like a light and woke up the next morning with a pounding headache. My lovely auntie and uncle naively hadn't realised that Babycham was alcoholic!

As I awoke each morning, the first thing I would see as my eyes slowly came into focus was an enormous wood carving which hung on the facing wall. Uncle Jack had created this with a pocket pen-knife. It was a depiction of the 'appearance' of the Angel of Mons, during the war. (This was so ironic as you will later see as 'Angels' feature here too) The intricacy was amazing. Even the rats in the trenches were perfectly formed, and two huge ANGELS stood on each side looking down, as though protecting all who gazed at them. As I said, the irony, how I wished *my* particular 'angels' were so magnanimous.

Now it was this very carving which was to be at the centre of such controversy. After my beloved uncle's death, this beautiful carving was to be donated to the village church, the village where he grew up. A wonderful gesture I thought. However, as Dora and I were walking along the village one day, we saw Carla emerging from the front door of my favourite cousin's house. She had paid a rare visit to her and her parents. Dora and I thought immediately how odd this was, as Carla rarely visited them at all, unlike the many hours, days and nights I had often stayed, and enjoyed. However odd it was, this section of my family did not speak to Dora or me for a very long time. I feel perhaps some things which had been said had been completely misinterpreted. Once again, whatever Carla had said that day, she was believed yet again.

Chapter Four

Motherhood

Gordon and I had now been married for almost two and a half years and it was soon to be my 21st birthday. I was already married and running a home, and still not officially an adult. Gordon still couldn't take me to a pub without being asked for proof of my age. I suppose my 4'11" frame was the problem. We'd had our ups and downs mainly because Gordon found it difficult to grasp the fact that I was definitely *not* his possession. I would not be trodden on like an old doormat, and *woe* betide any man who ever laid a hand on me! His ideas of the wife being at home chained to the kitchen sink were definitely outdated. He was soon to have this proved, when one day he didn't turn up to dinner on time. Arriving home late, his excuses were so lame, that the middle size of our shiny new set of saucepans was hurled at him from across the kitchen. The pointy end of the handle quivered as it stuck in the wooden panel of the door, not to mention the contents of which Gordon was now wearing as a shampoo! We had many occasions in the early days, where his 'townie' ways and my 'bumpkin' upbringing would clash. We would have pillow fights around the bedrooms to such an extent that the air was thick with feathers, and although we hadn't noticed we must have made a great deal of noise, as on night, a neighbour shouted to her husband to "Get t' police 'Arry, she's gonna kill 'im!" However, it was never anything too serious, and we would always end up in heaps of laughter. From then on the only topic we would differ over was my involvement with 'Dora and Joe every time I was called upon to sort out their dilemmas. But! Dora was the only sister I had and she always seemed inadequate in some way, unable to fend for herself, and wallowed in self-pity. Worst of all, there were now three little 'angels' and I could never bear the thought of any child being unhappy, for whatever reason.

As I said, my 21st birthday was approaching and I could plan a party. We had our own house, no-one to ask, or disturb. So I set about making plans. I ordered a cake, beautifully iced and decorated, invited all our friends and bought myself a dream of a dress in white lace with little pearl buttons fastening an organza panel at the front. I had to buy white underwear as the dress was ever so slightly see-through. I felt very daring and deliciously wicked. The memory of my bottle green knickers versus red lacy briefs came flooding back to me and made me smile. Yeah! Let's do it! The evening arrived and the party got under way. We had alcohol, cheap bubbly plonk and *Babycham*; I knew how alcoholic *that* was. I wore false nails and false eyelashes, very trendy and desirable back then. Well, I deserved to be a tart just *once* before I died. However, for me, this was to be the first experience of how alcohol could turn happiness into hell in the blink of an eye. Dora and Joe drank frequently, and tonight was no exception. In Joe's usual style (punch first-think later) he punched Gordon in the eye knocking him backwards. Gordon naturally wanted to punch Joe in return, but given that he was not generally violent, and Joe wearing his prosthetic leg was standing at the top of the steep stairs, Gordon instead punched the wall of this old house, and the weak plaster immediately caved in, thereby leaving two gaping holes in the wall. Meanwhile as I tended to Gordon's cut and bleeding eye, my white lace dress was now stained with his blood. In Dora's usual style she whipped it from me and draped it into some very hot water, just as she had done years ago with my blue skirt, thereby reducing my lovely dress to a blouse! To top it all, someone sat on my lovely birthday cake until it resembled a trifle. I would never forget my 21st birthday.

This was the first time I had *ever* been so drunk, however when all the frivolity was over and the mess cleared away the result of this fracas was that now I was officially an adult and it was time to settle down a little. In my opinion, I have also never since dressed so tarty, others may think differently, but – Am I bothered?

We had recently become friends with a woman who introduced us to the Ouija board. We would cut up pieces of paper with letters and numbers on and space them around the table. A group of us would gather and place our forefingers on an upturned glass. I could not *do* this! I was an atheist and was greatly amused at everyone sitting with great concentration as the glass started to move around the board. If you don't believe in a God, then you cannot similarly believe in a Devil, for they are adversaries, opposites of each other. However, I didn't like the messages the board spelled out, and became quite spooked by the accuracy of it sometimes. Find new friends perhaps?

Both Dora and Carla now had families and although I only had a few years left to live, I found myself pregnant too. It was quite an easy pregnancy I thought. Although I had low blood pressure and would pass out occasionally I never suffered from morning sickness. All those months of illness as a child, and now I was virtually sailing through this with happy anticipation. My only concern was whether my 'dickey' heart would survive the onset of labour, and would I even see the face of this child growing inside me. Despite all else, I tried to concentrate on the forthcoming event. Planning names, would it be a girl, or a boy, what colour hair and eyes, what little personality would he or she have? Gordon would get the tin bath down for me, as our little house didn't have a bathroom, a step backwards from our new house in the village. As I sunk into the hot water breathing in the fragrance of the Lavender bath salts I'd thrown in, I would talk to this little, as yet unknown person, and sing as my mother had to me, thankful that the little ears yet forming could not clearly hear my dulcet tones.

I still worked whilst I was pregnant, until I could no longer reach the typewriter for the huge bump in front of me. At one time it was thought I may be expecting twins, as my mother had, and my cousin and aunt before me, although they had always died, but to my relief there was only the *one* foetus. My mother-in-law told tales of Gordon weighing 10lbs at birth. This bothered me slightly as I felt my tiny frame would split in two!

At this point Gordon had started working for a double glazing company. This I found quite difficult as it often meant him working until very late at night. I would sit on my own and feel desolate. I was by now heavily pregnant and longed for company. After an evening's work Gordon and his boss would then go to a night club or two, maybe Stringfellows, which was an early venture of Pete Stringfellow before he made his millions. There were 'go-go' dancers and champagne, and on one of these lonely nights of mine, I'd had enough, and decided to ring the club. I spoke to the doorman, who knew Gordon by now, and told him to ask Gordon to please come home. My ultimatum was that if he was not home by midnight, I would be down there and sit cross-legged in the midst of their 'go-go' dancers until he did so. I also informed him of my huge fecund shape just so he knew I wouldn't blend in. I didn't care because by now I had foolishly downed half a bottle of brandy, but I meant it. However Gordon knew me so well, and he therefore knew that I actually *would* do it, and sure enough the next night be was home by 11p.m.

It was now almost four years into our marriage and we were still together, why was I here, why was I now pregnant? It suddenly dawned on me how totally selfish I was, to have married Gordon, knowing it wouldn't be for long, to be having a child whom I would soon be leaving motherless. I had wanted to cram *so* much into my short life while I had it, and hadn't stopped to think of anyone else. I decided none of this was fair on any of us and decide to leave. My 'life' wasn't working out as I had planned at all. I walked out and returned home to my parents. I left Gordon a note to say I would let him know when the baby was born, its weight, name, girl boy etc. My parents were wonderful and didn't ask me anything, although I am happy to say, Gordon gave up this awful job and came after me. He took a new job locally as a milkman, less exciting I know but more conducive to our situation, and we tried to settle back into family life. How cruel we had been to each other.

The day I went into labour, I was perming my mother's hair. As Gordon prepared to go to work, I said I might not be here when he came home, hoping he would do what other new fathers do, and go into a panic and whiz me off to the hospital. Not Gordon! Never a man to panic, he donned his coat and said if I wasn't there when he arrived home he would know where to find me, and off he went on his milk round. I finished mum's hair and lacquered it to perfection, all the while she was fussing as I repeatedly bent double as the contractions came and went. I did the dusting, and donned my favourite pink and white maternity dress, then made sure my very long hair was curled and pinned into swirls on top of my head, and the slap on my face was painted like a Picasso. *I* was not going to be one of those sweaty, dishevelled women; *I* would give birth with dignity, just like those women in the movies. By now the contractions were every three minutes, so I decided now would be a good time to get myself to the hospital.

However, at approximately 9 p.m. on the fifth of December, 1970 my daughter came into the world. She weighed 6 ½ lbs, had hardly any hair to speak of, big –no – *huge* blue eyes and a little button nose. One ear was squished and crumpled out of shape, and the skin all over her little body was scaly and peeling. Apparently she was overdue; I called her my little frog.

However, all this said, she had grown into the most beautiful young woman. We called her Angeline Melanie. As I gazed at this little miracle before me, and counted her tiny little fingers and toes, the nurse came in to tidy me up. As she stood in the brightly lit delivery room, she looked at me and commented on how glamorous I looked, and how lovely my hair was. *Result!* I had achieved it; I had given birth with dignity! The pride in my new born infant was over-taken by pride in my abilities. As I returned the nurse's smile, I noticed a mischievous grin on her face as she collapsed in a heap of laughter, and pointed out to me the pile of hairpins on the floor, the long curls of springy hair now protruding from my head, rather like the Medusa, not to mention the black streaks of my mascara which had deserted my lashes, and was now travelling down my cheeks, chin and beyond! Giving birth was not as easy as I had imagined, and when I was informed that she had been born with *three teeth*, I decided that breast feeding was definitely OUT!

Seriously, it didn't matter to me what my baby looked like. My little frog was beautiful, she was part of me and a miracle to have survived, she was mine, and she was something wonderful I had achieved in my life. Only another four years of it to go.

It took us a while to get used to night feeds, nappy changes etc., just like any other young couple. Gordon did his share and was a doting father, therefore quelling my fears of leaving them. I knew instinctively he would be a good dad, and take good care of her no matter what. This marriage had stayed stable much longer than I anticipated. I never imagined it would get this far, and even to start a family. Anyhow we plodded along; Gordon worked hard to provide for us, as I now obviously had to stay at home with my baby. I enjoyed motherhood. Making a child happy and contented was a wonderful feeling, seeing the smiling face and progress day by day was so rewarding. As I watched Angeline growing and learning I felt sadder for poor Dana, Tina, and Sally who were finding life with Dora and Joe so difficult. They didn't go to school; they witnessed frequent fights and arguments which made them very insecure and afraid.

I didn't drive in those days and each time I visited Dora, it required two bus journeys. Gordon's mother also needed more care at this time, she couldn't get about like she used to. When Gordon was thirteen years old his father had died of cancer, so he had always needed to be grown-up and look out for his mum.

Whenever Dora would cry for help, it was almost always late at night. I would receive a call and climb on the first buses I could, to get me there as quickly as possible. I had just taken a bath and washed my hair. My mother was staying for the weekend and Gordon was on night-shift. I had just made us a cup of tea when the 'phone rang. It was Dora; she was ringing from a call box at the corner of the maisonettes. I could barely hear her words as she was so distraught. I dressed and put on my coat, wet hair blowing in the wind and travelled the two bus rides to the other side of the city. Dora was still standing in the 'phone box to keep warm and for fear of Joe. He had apparently threatened her with an old knife he had from his navy days. He told her he kept it under his pillow, for when he needed to use it. He also had a gun in the cupboard. Dora was terrified, *I* was furious. I took Dora by the arm and together, she reluctantly, we marched up to the door of the maisonette. I was so angry I didn't wait to knock. I pushed my way in and gave Joe a very verbal warning of what would happen if he continued this abuse. I was not afraid of him. If he decided to take my life, after all he would only shorten it by a couple of years or so. Once more, my anger obliterated my selfishness. I wasn't afraid, but Dora was, and he could have taken her life too!

I explained to him very carefully, that just as he kept the knife and the gun, and Dora couldn't sleep for fear, he also should not sleep, or alternatively keep his prosthetic limb firmly attached at all times. Otherwise one night *I* might creep in and discard it down the rubbish chute at the end of the block. Would you believe, this violent bad tempered man did not say a word?

There were to be many such occasions in the years to come. Dora cut her feet on broken glass when windows were smashed, she even turned up at our door with a dislocated jaw, Joe soon followed wanting to talk to her but I refused to let him over my doorstep.

That idyllic childhood now seemed so far away, and life was fraught with traumas, one after the other. We were constantly battling to restore peace and sanity but to no avail. I had even forgotten my ever-shortening life span, there wasn't time or energy to think about it, and yet I felt surprisingly well, and hardly ailed more than the occasional 'cold.' Not only this, but my mother-in-law required more and more help, and plus I felt the need still to visit my parents frequently simply because I loved them, and travelled back to the Styx every week to visit, or even to stay a night or two. Here is another lesson I have learned, and that is that children need as many loving adults in their lives as possible, and I was going to make sure Angeline experienced the love of grandparents, as I never had.

Dana was now growing and had a strangely mischievous streak to her personality, which was not always amusing. One day there was such a panic, as Dana had gone missing. We searched the house, calling her name as loudly as we could. We then, with fear and trepidation, turned our attentions to the nearby woods. Just as we were discussing whether we should call the police, out popped Dana – from the laundry cupboard. She had buried herself amongst the week's laundry, my goodness; she could have been gone forever! She was clearly ecstatic at the worried looks on our faces and the stir she had created deliberately. I began to have a very uncomfortable feeling that night. Something about her behaviour reminded me of Carla. However, I quickly dismissed this, and my fondness for Dana outweighed my anger, and I felt only relief that she was o.k.

There was another occasion, when Dora went into hospital, and Gordon and I had called in to see how Joe and the kids were coping. As we knocked, Dana came to the door, and told us that her dad had gone to the pub and she was looking after the young ones! Dana was no more than nine or ten years old. Gordon was so incensed by this, that we bundled them all into the car, but we only had room for one more in our small house. Now as anyone who knows Gordon will tell you, he gets to the point. The maternal family name was Sherman, his grandfather had been a Sergeant Major in the

Royal Horse Artillery, and was stationed in India for many years. Gordon's mother was a straight talking woman, and so therefore was Gordon. As I was one day to discover, so would be Angeline. It's quite an amusing allegory when you think about it; they were like a set of 'Sherman Tanks!' pushing their way to victory. So anyway, Gordon took Tina and Sally by their tiny hands and led them into the pub, straight up to the bar – to Joe, who by now was well into a boozy chat with his mates. Gordon's words were short and sweet as always. "These are *your* kids now *you* look after 'em!" There was little else we could do. Joe came running after us out of the pub as we drove away. I wickedly felt good that he had been shown up in front of all his drinking friends, but couldn't help my overwhelming sadness as I watched Tina and Sally's crumpled and tear stained little faces becoming ever smaller in the distance, my gaze fixed on them through the rear window of the car as we sped away. We took Dana home and kept her with us until Dora returned from hospital.

Now my parents were understandably horrified by all of this happening to their eldest daughter, and their grandchildren. My father offered all kinds of help to Dora, if she would leave Joe. He would finance the divorce and provide her with anything she needed, but Dora seemed unable to walk away from her abusive life, and so it continued. Events were now turning in our family, into situations we had never encountered before.

Motherhood however, was happening to all of us. A whole new generation was changing the equilibrium of family life. Some of us coped with and enjoyed our 'mini-me's' while others like Dora found it difficult. Carla also found it to be a problem and announced to her daughter, Carrie, that *she* being born had ruined her life! What a dreadful burden for a child to live with.

Another person in my life, my friend Janine was also to become a mother again. Janine was a very attractive young woman, and yet she always seemed to be trying to prove somehow, that she had 'what it takes,' and embarked on numerous affairs, all of which she would sit and discuss with me and ask my opinion. However, when she asked me whether or not she should terminate her latest pregnancy, I gave her my opinion and of course used scripture to back up my thoughts. Janine was Catholic and would always take an interest in the scriptures, although her priest had told her not to question the Bible. How ridiculous, should we be puppets and have our strings pulled? Or should we not confirm and obtain proof of what we have put our faith in? I may not have mentioned before that Janine had always wanted to become a Nun, but her status as wife and mother prevented her, and indeed she had another friend she would talk to about her problems. This lady was a Carmelite Nun who lived in a convent on the outskirts of Sheffield. Now the Carmelites were different from most orders. To begin with the Habits they wore were brown rather than the traditional black. Unusually, this was also an enclosed order, which meant that the nuns dedicated their lives to prayer, and stayed within the convent walls. During my chats with Janine my worst fears were founded one day when she asked me if I would visit her friend, with special dispensation. I feel with hindsight, Janine possibly wanted to watch and listen to us battling out our different beliefs, but it was not like that at all.

I agreed to go along with Janine to the convent. It was a murky day as we walked up the drive and raised the iron knocker which hung on the large studded oak door. Our knocks were answered by a man dressed in black; he was very austere although very polite as he showed us into a waiting room. He was the only outsider to gain entry and handled all the day to day secular needs

This place was cold, not only in a physical sense, but also because it was so sparsely furnished, just two upright wooden chairs, and grey stone walls with no décor at all. Eventually we were shown into another larger room at the top of several flights of stone stairs. This room was equally bare, although it did have a strange sort of metal grill in the wall with spikes on all joints, and an equally strange long oak drawer beneath it. The two chairs in this room were situated facing the metal grill, therefore we naturally took up position on them as there was nowhere else to sit. I sat gazing at the grill in the wall with mystified curiosity, although Janine clearly knew the procedure. After a few moments wait, the wooden shutters I could see beyond, opened loudly, and the sound echoed around the grey stone walls. There was a space beyond, connecting to another grill in the wall of the adjacent room we could now see into. Sitting on a wooden chair, similar to ours, was a very frail elderly lady dressed in the Carmelite Habit.

As she began to speak, I listened carefully to her soft voice. She was a kindly lady with good intentions; she had devoted her life to prayer for the less fortunate. I began to wonder how less fortunate one could be, than to live in a place like this. However, as she spoke and gave us her blessing, Janine seemed to be urging me to discuss Satan, The Devil, Lucifer, with great enthusiasm. I asked the Sister what her thoughts were regarding the Devil, she answered that the Devil was not a real being, but was a 'quality' that was to some extent in all of us. (There will be times in the future when I quite agree with this in a certain light.) However I felt obliged to point out to her that in the book of Genesis, the Devil had been a real being, who had tempted Eve. He had later tried to tempt

Jesus in the wilderness, and offered Jesus all the kingdoms of the world, which if we think about it must have been given to *him* at some point. Also that he had been created by God as an Angel and was given the name Lucifer. AH! The first angel who told a lie, however *this* one had wings *and* horns! As the conversation continued this lady clearly could not argue with the writings in the very Bible she so clearly did not fully understand. She then asked me if I had any other questions. I had just one; I asked her how long it had been since she had left the convent? Her reply? Fifty three years!

Now Janine and her husband Jack, had everything, a beautiful home, own business, and money no object. They decide to move out to Derbyshire. Not far from my place of birth, and bought a cow shed, barn and stables, and had it transformed into the most desirable dwelling you could wish for. Now, being an expert of sorts on village life, I had explained to Janine the necessity for discretion, living in these small villages, but Janine seemed to disbelieve my good intentions and soon after, began yet another affair with a local farmer. His land was above their new dwelling place, and he would wave to her as he drove his tractor across the fields. Eventually Janine gave birth to yet another child which she confided in me, belonged to her farmer friend. Sadly one day, for whatever reason we never knew, he threw a rope around the safety rail over a disused mine shaft, put it around his neck and jumped! Janine ended up in the psychiatric hospital for quite a while. However, when she recovered, and moved house yet again, she started another affair with the vicar, and disappeared with him to America! I much later asked her how she met him, and she explained to me that she had become an embalmer and met him at the funeral parlour where she worked. Yes! I'm afraid I couldn't help myself, I asked her if he blessed 'em and she stuffed 'em!

By now I was beginning to realise that there were several little children who were suffering emotional abuse as a result of their parent's selfishness. Where was it all going to end? I had been so protected from all of this in my youth, and found it quite heartbreaking that all children couldn't have a wonderful childhood like mine, where there was an endless supply of love.

Chapter Five

Rescue and Reprieve

As I pushed Angeline in her buggy up the hill to the bus stop, I was gasping for air. This was becoming an ever increasing problem, and at the age of twenty six, my thoughts turned to those dark days as a child, lying in bed in pain, being told I would not reach thirty. It had meant nothing to me then, thirty was ancient, but now, as my life was really just beginning, it was also ebbing away. I had a beautiful daughter, and I really didn't want to die, but I said nothing to anyone, not even Gordon about my feelings.

I had spoken to Dora about her life being in upheaval but felt so helpless. I had a husband and child of my own to consider, and couldn't just take in someone else's child. However, I needn't have worried, Gordon could also see the neglect that Dana in particular was suffering, not being Joe's natural child and Gordon was the one who decided she should come and live with us for a while. I put this to Dora and she readily agreed, hoping that she and Joe could patch things up, repair their marriage and then Dana could return to them. We replaced Angeline's bed with a set of bunks, and she and Dana shared her little room, it would only be a temporary arrangement. Gordon 'kept' Dana without a penny from anyone, cared for her like his own, more than her step-father could even do. He fed her, clothed her, and took her on holidays, with no reward, except the knowledge that we had rescued her from her confused life.

I was now working for Sheffield Newspapers, for the 'Women's Circle.' I wanted to return to some sort of part-time work, now that Angeline was growing. I saw the ad' for couriers to take groups from the 'Women's Circle' on outings and holidays etc., and so applied. I was selected along with half a dozen others, from over two hundred applicants and was thrilled. It wasn't my usual shorthand dictation and typing, it was completely different and exciting.

On one occasion I had taken thirty or forty people on a canal barge tour for the day. It was summer and my group looked so relaxed as the barge slowly moved among the reeds, and flowers along the canal bank. I had left Dana and Angeline with my mother-in-law, as she was always willing to baby sit for work – not pleasure, and I called to collect the girls on my return to Sheffield. I was not feeling too well, and appeared to be finding it quite difficult to breathe. However, we made it home on the bus, and walked up the hill from the bus stop. As we entered the house I was by now, gasping for air, my lungs felt as though they were not big enough and my head was about to explode. I verbally guided Dana to call the doctor's number, and immediately collapsed onto the sofa. Got to keep alert, couldn't leave the children even to pass out. Although it must have been minutes, it felt like hours before the doctor arrived, he examined me then sat back and said, "You're having an asthma attack!" The pollen along the river bank had had a drastic effect, but ASTHMA!? Was I not going to die tonight then?

I did recover from this attack, and had several visits from my G.P. in the days that followed. I talked to him about my rheumatic fever, about my time being almost UP! "Don't be ridiculous!" he said with a bemused look. "Yes, you have a heart murmur which is a result of the rheumatic fever, but it's nothing to worry about, and we'll soon get your asthma under control." My head was buzzing. Was I not going to die then? From that day to this, I have never had another asthma attack! Yes I get more breathless at some times of year when the weather changes, but the asthma is mild and well controlled. *And* best of all, I was going to LIVE! As I write this book I have up to now almost doubled my thirty years, but it was not to be plain sailing, Oh no! As you will soon see, life in our family was about to go rapidly downhill, and you'll never guess who would be the main instigator!

My little Angel was now living with us and sharing our home. Angeline was so small and a good child. She rarely complained and we gave her all the love and attention our parents had lavished on us, not to mention the love and attention we also gave to Dana. Because of my early memories of not being offered sweets in a group etc., it had left me with very defined feelings about equality. I never wanted my children to experience those awful sinking feelings, which meant that whatever my own child had, Dana had also. This didn't just apply to material things, but also to hugs and kisses and praise etc. *All* children deserve to be treated equally. However, Angeline did not always appear to be happy following this addition to our family. She seemed at times unhappy and unsettled. She would tell me how she couldn't sleep at night for Dana teasing her and telling her things which would upset her. I couldn't see any reason at the time for Dana to do this, and wondered if Angeline was feeling a little sensitive and 'pushed out', maybe a little more attention would solve this 'minor' problem and after all, we had taken Dana on the understanding that as soon as Dora and Joe could sort out their differences, and make a few changes in their lives, Dana could return to them 'unscathed.' How naïve, I had no experience in the damage children could sustain emotionally from such upheaval, my maternal instincts were just the natural ones that every mother *surely* had after giving birth, were they not?

As the weeks and months passed, Dana progressed in every way. The school was so pleased that in the time she had been with us, she hadn't missed a day. She grew and filled out, she enjoyed being dressed in clean, well fitting clothes, having her hair brushed and braided and tied in ribbons. After six months with us, Dora and Joe appeared ready to take Dana back. So we packed all her newly acquired clothes, toys and belongings and returned her to the bosom of her family in the maisonettes on the council estate, hoping she would rehabilitate into her old life, hoping the fights and the arguments would now stop, and Dora would get up in the mornings and take the children to school, of course, I was wrong yet again!

It was now time to concentrate a little more on Angeline. By now my parents had four grandchildren, but sadly saw only Angeline on a regular basis, as it was just too much effort for Dora to get on the bus to Derbyshire. I still had a wonderful relationship with my mum and dad and visited them frequently. Sometimes Gordon would be going to work at 6 a.m. but would wake up Angeline and we would climb into the car half asleep. Gordon would drop us off at my parent's house on his way to work in the next village. We would sometimes stay the weekend and Gordon would collect us on Sunday evening to bring us home. Angeline was surrounded by love. She adored her daddy, he was her hero, her grandparents were the best thing since sliced bread, as they say, and she would take walks in the countryside with my mother as I had done.

One day when Gordon was at work, his friend knocked on the door, and asked if we were interested in a 'new' car. Obviously I knew nothing about cars but it *looked* nice, it was an Austin A40 Farina, aubergine, the latest colour, and he wanted fifteen pounds for it. This needed some consideration as fifteen pounds was almost a week's wage, but I thought Gordon would be pleased and surprised. However he was *not* pleased. When he came home and saw the car, looked under the bonnet, and under the chassis, he was *not* pleased at all! I had apparently bought a wreck. Each time we drove out in it, we would periodically have to stop to pick up the quarter light which had popped out and landed half a mile back on the road, and this was one of the minor problems. Not to mention the night we had gone out with Phillip and Diane, and on the way back, Gordon and Phillip felt the urge to stop and visit a tree in the woods at the roadside, whilst Diane and I sat chatting in the car, waiting, and watching the trees slowly passing the windows. Apparently the handbrake didn't work either, and we were careering down the road – with no driver. It was rather amusing though, watching our two spouses chasing after us on foot. Eventually the car had to go however!

As Angeline grew and started school, I continued my free-lance work as a courier, and travelled far and wide. Gordon was always willing to stay with Angeline if I needed to go away. This was great, especially if I needed to go abroad. One such event took me to France; I took two coaches full of people with the aid of one photographer, a reporter, one driver and a co-driver, by road. We drove down to Dover and boarded the Hovercraft for Bologne. It was a rough crossing and most of the passengers were sea sick, *I* was not. My fear of water occupied my mind so much I had no time to be sick. I overcame my fear by sitting below, therefore unable to see the rolling deep relentless ocean through the window. I was so relieved when the huge craft floated up on the shores of France. We had quite a busy itinerary, and we arrived at the beautiful hotel feeling very tired after the eighteen hour journey, and ready for a meal and some sleep in our five star rooms. However, on arrival at our destination, in Rheims, I discovered that the travel company had double booked and some of us were forced to stay in a very grotty boarding house across the road. Naturally there were a lot of angry people that day, but I sought out the driver, who actually owned the company and told him he must carry the can and apologise to our passengers. This didn't go down too well with him, especially as I had barged into his five star, en-suite bedroom and disturbed his rest on his five star bed, but I was determined he would do his duty. After such a hard day, I decided to spend the evening with a couple of my passengers, a mother and her daughter, who was about my age. We had a meal and a long chat and then returned to our respective lodgings for the night. These two were in the posh hotel; I was in the awful place over the road. As I approached the door to climb the worn stairs to my room, I found to my amazement that it was locked and bolted. I trudged my way across the street to the posh five star place and asked the concierge to call the manager for advice. He decided that he could not understand me; obviously my English qualifications were invalid here, oh how I wished I had studied French. However, when I discreetly informed him in *English*, that if I didn't speak to the manager, right away, I would be spending the night on the floor of the foyer, right in front of the reception desk, he called for the manager! The next evening we had a meal arranged for the whole group in the Champagne Caves of the famous Moet and Chandon. Just about everyone was drunk by the end o the evening as magnums of champagne had freely flowed. I spent most of the night putting people to bed, retrieving a set of dentures from down the loo, and informing a rather hoity-toity lady that she had broken her wrist when attempting the French folk dancing, (I was in raptures when I *had* to break the news that she was to be given pain relief –by suppository!) Then eighteen hours back to England.

However, I continued with my work, it was a challenge and kept me alert. Gordon continued with his, by now he was working in a local hospital, mostly in the mortuary, his charges were much less challenging than mine and a lot quieter. I was also asked at this time by a neighbour over the road, if I would look after her two little girls whilst she went out to work. One was two years old; the other was a few months. I didn't have too many friends around here, so I readily agreed, despite having two prams stood side by side in the kitchen, I wanted to help out. I couldn't seem to blend in with some of the young mums who went down to school every day. They would walk out the front door wearing curlers, with a 'fag' hanging out of the corner of their mouths, and fluffy slippers on their feet. This was completely alien to me, I didn't smoke, and my curly hair certainly did not need curlers, not that I would *ever* have set foot over the doorstep in them. Anyhow these two children screamed from the minute their mum walked out the door, 'til she walked back in several hours later. These little girls really missed their mummy, so after a week, I told her they should come first, she needed to be with them and I wouldn't have them again. Another lesson, children *must* come first!

As you can imagine, life was quite hectic, with Gordon working very hard every day, including most weekends, whilst I was caring for Angeline, which was about the only thing I enjoyed amidst all the problems I seemed to be continually sorting out, and people I seemed to always be placating. We never had time to go out anymore, and Angeline was seeing less and less of her daddy. He would come home in the evening after a long day; I would have his meal ready for him. I felt so sorry for him, working so hard whilst I had been at home, keeping the house tidy, and playing with Angeline when she came home from school. Sometimes he would feel like going out for a pint with his mates and I felt he deserved a little relaxation. So, I would iron his favourite shirt and sew a button on his jacket, and then I would give him some money from the housekeeping. I didn't mind this, as Gordon was never mean with his earnings. He always handed them over for me to sort out and pay the bills. As these evenings became more and more frequent, I found that we as a family were going out less and less, and if I asked if we could just go for a drive in the car, a simple pleasure which I really enjoyed, sad I know, but the answer was that we didn't have enough money to put petrol in the car. This I found odd as I was giving him any money spare!

Chapter Six

The Phoenix Rises

I had very strange, confused feelings around this time. So many good things had happened, and yet somehow I was so very unhappy. After taking Angeline to school one morning, I trudged my way down to the local supermarket, to do the weekly shopping. My mind was spinning and everything in it was swirling before my mind's eye like the colours and patterns in a kaleidoscope. I had never felt like this before, and as I looked back over my life I tried to count my blessing, perhaps this would lift the black cloud hanging over me. The perfect childhood, my wonderful parents, my beautiful blonde-haired, blue-eyed daughter, my new lease of life, being told I was not yet to die! What more could I want? The answer of course, was a real family life, with the three of us spending time together. I day-dreamed about trips to the zoo, even just the park, Gordon, Angeline and me, and maybe one day, a new addition. Ha! How I laugh now at *this* thought, for there were to be *many* additions, from a different source. However, I'm not quite sure what I bought that day at the supermarket. I trod the aisles, picking up familiar items in a daze, like an automaton. I made my way back up the hill laden with carrier bags full of goodness knows what. I breathed a heavy sigh of relief as I finally made it to the back door, but as I pushed my key into the lock, I could hear the shrill sound of my 'Trim Phone' ringing inside. I instinctively dropped the bags on the path outside and ran into the lounge to answer it. The voice on the end of the line was unfamiliar but friendly. Her name was Jenny, and she was asking for Gordon. I assumed it was a work related call, as he was also now involved in part-time selling and often recruited new salespeople. I told her that Gordon was at work, but that I would ask him to ring her as soon as he came home. Her reply would ricochet around my already troubled head like a bullet from a revolver! "He's supposed to be taking me out tonight, but he hasn't let me know what time he will pick me up." Somehow I verbally reassured her that I *would* remind him to call. As I replaced the receiver on its cradle I sank into the chair beside me, and wished it would swallow me up. This black cloud over me now became a crashing thunderstorm. Crashes, bangs and bolts of lightning – the works- were now filling my head. It all made sense now, the nights out, the lateness. Gordon was having some sort of affair and I was so naïve I hadn't realised. I was numb for a while, then I was devastated, then *bloody* furious! The marriage I thought would be o.k. while it lasted was now coming to an end, and I was surprised at how much I didn't want it to.

However, I had the rest of the day to compose myself before Angeline came home. Somehow

I managed to cook tea for Angeline and Gordon, as always, except the usual pride and joy wasn't present as it normally would have been, but then things were far from normal. I was a little short-tempered with Angeline that night and hated myself for it. None of this was her fault she was a young child and knew nothing of how I felt or why. I put her to bed early, and sat and waited for Gordon to put in an appearance. As he walked in the door, I consciously regained my composure and re-heated his meal in the microwave. As he took off his coat, and sat down to eat. I asked him what kind of a day he'd had at work, and chatted about the latest painting Angeline had done at school. Once the meal was over, I poured him a drink as he settled into the armchair. After a very very long ten minutes I announced: - "Oh! By the way, Jenny rang today; she wants you to ring her back with the time you'll be picking her up tonight!" I didn't have to wait for a reaction. His face bore an expression I cannot describe, and to top all that he was completely speechless! I passed him the 'phone and insisted he ring Jenny there and then. I did give him a choice, either he could tell her what time he was meeting her – and not come back! Or, he could tell her he didn't want to see her any more. My only reason for the choice at the time was Angeline. She worshipped her daddy and I couldn't visualise either of us living without him. As he picked up the 'phone and dialled the number I had jotted down earlier, I waited with anticipation, to hear what our fate would be, would one of us be leaving or two of us, because there was no way Angeline was going *anywhere* but with me. The only words Gordon spoke were, "I won't be seeing you any more" to Jenny. I may never know the true reason for his answer. Was it also because of Angeline that he chose to stay?

The next morning I was to find out once more, how little understanding some people have for children. Gordon went off to work in stony silence, perhaps borne out of lack of things to say. At 9.15 a.m. the 'phone rang, and it was Jenny. For an hour and a half she poured out her heart to me, telling me how much she wanted Gordon. I remember thinking how wrong my mother had been about him, everybody wanted him, he must have been quite a catch. Jenny proceeded to tell me how they had arranged to move in together after Christmas etc. Then her next words hit me like a bolt of lightning. She said that if Gordon wouldn't move in with her because of Angeline, she would take *her* also!! This woman clearly had no understanding of real feelings, and there I ended the conversation. However, she called me every morning with her tales of woe, and I listened, and sympathised. After several days of this I asked Gordon to leave, gave him a carrier bag containing the essentials, and told him I would pack the rest later. However at 11 p.m. that night, he knocked on the door and said he wished to stay.

By now I had given this, much thought and had made decisions.

In the days that followed, Jenny would ring each morning with her woes, she had found an unlikely listening ear, and I *did* listen. As a rule, certain members of my family, of my generation, would by now have gone out and got well and truly 'bladdered' as they say. I decided I ought to give it a go; it might numb the pain or blot it out completely. I went to a pub in town one lunch time with Dora and Carla. They knew how to drink alcohol successfully, I didn't and hoped they could teach me. They did! I neither knew nor cared what I drank, as long as it did the trick. I continued for the rest of the afternoon and somehow managed to find my way home. Another lesson learned! Alcohol *never* solves the problem, in fact the problems were now tenfold, because I had a raging, blinding headache, and the original problems were still there!

The following weekend, my mother was coming to stay. I hadn't told my parents about all this. I didn't want to worry them, plus they had told me when I decided to marry, "You make your bed, you lie on it!" Of course they never meant these things because they were always ready to help out in a crisis, but I decided this was one I had to sort myself. Gordon came home that night, and my mother suggested that she baby sit for us to have a night out together. This was a rare opportunity for us at the best of times, so I had a brilliantly wicked idea; I was getting good at being wicked! I accepted mum's kind offer, and ran upstairs to prepare. I put on my most glamorous dress, tidied my hair and put on some makeup. There was a method in my madness, for as I climbed into the car, I knew Gordon would ask where I wanted to go. My reply was, "to see Jenny please." Naturally he protested, but I had dressed 'to kill', to meet the opposition and was very determined. There were lots of excuses as to where she would be, but Gordon was unaware of my conversations with her and I possible knew more about her than he did. I sat in the car whilst Gordon went to check if she was home. As I then ventured up the garden path to the door, I was preparing myself to face this glamorous woman. I checked my hair, and raised myself up as usual, to the full 4'11", but when I saw her there, at the door, I was amazed, and a little insulted at her plainness. However, I felt so sorry for her, and gave Gordon an immediate ultimatum, either leave now, or come home. He chose to come home, after which only two things were left to do. One was for Gordon to apologise to Jenny for the hurt she was feeling, and the other, was to lay bare the conditions under which Gordon would return, e.g. double housekeeping, heaps of respect, and no arguments when I went out with other men! To all of which he agreed, poor Gordon, looking back he was not completely to blame at all. To begin with Jenny knew he was married and it takes two to tango as they say, also he had been receiving little attention from me, who could blame him? To be honest, I *did* go out, and stayed out until the early hours of the morning. I would visit Dora or friends and return home in a taxi. After doing this a few times, Gordon worried where I was, and I decided I had made my point, he had felt what I had been feeling all those weeks. I feel I *must* stress at this crucial point, that from that day to this, Gordon became the best father and husband *ever!*

It was now time to make some changes. The compliant little housewife had to go, another woman, in my little body, rose like a Phoenix from the ashes of her life, and from then on a stronger, more determined person than ever, emerged. One who was now going to be completely in control, and remain in control. A whole life was ahead of me and I wasn't about to waste it, I was going to make the most of every minute, or so I thought.

Chapter Seven

Faith, Belief and Conversion

As I said I decided it was not entirely Gordon's fault that he had sought company elsewhere, I had to take my share of the blame. It turned out not to have been a serious relationship, their meeting was apparently work-related, and I realised that I had been so wrapped up in everything else, that he must have felt very neglected and I had become very boring company. Going out at night and having fun, had not been high on my list of priorities.

We settled back into some kind of family life. There was a lot of healing to be done, and I must confess, there were times when I felt it was more than I could handle and I did have thoughts of leaving. Then as I was hanging out the washing one morning. A young woman came to the garden gate. She had a happy friendly face, and introduced herself as one of Jehovah's Witnesses. Now I had heard of this group of people many years ago as a child but had never spoken to one. This was because my mother would see them coming down the road, preaching from door to door, and tell Dora and I to hide behind the sofa, as they had to pass the window on their way to the back door. She would turn off the radio and lock all the doors. We had to be very quiet, until they had gone. I grew up terrified of these people as I had no idea for what reason they came to people's houses, or why we had to keep them out and hide. If my dad was at home, he would always answer the door and buy the Watchtower and Awake magazines as he believed this would send them on their way.

So this particular day, I had at last the opportunity to speak to one of them to ask her to explain what it was all about. As she began to open her Bible. I bristled. All those years ago my early experiences of religion had turned me into an atheist, as far as I was concerned, the Bible was a load of twaddle, like a fairy story that someone had made up. However, as we chatted this young woman appeared to be very confident in what she was saying, she had conviction in what she believed. I admired that, and invited her back another day for further debate.

She lifted my spirits with her cheery demeanour, and as I made us a cup of tea, I fired questions at her, and in a friendly manner, insisted that she show me the answer in her Bible! I was given a Bible as a child and encouraged to read it from cover to cover, which I did, but none of it made any sense whatsoever. It was a King James Version, the one commonly used in churches even today. Every other word was 'thee' and 'thou.' This girl, however, had a copy called The New World Translation, it was in a more modern language and much easier to understand, but otherwise exactly the same. I argued with her about such things as the trinity or triad, that the father, son and Holy Spirit were one, how could they be. She therefore showed me in her Bible, that my thoughts were totally logical, it speaks of Jesus baptism, as he was rising from the Jordan river, after being baptised by his cousin John, when a voice from heaven spoke and said, "This is my beloved son in whom I am well pleased" and the Holy Spirit descended in the form of a dove. Three beings in three separate places, as I had thought, they could not all be 'one.' I also questioned the name of Jehovah, had somebody made it up? Exodus chapter six, verses six to eight. It all made sense.

There would be many many things I would question over the coming years, always trying to catch them out. By this time I had not only read but studied the Bible cover to cover, but this time I understood it. This time it made sense. If the Messiah was a new born infant, in a stable, in Bethlehem when King Herod sent the three wise men or 'Magi' to kill him, why did he ask for all male children under the age of two to be slaughtered? Because people travelled by camel in those days and it would have taken a very long time to travel the desert. This was all so exciting! There was *one* draw back though. My parents were not happy. Mum still a Methodist, dad still and atheist. Once again I was given an ultimatum, "If you become one of those, don't darken our doorstep again!" They needed a little time for this to sink in. The people they had so diligently protected their daughters from, had now ensnared the youngest, wilful one. Week by week, day by day, I was learning more and more. There was nothing, try as I may, that I could discredit, or that they couldn't prove to me from the Bible itself.

Considering how Jehovah's Witnesses were viewed, in these small villages, and still are today my mother was ashamed for anyone to find out what I had become. So for her sake, I tried to keep my enthusiasm under wraps when with her. Apart from which, I was never one of those over-zealous, over-the-top preachers. If people didn't want to listen, then I didn't force it upon them. Gordon was also oppositional in the beginning, but he then became interested in the logic of what they were saying, the Bible is made up of sixty six books, and yet they all interlink like a jigsaw, with no pieces missing.

This now became a whole new way of life for us, we made many new friends. We did things as a family unit, and everyone had great consideration for one another. Some may even say, the very timely visit from that young woman that day, was meant to be. Who knows what might have happened if our paths had not crossed, and our direction in life had not changed that day.

Suddenly life had real meaning, it was rich and full, we all cared for one another and helped each other when needed. This was challenged for us one day when we discovered a member of our congregation had been evicted by her mother. There were several reasons for this, one was of course because she wished to become one of Jehovah's Witnesses, but also being black, she had given birth to a 'white' child and this would 'never do.' Gordon and I felt it was completely unacceptable for her mother to do this. All we knew was that she had gone to a hostel for mother and child in the city. That night we tracked her and her son down and brought them home to stay with us until they could find somewhere to live. They were with us for a few weeks, which didn't go down well with some of our neighbours, who wondered how on earth we could have a black person living in our home, but we loved her as we would one of our own family.

There was also Katrina, who was a very troubled girl, married with a young son. She had so many problems and obsessions. She later confessed that when she first met me, she thought I was snobbish and wouldn't wish to know her. (This was to be a common assumption that I encountered more than once) but I took to this young woman, despite her problems. One morning the telephone rang at about 5.30 a.m. I lifted the receiver with trepidation, as Gordon would shortly be finishing a nightshift, his job was quite dangerous, and I was hoping with all my heart that there was nothing wrong. However it was Katrina, she was in Skegness, miles away on holiday, but couldn't bear to be so far away and was asking us to go and bring her home. Gordon walked in the door at 6.30 am and without hesitation, was driving to Skegness to pick up Katrina. We brought her back and she stayed with us for two or three weeks. I thought perhaps she had schizophrenic tendencies, she said she could hear voices telling her to kill someone. I found her one day standing at the front door with knife in her hand! We organised a psychiatrist to visit her at our home, as she desperately needed help. Many years later, Katrina would reveal to me that memories of abuse were coming back to her. She had needed to feel someone cared and yet some of those who should have helped, Jehovah's Witnesses, Christians, had turned her away from their doors as they saw her as some kind of nuisance, and wouldn't let her in. This hypocrisy astounded me.

We had given up a lot for this way of life. Some of our old life-long friends had refused to speak to us now we were 'Witnesses' and Gordon had to give up smoking. This was no mean feat for him as he had smoked since he was eight or nine years old, picking up 'dog ends' where he could find them, here and there.

He would smoke virtually *anything* he could roll up, stick in his mouth and set fire to! When he was asked to give up for his faith, he was smoking thirty or forty miniature cigars a day!! But, he made his decision just as I was going to France for a few days. When I returned, he had stopped completely, suffering cold turkey and the horrors that went with it, but he had succeeded, and has never smoked since. He also cut his precious hair which was shoulder length with a beard to match which he shaved off. I on the other hand, had made a conscious decision at a very early age, never to smoke, that is of course, unless you count a pack of ten Woodbines, my friend Lorraine and I bought to try out. We hung our heads out of the window and smoked five each, then promptly vomited! The decision was made, however, following a very memorable physiology class, where we were shown the differences between a healthy lung and a cancerous one.

Many things were now happening in our lives. I had been 'spotted' on a night out and offered some photographic modelling work which brought in some extra cash, and made me feel quite important for once. This was frowned upon by the Witnesses, as women were second to men and should be kept in their place. This, as you can imagine by now, did not go down too well with me and I guess I never did get the hang of being in submission to my husband, as was expected of me. Many things about being a

Jehovah's Witness were difficult for me, and there were many other occasions to come where I would not lie down and be quiet. I remember one of the Elders ringing one day to speak to Gordon, who was unfortunately at work. As I raised the beeping Trimphone to my ear the caller's voice said "Good evening, is the master of the house in?" In my true wicked style, I silently chuckled to myself and replied: - "Speaking." This was followed by what felt like a very long silence. He did not find this remotely amusing; my sense of humour was totally unacceptable. When I continued to explain that I was just eating tea, I was then reprimanded for eating before my husband was home. It was just *too* tempting; he was playing right into my hands. Gordon was actually not going to be home until 10.30 p.m. and I wasn't about to wait, but once more, I decided to be really wicked and told him that if my husband couldn't turn up on time when his food was on the table, then it was tough! They must have thought I was the true spawn of Satan.

Chapter Eight

Loss Takes Many Forms

Just as we thought everything was running smoothly and life was quite peaceful, events in Dora's household took a turn for the worst yet again. This time Dora begged us to take Dana to live with us once more. By this time she was about fifteen years old. Gordon and I had a discussion about the implications of this and decided we needed to help. However, we asked Dora to make certain promises. As Dana was now fifteen, we felt it would be better to allow her to settle with us and stay until she decided what she wanted to do with her life. My dad had persuaded Dora to put some of the insurance money she received after Vince's death, into a savings account for Dana, and dad added to this each month out of concern for his then, only granddaughter. We therefore knew that with the right guidance when the time came, she could set herself up in a business of her own. She cleverly realised it was much easier to sit about and do absolutely nothing, and therefore was making little effort with her education, despite every encouragement, and regardless of her young age found herself a boyfriend. I honestly believe that Dana enjoyed living with us even though we had fairly strict boundaries. She had peace, and refuge from the relentless fights and arguments at home. We took her on holidays and treated her as our own, why wouldn't we, she was still my little angel. However she and my very own little angel, Angeline, who was about seven by now, still didn't always see eye to eye. Angeline would often seem quiet and take herself off to play with her toys, whilst Dana would then be happy and cheerful, such a 'pleasant' young person!

We were still attending meetings of Jehovah's Witnesses each week, and Dana would come along with us, everyone liked her, she was so very affable with all our friends and we had many. There was Laurence, and his wife Helen, two of the most genuine people I have ever known. Tragically Laurence was to later pass away in his mid-forties from cancer, and Helen only two years or so after him. We miss them terribly. There was Wendy, who through our matchmaking, befriended and married Frank, yet again we lost dear Wendy, to the big 'C' also. Aileen and Michael whom we love dearly and wish we could see more of them, but time and work are our enemies. However we value their friendship and enjoy their company when circumstances allow. Rita and George was an older retired couple who had led an army life and often transfixed us with their tales of life in Burma during the war. There were many others, largely of an older generation, whom we seemed to take under our ever accommodating wings. One of these was Doris a rather frail old lady who had never married and lived alone in her little flat about ten minutes away from us. We would pick up Doris each week and take her to the meetings at the Kingdom Hall and take her home afterwards. One day we received a 'phone call from another congregation member to tell us that Doris was very poorly and had been taken into hospital. We took ourselves off to the isolation hospital on the outskirts of the city to see Doris and to be informed that she had tuberculosis. This was the beginning of a very long illness and recovery for her and we knew she would need much help and encouragement. Having no family to speak of, we knew we would need to be involved. After a three month stay in hospital, Doris came home to her little flat and spent much of her day, sitting in her rocking chair in front of the T.V. When we had finished work, I would cook a meal for Gordon, Angeline, Dana and me, and make a little extra for Doris, which Gordon would then take over in the car to encourage her to eat. Gordon also fitted her front door with a safety chain which had a key, so that when we arrived with her meals etc., she wouldn't have to walk down the long hallway to answer our knocks. She could still be safe but, *we* could gain access with her food.

It was a Monday morning, as I had stripped the sheets from all of the beds, and the kitchen floor resembled a Chinese laundry. The twin-tub washing machine was labouring away at its heavy load, when the 'phone rang. One of the

Witnesses had been on door to door preaching, and decided to call in to see Doris. However after knocking, she'd had no response and was a little concerned, and knew that we had a key so thought we might know what was happening. Where could Doris be? She could barely get to the kitchen let alone go out! I switched off the washing machine, put on my coat, and started my trek up the hill. It was only ten minutes away in the car, but I didn't drive then so when Gordon was at work it was Shank's Pony for me. As I arrived at Doris's front door, I had a feeling of foreboding. I knocked very firmly but there was no response. By now of course, I had also tried to unlock the door with the keys we had, and became very alarmed to find that she had disregarded the new chain with lock and key which Gordon had fitted and instead had attached the *old* chain preventing me from entering. Of course, I was now understandably *very* concerned. I decided to walk to the house of the warden by whom the flats were monitored, to ask of Doris's movements that day. She was a woman who intensely disliked the Witnesses and was very abrupt and off-hand with me, brushing my worries aside as though I were a nuisance. She sharply advised me that Doris had taken her morning pills and would have removed her hearing aid and nodded off in her rocking chair, and anyhow, she would be going back again at four p.m. to give her, her afternoon pills, (it was now around midday.) This woman by now was beginning to annoy me enormously, urgency was causing my mind to race and all etiquette evaporated into thin air. I had no training back then, in patience and procedure, I cannot bring myself to write in this book, the words I used that day! I was a Christian, obviously once again, I had proved myself not to be a very good one, as strong language was *not* in our vocabulary, and I was a diminutive little blonde, who tried to appease everyone, needless to say, by the time my lips had stopped moving, the woman grabbed her keys, said not another word and followed me back to Doris's flat. She also could not gain access, so I asked her where the nearest telephone was (no mobile 'phones back then) as I was now going to ring the Police to break down the door. For the first time in half an hour she spoke, only to say she would not be responsible for the broken door, *I* said the door was nothing compared to what she may find at four p.m. if we didn't get inside *now*, as instinct was telling me loud and clear, that we were wasting precious time somehow. An officer arrived and in an instant he had snapped the chain and we were in! Not surprisingly the warden stayed at the front door as the officer and I rushed down the hallway to the sitting room. There was Doris, sitting in her favourite old rocking chair, eyes closed, hands loosely resting in her lap, which was crimson with blood! The large carving knife was resting on the edge of the table, blood dripping from its blade; it was like a butcher's shop. Doris had, for whatever reason slit both her wrists and her life was ebbing away. My feeling of foreboding had been well justified, and I left the warden with my words ringing in her ears, as to the shock at possibly finding a dead body had she waited until four p.m.

Doris survived, but she had been taking so many prescribed drugs since contracting tuberculosis, that I couldn't help feeling that they had some part to play in hr actions. She was now back in hospital, and was hearing voices telling her to jump out of the fifth floor window, tried to swallow her hearing aid, even stood on the bed and took out the light bulb and stuck her finger in the socket. When I visited she would drag me with incredible strength into the toilet, to 'talk' as she was convinced the curtain runner around the bed was some kind of 'telecom' and 'they' were listening to every word. The distant family Doris had, seemed uninterested in helping her, someone had to, and so I asked to speak to her consultant, and put to him my concerns regarding the cocktail of drugs she was taking, and how I felt they were contributing to her deranged state of mind, he readily agreed that this was a possibility and promised he would review her medication. Sadly, sometime after, Doris passed away, we lost her too.

It was also around this time that I received a call to tell me my favourite cousin, Bernice had died, followed by my cousin Edna, and Cyril then Jean. People close to me were leaving one by one, which left me with an unbearable fear for my family's mortality, life itself seemed so very fragile, yet I, the one who had lived with a death sentence for so long, was alive and kicking,. Oh! The irony of it all.

All this time Dana was still with us and growing older. However one Saturday morning, as Dana was having a lie-in, a knock came at the door. As I opened it, her stepfather Joe pushed his way in and demanded he take her home *now*! It would appear they were missing their built-in baby sitter and wanted her home. Dana's place with us was a private arrangement between Dora, myself and Gordon. We had no legal backing, no Social Services to support us, and no knowledge of how the court systems worked, and therefore nothing we could do about it. Joe demanded that I pack her bags *now*! As I stood at the top of the stairs, suitcase in hand, I had a flashback to the night of my twenty first birthday, and how Gordon had punched the wall because he didn't want to hit Joe and unsteady him with his artificial limb. As I thought of this, that wicked little demon inside me chuckled. My wicked side was normally weak and feeble, wickedness gave me no joy as a rule, but at that moment I decided I wasn't going to make it easy for him, and with a glint in my eye, and a wry smile on my face, I uttered the word 'catch' as I let the suitcase tumble out of my hands and down the stairs. As it somersaulted down every steep, wooden step, its contents spilled endlessly as I watched, it seemed in slow motion, as Joe stumbled back and forth as jeans, tee-shirts, shoes, socks and pants engulfed him. My pleasure was indescribable as I said the words "Now pick them up." He duly did so and bundled Dana into the car and sped off.

The sight of her empty bunk made me feel desolate once more. This ever familiar sense of loss swept over me once again like a wave. This was a bereavement of a very different kind. However, much as I had to outwardly appear strong, this was beginning to have its effect upon me. If I so much as saw a funeral car pass in the street I would want to weep for the families within, as I gazed at their tear-stained faces even though I had never met them.

Despite the fact that Dana was back 'home' she was never far from my thoughts, or deeds. Whenever there was a problem at school, the headmaster would always by-pass Dora and ring me. It was a another normal school day when he rang to ask if I could go down to the school as there was something serious he wished to discuss with me. As I sat in his office, he closed the door behind me and looked at me with an expression which said, he wasn't quite sure how to explain. In so many words I encouraged him to 'spit it out.' The problem was that Dana had been to him with a story about her stepfather touching her inappropriately when Dora was out of the room. I assured him that I would look into this and get to the bottom of it somehow. I decided the best place to start may be with Dana herself, so I took her to one side and asked her to explain what had happened. She told me that whenever her mother was in the kitchen cooking tea, Joe would 'touch' her. The next step was to talk to Dora who was quite astonished! She agreed that Dana and Joe didn't always get along, and Joe had his ways but I was inclined to agree, he was a belligerent man, who lost his temper easily, but nothing about him ever suggested to me that he had this perversion. Therefore Dora and I planned a strategy to uncover the truth. We spoke discreetly to Dana and told her that whenever this happened she should call Dora immediately and tell her. One evening, as Dora went into the kitchen to cook the evening meal, Joe was sitting on the sofa, watching the day's news; Dana was sprawled on the floor, with a book. "He's touching me again mum!" came the words loud and clear, but little did Dana realise that Dora was watching through the hinged gap of the door. Joe was still nodding off on the sofa, Dana on the floor, lazily turning the pages of her book, nowhere *near* Joe! We soon realised that Dana was getting her own back on Joe for whatever had recently upset her, and she was clever enough to know that had this been believed, it would have had serious repercussions. Another lesson, and perhaps the most useful one to date, was about to be learned, Angels *do* tell lies!!

Meanwhile, our now smaller family was still plodding on as Jehovah's Witnesses, and as I said before, there were occasions when I felt I was definitely *not* a good Christian the way that the rest of them were. They did everything by the book, but sometimes practicality took precedence as far as I was concerned. For example, women came second to men, and there were some things we weren't allowed to do. We couldn't lead the way in sharing the bible with others in the presence of a man; we would have to cover our heads, as a sign of respect. This took me back to my school days when I had to put my hanky on my head. What a load of old twaddle!! How petty, if I didn't have a hat on my head it didn't mean I was inferior to any man did it? My brain and my mouth still worked the same. I rarely wore my wedding ring and still don't, despite having copious amounts of gold and gemstones. It just bothered me if worn all the time, or perhaps I'm just allergic to marriage. I was once told that I *should* wear it and it didn't go down well with one of the Elders, when I asked him why he was not wearing one also, and reminded him that it was after all, introduced by the Pagans as a symbol of eternity, a never ending circle et., etc. *I* knew I was married, and I didn't need a metal band on my finger to remind me. No-one, could forget being married to Gordon! I wouldn't be told where I should sit at a meeting either, rebellious or not, I was an individual, *not* an appendage of my husband. Please don't misunderstand me, I will go out of my way to be accommodating but I do not feel that the male species is in any way superior to the female. We each have our individual attributes and should therefore complement each other. Each gender has it's own qualities. *Good grief*!! People are dying, children are starving, and being abused, who cares who wears a hat or not, or who should be superior to whom, or where we sit, or whether I wear a wedding band, how petty!

Chapter Nine

Moving on

It's now the early eighties and ten or twelve years since our delayed honeymoon in Spain. We had had many British holidays on a shoestring, but I decided it was time Angeline saw a bit of the world and broadened her horizons. Gordon announced that he did not want to go abroad, and that we weren't going. Oh dear! A red rag to a bull situation, you'd think he would have learned by now wouldn't you. Of course this made me all the more determined that we would go. However when I made it clear that I would be taking Angeline and whether he joined us or not was his decision, he decided to come along. Spain was still the main tourist destination then so we decided another trip would be good. Life hadn't been too kind in many ways, and a holiday would be good for all of us.

You may be wondering why I haven't mentioned a great deal about Angeline, after all, she is my only child, but the simple answer is, that she was such a well behaved little girl '*my*' angel, but despite our overwhelming love for her, we had firm and consistent boundaries and certain values were taught. Looking back, this was one of the advantages about studying the Bible, it has excellent values that we can all learn. However, once more we set off for

Spain, but this time there were three of us. We had a lovely time, Gordon had been taking Angeline for horse riding lessons and they were able to use their skills on pony treks in the hills of the Spanish countryside. Gordon had always been interested in horses and in fact we had made an attempt on our first trip, a few years previously. Now, I know I am a country girl born and bred, but horses were, in my opinion, beautiful equine quadrupeds, to be watched gracefully and artistically cantering around a field. I never felt these poor creatures deserved the dubious honour of accommodating some of the very large and unsavoury human rear-ends which sit astride them. Now, on our previous honeymoon trip, I had decided I would humour Gordon's interest and as the stable hands had gone to so much trouble to secure the smallest horse, with the shortest legs for *me*, I unceremoniously scrambled my way around its body with great trepidation, and to my amazement managed to finally sit facing the front end of the poor unfortunate creature, the end with a head. As they fussed and fiddled and adjusted the stirrups as high as they would go to accommodate my short legs, I grabbed the reins and sat high in the saddle like Joan of Arc, or Bodicia, ready to ride into battle! I wasn't far wrong. First and foremost, I may have been bitten by geese, head butted by sheep and pigs, and chased by a gang of marauding cows, who probably though I was going to milk them, but the largest creature I had ever sat astride was a donkey on Blackpool beach. I had certainly *never* sat on the back of such a huge and powerful animal in my life! We set off quite well, we did all, the very young and lively female leader instructed us to do, the animals also appeared to be well disciplined, but as we moved further into the hills, I became astutely aware that *my* horse, was not best buddies with the one next to it, as they kept biting each other, totally ignoring my right leg which was very much in their way! The rest of the group, including Gordon, moved further and further into the distance as I lagged behind, but I didn't care, this was quite pleasant, plodding along in the sunshine looking at the scenery going very slowly by. The horse, bless it, seemed to know his way, it was a path he must have trodden a million times before, so I knew we would catch up with the others eventually.

It was a very faint little 'chugging' sound, in the distance, which broke the silence, and my solitude. I turned very confidently in my saddle, to see a small tractor-type vehicle chugging ever closer behind me. My dilemma now was, how will it pass me? For either side of me were beautifully ploughed and furrowed fields full of newly planted crops. The decision was rapidly taken out of my control when the 'chug chug' spooked the horse from behind and it exited stage left and galloped furiously among the crops, its hooves uprooting whatever had been lovingly planted. In fear I tried to stop the horse by mainly shaking the reins and shouting "*STOP!*" He obviously didn't understand English, why should he? He was a Spanish horse. However, the swift pace at which I was now almost flying was nothing compared to the large angry looking farmer's wife who was running towards me brandishing her best carving knife. No sooner had I said what I thought would be my last prayer, than a voice behind me called sternly in Spanish and the horse turned and meekly followed our young leader who had returned to find me. Now! Back to this second trip to Espana! Gordon and Angeline had had lots of practice and were determined they would use it, so Gordon decided a few lessons at the equestrian centre would do the trick for me, before we went. However, when we arrived at the Spanish stables this second time, and the horses were rearing, and sneering at each other in their stalls as we waited to be tended to, my earlier memory came flooding back and I decided I would rather be a 'clothes horse' and chickened out to a day's shopping alone, well someone's got to do it

Despite this, it was a great holiday and a great adventure for Angeline and two weeks of the three 'S's' Sun, Sangria and Shopping for me. Upon our return to England, all looking bronzed and fat from Sangria and paella with hilarious tales to tell, Angeline clutching her stuffed obligatory Spanish Donkey, we felt rejuvenated. However this euphoria was short-lived as we discovered on our return that there had been a huge 'war' at Dora's house and Dana had walked out, declaring Joe had thrown her out, all the while both Joe and Dora denying this was true. I didn't know who to believe. If it *were* true, how could they do this to my Dana? Thankfully, Dana had secured a room in a house for homeless teenagers but alas, it was situated in the red-light district of Sheffield. In fact, exactly where, in the near future the Yorkshire Ripper was to be caught. My loyalties were torn. Angeline was now getting older and seemed reluctant to want Dana back in our small house. I *had* to make a choice and Angeline was my daughter, she was the one ultimately that I had a responsibility to. However, when I visited Dana at this house, she actually appeared to be happy with this new found independence, but there was one fly in the ointment – Kevin!

Kevin was a larger than life seventeen year old who occupied one of the rooms of the house. As Kevin walked into the sitting room, I was chatting away to Dana and fussing over her unhealthy eating habits. I was just emptying the carrier bags full of food I had taken her and instructing her on how to cook it, when the lulled conversation around us went abruptly silent. I turned in curiosity to see what was the cause of this sound of silence, as though a T.V.

had been switched off, and set eyes upon the only person who had not been in the room when I arrived, said "Hi" and continued my conversation with little consequence, but the faces all around, were filled with fear, and those behind Kevin, were gesturing to me silently to shut up! I think *not*. I obligingly introduced myself and asked his name. His lips didn't move, but certain faint little whispers informed me that this was Kevin. Apparently he was 'king of the roost', and he glared with what was to me, an amusing malevolence in his eyes. Just *who* did this young man think he was, looking at me in such a way? I queried those around us as to why they were so obviously afraid, but no-one answered. Kevin hadn't given them permission to speak. I continued to talk to these silent frightened young faces, and explain that Kevin could only be 'king' if *they* were willing to be his obedient subjects, otherwise, who would he govern? Dana took me to one side and explained that, as I had first assumed, Kevin was a very angry young man with a huge chip on his shoulder, and he had recently attempted suicide. Now, of course I had no training in such matters, but had a desperate need to help, to tell this young person there could be a better life, and as I was, without a second thought, telling him all this, I spotted a Bible on the mantelpiece. It was as though it was shouting at me. I picked it up and as I thumbed the pages, I read various scriptures to him about taking one's life, and offered the book for him to read for himself. Until now, Kevin had not said a word to me just glared at me with utter disdain. As I placed the book in his hands, and dexterously pointed out the relevant passages; he slammed it shut and promptly threw it at me! Now this was quite a hefty volume, and not what you could call at all portable, therefore I instinctively felt it best to 'duck' and the heavy tome flew straight through the open window. All the silent mouths opened in unison with a stifled gasp. I on the other hand did what I usually do best. Yes – I straightened myself up, to my full 4'11", my calf muscles straining as I carefully repositioned myself on my three inch heels and looked at Kevin with a wry shake of the head, and said:- "What a very childish and selfish thing for someone who is becoming an adult to do! You have now deprived all these other young people of the pleasure of reading that!" I pointed to these 'other young people' as I spoke and noticed that their heads were turning from left to right as they looked from Kevin to me, and back again. Like spectators at a tennis tournament. I wasn't quite sure what would happen next and obviously neither were they, no-one had moved from where they sat or stood. However, within a couple of very long seconds, Kevin burst into tears and sat down heavily with head in hands. I sat on the arm of the chair and put my hand gently on his shoulder and told him it was o.k. to cry.

I made several visits to the house following this, and Kevin was always welcoming and appeared genuinely pleased to see me. I would collect fish and chips for everyone on the way, as none of them had much money. I noticed shortly, that everyone in the house seemed much more cheery and relaxed, and Kevin would laugh and joke. All it needed was someone to let him know that he had a right to be angry, but he needed to channel it appropriately, and not at the expense of those around him. A few months later, I saw Kevin in town pushing a pram, laden with packets of disposable nappies. It turns out, Kevin's new-found amenable persona had led him so far as to get a girl pregnant, and who then left him and dumped the baby with him when it was born. He however was enjoying fatherhood. He came to visit me and told me he had his son to live for and was so glad he hadn't taken his own life.

Another lesson I learned here. Don't judge people by their behaviour; let them know it's what they do that you may dislike not *them*!

Chapter Ten

Bitter Sweet

Life was moving pretty much at the same pace. Dora still had her problems, which every now and then needed some attention. We were still Jehovah's Witnesses, and I was still trying desperately to be one of those Christian wives, who did whatever her husband said without question, and put the preaching work above everything else, but try as I may, I was constantly failing miserably. Looking back I think my logical and practical way of thinking was to blame. There were just some things which were *not* practical, in fact were so petty I couldn't accept them, but I wanted a faith after years of nothingness, and so I kept trying, and Gordon kept encouraging me. He never, of course, expected me to do as I was told, he knew me too well and didn't even *try* to control me, but we had some good friends, as you may remember I mentioned earlier, George and Rita were two of our very good friends. Despite them being a generation older than us we got along well together. George had been a Sergeant Major in the British Army and was stationed in Burma during the war. Rita had been a nurse all her life, and eventually had become Matron of a very large hospital. I would imagine her being an excellent Matron, for she had very prim and proper ways. Her hospital would have been spotless. They both would tell us tales about their lives in Burma and how, when war broke out they climbed the steps of the only 'plane bound for England in order to escape. All they were allowed to take with them was as much as they could put into a blanket and tie at all four corners. They had four children and as they hurriedly clambered to board the waiting aeroplane with engines revving, the soldiers took the blankets each of the children were carrying, and threw them into the surrounding jungle. They arrived in England with little more than what they stood up in.

However, here they were, many years later, about to retire. They dropped the bombshell one day, as they invited us to tea. They had a son living in Australia and had spent a couple of months with him and his family near Perth W.A. Now, they had decided to emigrate there! How we would miss them this was yet another loss but of a different kind, *but*, not for long, because two or three years after they left, they invited us to visit them twelve thousand miles away at the other side of the world! What an opportunity for us and Angeline. We made plans; we took time off work without pay. I did have a struggle to convince school that Angeline would only be gone for a couple of months, and would be back. We live in a very multicultural area of the city, and they were used to the Asian children going off to Pakistan, which must have been a great adventure for them also, visiting their country of origin and learning about their culture, but then they may not be seen again for a couple of years, then walk back into school as though they had never been away, so I understood their concern, but assured them I would set Angeline some work and she *would* be back in a few short weeks.

It was April when we arrived at Heathrow Airport. Angeline was so excited, thinking of kangaroos and koala bears. We boarded the huge Jumbo Jet and took our seats. This was very different from the little 'plane with its propellers which took us to Spain.

This one had two aisles and banks of three seats down each side and four down the middle. It was a very long flight, about twenty eight hours I think, stopping in Bombay and Kuala Lumpur, and I remember the palm trees were bending almost in half with the winds, and water was pouring down the windows in such sheets I thought they were hosing down the 'plane, before it even ground to a halt. It was monsoon season. However pretty soon we were in the Antipodes and our friends George and Rita were there to meet us. They had also told the congregation they had joined in W.A. of our arrival, and half of them were there to greet us too. Unfortunately one of our suitcases had gone astray from the carousel, and by the time we had reported this, it was the early hours of the morning and our flight was already delayed due to engine failure before landing in Kuala Lumpur, everyone had been quite concerned, but we had eventually landed safe and well, but tired.

Please feel free to smile when I remind you that our wedding anniversary is on first of April (April Fool's Day) and George and Rita's was the day after. They had told us not to celebrate until we arrived with them, where they had organised a party, which was a wonderful way for us to get to meet new friends. Of course I had prepared for this party in true 'Brit' style with a black and gold chiffon dress with my nails to match, gold stilettos and bag, my favourite perfume wafting as I moved. People began to arrive and we were correctly introduced. However, the trend in the early eighties in Australia was 'tracki' bottoms and a T shirt. I stood out like a koala in the North Pole! But hey – I always liked to be different, so here I was, with a bang! We mingled with everyone, chatting to all, and I got talking to a very nice young couple, with a pair of cute little boys, but the wife Kathy, took off and made a bee line for Rita. She had taken one look at me and assumed this hussy in black and gold was after her husband! After Rita assured her that I had my hands well and truly full with Gordon, and I didn't want *anybody's* husband, she and I

became firm 'Sheila' friends. In fact they invited us out to their farm in the Australian Bush, and took us out through the trees
and scrubland on a flat-backed land rover. Seeing kangaroos leaping in groups, snakes slithering away as the vehicle trundled towards them, foxes and eagles etc. These friends were also amazed at this little blonde who a few nights before, had teetered out in three inch heels and gold 'fuss' now in shorts and T shirt, revelling at antipodean nature. It was one of the most memorable and enjoyable days of my life.

We had a great time; Gordon and Angeline were able to pursue their love of horse riding in the Aussie Bush. At the stables, Gordon had spotted some mounds of manure, and as George was establishing his new garden, Gordon offered to obtain some. He hired a trailer, and asked the stable owner if he could fill it. He laboured very hard that day, until the trailer was full to the brim. He drove back to the house, and unloaded it onto the drive. George was overjoyed, and lovingly shovelled the succulent and very ripe manure around his carrots, onions and various other vegetables, plus his beautiful banana tree, tucking them into a circle of cosy manure like you would tuck a child lovingly into bed, and said goodnight!

It rained quite heavily during the night, the best time, I thought to myself as I listened to the pitter-patter on the sky-light above me. When we woke the next morning, the sun was beaming down as we sat and ate breakfast under the Pergola. George sauntered slowly down to his veg' patch to check that his beloved plants were rousing from their slumbers. Oh-my-goodness! None of us had realised that horses do not digest the kernel of the barley, they pass straight through into the intestines and are passed out as nature takes its course. The heavy rain in the night was all the dormant seeds needed and had quite literally sprung up about four inches and choked the little plants! Quite ironic really, when you read the verses in the book of Mathew, about the seed that fell upon stony ground etc. Could these be the ones that choked? We were Christians for goodness sake, shouldn't we have preferential treatment?!

However, all in all we had a wonderful two months in W.A. and smiled together so often at the memories we had and yet I couldn't help feeling 'loss' yet again, as we had made some new and wonderful friends and the chances of seeing them ever again were remote in the least.

We came back down to earth with a bump and I don't just mean when the 'plane landed on British tarmac. We had returned home to the news that Dana was pregnant! How I suddenly missed the azure blue of the Indian Ocean, the white sandy beaches, the burning sun and the aroma of prawns on the 'barbie'. Life now had to continue on from where we left off and the last few weeks were like a distant dream.

Of course Dana could no longer stay in the hostel for the homeless. Her boyfriend Pete took her home to his house. His mother had had ten children and now had one more. Dana stayed at Pete's house whilst we had to think what we could do about the situation. It was a process of elimination really, they couldn't possibly live with us, there was *no* space for three more people. There was no space for them to live permanently with Pete's family, and Dora and Joe couldn't even consider it. Eventually however, a council property was allocated, the only problem then was, the wedding. No-one seemed too interested, but I couldn't allow Dana to marry without ceremony of some kind. My dreams of her in a white wedding gown, with perhaps me or Gordon giving her away, were gone. As plans progressed she was quite heavily pregnant by the time the arrangements were complete. I made Dana a dress from deep blue velvet with pale blue shoes and accessories; I put together a bouquet of silk flowers and arranged an appointment at the hairdresser. Angeline was bridesmaid and I made a pink velvet dress for her. It was a simple registry office wedding followed by a buffet at our house attended by a few relatives, including my mum and dad. Thankfully Pete's parents arranged a small reception somewhere local for the evening.

A couple of weeks later we received a 'phone call to say Dana was delivered of a baby boy. He was slightly jaundiced and on the small side, therefore in an incubator the first time I laid eyes on him, but he was perfect, and 'the image of his dad!' I couldn't possibly have known then, how important that thought would later become.

I was thrilled for Dana and Pete, they had a son, and I was a great-auntie. This was Dana's child, she was the apple of my eye along with my Angeline, and I hoped I would have the same overwhelming love for this child. They named him Andre.

Now, since we had returned from Australia, Gordon found it difficult to settle in our two-up-two-down, with 'postage stamp' garden, so he decided we *had* to move. He desperately wanted to emigrate at that time, and in the immortal words of Rolf Harris, he wanted 'to go back to W.A.' but I felt I couldn't leave my parents. I was already twenty miles away, and saw them as often as I could. Another twelve thousand miles would be unbearable, and anyway, they were getting older and would need us one day, as would Gordon's mother too. So I agreed to move house, it was the least I could do, but it was quite scary, I had only ever moved home twice in my life and wondered where we would go. We were thinking of perhaps having more family of our own now that events with Dora and co. appeared more settled, so we had to bear this in mind when house-hunting. There was a lovely property opposite the park, but with about twenty odd steps to the front door, not conducive with manoeuvring a pram. There were several others but quite surprisingly we found one only ten minutes from home, which we never knew was there. It was built high on the hill with views of the park, the roads below etc, and was in a cul-de-sac, so no noisy traffic trundling by. It was a semi town house, built only about five years earlier. There were a few amenities which were new to us. The lounge window was a good ten feet wide and six foot high, with a positive vista beyond, separate toilet, shower and quite a lengthy garden. I could now, to some extent, enjoy my artistic flair which had been denied me so many years before. We painted, papered, altered, ripped out; I sewed curtains and decorated until we had stamped our mark well and truly on this property. Here we also had three bedrooms which meant we had a spare, Angeline had a lovely room of her own and decorated to her liking. Dora had no further children, Dana was married, and Sally and Tina were growing up, therefore no more children needed us, and so I made the third bedroom into a sort of study-cum-boudoir, with drawers and long worktops, long mirrors and lights where I could dry my hair, or sit and write etc. This was *our* life now.

We continued on here, in relative peace. Visiting and caring for our parents. They were getting older now, and my mother-in law had moved to a more manageable flat, and as for my mum and dad, well, dad was now finding the huge garden which had been his pride and joy, his hobby, to be rather a burden, and the large house was more than mum wanted to clean. They had had their eye on a small bungalow further into the village, and when it became vacant they were thrilled. There would be no stairs to climb and no garden to speak of. We had to travel to Bakewell, the nearest town for the key, Gordon took dad in the car, the keys were handed over and they returned to Bradwell, with great excitement. We all walked up to the front door of the bungalow. It was situated further upstream from the babbling brook, in fact its Spring was right behind the bungalow, still in the shadow of the hills, the 'world's end', it was very peaceful and pretty, just what they had been waiting for, it was perfect for them. However as Dad turned the key in the door to their prospective new home, my mother's face fell. It was very sparsely decorated, white, complete with all the brush marks, the kitchen was bedecked with blue tiles, it was the furthest thing from 'home' as they knew it. I found this so distressing for my mum. She was a wonderful homemaker and I could imagine what a daunting task this must have been for her. They were moving here to retire, for *less* work and maintenance and they were now faced with an uphill struggle greater than Everest! No way! I walked into the village to the local and *only* D.I.Y. shop up yet another hill, and bought rolls of wallpaper of various patterns, tins of paint and paste etc., I had to make two or three journeys to carry it all, Gordon was at work and unable to do much, although the previous day he had taken up the lounge carpet at the old house. I set about pasting, cutting and papering. A nice subtle beige design over the fireplace wall with toning emulsion paint on the remaining three walls. Then I moved on to the bedroom, a delicate pink with a little rainbow design and the rest in the palest pink. Gordon had called in after work, and I asked him to go and see to stuff at home, in Sheffield, but he did pick up the carpet and dropped it off at the bungalow. At just after midnight my dad donned his coat and cap and walked over to see where I was, he strode in the door just as I was cutting the last bit of carpet around the hearth. I was shattered and he insisted that I stop and go home with him for supper. I can tell you, I was glad to, but at least I felt satisfied and pleased that all the painting, papering and carpet fitting had transformed and reinvented the place. The next morning my mum and I had a walk back to the bungalow. Her face lit up when she stood and gazed at the transformation. She could now see what a difference we could make with a bit of paint and paper, some imagination and a lot of hard work.

In the days that followed we soon had the place ship shape and as we moved in familiar bits and pieces, it began to look like home sweet home. They came to love this place, it would be their haven and we had many happy times there. However, I couldn't help feeling yet another loss. The old house and the garden had been such a big part of our lives for so long, and I wondered how mum and dad were feeling also.

Anyhow, in the days that followed, much time and effort was spent on settling them in, and making the place look and feel comfortable. It was also much easier for mum to pop in and see her sister Gwyneth; we could even see her bungalow from the lounge window. This was to be a bonus, as Gwyneth was becoming increasingly less well in herself and needed mum and dad's help on a daily basis. Carla showed herself now and then, when she needed money.

Gwyneth was certainly not well, but despite visits from the doctor, no-one seemed to know what was wrong. Mum and dad had to do more and more for her. Dad took care of collecting her pension and paying the bills; mum would go daily and tidy round the bungalow and make her some breakfast. Both would do her shopping along with their own. This entire time mum was also still working. She was like a little bullet, always on the go despite her age, scuttling around from here to there. When mum cooked a meal, the dishes didn't stay dirty for one second longer than necessary. She would practically whip them from under your nose as fork lifted to mouth with the last morsel of food from the plate. Sunday seemed to be an equally busy day, dad would go for his usual pint at the Bath Hotel, and mum would put the roast in the oven, and veg' in the saucepans, and while this was cooking she would whip out the vacuum cleaner, and flick round the duster, set the table and all would be neat and ready when dad came back to carve the roast, and serve Sunday lunch. It was one such Sunday that the usual household routine was in full flow, and mum was mopping the kitchen floor, when she felt her feet were sticking to the tiles and she couldn't move them. Fortunately by now, I had convinced dad it really would be a good idea to have a telephone installed. As mum eventually prized her feet free, she awkwardly made her way to the 'phone to call the Bath Hotel to get dad, but the landlord couldn't understand what she was saying and all he heard was 'Tim.' He told my dad he should go as something didn't seem right. Dad rang me at home that day, and I had to inform him that it sounded to me as though mum had had some sort of stroke; he had already called the doctor when I arrived from Sheffield.

In the days that followed we had to convince mum to slow down, to give up her job. She did recover from the stroke, but it was a warning, and she never seemed to have the same energy in her step afterwards.

Of course Dora was still having her problems to be sorted, back in Sheffield and I knew now that I would have to visit mum and dad more to help them. Dad continued the care that Gwyneth needed, all the wile having to counter the actions of Carla, who would always be intoxicated, but we were also still dealing with Dora *and* now Dana, who had their own special little ways.

Fortunately I was between jobs at this time. I had been working for an insurance assessor, but found myself completely running his office, and with all that was going on around me, I felt it was too much, however I was later offered a job as a medical secretary part-time, in a busy General Practice. I had dallied with my application a year before, but left it too late and the position was filled, but early one morning the 'phone rang and as I lifted my sleepy head off the pillow. I realised it was the Practice Manager, ringing to see if I was still interested in a position, as now one year later there was another vacancy. I had sent my application on bright orange notepaper, with matching envelope in true Sandy style, and thought perhaps it was too much, but it just goes to show, that it was this that was so striking. Lesson – never change yourself to suit others, stick with what *you* think is good, you never know, *be individual.* Anyway, I decided it would be a new challenge not to mention a diversion. Diversion it was, although some of the material I had to read could be equally depressing, post-mortem reports, someone else's progressive illness, etc., but they gave me lots of training to add to my qualifications and soon I knew the difference between an 'otomy, 'ectomy or an 'ostomy, otherwise during my shorthand translation, someone could end up having the wrong bits cut off, cut out etc.

I especially remember one occasion when Bob, a colleague and one of the G.P.'s rang in desperation and asked if I could go to the address of one of our patients. Apparently the lady's husband had recently died and she had become particularly depressed, he therefore feared she may do something drastic and was keeping a close eye on her, hence his routine visit. When there was no response to his knocking, he broke down the door, but the lady, it appeared had gone out shopping. I abandoned the clinics I was preparing, and sped over there. He felt so awful when I arrived as he had virtually destroyed the front door for nothing, but I remembered having a door broken down and finding Doris with her wrists slashed, and assured him I felt he had done the right thing. However he wanted me to stay to explain to the patient when she arrived home as he had to leave for he had a surgery starting. As I waited for her return, going over in my mind, what I would say to her, how I would explain why the doctor had demolished her front door, I busied myself sweeping up the glass and debris. She was understandably shocked when she arrived home, there was no way I could say 'bye' and walk right out the door and back to work, so, I made us both a cup of tea, and rang the office to say I would be a while, and she poured out her sadness at the loss of her husband. I later thought that, this was all the lady needed – someone to talk to.

On another evening as surgery was nearing its end, all the drug addicts had sadly left without their spuriously requested prescriptions, a lady walked in clutching a paper bag which obviously contained a bottle. She sat in the waiting room swigging from the 'concealed' bottle, profanities streaming from her uncontrollable mouth. As I watched with caution, I realised the remaining patients in the waiting room were becoming increasingly disturbed by her behaviour, so I invited her into the interview room. She actually took hold of my arm in a vice-like grip and calmly announced that she had just killed a man and left him for dead under a bench. As her grip tightened around my arm I offered her a cup of tea and a biscuit, as I could see she had obviously been sleeping rough for some time.

She very readily accepted my offer, but I then pointed out to her that she would have to let go of my arm in order for me to make the tea. She released me, went in to the doctor who then threw her out, but for weeks afterwards I scanned the newspapers for any mention of a body being found but fortunately there was nothing. This was just the ramblings of a sad alcoholic, but the rules of confidentiality could not be broken,

So for a while, this is how life would continue, I would go to work every day, Gordon to his job in a private hospital, so at least we had our work in common, working with the medical profession. Thursday was my day off, so I would take two bus journeys to mum and dad's, visit auntie Gwyneth for a while, do whatever they needed and back home on the late bus, back to work again on Friday morning. I enjoyed my job, as I had always been fascinated by physiology etc., and the people I worked with were friendly and caring, but there was little time for much else, as Gordon worked shifts; we were like ships passing in the night. Angeline was becoming a teenager, and anyway weekends were mostly spent with mum and dad. Although Angeline would come with me often and help with the chores, and spend time talking to mum and dad. I felt at times that she should be having fun at this age, but remember we were still Jehovah's Witnesses and fun was not a priority, meetings were, and sometimes on

Thursdays we would arrive back in Sheffield in time to attend, sometimes we wouldn't. Therefore, on a weekend when all the work was done, I would occasionally walk over to the pub with Angeline. We would sit and chat to old friends I knew or neighbours, and pretty soon, Angeline was getting to know *their* sons and daughters. But it was mostly the boys who gathered round my very attractive daughter, like bees round a honey pot, but these lads took to me too, and we would all have a good old laugh, it lightened the load a little. One of them, (the grandson of the local undertaker) even remembered having a crush on *me* bless him, when my 'photo's used to appear in the 'Star' when I did promotion work. He had been about ten years old at the time. He had remembered as my 'photo used to be frequently in the newspaper. When I had worked as a courier for the Women's Circle, the promotion department had asked if I would do something quite different, they had thought up something called the 'Paper Dollies.' We were a group of about four or five girls who would dress in 'Hot Pants' and wear a sash, declaring various promotions. One week it may be 'Pet's Week' another 'Laughter Week, or 'Quiz Week' etc. I loved it, it was such fun meeting people in the streets and chatting to them. Each week a question would be put in the newspaper, anyone carrying a copy of the 'paper could approach one of us and if they gave the correct answer would win a bottle of champagne, and I was even being paid for this fun! Anyhow, the fun was shortly to come to an end. One week a reporter had inadvertently printed my address below a 'photo and I began receiving some very disturbing letters and 'phone calls. One such letter was inviting me to meet the perpetrator outside the Odeon Cinema one evening. I knew it was now time to contact the police, and the C.I.D. was called in. The detective I was dealing with, asked if I was brave enough to actually meet this man, and that they would be discreetly hiding, to pounce on him when he approached me. Gordon also made it clear that he too would be hiding! I was not at all brave, but I knew this man had to be caught and therefore agreed. When the evening arrived, I stood prominently on the steps of the cinema; my eyes peeled and focussed on every man I saw pass by, or climb the steps innocently to make an entry to see a movie. It was a very uncomfortable feeling, and I wondered what people must think of me standing there, watching men rather like a prostitute touting for business, but I didn't care, I just wanted to know who this man was. Sadly something must have spooked him, he didn't show, but at least I never heard from him again.

As things were going, with work every day, mum and dad on Thursdays and most weekends, I began to realise that I needed to do what I had put off all those years ago- *drive*! Angeline and I started lessons around the same time; Gordon would give us both plenty of practice in the meantime whenever he could. Pretty soon I was becoming more confident, despite hating every minute of it, but I took my test, and one thing in my life I am proud of is the comment the instructor made upon our return to the test centre. He said: - "That was a good drive, I really enjoyed it." Given that I hadn't at all enjoyed learning to drive, I was over the moon. I'd never had much praise for anything, there wasn't time, or felt I needed it, but considering what a chore it had been, I realised at the age of forty one, I had achieved something valuable. This now meant that I could get out to the village more quickly and easily, to work and back more easily, also I could take mum, dad, Gwyneth or anyone to hospital appointments, shopping etc., whenever they needed it. Of course, as anyone would think, I did wish I had done it years ago, it opened up a whole new found freedom.

I soon bought myself a car, and life was considerably easier with this freedom of movement and not being governed by the unpredictability of public transport. I could flit here and there in no time. Angeline was also progressing nicely with her driving, the difference was, she was young, and also enjoyed it. In those days, once you had a full licence, you could sit beside a learner driver, and so I did with Angeline. One evening the two of us went out with a couple of my friends Val, and Aileen. Angeline was always a sensible girl and would wisely refuse alcohol when she was driving. I had allowed her to drive on this occasion, as her test was due in a couple to weeks and she needed all the practice she could get. As she drove home with Val and Aileen in the back seat and me beside her, I felt proud of her driving skill, and was quite certain she was going to pass first time. As we were a mile or two from home it was ten thirty p.m. on a Friday night and people were already leaving the pubs and making for the 'chip shop' on the corner. Angeline was concentrating on her driving and I was also observing her manoeuvres, when I spotted a young man coming towards us balancing one foot in front of the other along the edge of the kerb. I cautioned Angeline to slow down, and pointed out that the man was possibly drunk and could run into the road at any second. Before I had finished my sentence he flung out his arms like an aeroplane and ran towards the car. Angeline responded immediately, her emergency stop was perfect; it would have been so easy for her to swerve to the other side of the road and hit an oncoming vehicle. Nevertheless, the young man *didn't* stop, he continued to hurl himself towards us and even at our low speed, it was a huge impact. My shiny red Charade was now red with blood. His legs were first to make contact with the bumper, his chin then dented the door frame on the passenger side, as he rolled down the door he took the wing mirror with him and left a very large indentation in the door with his head! I was furious. This was a deliberate act of someone under the influence of whatever! It all happened in seconds, although as he flew through the air and landed with a thud at my side, it felt like ages. I opened the car door, strode over him and knocked on the door of the nearest dwelling for them to call an ambulance. *THEN* , I strode back to this person who was struggling to stand up, like an injured animal. I took him gently by the neck of his T shirt and drew him quickly towards my angry face. As I looked into his eyes, his pupils were moving in various directions, and with my experience of drug abusers at the surgery, I could see that he had taken some sort of illegal substance, blood was pouring from his ears, nose, legs, his shoes were completely missing, but all I wanted was his name. My friend Val took his face gently in her cupped hands to comfort him. *I* shoved her off I'm ashamed to say, telling her to "Leave him alone! He's mine!" This was one occasion where my usually caring attitude had disappeared. This man had caused untold damage to my car, but far worse than that, he had put all our lives in danger and completely traumatised Angeline, who was by now distraught. Her emotions were swinging from anger to worry about what her dad would say over the state of the car. I told her it wasn't her fault, and the car could be repaired, she was more important right now. Needless to say, a week or so later, she took her driving test and passed with flying colours. Well done!

Now things were really looking up. The car was repaired, and there were now two of us who could drive, and therefore able to offer much more help to mum and dad. I was however, starting to have dreams of dad dying, literally, in a pool of blood, it was very distressing and I didn't know how to interpret it, but this particular dream recurred on many occasions, always the same, dad lay dying, blood oozing from everywhere and I was standing helplessly watching, his life slowly ebbing away, maybe it was just my morbid fear of death.

The next wonderful news was from Dora would you believe; yes let's not forget Dora and my angels. On one of her rare visits to mum and dad's she announced that she had decided at long last to divorce Joe. We all felt life would be better for all if they parted. Despite Joe being quick tempered, I understood more than anyone to some degree how difficult it must have been living with Dora's odd ways. However, Dora decided that as soon as a place could be found she would move out of the marital home, taking Tina with her. Sally had decided to stay with her dad. She was involved with horses near her home and I would imagine wanted to continue with her interest, and may also have found her dad at the time, easier to live with.

Home life for them had gone from dreadful to diabolical. Dora was frequently going out with her friend, as Joe also frequently drank with his buddies. Dora had an arrangement with one of her friends that at the end of their evening out in town, they would walk to the taxi rank together for safety and leave for home in their respective ways. As they waited in the queue one evening, Dora's friend had waved goodnight and climbed into her taxi, as Dora moved to the front of the long queue, she reached out to open the door of the next available cab and climbed inside, to find a tall young black man, had climbed in at the other side. Realising that everyone had been waiting a while, she agreed with the driver that he take this young man to wherever he was going and then onto her home. Twenty minutes or so later, the young man had arrived at his destination, paid the driver, grabbed Dora by her arm and dragged her out onto the road. The taxi driver assumed they were a couple having a 'domestic' and promptly drove off. My sister found herself in an area of Sheffield, late at night in the dark, where she had never been before. Everything was totally unfamiliar to her, and she became much disorientated. As she picked herself up and looked around to grasp her bearings, she noticed the young man was still standing beside her. As she began questioning his actions and where she was, he produced a knife from his pocket. As Dora saw the street light glinting on the blade, she began to run in fear for her life! As she ran down the street, she banged on doors, screaming to people to help, to let her in, but no-one would. One young woman however, pushed open her bedroom window and saw the chase. She would not go down or open her door, as she had two young children in the house, but as she saw the man with the knife grab Dora, under the street lamp on the corner, she did call the police.

After Dora had been attacked, held at knife-point and raped by this man, he then forced her, still at knife-point, into a 'phone box to call a taxi. When it arrived he told her to give the driver her address, and instructed him to take them there. Now at this time Dora lived at the bottom of a very steep, small cul-de-sac, and on arrival the driver refused to go down. This was February and we had had a very heavy snow-fall and he feared he would not get the vehicle out again. Dora's attacker had also stolen her money and her purse was empty, therefore rendering her unable to pay the driver. This is one occasion when Dora showed a modicum of intelligence. She offered to go inside and find the money to pay her fare, at the same time taking a mental note of the licence number on display *inside* the cab. As she approached her front door, she ran inside and locked it behind her, desperately fumbling for the 'phone and calling the police, she dialled 999. As she sobbed out her story to Joe, he dismissed her with a wave of the hand and said she was being over dramatic. When the police arrived, they appeared to be equally unsympathetic, pulling her story to pieces, asking her where all this took place, and of course, poor Dora had no idea, it was not familiar to her. They made a feeble offer to 'check it out,' when Dora remembered the cab number, and gave it to them, which they duly noted.

They tracked down the cab driver who informed them that this man had also refused to pay his taxi fare on arrival at his address, which the driver gave to the police. He was arrested and so began a period of worry and distress. Poor Dora, she made me angry and frustrated most of the time. Her life made me very sad *all* of the time but she was my sister, and I loved her. For all her apparent failings, she would never deliberately harm anyone, and she certainly did not deserve this, no-one did.

It was almost a year later that the case came to court, and Dora had needed a great deal of support and sympathy to help her to deal with this, now she would need even more. I was amazed to see how unsympathetic my angel, Dana had been, in fact her derogatory remarks had only made Dora feel worse if anything.

The first day of the trial arrived, and no-one offered her any support or even wished her luck. Even her friend who had been with her that night was nowhere to be seen. I decided to go with her, she needed somebody and although this was a very daunting prospect as I had never seen the inside of a courtroom in my life, I agreed to attend. As the proceedings began, we sat in the courtroom together. I had told her to hold her head high, she was the victim here, and she had nothing to hide. She was afraid of how she would feel if her attacker looked at her. I advised her to look at the Judge, or *anywhere* but in *his* direction. The accused, however had no such fear, he sat calmly in the dock, wearing sunglasses, and reading a newspaper, with his feet up on the rails in front of him. This pleased me greatly, because I felt confident that the judge in his wisdom would be unsympathetic toward such an arrogant specimen of humanity.

As evidence unfolded in the court, he was asked many questions. One of them was, why had he taken her money, his answer was that *she* had asked *him* for sex! When asked why he carried a six inch knife, he replied that he used it for cleaning his nails. The young woman who rang the police described how she had seen him chasing Dora down the street, with the knife in his hand. I was amazed it had come to court, given that no-one seemed to have believed Dora at the time, although upon checking when the police tracked down the cab driver that night, he was able to inform them exactly where he had picked them both up, and the police had eventually found pieces of Dora's clothing and buttons which had been ripped from her coat. Only then had they taken her seriously.

The accused was given three years imprisonment for assault, rape and carrying an offensive weapon. *Three years*! British justice does not allow previous convictions to be read out in court, unless the accused is actually convicted. After sentencing, the policeman on the case stood up with a note book and it took him ten minutes to read out his list of 'previous' which began with 'living off immoral earnings' etc. etc. The man was nothing more than a pimp, a violent individual who thrived on the control and fear of women.

My poor parents. They also found Dora difficult to understand at times, but they loved her also. She was their first born, but their age and failing health made it difficult to do anything other than give her moral support where possible.

Meanwhile life drifted by in a buzz of activity. Mum and dad's Golden Wedding was approaching, so I thought it would lighten the atmosphere somewhat and so we'd have a party. I felt as the two daughters Dora and I should plan it together, and it would also be therapeutic for Dora to be involved, although I wasn't sure to what extent she would be willing. Happily Dora agreed and yet again surprised me by making suggestions and to the best of her ability, carrying through. We kept it a complete surprise for mum and dad. We organised a buffet at the Bath Hotel, their favourite local. We invited as many friends and relatives as we could find. I had table arrangements made from fresh cream-coloured roses, which my mother had had in her bridal bouquet. On the day, Dora and I went to stay at mum and dad's and told them we would just like to take them for a drink to celebrate. I had ordered a beautiful bouquet to be delivered, and remember my lovely cousin Jayne, who made cakes for me when I was a child? Well, she was also very talented at flower arrangements and visited with a beautiful arrangement she had put together. I also had a cake made, and many friends and neighbours brought cards and little gifts to wish them well. In the evening we took them to the pub, and as they walked through the door, they saw the table beautifully laid out with food and flowers. They then started to notice old friends they hadn't seen for a while and my mother's comment was "Somebody must be having a bit of a 'Do.' I answered – "Yes, it's you!"

We had a wonderful evening, despite Dana being her usual intoxicated self, and standing up and *straining* the theme tune from Prisoner Cell Block H! There was lots of reminiscing, and mum stood up to sing also, though much more professionally with her brother James, exercising their beautiful welsh voices together in ethereal harmony. This was to be the last time I would hear my mother's lovely soprano voice in song.

Chapter Eleven

A Merciless Angel

Now I know it must be very hard to keep up, but the real decline was about to set in, and Carla would play a very large part. Gwyneth's health had taken a turn for the worse, and ultimately she had a stroke. It turned out to be far worse than mum's had been and she wound up in a hospital which was several miles away. No-one visited Gwyneth much but some neighbours in the village were very kind, and would offer to take mum to see her. We would also visit whenever time permitted. We knew she would be there for some time, so dad had a key to her bungalow and would pop in daily, keep the heating on, pay the bills and collect her pension. I was visiting mum and dad one day to find neither of them at home, which was unusual. I decided to have a stroll into the village to see if dad had gone for his tobacco or to the post office. I popped my head round the shop door and asked if dad had been in. Mr. 'W' the shop keeper said he had seen dad passing earlier and "By the way, I'm sorry to hear about Gwyneth!" he said. I was a little puzzled at this because surely if anything had happened dad would have let me know straight away. However Mr 'W' said that someone with a large truck had called in early that morning asking where my auntie lived and said they had come to empty the bungalow due to Gwyneth's recent death. I was very anxious and very confused. Carla had recently been harassing my parents on the 'phone being verbally aggressive towards them and demanding the key to her mother's house. I advised my parents to hand over the key to her, (to my regret) she *was* Gwyneth's daughter, and I was not going to continue to allow her to upset them like this. They handed over the key.

Getting back to confusion, I always seemed to have a dilemma going on, protecting my parents, or protecting Auntie Gwyneth for instance. I rushed through the village that day, and found dad in the post office and hurriedly questioned him regarding Auntie Gwyneth. Dad was amazingly calm, as always, and said "Your mother's gone to visit her today, and she was very mush alive this morning when we spoke to the hospital staff!" As dad and I made our way back home we detoured past Gwyneth's home and peered through the window. The place was completely empty! Not a curtain, not a rug – *nothing*! Yet in the garden were the remains of a fire, still smouldering, remains of family 'photos and documents singed at the edges. *CARLA*! She had removed everything her mother owned and sold it to finance her alcoholic habit – priceless! She had burnt what she considered useless and one of the 'photo's she had burned was of my grandmother as a young girl, with bustle, curled hair and looking beautiful, the only one anybody had – gone. Where were Auntie Gwyneth's possessions? Where was her jewellery, clothes even?

I decided the next day, to visit her in hospital, as she *was* very much alive and completely unaware of recent events. As I approached the bed, she was sitting alone, crying, as a nurse approached me and asked me what was happening. She complained that Carla had not visited her for at least a couple of weeks and they needed some clothes, to teach Gwyneth how to dress herself after the stroke. I took the nurse to one wide and told her we didn't have any clothes we didn't have *anything*! She looked at me in total disbelief. As I sat beside the hospital bed, once more I couldn't bring myself to tell Gwyneth what had happened, just like all those other times years ago, I was once again protecting the guilty in order to protect the innocent. Instead, I decided to comfort Auntie Gwyneth and ask her what exactly was upsetting her. As her story unfolded she explained that, amongst other things, she had requested a new cheque book from the bank but had not received it, and needed money to buy magazines and biscuits. That was soon rectified as I left her a few pounds temporarily. Her hospital social worker assured her he had been onto the bank and they had sent a book, and she shouldn't worry because Carla was taking care of everything. *THIS* worried me! Gwyneth was understandably upset, due to Carla not being anywhere near for weeks, she was helpless in that hospital bed and her life was falling apart in front of her, only she wasn't aware of *just* how bad it really was. With the exception of mum and dad, most of the family had never believed me when I tried to tell them how truly evil Carla could be, and I knew they wouldn't believe now, after all Carla *was* an 'angel' and therefore very expert at lying and I felt I must have been more of a devil the way no-one ever listened, I was not good at lying either. I was beginning to feel as helpless as Auntie Gwyneth.

I returned to the bedside. I assured Gwyneth that I was going to find out what was happening, still keeping from her that she now owned *nothing*. Carla had not visited her dad when he was dying, why did I think she would visit her mum? Then I remembered, my uncle had left Gwyneth well provided for. She had money in the bank, he had a private pension, and Gordon had sold the car for her. I told her, I could only find out the truth if she agree, and she readily did so and therefore needed someone to sort it out. I asked if she was happy for me to look into her financial affairs, and if so I would need her written permission to do so. She had no doubts, she wanted to know.

The next time I visited, I went armed with a typed letter stating her wishes, with a place for her to sign, me to sign, plus a witness. I barged into the social worker's office, and was looked at with a gaze that assured I had interrupted whatever it was he was doing. GOOD I thought, I had his attention. I then demanded that he follow me. We found Gwyneth still sitting in bed crying in utter desperation. I thrust the letters under his nose, suggested that he read them. The 'Squib' was now in full explosion. As the man read, Gwyneth also read her copy. She agreed with all I had written and readily and eagerly signed. I offered the pen to the social worker, who was still protesting that Carla was sorting this, and once more made my demand for him to sign, to witness that Gwyneth knew what she was doing. That same day I took off to the village of Hathersage, to the bank and asked if I could speak to the manager. He was a very nice man and very diplomatic as I expected he would be. He reservedly told me that he had some concerns regarding my auntie's account, but was unable to discuss them with me without her permission. I could sense from this man, that he desperately wanted to tell me something but knew that protocol and confidentiality prevented him. However, when I produced the signed letters from Gwyneth he almost smiled. The grave look of concern lifted from his friendly face and he assured me with confidence that he would look into this immediately and let me know within a day or two what the exact situation was. There was just one drawback for me, we were going on holiday to the Scottish Highlands and wouldn't be around after the weekend, for the next two weeks. Never fear, I visited my uncle James who was always willing to help in a crisis and asked him if he would just humour me by following this up in my absence, even though I knew none of them would listen to me, just as they hadn't when the family fell out over goodness knows *what* Carla had told them way back. I promised that if I was wrong, I would apologise to everyone, especially to Carla! I knew I wouldn't have to.

A few days into our holiday I rang my dad to ask if there was any news. He told me that Gwyneth's bank account was *EMPTY!* Carla had got her hands on the cheque book and had slowly and systematically drained the account of *thousands* of pounds. Poor Gwyneth. What would this do to her? This was one I couldn't keep from her. I could no longer protect the innocent *nor* the guilty. It was all going to come out.

It must have come as a great shock to the residents and particularly the family, in this small village. Little did they know what was happening back in Sheffield? The evil was spreading, how could anyone do such things to their own mother? Apparently prior to this revelation, suspicions were aroused when Carla had visited the village with Gwyneth's pension book and told the lady in the post office she needed to cash it as she had no money to go home. Way back, these small communities would be helpful to one another and Carla cashed the Gyro slip, even though not signed, on the promise from Carla to the post office assistant, that she would pay it back the following week when they were signed by her mother. She immediately enlisted the local taxi driver to drive her all the way home to Sheffield, about twenty miles, *after* she had squatted down and urinated on the pavement. This behaviour to a large extent could be attributed to the alcoholism, but I *knew* Carla, this was the evil, it was just that on this occasion the alcohol had clouded her inhibitions and prevented her from cunningly concealing her normal methods.

I was devastated that so much was going to be revealed about Carla, for Gwyneth's sake. She didn't deserve to be treated this way, by her only daughter. The only consolation for me was that maybe at least the family would now believe what I had been saying and yet they really knew nothing. This incident was just the straw that broke the camel's back.

However, as Gwyneth progressed, mum and I bought her some new clothes and eventually she came out of hospital and moved into a residential home where she could be cared for and protected. Now at least she was out of Carla's grip, and although she was now penniless, she was reasonably happy.

By now Gwyneth was well and truly aware of what Carla had been up to, and asked that we didn't let Carla know where she was. All she had now was the continued private pension from her husband, although minus a large chunk as Carla had forged these cheques also, for months and drunk away the proceeds. However Gwyneth refused to have her prosecuted.

Chapter Twelve

A New Generation and Decline

I was so glad my heart was working so hard to keep up with my body. Gordon and I were flat out. There was his own mother, who had failing sight and often lost her balance, my parents, whom I spent as much time with as I possibly could, Dora of course, and Angeline, who thankfully was quite self-supporting, considerate of what we needed to do and helped where she could, and we were still Jehovah's Witnesses, attending five meetings a week. Of course don't forget Dana, baby Andre was already staying with us at weekends, just like his mother had when she was young. He was now becoming a toddler, and a cheeky little chappy, full of energy and life. Whenever I visited, he would greet me at the door, grasping my bags as I entered saying, "Let me help you with those heavy bags auntie Sandra" as he held his little arms as high in the air as he could to prevent the bags trailing on the floor. He also knew that they would contain goodies and treats for them all, and it was a good method of teaching him manners, for he knew he had to say his please and thank you's to get his sweeties. Dana had by now given birth to her second child, a daughter this time, named Leah. Leah was, from the beginning, a wilful child. I could see it in her eyes. She would sit in her high chair and bang the handle of her spoon on the tray, wearing the most ferocious frown until her food was served. Leah never did stay over at our house; I don't think she ever wanted to. However, Leah was followed shortly by Adam. A whole new generation was emerging.

So, all in all, life was full to overflowing, with all of this not to mention going to work, oh! And then of course, there was that small thing called housework, for our house was a fair size built on three levels, with two staircases but somehow, working as a team Gordon and I managed. We even had a rare night out now and then, and the odd holiday when we could. My goodness! When I look back and think of all this, I can't imagine how we kept sane, but somehow we did. I was however, still having the same recurring nightmare of dad dying surrounded by copious quantities of blood. I put this all down to the stress I was under at the time, and they say dreams are usually the opposite to what they appear, so I imagined it was once more, down to my morbid fear of people dying and the fact that I loved him so much and couldn't bear to lose him.

On Friday night I would still visit Dana. Whenever Gordon and I re-decorated or bought new furniture, I would take anything we didn't need for Dana, she couldn't afford much, and pretty soon her house was furnished with lamps, cushions tables and chairs, curtains and rugs etc.

I kept my visits to Friday evenings after work when I had locked up the surgery, after the last patient had gone, whether it be six p.m. or seven p.m because whenever I saw Andre, he would beg me to bring him home, and Friday was the only day I could do this, as each weekday there was work, my day off was Thursday and spent at mum and dad's, so the weekends were good, plus I could take Andre with me to Bradwell and drop him home on Sunday evening on my way back to Sheffield. Mum and dad loved to see him; he was their first great-grandson. Dad would throw his coppers into a jar and Andre would spend his time trying to count them, and show us his big broad smile as he announced how rich he was.

As we would climb into the car on those Sunday evenings to return home, he would beg me to put his favourite song on the stereo. "Walking in the Air." He would sit back and relax and fall slowly and reluctantly to sleep. His little eyelids drooping, his head nodding 'till the restraint of the seat-belt jolted him back to reality, but eventually he could resist no more and he would nestle comfortably in his seat and dream of flying through the air with the 'Snowman.' I always tried to get him home for a reasonable bedtime because he was by now, starting nursery and needed his sleep. This was however, quite futile, as he rarely went, Dana just couldn't be bothered to get him up and ready. It's quite difficult when you've been up until three or four a.m. drinking and smoking. When he did make it to school, he was often bullied because he smelled, and his clothes were badly fitted, and often torn and dirty. I would bring him clothes to wear when he stayed with us so that he could shower on a Friday night and at least be clean for the weekend. I would wash his clothes and he would return home in them on Sunday, otherwise the new ones would be swallowed up in the 'abyss.'

One weekend I remember bringing Andre home from his grandparent's following an argument with his mum, when the 'phone rang. It was Dana asking if she could speak to Andre for just a minute. I could hear the noises of pub life in the background, but nevertheless allowed her to say goodnight to him. I listened as best I could to the conversation only to find that she was informing Andre that the police were looking for him for 'stealing a car and wrapping it around a lamp post .' Little eight year old Andre wouldn't even be able to reach the pedals let alone drive it! I reassured him as best I could, his mummy was kidding and the police were *not* after him.

Dora now, had divorced Joe and moved into a huge complex of flats called Kelvin. It was an awful place; a mountain of concrete steps faced me as I approached the buildings. As I looked upwards, it felt rather like starting the ascent of

Machu Pechu, except the 'jungle' around it was also concrete. The lift was not a desirable option either, as it often didn't work, and even when it did, the odour of stale urine was so overpowering I felt like I was in a moving gas chamber, and couldn't breathe. Dana would often take her brood and stay over a t Dora's, it was great to have a built-in babysitter I guess, just as Dana herself had been for her mum and Joe when young. One night as our household had drifted peacefully off to sleep; we were woken by the shrill sound of the telephone in the dead of night. I sat bolt upright in bed as I fumbled for the receiver in the dark. It was Dora, but her mumblings down the 'phone were incoherent, and I was not fully awake. I had to blearily urge her to slow down and speak more calmly. As Dora's story unfolded, between her sobs, I could barely grasp what had happened, but enough to understand that she was at the hospital and Dana had jumped from the balcony of the flats! It was a long way to the top of Machu Pechu, and an equally long way to the bottom, but as the crow fly's quicker than the stairs, and I couldn't help wondering if in a drunken state, she had decided not to face the 'gas chamber.' As I climbed out of bed, Gordon urging me to 'leave them to it' I knew that Dana would have very serious, if not fatal injuries after such an impact. I fled to the hospital ignoring every red light I could. The Accident and Emergency department was overcrowded that night, full of drunks who had been in fights. I scanned the waiting room for Dora, but couldn't find her. I surged from one nurse to another until someone pointed to a small room, and there through the glass window, I could just make out Dora's sad face. I thought it must be *very* bad news indeed if they had put her in a room alone. As I entered, I searched Dora's face for answers. She explained how there had been a knock on the door of her flat, neighbours were there to tell her Dana had been found at the bottom of the stairwell, unable to stand and telling them she had jumped. Poor Dora was distraught; this was her daughter, Vince's daughter. This just didn't add up to me. If Dana had jumped from this concrete mountain, she would either be dead, or at the very least unconscious when found. I was, by now starting to read Dana's mind as always, and could pre-empt her next moves, and decided I should find out the truth behind this tale. I made enquiries as to where Dana had been taken and was told she was about to go down for X-ray. As we spoke I noticed Dana on a stretcher wearing full neck brace to immobilise her movements, although it hadn't immobilised her mouth. She was drunkenly dishing out orders to doctors and nurses and spitting her usual venom. Upon hearing Dana's voice, Dora immediately ran to her side, all the while, Dana is telling her mother, she is going to join Vince! This of course was terrifying for poor Dora, but that was the whole idea! What perfect emotional blackmail. However Dana was completely unaware of my presence at this point and as I carefully approached the moving trolley from the 'top' end, I leaned over and gazed into her upside-down eyes and said, "You should be so lucky!" I was by now, beginning to realise that Dana had carefully placed herself at the foot of the stairwell and waited until passers-by discovered her, as she spun her usual web of lies, but hang on! She was and 'angel' wasn't she?

Eventually the doctors were tiring of Dana wasting their time, and concluded that they could find no physical injury. Amazing, after jumping from 'Machu Pechu' to the tarmac below, and so they were discharging her, much to Dana's surprise and very verbal objections. She was now insisting that her legs and ankles hurt due to the 'landing' (very clever to land on you feet after jumping from such a high building) The doctors were by now looking at me with a gaze that said 'take her away' Dana on the other hand was enjoying their dilemma, not to mention Dora's obvious distress and insisting she should stay. A little psychology was called for here. I immediately turned to Dora, who by now was also angry at being so upset for nothing, that she was actually feeding Dana's ego with a retaliating argument. I gently put my hand on her shoulder, and said that she and I should now go home leave Dana there, and take control of what would happen to the children. Dana quickly jumped down from the bed and declared they were *her* children and *she* was in control. Just the response I wanted and expected. To her, I really *was* a child predator.

One can often make excuses for alcoholism, but Dana had a husband who tried his best and three lovely children, and a home which some people didn't have, I could see no reason for her turning to drink other than she enjoyed it. Often I would visit, and the bin would be full to overflowing with empty lager cans, spilling out onto the surrounding lounge floor. She would often not get out of bed until mid-afternoon, which meant Andre and Leah didn't go to school, and Adam was still in his cot, in his bedtime nappy. History was repeating itself, and now I was the one cajoling and trying to encourage Dana to get up and do her duty as a mother. Just as my mother had done years before with Dora. Of course situations like these can only go on for so long before disintegration sets in. Pete was the first to leave; he could no longer tolerate Dana's drunken moods, and moved out. He didn't go far, just around the corner to his parent's, so that he could still see the children. However he didn't even manage this because Dana had told him he could not see them. I knew this was not good for the children, and felt so sorry for them and for Pete. He was accepting his role as a father trying his best with an impossible situation, and failing miserably to control Dana's demands.

Anyhow, on one of my Friday night visits to take sweeties, I was met at the door, as usual, by Andre, only this time he didn't grab my bags but held on tightly to my arm leading me into the house. He was so excited as he told me his daddy was coming for him at seven p.m. I thought this was very strange for Dana to have changed her mind so quickly and easily. Dana offered me a cup of coffee, she was usually glad to see me as, taking Andre home meant she was free of him for the weekend. I accepted the offer of coffee, it was six fifteen p.m. so I decided to hang around and see what happened at seven o'clock. Once more, I was pre-empting her behaviour patterns. All the while, little Andre was performing his 'Tigger' bounce up and down and every five minutes asked me "What time is it now, auntie Sandra?" the next forty five minutes must have passed very slowly for him as he anticipated his daddy's arrival. I had shown him where the hands needed to be on the clock as it ticked slowly by, and as the 'big' hand edged its way *past* the seven, Andre's little face fell, the excited smile disappeared and the 'Tigger-like' bounce had gone from his legs, he started to cry. His mother stood with hands on hips and told him it was to be expected, as his dad didn't care and didn't really want him. I couldn't help feeling that Dana had engineered this situation. I told Andre to put his coat on, and we would go and find out what had happened as I was sure daddy must have a good reason for letting him down, we'll go and see daddy to find out. Dana was *gob-smacked*! She obviously hadn't anticipated my determination to uncover her little game. We climbed into the car and drove to grandma's. Pete was there, having his evening meal, and as we were invited in, seemed so pleased to see Andre with me. As we informed Pete what was wrong, he knew nothing about his expected visit, as he had been told by Dana that he couldn't see the children. Just as I had expected! Pete couldn't keep him that night as he was going to work, so as usual I took Andre home with me, but at least he was happy because he had seen his daddy and knew he *was* wanted by him. We spent the weekend gardening and Andre loved it. Picking up worms and throwing them at me, digging the soil furiously, and receiving some 'wages' at the end of the day for his hard labours. Unfortunately, his green waxed jacket was covered in mud so I popped it in the washing machine before he went home! I knew nothing of these waxed jackets and of course it came out of the machine with cracks and marks all over it. On his return to Dana, I promised I would buy him a new one. The following week I took a few days leave from the surgery, and on my next visit to see Andre, took along the new coat I had bought. Andre was lying on the settee with just a dirty thin duvet covering him. As soon as I sat down, Dana ordered him off to bed, but a few minutes later he was crying and calling down that he had been sick. Dana rushed upstairs, fag still in hand and was quickly back down again saying he had *not* been sick at all and just wanted attention. Understandable, Auntie Sandra had come to see him. However, when I asked Dana if I could pop up and try on him the new coat, to make sure it fitted, she protested that he wasn't well, and needed to go to sleep. By the time I said it wouldn't take a minute I was half way up the stairs. Andre was indeed not well. I had seen by the pallor on his face that he was quite poorly but I was appalled by what I saw when I entered his bedroom. There were no curtains to the window, no carpet on the floor, a pile of vomit beside the bare bunk beds but worst of all, no sheets or pillows on his bed. It was the middle of winter and I could see my breath before me as I walked across the freezing cold room. I scooped this sick child up in my arms and carried him as best I could down the stairs, wrapped in his new coat and took him home with me. I laid him on the settee with a clean duvet, and slept on the floor beside him for three nights until he recovered, he had a fever and was hallucinating, I had called the doctor to him and was told he was quite poorly, and he was given antibiotics. After about a week, Andre had recovered well enough to go back once more, into battle, and I returned to work.

The decline was really setting in. In the weeks that followed there would be many more incidents of emotional abuse. Dana would sit the children down and give them a 'nice drink' in a pretty mug, then tell them they must drink it quickly, as it was poison and they were all going to die. She would put on their coats and tell them she didn't love them anymore and they were going to live in a children's home.

There was an evening when Dana took out Adam in his pushchair with Leah grasping the handle for security. In her drunken state that evening, Dana fell down in the middle of the road, and Adam was tipped out of his pram in the process. Leah ran to a neighbour because she couldn't pick mummy up, she was six years old. Ultimately, the police were called and Dana was arrested for being drunk and disorderly, whereupon she had a screwdriver from somewhere, and used it to stab the arresting officer. The children were taken to grandma's, thankfully Andre was already here with us, but despite this, and our protection, he guessed from the 'phone call we had, that his mother was in trouble once again.

Dana had started seeing a new man. His name was Damien, and he was a tall, well-built young man and also unfortunately, a 'schedule one' offender. I could almost see the '666' imprinted on his forehead every time I saw him. He and Dana would stay in bed all day, and this resulted in Adam becoming malnourished because he wasn't fed. Andre and Leah would just go downstairs and help themselves to the dregs of last night's tea cups, and the remains of the scraps left on the unwashed plates. Poor Adam could not help himself; he was a prisoner of the bars on his cot and his as yet less agile little legs. Andre could only take so much on these occasions, before he would run off to grandma's, often in his pyjamas and bare feet, whenever Dana had succeeded in winding him up. Grandma would then ring Gordon and me to tell us, that he had lashed out at everyone violently and had then fallen into a catatonic state, and she didn't know what to do. Social Services had by now been involved, but nothing seemed to be happening. This was to occur many times when we would answer the call and take Andre home with us in his trance-like state, until he came out of it.

One particular evening, events reached a crescendo, when Dana had knocked on a neighbour's door to borrow a cigarette. As the door closed behind her, Andre seized his opportunity for revenge. He locked the door, keeping Dana out, and wouldn't let her back into the house. The police, doctor, and social worker were called. Eventually someone gained entry to the house through an upstairs window and reached Andre, who was by now once more, in his catatonic state of mind. Of course Dana made up some cock and bull story about him taking a shovel to Adam and threatening to hit him on the head. Andre loved his little brother, and would never hurt him, but

Andre and Leah were once again taken to gran's and Adam was left with Dana. I returned at 11 p.m. to see if she and Adam were o.k. to find her just leaving the house, going who knows where with a baby at such a late hour.

The bombshell came a week or two later, when Dana announced that she and Damien were going to be married! The Social Services pointed out that if she did so, they would have to remove all three children, and take them into care, (even though they had let them stay whilst Damien had been living there.) However, Dana rather impolitely told them that if that's how they felt they could take them, "I'll just have three more!" This time the Social Services had to do *something*, and so the three children, Andre, Leah and Adam, were taken one day, by their social worker, into care.

We have to remember here, how many times these children had been told they weren't loved and were going to live in a children's home. We can only imagine the true horror they must have felt, and the fear they must have endured, when it actually happened, their worst nightmare was now a reality. Let's be honest here, it was probably the first actual truth their mother had really told them.

Chapter Thirteen

Mixed Blessings

As Dana's little world seemed to be falling apart, we were trying to keep ours on an even keel. We enjoyed some the friendships we had made over the years as Jehovah's Witnesses, and some of us would invite each other for a barbeque or an evening chat, and supper.

Angeline had had a few boys hanging around, now and then, but there was one young man in particular that she seemed to really hit it off with. He was a lovely young man, and very handsome with olive skin and dark eyes, and beautiful dark wavy hair, his name was Dan. I took to this young person immediately; he was softly spoken and very pleasant and polite. Very unlike most you meet these days.

A group of us decided to take a holiday together, and so Gordon and I organised a week in the Scottish Highlands. We had been a couple of years ago and had great fun. The place we had stayed in was called Kindrochet Lodge, and it was the most unforgettable place, for many reasons. An old hunting lodge, nestling in the forest, on the Blair Athol Estate, Kindrochet was built in 1816, which was etched into the stone lintel above the front door. As the large and heavy key was turned in the lock of the equally heavy oak front door, it felt as though a time warp had sent us back to the eighteen hundreds. There were three sitting rooms, several staircases, many bedrooms, each with a bell-pull by the fireplace, which would operate the big curly iron bells which sat in a row at the top staircase, in what would have been the servant's quarters. There was a large scullery kitchen with a long, worn pine table right down the middle, and all the windows had wooden shutters, which were riddled with woodworm. We felt we had stepped back in time.

Twenty one of us descended here in the summer of that year. Gordon organised a mini bus for those who didn't have cars, and drove it all the way there. One of our dear friends, Val, had just lost her husband to meningitis and she was feeling alone and bewildered, despite having six children. She couldn't afford this holiday, but needed it, and so Gordon and I paid her share. There was Robert, a young single boy, who had obsessive compulsive disorder, which was actually great for the rest of us, because he cleaned all the bathrooms! Poor Robert, by the time we left for Scotland he had no money to pay for the holiday either, so we financed his trip too! All in all, it was an expensive holiday for us, but very enjoyable nonetheless.

However, Angeline and Dan got to know each other better that week, and became girlfriend/boyfriend. We were quite pleased with this match, and they were a handsome couple together.

Not everything in the city was rosy though. Gwyneth was now settled in the 'Home' and Carla had no idea where she was, therefore she had to turn her attentions to some other mischief. She started ringing me every afternoon, possibly when she had just woken from her alcoholic induced daze, and maybe the bottle of vodka she left in the washing machine, the bathroom cupboard or the up-lighter etc., was no longer there.

Each day the 'phone call would begin with Carla crying to me with some sob story or another. During one call she asked if I would help her make funeral arrangements for her mother. I was astonished! Gwyneth was alive and well and recovering nicely. When I pointed this out to Carla, she replied:- "Well she's gonna die sooner or later, so I may as well do it now." I couldn't help feeling that there was a desire on Carla's part to perhaps speed up Gwyneth's demise. Once I had entered into conversation, and Carla had succeeded in grasping my sympathies, her whole attitude would change in the blink of an eye, from Jekyll to Hyde, and the next second she would venomously accuse me of something, anything, or perhaps spit out that Gordon had sold her dad's care and taken the money. Gordon *had* in fact sold the car for her, because Gwyneth didn't drive and knew nothing about cars or indeed what to do with this one. He got the best price he could, and she was very grateful for the cash along with receipt from the purchaser. Anyhow, Carla would then slam down the 'phone!

These 'phone calls persisted on a daily basis for some time, and despite being a fairly strong person, along with everything else, it was beginning to wear me down. I can truly say that this was the first time in my entire life, so far, that I was to experience the emotion of *HATE*! It's such c small word of only one syllable, and yet it has such a powerful meaning. I could only think of the wicked things Carla had done to her mother, and others, and realised I wanted no more to do with this person, ever. My strategy was that whenever I picked up the 'phone and Carla answered, I would immediately replace the receiver, until she finally got the message. It worked, and I would thankfully hear nothing more from Carla for a very long time.

As a Christian, I knew only too well that I should forgive, but I have forgiven all my life, and the cruelty Carla had shown her mother was something I could *never* forgive. One has to draw the line somewhere. I was now beginning to realise that Angels *do* tell lies and this 'Angel' was one of the worst I had come across and so once again I was not conforming to the 'Christian' way of life. Did Jesus forgive Judas? Will Judas enter into the Kingdom of Heaven? I still wonder.

Now on a lighter note, we communicate regularly with George and Rita whom we had visited in Australia. Gordon would also visit various members of the congregation and take with him an audio tape recorder. He would ask them to say a few words, and when the tape was full he would send it to our dear friends so that they could hear all the old familiar voices. We still missed them, but at least having been to Australia to visit, we could visualise them in their home, or imagine them sipping wine under the pergola. One day, as I was preparing to go to work, I received a call from their son. He was ringing to inform us that our dear friend George had died of a heart attack. I then had to hurry as I was late for work but as soon as I arrived there, I burst into tears as it hit me, another dear friend was gone!

Rita, of course, was devastated. They had just celebrated their Golden Wedding Anniversary, fifty years together is a long time. We couldn't go to the funeral, it wasn't practical, but Rita wanted to bring the ashes back to England, to Sheffield. George would have wanted them scattered on the river Don, and so we arranged that she would spend some time with us. As we communicated back and forth, Rita asked if

Gordon would go back with her to Australia, for a week or two to help her make decisions. Gordon is a very reliable sort and she and George had liked that quality in him. However the elders of the congregation decided it was inappropriate for him to be staying with her, alone. We have to remember here that Rita was by now in her late seventies and recently bereaved, Gordon was a relatively young man. She viewed him as a second son and treated him that way. Also *I* had no objection at all, but we must abide by the rules, so we decided that *I* should go, no-one could object to that. I prepared time off work, three weeks was the maximum I could have at that time, as this was my first year, so my whole annual leave was taken at once. Rita had been ill whilst here, although eventually returned to 'Oz' on her scheduled flight, but a seat for me wasn't available. Therefore we had some searching to do. However, eventually we found a flight with Singapore Airlines, changing 'planes in Singapore, and Dubai. A twenty-eight hour journey to the other side of the world lay ahead of me – alone!

It was a very sad time for Rita and the next three weeks were quite a strain, but I feel we talked over her options, fully, and she made the decision to move back to England. I returned home three weeks later, having missed Gordon and Angeline terribly.

Poor Angeline! When I look back, much time and attention that should have been lavished on her had been focused elsewhere yet again. Events just always seemed to take over our lives continually, but now it was time to place the focus on Angeline once more. She and Dan were getting more and more close, and decided to become engaged. It was such a happy time for a change. Dan and Angeline made plans to have their engagement party at a place half way between the city and the countryside so that it was easily accessible to friends from all over. It was early December, and the morning of the party had arrived. I rose early and opened the curtains to find there had been a heavy snowfall overnight. We soon received a call from the manager at the venue to say that the snow had brought down the power lines during the night and there was no electricity etc. Angeline was devastated. This was her dream day, I had made her a beautiful cream lace dress to her specifications, the disco had been arranged, the food, and they had had the most unusual designer engagement ring made, with rubies, sapphires and diamonds. However, I decided that 'the show must go on!' We contacted the disco company and cancelled. No electricity for strobe lights and dance music, no lights in the pub even. Pretty soon the evening arrived and all the worries and concerns of the day disappeared. Dan took a portable C.D. player, and when we arrived at the country pub, there was a huge roaring log fire, and the landlord had placed recycled wine bottles, each containing a candle, on every table. It looked so romantic in the dim candlelight, with the flickering Christmas coloured flames of the fire, licking the stout logs upon it, giving out both physical and internal warmth. It turned out to be the most memorable of occasions, despite being for all the wrong reasons- 'negative to positive!'

Happy times continued to be interspersed with sad time, the core of the family was still discordant, dysfunctional, or whatever was the politically correct term at the time,
In other words, Dora and Dana were still battling on – literally! Anyhow it wasn't long before Angeline and Dan decided to set the date for their wedding. September the 7th. I knew it was going to be a hectic time, all else considered, but I was determined that Angeline would have the best we could manage. The first item selected was the wedding gown I had visited a bridal shop and saw *the* gown, and could just picture Angeline wearing it, in my mind's eye. I took her along to see this beautiful sparkling creation on its pedestal in a glass case, begging to be worn.
She agreed, the minute she laid eyes on it, shimmering in all its glory proudly situated in the centre of the bridal shop, like Cinderella's ball gown, she fell in love with it. Angeline was very slim yet shapely; she had also inherited her grandmother's elegant legs with curves in all the right places. She was also average height,

not short like me, yet even so, we needed a few minor adjustments. The gown was very slim-fitting, covered in ivory lace and encrusted with tiny seed pearls and rainbow sequins. It fastened down the back with a dozen round pearl buttons and long lace sleeves which rested neatly to a point on the hands. From her hips at the back sat a full large 'curvy' bow from which trailed a wonderful 'waterfall' train of tulle, which spread out rather like an upturned fan. She wore satin shoes, and with a little of the lace left over from the dress alterations, I customised them to match. We found beautiful combs for her hair, headdress and veil which fitted perfectly. Several florists were visited until we discovered the perfect bouquet made from Arum Lillies and bear grass. Angeline managed to find a jeweller who would create a wedding band which fitted symmetrically with her unusually shaped engagement ring. Bridesmaids were selected, Kirsten, a childhood friend, would be Maid of Honour, Leah and Katie were smaller bridesmaids and Andre would be Page Boy. But what would they wear? Well, we decided on a fairytale wedding, so why not continue the theme. We bought yards of satin fabric in red, green, blue and a champagne colour and I got very busy every night after work, on my trusty sewing machine. I worked night after night with tulle and netting, ribbons and bows until all the dresses and bonnets were flounced and ready. Andre's little suit was in the style of Little Boy Blue, with a pale blue satin bolero and knickerbockers, a creamy lace shirt and cravat, accompanied by black patent shoes with big square silver buckles. He was however, slightly non-plussed by the tights he had to wear to complete the outfit. I also made a blue satin cushion with tassels at each corner, to bear the rings. The wedding cake was also a work of art and Angeline chose it because it was so uncommon. Rather than the usual frills of pink icing with plastic bride and groom wearing their plastic grins, arm in arm atop the cake, it was a wash of colour, each of the three tiers resembled an English summer garden with poppies, irises and roses climbing and reaching out to meet a softly clouded blue sky. On the very top was a bouquet of butterflies which appeared to be fluttering away into the blue icing sky.

The day went perfectly, Gordon told Angeline she would be travelling in his Skoda, much to her dismay. Early morning, Angeline took herself off the have her makeup professionally applied, whilst the florist delivered her bouquet. The Bridesmaids had stayed over and were busily 'glamming' themselves up. Kirsten in her champagne satin, Leah in bright red, and Katie in emerald green, all in the style of Little-Bo-Peep, like a collection of little jewels, not to mention Andre in his Boy-Blue outfit. All of them looked beautiful. When Angeline returned, we poured her into her close-fitting bridal gown, reminiscent of my own wedding day. I smiled at the thought of the crowd looking for my 'bump.' However, when everything was put together and Angeline slid the blue garter onto her shapely leg, she looked *so* ethereal! This was a *true* Angel, <u>never</u> had she caused us any concern, despite her young years, she had always been supportive in a crisis. She truly deserved this day, it was *her* day. As the finishing touches were being applied, and I donned my cream lace dress, fuchsia pink hat and shoes, we heard a strange 'beep.' It was the vintage car I had organised or Dan and Angeline. The chauffeur was decked out in full livery and looked stunning as the 1920's vehicle pulled up outside our garden gate. It had lovely lace curtains a small table holding a champagne bucket, containing a bottle of pink champagne, the brass work was bedecked with ribbons and the hood at the back was down, because the sun was shining brightly on them that day. The finishing touch was the 1920's gramophone which was later set up on the lawn in the park where the photographs were to be taken. The music wafting around our group in the park ensured we were all so happy, and along with the pink champagne, we were almost inclined to dance the Charleston.

The ceremony was conducted by a close friend of ours who was an ordained minister; our lovely friend Laurence married Dan and Angeline. He gave the most poignant speech, using the allegory of a three strand cord, and how, when they are intertwined, they become stronger. The three cords represented man, wife and God. We had two receptions, one was afternoon tea for about two hundred guests with a duo called Quando entertaining us whilst we ate, and in the evening there was a disco at another venue where alcohol could be served. The day was wonderful, I'm sure I enjoyed it equally as much as the bride and groom. I was ecstatic; they were such a well matched couple.

There were however, one or two situations which *could* have ruined the whole day. A few weeks before the wedding, Dan broke his leg in three places, whilst playing football. He had his leg in plaster, and was walking on crutches. Curiously the elders of the congregation insisted he did his preaching from door to door, and if he didn't then the Kingdom Hall couldn't be used for their wedding service. Gordon and I were so incensed, we rang several individuals of the body of elders, and expressed our disgust, and asked if God would want this young man to risk further injury to his leg in order to do the preaching work, then perhaps we should go to the local church! I'm happy to say for the sake of Dan and Angeline that they agreed to go ahead with the wedding ceremony.

Now on the evening of the wedding there were many friends, and family at the disco, all having a good time, except me! Thankfully, Carla was not there simply because she was not invited, but Dora and Dana *were*! Every few minutes, one or the other would seek me out, as I was mingling and say: - "Can I have a word?" which greatly amused our Australian friend Lional. They would then drag me off to a corner and proceed to pelt me with a deluge of sorrows from their sordid lives. Before the night was half over, I had to tell them in no uncertain terms, that this was my *only* daughter's wedding, a 'one-off' and I couldn't help them that night, but they would not leave me alone.

However, the wedding was otherwise wonderful; all the months of planning and hard work were worth every second. Dan and Angeline had bought a house ten minutes away from us, and so life was good. They went away on Honeymoon, and one week later as I was about to leave for work, Angeline burst in through the front door, in floods of tears. I was taken aback. One week!! Had it gone wrong already, was it a mistake? Thankfully no, Angeline was simply missing her mum and dad already, just as we were also missing having her around, but we worked through it and life settled to a peaceful 'norm' yet again.

Chapter Fourteen

Empty Nest – Refilled

Dana now, of course, had an empty nest, and was enjoying her new-found freedom; all three of her children were placed in care. Social Services had removed them, just as they said they would. She had also emphatically told them as you may recall, that she would have three more, and true to form she was now pregnant by Damien and they were planning to marry as soon as her divorce from Pete became final. Her empty nest would soon be refilled. Our empty nest of course would stay well and truly empty. Gordon and I were looking forward to some space, some time for ourselves, and no responsibility but for each other. I felt quite pleased our nest would not be refilled, even though it seemed very quiet, and we were rattling around this house like two marbles in a jar. How wrong could I be? Oh why do I tempt fate so?

Meanwhile, Adam being a young toddler appeared to thrive now he was being properly fed and nurtured by his foster carers. Andre and Leah, on the other hand, hated it. Gordon and I would visit them in their foster home each week, and whilst Leah was accepting where she was surprisingly quietly, Andre found it difficult, he was so very confused. His mother

had done a wonderful demolition job on his self-esteem. On a lovely sunny day, as we took Leah and Andre out for a picnic on one of our visits, I asked him what was so bad about where he was living, and he told me that his foster carers lavished all their attention onto their own daughter, who was a similar age, and he and Leah had to largely fend for themselves. Of course they were used to that, but wasn't this supposed to be better? With my strong feelings for equality, this incensed me. ALL children especially when together should be treated equally, how can they thrive and grow in confidence if they feel they are not quite as worthy as the next one? I sat at home that evening desperately trying to come up with an answer, I had no experience of how the Social Services system worked. How could I go against the authorities who had placed them where they were? From then on, I observed more closely when I visited, and Andre was right. They fussed and flounced around their daughter, yet grunted orders at Andre and Leah. "Get your shoes on" "Where's your coat?" or "No you can't have chocolate!" Something had to be done. It was almost like a scene from a Dickensian novel, where the poor, unwanted children were subservient in some way. I had stupidly idealised that all foster carers were 'saints.'
Once again, I had a lot to learn.

However, I didn't have to wait too long for a solution. Very shortly, Andre started to run away from his carers, of course only to be taken straight back. He *was* though, a very resourceful little chap and one such evening, already an expert, he managed to slip out in nothing but his pyjamas and bare feet once more, and ran off to the nearest pub. I can imagine the surprise on the faces of the punters that night, seeing a very small boy standing there in his P.J's amidst the hushed conversations, and the shouts and cheers as a dart hit the bull's eye. Someone wisely called the police, because when questioned, all Andre would say was "I want to go back to mummy" this seemed strange at the time, given the way he was emotionally abused at home, but of course if you are going to be ill treated, it may as well be where all else is familiar, and he must by now have been wondering why he couldn't be with mummy. It was decided by Social Services eventually that Andre should be allowed to stay with his mother for a while, at least I suppose they thought they knew where he was. Of course it was inevitable that Andre would return to his angry outbursts when he was unable to take the mind games anymore. So on one of these occasions. Dana decided she didn't need Andre; she had a new life now, a new partner and a new baby on the way. Andre's return was just an intrusion, like a cuckoo in the new nest. As Andre kicked and screamed and punched in anger, Dana whisked him off to the police station. This was the final straw for poor little Andre, he absolutely flipped, his mind couldn't take any more. It took four police officers to control this eight year old boy that night. When Andre had gone into, and come out of, his usual catatonic state, and was calm, the officers asked him where he would like to be. He had told them, the only place he would go was to Auntie Sandy's it was at this point, as we were woken from our sleep in the early hours of the morning, that we discovered what had happened. The officer on the other end of the line was asking us if we could just take him overnight or they would have to put him in a cell! *How* had it come to this? A small child should never have to endure the possibility of being placed in a police cell at the age of eight. I told the officer to bring him right away. It was one thirty a.m. when the knock came at the door. The policeman stood there with Andre, and Dana was also with them. Apparently she had insisted that she escort Andre here. As the officer left I knew Dana was enjoying this unfolding drama, playing the desperate mother with such a disastrous child she couldn't control, though all the time she knew she was the one who was instrumental in winding up his emotions like a yo-yo to the level where the string was taut, and with her finger through the loop, she could control every move of the game. Throwing him out and drawing him firmly back in again. However, *I* was determned that in *my* home, *I* controlled the game, and promptly invited her to leave, so that the child could go to bed, and as the police officer in his car had now left, she would have to find her own way home. Andre stood there, in my lounge, the saddest little boy I had ever seen. I had always loved him, but tonight, my whole heart went out to him, he was *so* damaged and I felt so helpless, that I had not succeeded in stopping it. I took from him the crumpled plastic carrier bag he was tightly clutching in his little hand. As I opened it and saw the contents, it broke my heart completely. Nestling amongst the polythene creases of the bag, were his old teddy, and his 'Little-Boy-Blue' wedding outfit, complete with tights! It was the only decent outfit he owned. The police had assured us that they would come back the next day to take him home. I convinced them there was no need, I would sort things out. The time had come for drastic action.

What had happened to our empty nest? It wasn't long since Angeline had left and set up her own home, and here we were again, with a new house guest. With Gordon working shifts we were able temporarily to care for Andre between us. At the surgery where I worked we had a resident social work, Ken, who gave me some excellent advice. He told me I needed to offer Andre a home with us, but also needed a childminder, as there was no way I could afford financially to give up my job. Andre's social worker promptly arrived the next day and filled in a mountain of paperwork, asked *me* to find a childminder in the area, and so Andre stayed. We found someone who was willing to pick him up from school until I finished work and pretty soon, we had a good system going. We were informed we were now Andre's 'De-Facto' foster carers, which basically meant we were not at all 'proper' foster carers, but designated just for Andre. We would be paid a pittance and the social worker would pay us a visit weekly and hand over the cash to me personally. It would just about cover school meals, and something towards the childminder fees. Food became a big issue for Andre, he would stuff everything in sight into his mouth, there was no filling him. I began to wonder if perhaps he had some sort of eating disorder, but eventually with observation I realised it was purely and simply that he was used to not knowing when and where the next meal would be coming from therefore it was a case of, eat as much as you can whilst it's there, but with consistent routine and mealtimes, he began to understand that food was regularly available, and his eating patterns settled down. We managed to organise his enrolment in a local school and for the first time ever, Andre was now attending every day. He was no longer smelly with torn clothes, but was smartly and cleanly dressed each day. Other than that, clothes, shoes, football boots and toys were down to us. We were back to square one again, but despite that, we enjoyed watching Andre thrive and grow. I loved seeing that broad smile stretch across his little face again, which made him look just like his grandfather Vince. He played football with the kids on the street, wore decent trainers and loved being clean. We had no trouble getting him up in the morning for school, as he wanted and needed to be independent. He would, without request, wash, dress, brush his teeth, and then come down and put a slice of toast in the toaster or make himself a bowl of cereal with pride, and off to school. He hardly had a minute away from school, we took him on holiday, a totally new experience, and he flourished. His bedroom was his pride and joy, curtains, carpet and duvet cover, bedecked with footballers on a pitch of the most insidious green but he loved it, and then there was the long mirror in which he could gaze at his reflection like a peacock. His greatest wish had been to own a suit, and so we bought him a neat little grey one, with a pale blue shirt and a red tie, the sort which is on elastic that he could just pop over his head, and shiny black lace-up shoes. The day we brought home his suit, we unwrapped everything with great excitement and I helped him put it all on. He gazed into the mirror and was obviously pleased with his reflection. He quickly attempted to lace up his shoes, with some help, and off we went to the meeting that night. He loved going to the Jehovah's Witness meeting with us and he was learning how to make choices, as to what to believe and what not. As we sat listening to the speaker, Andre constantly fiddled with his collar and tie, uncomfortable, I thought, he's not used to being dressed so formerly and I would discreetly and silently guide his hand away from his agitated neck. When the meeting was over we drove back home and as we entered the house, he asked "Can I take the cardboard out of the collar now Aunty Sandy?" Poor lamb!! He had sat for two hours with his little neck embraced and encircled with cardboard and never said a word! This was when I realised I knew very little about boys, being brought up in a predominantly girly family. How we laugh at this incident when we look back now.

Leah and Adam were still with their respective foster carers, although Leah's placement did also eventually break down, and she was then moved in with Adam and his carers and settled much better. Once again life had dramatically changed. Andre was to eventually stay with us for over two years, but it was not to be a peaceful respite for him. His mother would still taunt him with her machinations, and there would be many incidents of attempted emotional abuse, even from a distance. The first such occasion was to be her marriage to Damien, I had made it very clear that I wished to have absolutely no involvement at all, and even more so that Andre should be left out of it. However, Dana had other ideas, and during her weekly contact visit, she invited Andre to the wedding and in fact *insisted* that he be there. I later sat him down and asked him how he felt and what he would like to do. To begin with he was angry and flew into a rage, confused as to why his mum had chosen this man at the cost of his own happiness, he was adamant he would *not* go! I assured him he had nothing to worry about, he didn't have to go at all and that I would sort it out. However, we had all underestimated this little boy, who had missed so much of his education, for he had a inherent wisdom which was beyond secular reasoning and far beyond his years, and the very next morning, he dressed for school, and as he munched away on his cornflakes he announced that he had made the decision to attend his mother and Damien's wedding. I was astounded, and also slightly panic-stricken. This would surely be a disaster for this child, but as I beckoned for him to come and sit beside me, I asked him if he could help me understand what it meant to him and why it was so important that he should attend? His answer? "When people get married, there's a bit where you can stand up and say NO! And that's what I want to do." This was a very determined little lad, one who was obviously growing in confidence and independence. We chatted about the in's and out's of his decision, and mutually agreed it was not worth the upset it would cause him.

Dana's determination to emotionally destroy her children was relentless. The social worker would occasionally request contact take place at home when a neutral venue couldn't be found. I didn't mind this and it was far less stressful for Andre. Leah and Dana would be collected and brought here; I would make lunch for us all so that this 'happy' little family could dine together. I soon began to see that this was actually preferable, as having an eye and an ear for Dana's modus operandi, which no-one else had, meant that I could be blunt and open and put a stop to it immediately it began. As we ate, and Dana 'played' with the children on the floor, I could see her periodically whispering in their ears, obviously she was infiltrating their little minds with her poison, and the social worker was completely oblivious to her game, she didn't know Dana's every fibre and sinew as I did. This made me smile slightly; it had its advantages being on both sides of the fence, so to speak. I knew the workings of this family inside out, it was part of my own, and yet here I was, the foster carer, treated as though I knew nothing. As far as social services were concerned I had no training or 'experience' as a foster carer and in fact Gordon and I were turned down many years before, when Angeline was young. We had made the decision at the time to look into fostering and had attended an induction meeting with the Local Authority. Ironically, when we arrived, there also were our dear friends Laurence and Helen, they had had the same idea, unbeknown to us but we were refused because we were Jehovah's Witnesses. How ironic, how remiss of them.

However, Dana continued her attempts to undermine Andre's placement, with the determination of bulldozer, but I was equally determined she would no longer harm this little boy. Few people can understand unless they have lived through it, what effect this two-edged sword situation has on one's perspective of life. No longer does anything matter to you, other than protecting the child's feelings. Andre had been through so much, and at that time I would even have broken the law to protect him from returning to his mother's onslaughts. The children were initially 'accommodated', which means the parents have some control, and on one particular evening, I received a frantic call from Andre's social worker, hurriedly warning me that Dana was on her way to collect up all the children from their respective homes and was taking them back! Now, I thought, being on both sides of the fence could be useful yet again. I could behave as a proper dutiful foster carer, but then I didn't have any formal training did I? OR I could be the caring relative. I decided I had more experience as the caring relative, and therefore chose the latter. Andre had great trust in me, and I would not let him down. I informed the social worker that Dana would take him 'over my dead body.' I would go to court and prove her a negligent parent if necessary but she would not take him without a fight. The social worker was very concerned at my decision but I stood my ground, and ended the conversation by telling her this was just another ploy of Dana's to cause ripples, and that she knew my methods and would not come! She proved me right yet again, she didn't show up.

Nevertheless, some of her whisperings had already taken effect, and I noticed each time I mentioned his dad Andre would frown and walk away. I began to feel that he had been aptly cast in the role of Little-Boy-Blue for Angeline's wedding, for he frequently had the 'blues' when it came to discussing his dad. However, poor Pete was still on the fringes, and kept ringing enquiring after his son, who would have nothing to do with him, and no attempt was being made at *any* sort of contact. Pete was now settled with his new partner Mona, and yet he had continued to show interest in his children, whom he could not see. I sat Andre down one day when he was in a particularly relaxed mood. We had bought him a mini Pool table and a few other items. As you may be aware, as Jehovah's Witnesses we didn't have birthdays or Christmas, so I introduced 'Present Days' whereby for good behaviour, there would be a day, for no other reason, where there would be a few presents to unwrap and enjoy. This particular day, along with the Pool table Andre had a new football, football boots and pyjamas with footballers on them plus various other 'boy' things. As he unwrapped the gifts, and excitedly tore off the paper of the last one, he sat beside me exhausted but happy. I put my arm across his shoulders, and gently told him his dad had asked about him. My intention was not to spoil the moment, but without training, I was trying to associate dad with a happy time. It worked, out poured his little heart. He told me how he didn't need this man Pete, because he wasn't his real dad, he didn't know who his real daddy was, and therefore wanted nothing to do with him. Dana! She had done her worst yet again, the whisperings had proved to be a great forum for her to weave her web of deceit and lies and the children, Andre in particular were the hapless pawns in her most recent game.

I was incensed; this was the biggest lie ever! Andre was a walking, talking miniature of Pete. Every little mannerism, every smile, the glint in his eye, were identical to Pete's. Short of a D.N.A. test, what more did anyone need. We sat together. We covered eyes, we covered mouths, we covered noses, and compared them. Andre trusted me, and pretty soon he was smiling at the prospect of this *really* being his dad. He agreed to let Pete visit him, first for an hour, and then a day until without the unavailable help of a social worker, this little boy once more had a daddy who loved him. Eventually it was agreed that there could be overnight stays and alternate weekends. Pete's partner Mona had no children and she welcomed Andre then Leah into their home. No-one was completely sure of Adam's parentage, and so he continued in care, he was young, and Dana had not yet had much opportunity to play the mind games with him, there was little point, he was too young to be hurt and manipulated by her actions.

Life was becoming another roller coaster of ups and downs, and the day dawned, as we knew it would, that Gwyneth passed away, another loss and I didn't even attend the funeral, as it was a situation I wouldn't put Andre in by taking him, he had had enough. There always seemed to be impossible choices to be made. I'm not even sure whether Carla attended the funeral, neither do I care, at least I wouldn't have to see her ever again. I could consider her out of my life like one of the deceased, except that we keep the dearly departed alive in our memories, but Carla was not dear to me in any way, I just wanted to forget she ever existed. Would I be allowed I wonder?

Dana continued to grow in her new pregnancy with her new man, and Dora was sad that her grandchildren were dispersed, and for this, I really felt for her, therefore I made sure I took Andre to visit as much as possible, and contact visits were set up for her to see Leah and Adam. Looking back, the social worker had an easy time, I was unwittingly doing her job for her, but I didn't care, so long as the children and

Dora were happy. However for some reason which I cannot remember, Dora decided to move in with Dana! This was a recipe for disaster. Dana had no children to taunt; surely she would now turn her attentions to her mother. Sure enough, as soon as Dora had given up her home, and moved all her possessions into Dana's house, she was mercilessly thrown out! Dora was confused, and at times could be quite annoying, none of which she could help, but she had done nothing instrumental to deserve such treatment or loss. Thankfully, Andre and Leah had by now moved in permanently with Pete and Mona and continued to become more and more acquainted as a family. They were temporarily away from Dana's clutches.

Now I know in times of trouble (which were many) you would expect me to turn to the Bible, as it does give many words of wisdom and comfort, but I couldn't help my mind from reciting Rudyard Kipling as though somehow I would be given half a crown if I got it right, as I did as a child.

'If you can keep your head, when all about you
Are losing theirs and blaming it on you,

If you can trust yourself when all men doubt you but
Make allowance for their doubting too

Yes, I had been doubted about Carla, now I was being doubted about Dana, because once again she was an 'Angel!' and although social services knew she needed help, she could turn on the tears like a dripping tap. However, as Kipling said, I trusted myself because I *knew* the truth, and for a change, to quote the Bible, the 'truth' will set you free!' So I had faith that one day all would come out, and these 'Angels' would reap what they had sown.

Speaking of the Bible, another little aspect of our faith was to teach the scriptures to others. I knew the scriptures back to front, and any question that was asked, I could flick through the thirty three books therein and find the corresponding passage, and if I couldn't I would go away and research until I could. Now there was a particular young woman who attended our meetings, who was also a patient at my workplace. This person had had many problems in her life, the effects of which manifested themselves in various ways. She would come into the surgery for whatever reason and most of the staff found her very odd. It has to be said that throughout my life I have become a magnet for people who are 'odd' or different and this young woman was no exception.

For reasons of confidentiality, I will refer to her as X. It wasn't long before, each time X came in for a prescription or appointment, she would always ask for me! She would then stand at the other side of the desk and hand me a piece of paper bearing her request, which I would deal with and hand it back to her, with a cheery smile. In time she found the courage to actually speak and, then to even smile. She was a very well-built person with a physical strength, which I later discovered, belied her lack of confidence. As our acquaintance grew, she invited me to her home for lunch as a thank you, and I accepted. Her home was sparsely furnished and decorated, but nonetheless, neat and clean. Over time I bought her, and gave her, various little items for her home. As we chatted, she would unfold her life story, how her mother had tied her to the clothes post, and left her there in the rain, how she had been raped by a gang of youths, and her son, who was in care, was the result. She had later cared for her mother when dying of cancer, but now, she often sees her mother sitting in the corner! Why me?

However, she was studying the Bible with one of the Elders in the congregation, but decided she wanted me to take over the studies. I tried to explain to her that I had so little time, with work, Andre, meetings, visiting my parents and mother –in-law, with Dana and Dora on my back also, but even so, we managed to fit in an hour, once a week after I finished work, which continued quite well.

One lunchtime as I flounced into the surgery, with a big sigh of relief after a morning of the usual 'phone calls with the usual mundane crises; I was met by a mountain of boxes and bags of objects, stuffed under the desk. X had been in and dumped everything I had ever given, or bought for her. I was seething, and had to seethe through 'till six o'clock, my anger building with every hour that passed. I was the typical 'dragon' you meet in all doctor's surgeries, that day. The poor patients got 'short change' and so did the doctors. I knew X was unpredictable, I had heard one of the doctors one day, discussing how she had thrown a hammer through the window in temper. However, six then seven o'clock came round, the surgery had run late, and Angeline had borrowed my car, but as the last patient left, and I barred and bolted the doors, Angeline was waiting with my car to take me home. I calmly asked her, just to pop round to X's house, which was in fact the top floor of a block of maisonettes. As we pulled up outside, Angeline said she would wait in the car. I climbed the steps like a young teenager, fury and anticipation seemed to have put my asthma on hold and supplied me with newfound energy. As I approached the door, the place was in darkness. I knocked and knocked until my knuckles ached. I shouted through the letter-box and told her all her neighbours were listening and I was not going away until she spoke to me. The prospect of the neighbours knowing her business with me was enough to prompt X to open the door, just enough for her large, shovel-like hand, to extend towards me. Before I knew it, my tiny feet left the ground as I was lifted by this one hand, grasping my ugly surgery uniform blouse, the buttons pinging off as I was unceremoniously hauled through the gap in the half open door, just big enough for my frame to fit. As I look back, it must have been reminiscent of a scene from a cartoon, with me two feet in the air, choked by my garments, legs swinging, as I pointed and wagged my extended finger, giving her the biggest telling off she had possibly ever had in her life, my voice rasping as I was throttled. As she let go, and my three inch heels clicked to the floor, I saw this large ferocious woman, dissolve into tears, and a very soft 'sorry' was spoke. When the 'Squib' side of my personality came to the fore, although extremely rare, nothing mattered, other than the task in hand. I didn't care if the Queen were in attendance, she would have no choice but to pay attention to what had to come out, there were no inhibitions, things had to be said. However, X had apologised for her unnecessary childish behaviour, and gave me a hug, which almost crushed my ribs and bent my spine, before rushing up the stairs. Very shortly, I heard a rhythmic knocking on the ceiling and called up to X from the bottom of the stairs, but had no reply. Against my better judgment, I ventured up the stairs to find her face down on the bare floor, having what appeared to be an epileptic fit. Silly girl! Did she not realise that working in a surgery, I would know what a genuine epileptic fit looked like? And this was definitely *not* genuine. I called an ambulance and had her hauled off to hospital.

As I clambered my way back down the steps with shaky legs, Angeline was still waiting in the car. She knew me well, and knew I wouldn't want interference, but informed me as we drove away that the whole neighbourhood had heard me, plus from inside the car, she had also heard every word!

It seemed that every time I had people's troubles inflicted upon me, the more I tried to help, the more I was left defeated by them. Perhaps it was time I left everyone alone, it appeared that those who were more self-centred seemed to be happy and had no problems, or were they? Either way, try as I may in the future, I couldn't change so easily.

As time passed, with a little patience we had managed to rekindle the relationship between Andre and his dad. Before long both he and Pete were eager for Andre to move in, and be a real family together. We were overjoyed that this reunion was taking place, despite a two year struggle it had all been worth it. Of course to me it was yet another loss, although Pete, Mona and the children would not live far away, and I hoped I could still see them all. Andre was very dear to my heart and I would always have an extra special place for him there. The saddest news came a few weeks later, when it was decided by the courts, that Adam should be adopted. How could this be happening within our family? This, to me was a very great irony. I had two cousins one on my mother's side and one on my father's side, both of whom had found it necessary to adopt, as they had suffered traumas giving birth. Now here we were,. Having members of our family adopted out. It made no sense. As the summer of that year came and went, Andre and Leah settled well into family life, despite Dana's continued best efforts to sabotage their happiness, they attempted to overcome her onslaughts. As the winter drew ever closer, the days once more grew shorter, and therefore left us with less time to squeeze everything in. Mum often wasn't well and needed lots of medication. Life was very different in the country. In the surgery where I worked, it was often difficult if one needed a home visit. In the country however, the resident G.P. would do regular rounds, especially on the elderly, and would call in on mum, with her little dog, 'porridge' at her heels, and he enjoyed the visits, and the fuss he received equally. I had good communication with mum's G.P. and was occasionally there when she visited. I asked her on one such visit if she could have a look at dad, as he was looking after mum during the week, and tending to her every need, but I was wondering if this was becoming too much for him as I'd noticed lately he was looking a little frail. Our concerns were expressed and we jointly persuaded dad he should have a check-up. The doctor checked his pulse, took his blood pressure, and booked him in at the hospital in Bakewell. On the day of his appointment, I had a feeling of foreboding as we sat there in silence in the waiting room of the X-Ray department. So much attention had been given for so long to Mum, Gwyneth, Dora, Dana, Andre and Leah etc., that my dad, as always, had taken a back seat, just carrying on in his own quiet way. He was certainly not an attention seeker, and sorted things out in a calm solitary manner. No-one had noticed he didn't appear well, and he had said nothing. Within a short time, the X-Rays were done and we were on our way home, with instructions to ring in a couple of weeks for the results.

It was almost Christmas, and the local old-people's home needed someone to transport staff to and fro' over the holiday period. Gordon was almost always working at Christmas, hospitals don't stop for holidays and it didn't mean much to us anyway, so I volunteered. It was great on Christmas morning as the roads were empty. I mean *empty*! Like a scene from Day of the Triffids, I could go from A to B in no time at all. I even once went through a red light, after carefully checking to ensure there were *no* vehicles, not to mention any police cars to be seen, just for the devil of it. It was an excitingly wicked moment! When all the staff had been ferried to work or home, I would then drive out to Derbyshire and cook Christmas dinner for my parents. Angeline would often come along and help too. We'd spend the afternoon there and then return so that I could shunt the evening staff around once more.

However, in the days between Christmas and New Year I decided we should find out the results of dad's tests. I rang the surgery in Eyam, and was told my lovely dad had cancer!!

I was devastated. Beside myself, what did I do, Gordon was at work, and I had more 'pick-ups' for the Home to do. I drove around in a blurry silence and did my duty automatically. I didn't know what else to do. Should I tell dad, would they tell him? Should I tell mum? I had a lot of thinking to do, many decisions to make. The first decision I made was not to tell dad, unless he asked. The second was not to tell mum at all, yet, she was a compulsive worrier and it would do her more harm than good, but I did decide to tell Dora, as I felt she had a right to know, at least as much as I did, and of course, Angeline. She was equally devastated. She loved both her grandparents dearly and had a wonderful relationship with them. Angeline was soon to feel her first sense of *real* loss, the only thing we didn't know, was how soon. I had decided not to ask, and just to take each day as it came.

These were very gloomy days indeed, we continued to function as normally as we could and all the time, keeping this terrible secret. Dora seemed to take it in her stride, although, looking back perhaps she just didn't know where to put her feelings. Mum continued much the same and dad continued his care for her, and on reflection, perhaps for him, it kept things near normal. He still hadn't asked about his condition.

As always, I tried to think positively about everything, it was the only way I could get through it, and this was no exception, though what positive note I could put on this was beyond me, until I remembered my dreams of dad dying, drenched in blood, and I thought to myself, at least I knew he wasn't going to be shot or stabbed, we would have to keep and eye on him, but I dreaded the day he would have to go into hospital, he hated hospitals.

Gordon was my rock, he supported me, and mum, and Angeline and did anything and everything he could. I was also, so very grateful that he had practically forced me to learn to drive, because now I really needed to move around freely and quickly.

Spring was approaching, and with it, our wedding anniversary. This should have been a special one, it was a twenty fifth, our silver wedding, but the excitement and enthusiasm were non-existent, and yet as it grew nearer, I had mixed feelings. On the one hand it was an occasion which would only happen once in a life-time and should be marked in some way, but on the other hand, the way I felt, it didn't seem appropriate.

When the first of April arrived, Angeline encouraged us to have an evening out with our friends Laurence and Helen. We contacted them and they seemed more than eager to join us, in fact they agreed to pick us up and take us to a nearby pub for a meal. As we drove to the venue, Helen explained there was a 'sixties' night there, that would cheer us up a bit, I thought. We eventually arrived, and as we followed Helen and Laurence into the bar and up the stairs to the function room, it seemed eerily silent. I questioned our dear friends as to whether they had the right place, but they ignored my pleas and led us to the large double doors at the top of the stairs. As the doors were gently pushed open, the room beyond was bathed in blackness, and still silent, my heart sank, but as I was about to protest once more, the light flickered on and the room became visible as our eyes adjusted, we were both stunned! All our lovely friends and work colleagues were there, Dan was smiling and holding a video camera which he had trained on Gordon and me. Everyone cheered and applauded as we entered the room. My friends from work were there and even my cousin Jayne and her husband and about half an hour later someone brought my mum, how wonderful. Dad wasn't feeling well and stayed at home.

Angeline had gone to so much trouble to organise all this. It was a wonderful surprise, and for once, someone had done something for *us*! For the rest of that evening, all sorrows were forgotten and we had such an unforgettable time. Our daughter had put a lot of thought into all of this. All our friends together in once place, what a task that must have been, a lovely buffet and a cake to *die* for. It was peachy coloured, sat atop a wonderful fountain of cascading water, and lit from below to reveal flower petals floating in a circle. It was an evening we will never forget, and Angeline had especially taken care that Dora and Dana were not invited. Sad, I know, but she wanted this to be *our* evening, with no traumas.

This memorable occasion, and the 'photos and video later produced by Dan, were to lighten the load for a while. My colleagues at work also made an effort, as they knew what life had been like for a long time and this was one advantage of working in a confidential environment. We could use each other as sounding boards and let off steam about very private matters. However, I thank Angeline from the bottom of my heart.

Now, I wasn't fooled by the lull in the game of life. Dana was now very advanced in her pregnancy, the start of her new 'brood' and I just knew that things would soon be hotting up again. I wasn't far wrong, I had gone away to London for the weekend involving work, and when I returned, the first thing I did, as always, was to call mum. I heard her concerned voice, telling me how Dana's new husband, Damien, had arrived banging at the door, demanding to know where I was. He had travelled all the way to Derbyshire *just* to find me. Mum was petrified, dad was mystified, and both begged me to be careful. Now Gordon was at work and I couldn't wait for his return to sort this out. I was eager to know what was so important for me to be found. I made some enquiries and discovered that Damien was at Dora's house, along with Dana, and promptly made my way over there. As I ascended 'Machu Pechu' my anger was rising. I burst through the door, unannounced to find Damien standing there in the kitchen. Once more, I rose to my full 4'11" and looked a further twelve inches or so upward, my index finger almost touching his nostrils. He backed away from me, and This huge man was now against the wall, looking down on me. He had frightened and intimidated my parents; he would not do the same to me. As his story unfolded, urgently, for he was clearly not used to a woman scorned, it emerged that Dana was up to her games again, she had now even turned her venomous attentions to her violent husband, who else was there? She had told him that I had arranged an abortion for her, and I was to take her to do this. She was even using her unborn child as a silent undeveloped pawn. Understandably Damien was upset, this was to be his first child. This however, revealed to me that this man may have been violent, and controlling, but he was also not very intelligent. Dana was eight months pregnant plus, therefore a termination at this stage was a highly unlikely option. Also he didn't know me well enough to realise that I would never agree to such a thing. There was no end to the gratification this woman gained from seeing people's lives destroyed. I felt anguish and pity already for this unborn child, the beginning of this new brood, for I knew there would be more to come, more lives to be destroyed.

Chapter Sixteen

Monumental Changes

Once more, life continued, not as normal, I can't honestly say life has ever been normal. In fact as I read what I have already written in these pages, it is a more dramatic story than most fictional soap-operas I have seen, although every word is fact. We so far have, murder, rape, death and grief, alcoholism, adultery, domestic violence and most of all, 'lies' for this is the root of all misery.

However, Dana gave birth to a beautiful blue-eyed, blonde haired baby girl. They named her Anna, she was so cute, the kind of baby that drew extra attention and to begin with appeared to thrive. She gained weight appropriately and all seemed surprisingly well. Some things worried me slightly though. I knew nothing of attachment back then, but couldn't help noticing that rather than pick up Anna at feed times and cuddle her, Dana would sit her in her bouncy chair and stick the bottle in Anna's hungry little mouth from the end of an extended arm. Surely this couldn't help with bonding, although Dana had never bonded with any of her children, and as we recall when the first three children were removed, she said she would have three more, Anna was the beginning of yet the next three – to Damien.

Now, Angeline and Dan were enjoying building up their new home, and working hard into the process. Dan worked for the University, and Angeline was responsible for dealing with confidential documents being put onto microfiche. They had no plans for a family as yet, but Angeline would sometimes visit Dana and Dora with me to see the new baby, but she would also feel that the child was largely laid on the sofa and ignored. She began to take Anna home at weekends much to Dana's pleasure. Angeline and Dan would enjoy surrogate parenthood each weekend, taking Anna out, buying her toys etc., much as Gordon and I had done with Andre, *and* Dana before him, therefore I couldn't fault them for caring how this child fared. They were young and could have been out living their lives, but they seemed happy, and gained enjoyment from this child. I on the other hand was trying to keep my distance, both emotionally and physically, I had had enough and it felt desperately like history repeating itself. However, try as I may, as Angeline brought this little girl more and more, I couldn't help falling in love with her and soon became equally involved.

Gordon and I tried to settle down to a life of our own. We still had all our friends at the Kingdom Hall and would invite different ones around for a meal and drinks etc. Our friend Val whom you may remember, came to

Scotland with us after the death of her husband, was no exception. She had been very restless since her loss and didn't quite know what to do with her life. However, she one day announced to me that she was leaving for Ireland. I was happy for her, and said I thought the holiday would be good for her. However, that was not what Val had in mind, oh no, I should have known, everyone leaves in some way or another, she was going for good! She had a friend who lived there and was going to stay with her until she could find a place of her own. She had previously sold the house she owned with her husband, and rented a small terraced house, therefore freeing up some capitol so now she was going to make good use of it. She promptly thrust an envelope into my hand and said "I'm leaving tomorrow." The envelope contained a cheque for £1,000.00 and instructions on how to pay the rent, pay the utility bills, give notice on the house, and arrange for all her possessions to be shipped out to Ireland. I couldn't believe it! Once more there would be loss, and we were left holding the 'baby' only this time in a different way. It took weeks to sort stuff out and many 'phone calls, was this the end of yet another era?

But, as I said we had many friends and Jessie, Vic and Reg were also members of the congregation and lived in the next street to us. They were brothers and sister, and none of them had ever married. They had lived together, and cared for each other, all their lives. Each of them was very private if not a little eccentric. Their existence reminded me a little, in an affectionate way, of the Wombles, in as much as they would make other uses of items they already owned or collected rather than buy new ones. Very frugal. For example, when Jessie wanted a rocking chair, Vic took an existing old chair and created 'rockers' for the bottom out of wooden coat hangers. The bolt on the door was a huge metal bar placed across the middle with a very simple but effective mechanism. Cooking was done on a single gas ring, connected by a rubber hose to the gas tap by the kitchen sink! Money was not spent lightly in this house; in fact it was rarely spent at all. Jessie was an extremely kind and gentle soul, and frugal by nature, with a truly Christian attitude towards people, she was also therefore, very submissive and calmly went along with everything her two brothers decided. Reg went out to work every day, while Vic and Jessie would spend most of theirs engaged in the preaching work from door to door. We all knew they lived a little differently from the rest of us, and some of the witnesses would visit and help out with shopping etc. However, Reg suddenly died, leaving Vic and Jessie on their own. The two of them plodded on in their own sweet way for some time, both were getting older and Jessie was becoming frailer. Their main source of income had been from Reg's job, and Vic would do odd jobs for people now and then.

Surprisingly Vic was the next to pass away, once more very suddenly, meaning that Jessie was now left alone. Poor Jessie, she didn't know how to cope on her own. She had never had to take responsibility for anything in her entire life. For her, it must have felt like being adrift in a boat in open sea, buffeted in different directions by the wind of change. We tried to help where we could, and found ourselves once more cooking a little extra and taking it round to Jessie to ensure she ate properly. Then we decided that perhaps she would benefit from visiting us for a meal, and so Gordon would bring her round for the evening and she would sit and marvel at the wonderful colours on our television screen, and would become mesmerised by the landscapes and animals she saw on the nature programmes which she loved. She couldn't take her eyes from the screen.

Now Jessie was understandably concerned about where her living would come from, but we assured her there would be benefits and pensions etc., and one of the Witnesses who knew about such things would look into it for her. Nevertheless, it was the small, unthinkable things in life which were to be the biggest problems, such as for instance, changing a light bulb, and sure enough, one night Jessie rang in a panic, as the bedroom light had gone with a bang and she was plunged into darkness. It was here that our eyes would be truly opened. Jessie had to explain where the new light bulbs were kept. So, Gordon, following instructions, ventured up the stairs and found Vic's bedroom. As he entered the room, he looked around for the wardrobe in which he would apparently find them and spotted a home-made, painted cupboard, and neatly placed on newspaper across the floor, were the various parts of a complete motorbike.

He made his way around these objects, to the cupboard and opened the door. On the shelf at the top were several neatly stacked light bulbs in their cardboard packets. He reached in and selected one. However, when the packet was opened, instead of the much sought after light bulb, there were several hundred pounds rolled up inside, and secured with a rubber band, and upon inspection there were further packets containing the same. When he found an actual, suitable bulb, he ventured then into Jessie's room to replace the old one. Here was another strange sight to behold! The bed was neatly made and the room tidy. The bedding however consisted of grey army blankets which over the years had been in a war with an army of moths, but each hole had been carefully and lovingly crocheted around the edges to prevent them from fraying further. Jessie's slippers were made from pieces of blanket folded over and stitched along the top. The most horrifying sight was the electric blanket and electric fire, wired up to the metal bed frame, which was used to 'earth' the said appliance!! Poor Jessie could have been fried alive!

Gordon soon began to realise that there had possibly been something subversive happening in this household, and he was good at putting himself into the minds of others, and so he began a quest for fortune hunting around the place. He began at the top of the cellar and uncovered a large metal chest. The locking mechanism was obviously Vic and Reg's own device, but Gordon soon figured it out and upon opening, discovered approximately £3,000 in various denominations of notes and coins. Next was a hole in the sitting room floor covered with a piece of wood. This however yielded nothing but was explained by Jessie, as the hiding place for money during the war. Eventually, Gordon moved on to the garden shed which was more of an extension to the house, and located a drawer in the bench, which appeared not to open to its fullest extent. After encouraging it to be removed, several more thousand pounds were discovered, strangely also a bank book for the man who did not believe in banks. Jessie was overjoyed at her newfound wealth, and at the same time astonished at these revelations. One revelation Gordon did not make however, was the diary and 'photos of holidays, plus his feelings for a young girl in the congregation. Whilst he had holidayed abroad, Jessie had been wired up to the bedpost, and rocked away her evenings on wooden coat hangers, to save money. It was a truly humbling experience

As you may imagine, life was constantly pretty grim, knowing my dad was dying, wondering each day, how he was going to be. He had an appointment to return to the hospital to make decisions regarding his health but he refused, saying "There are people worse off than me who need it more." My visits now increased, although I don't know how it was fitted in, but somehow it was. I tried to do everything as normal, yet dreaded the day dad would ask me about his health, and I practised over and over, what I might say, but tried to avoid such conversation wherever possible. What a coward I am!

Dad never asked me, but I'm sure he knew, he was not a stupid man, but a very private one and he wouldn't have wanted anyone else to have known, especially not my mother. Despite looking a little frail, he plodded on in his own way, still making tea for mum and doing most of the cooking. Mum actually appeared to be less active, and now needed a walking frame, but looking after her was normality for dad, and so I said nothing and they carried on as usual. One thing dad did find difficult though, was shopping. He could no longer trot into the village and trot back with heavy bags, so I took over the chore. They would ring me with a list of items and I would call at the supermarket on my way out to Derbyshire, with everything they needed. I was at first rather concerned that dad was asking for a bottle of whiskey every week plus a few cans of beer. As I have mentioned before, he was never a big drinker, and only once was intoxicated which was when he retired, yet now he appeared to be drinking this each week. Who knows, perhaps it eased the pain, both physically and mentally, we had an unspoken knowledge between us, he and I, and my feelings were, why not, it can't do him any more harm. Yet again I felt like a coward, I should have been telling him it was too much, and yet I never saw him remotely drunk, and true to his normal routine, when it was his bedtime, he would say goodnight and quietly retire to bed.

Now occasionally I would encourage Dora to come with me and help, it wasn't easy, but sometimes it worked and on one of the many weekends, I decided to change the sheets and towels, to bath mum and wash and perm her hair, Dora came with me. After a full day cleaning the bungalow from top to bottom, we all sat down to watch T.V. it was a Saturday evening, and dad had his two daughters together, which was rare, and on these occasions it must have reminded him of when we were children and therefore he wanted to treat us. He would get up and venture into the kitchen and return with sweets or crisps, a little treat for us as we all sat together watching T.V. It was about 10 p.m., his bedtime, and as he gently eased himself out of his favourite armchair, with the usual words "Well, I'm off," I noticed him falling sideways towards the fireplace. Looking back, it was rather like a slow motion scene in an action movie, as I realised he was falling, I lunged forward and grabbed him around his middle, catching him before he struck his head on the mantelpiece. As I stood there, with the full weight of my father hanging over my arms I pleaded with Dora to move the chair, so that I could lower him to the floor, but she just stood there, hands covering her face sobbing, this was too much for her. The only course left to me, was to kick the chair away with my left foot as hard as I could. This left me just enough space to lower him to the carpet before my arms gave way. Was this *it*!? Had my dad gone, just like that? I was so glad I'd had my First Aid training at the surgery, I checked his pulse and also that he was breathing, which thankfully he was. Slowly he came round, although a little dazed, and managed with help, to get to the chair. Mum was understandably shocked and upset, Dora was much the same. The first job in hand was to get dad into his bed. We walked slowly together to the bedroom, as I supported him, and I asked him to stand against the wall whilst I turned down the duvet. As I turned away, he slid along the wall, and into the wardrobe. My rescue attempt near the fireplace had been in vain, he now had a cut on his head and blood was running down his face. I fleetingly reflected on my dreams, perhaps this represented the gallons of blood I had 'seen.'

He would not allow me to call the doctor. I cleaned up his wound and dressed it and got him settled into bed, then quietly left him, to attend to mum, and Dora. Dora went to bed in the spare room, we didn't want to disturb dad, so mum laid on the sofa, and I lay on the floor beside her, neither of us slept that night. I kept making excuses to go to the bathroom, but in actual fact, I was checking to make sure my dad was still breathing.

Now with all of this happening, and knowing my dad was dying, I knew my mother would have problems from certain members of the family descending like vultures. Dad had often said they were to have nothing! That was easier said than done and Gordon and I encouraged dad to make a Will, but he would rarely even discuss it. At the time, Gordon was a Will Councillor and could have helped him professionally, and we wanted to make life easier for mum, but neither of them, understandably, wanted to talk about such things, and so we knew we would just have to deal with the onslaught when the time came, and so we let the subject rest.

August was approaching, and with it came the village Gala. Many ancient traditions still linger throughout Derbyshire, and a major one of them is the art of Well-Dressing. A large wooden frame would be filled with wet clay and a biblical scene marked out. Flower petals, sheep's wool, leaves and twigs etc., or any other natural substance that could be found, would be lovingly, and carefully pressed into the design in the clay to create the scene. The results are always spectacular. The locals would then gather around the said 'Well' for the service, aptly called, the 'Blessing of the Wells' to thank God for the rain, whereupon, more often than not, the heavens would open, and they would then promptly complain about the weather, and the fact that they had got soaked! God *must* have a sense of humour, I thought, he gave us ours after all, we are made in his image are we not? Or perhaps the Devil has one too, because mine is often very wicked.The whole week, which used to be known as 'Wakes' week the true meaning of which I have never been sure, was filled with activities. There would be stalls of home-made jams and cakes run by the Women's Institute, jumble sales, and bric-a-brac by the Boy Scouts and Girl Guides, and Tombola to mention but a few. There would be the traditional sheep roast, where three or four able men of the village would unceremoniously skewer a whole sheep onto a spit in the field, and light the fire under it. It would take practically the whole day to roast, periodically being turned and basted, the smell would fill the air and when it was cooked to perfection it would almost feed the whole village with a slice of sheep on a lovely soft bread cake, with mint sauce. This was not all, as this pungent aroma of burnt sheep permeated everyone's nostrils, the village children would parade the field in their fancy dress costumes, to be judged for authenticity and imagination. The brass bands would play their best tunes, cars, lorries and drays would trail slowly through the main street as everyone stood on the kerb edges, throwing money into their collection tins, which ultimately was shared out amongst the older village residents for hampers at Christmas.

We mustn't forget, of course, all the May Queens, who came from every village and gathered together to be judged on their poise and presentation. Pubescent young ladies, performing their best curtsey, and a delicate wave of the hand as they appeared to float ethereally across the ground in their flowing gowns.

It was a wonderful week, everyone was out there, and now as I attended every year, I would see old school friends and neighbours, I had not seen in a long time.

Dad always loved his sheep sandwich, and I would always go into the village for a stroll with him, buy the sandwich and he would eat it as we strolled down to the pub for a pint with which to wash it down. It was also dad's birthday during Wakes week, 8th august, so it would be a double celebration, but this particular year, he couldn't make it for a walk, he was understandably feeling tired. However, he did surprise us that day as he said he had decided to make a Will! I was so relieved, because I knew everything would be so much easier for mum, and if I'm honest, for me too. It meant I wouldn't have to go through any questions with the rest of the family. So dad and Gordon sat down together, and I took mum out in her wheelchair, whilst they got to grips with it. Dad didn't have a lot, some money in the bank and a few personal items he wanted specific people to have, so Gordon put all his requests down on paper, and the very next day, delivered it to the solicitors to be legally put together.

Visiting the village was light relief for me, but especially so as it may be the last Wakes week I would spend with dad. Following this Gordon and I had decided to arrange a group trip to a safari park for the congregation at the Kingdom Hall. Spirits were low lately and we felt a group activity would inject some life into everyone. We spoke to one of the elders about the information we had gathered and he agreed it was a wonderful idea, and told us he would announce it from the platform at Thursday's meeting. Thursday came, and he made his way to the podium to make various announcements, including this forthcoming event and advised interested people to give me their names etc., afterwards. When the meeting was over, and all proceedings were done, I was astounded as everyone advanced towards me, eagerly wanting to be placed on the list and offering money to pay for their places. Whereupon, the elder who had so willingly read out the details of said trip, pounced on me like a lion out of Daniel's den! He accused me of dealing with money and profiting in a place of worship. Who did he think he was, Jesus in the temple, upturning the tables of vendors? There was *no* profit to be made here, it was for the good of the congregation, and as always, Gordon and I would be out of pocket at the end of the day, but did that matter? On this occasion I bit my lip *because* I was in a place of worship and promptly walked outside, and to my amazement, half the congregation walked out with me and still offered their money, they were so eager for this trip.

This was the final straw for me, the straw that broke the camel's back. These biblical phrases do keep leaping into my head, don't they?

After walking out that night, I vowed and declared, I would never return. I couldn't speak to this man, as I was trying to suppress the 'squib' within, and had she opened her mouth, the explosion of her anger would have consumed us all. However, Gordon decided he would go and talk to the elder concerned at his home to establish exactly what had been the cause of his sudden and dramatic change of heart. Upon arriving, Gordon asked him if he could spare a few moments, to be told in rebuke, that he had not yet had his tea! He also denied prior knowledge of what was written on the piece of paper he had read out that night. Gordon was in disbelief that this elder, this man of God, with prominent position in the congregation, was performing an outright lie. However, Gordon turned and left with the last word. He advised this man that he, Gordon, would be watching him and listening to every word he now spoke from the platform, and woe betide him if he was caught out in yet another lie.

Following this fateful night, I stuck to my word, as always, and never went back, Gordon, however did return for a few of the meetings. I would never wish to influence anyone to do anything which went against their principles simply because they didn't match my own, and in fact encouraged him to continue. The fateful outcome was the knowledge that this religion that we had considered to be different, more logical, was in actual fact no different from all the rest. It, also contained liars, thieves and adulterers, yet I still held on to the teachings of the Bible and maintain that to this day. I no longer feel the need for organised religion, as I

firmly believe God will judge us individually on our own merits, not on our ability to follow the instruction of mere imperfect mortals.
Eventually, when Gordon had made his point, he too decided this was no longer for him. As part of this organisation we felt we had been set apart from the rest of this wicked world, only to discover we were still amongst the evildoers we had been cautioned to stay away from. We felt at this point, we had wasted twenty years of our lives.

It was two days later, after all this fracas, and two days after dad's eighty second birthday, 10th August, that I had decided to take an early bath after work, and was ready for bed when our two good friends Wendy and Frank, came to visit to discuss the issues at the Kingdom Hall, and despite being tired, we were always glad to see them. They were tireless in their pursuits to try to encourage us back to the meetings, although unsuccessful. *I* had made my decision and was standing firm. However, Wendy helped me with the safari trip in as much as she collected the rest of the money to cover the fees, as I was determined to see it through. However, we chatted as the evening wore on and around 10 p.m. the 'phone rang. As I reluctantly lifted the receiver, I knew, at this time of night, it must be Dora or Dana with some tale of woe or needing to relay some argument or other. I was mistaken and surprised however, to hear mum's voice, she was breathing heavily, and very distressed. I asked her to slow down and tell me what was wrong, when she uttered the words – "Your dad's just coughed up a bucket full of blood!" Now, I know my mum could be prone to slight exaggeration at times, but I also knew that if dad *was* coughing up blood, this was *it*! I hurriedly told her we would be there A.S.A.P. I threw on some clothes and we left, Frank and Wendy leaving simultaneously. Gordon drove like the wind that night. We seemed to hit *every* red light, but it took us about twenty minutes to do what was normally a forty minute journey. As we turned the corner, I could see the ambulance just arriving and turning round. All reality had gone from my mind, and I didn't realise that the car hadn't stopped, before I was opening the door to get out. I could see my mum's neighbour standing on the doorstep as I ran across the grass verge. She took me by the shoulders and urged me not to go inside, but her words were meaningless as I pushed my way past.

NOTHING – could have prepared me for what I saw that night. When mum had said 'a bucket full of blood' she was not exaggerating, rather underestimating. My dad was sitting in his favourite chair, and as I walked in, I could only see him from the back, and he looked as though he had just perched himself on the edge of the chair. As I approached, my eyes fell upon the bucket, which mum had managed to place in front of him, and it *was* full to the brim with blood. There was blood dripping from the coffee table in front of dad, it was awash. As I ran to him I took hold of his lifeless upright body, only to see that his face and spectacles were also spattered with blood and his lap was soaked through to the chair beneath him. The carpet had an ever- growing squishy puddle beside him. Strange how the mind works when overwhelmingly distressed, shock I suppose, but as I gazed in disbelief at the sight before me, I remember thinking that a human body can't possibly contain this amount of blood; it was as though he had been drained. My dreams, my nightmare, had been horribly fulfilled! The visions of dad lying there with his life blood ebbing away had now become a reality, except it was a bloodbath as opposed to a 'pool.'

Hereon in, my life would change forever. Ironically as I write this page, it is once again, the 10th of august.

As the paramedics and the doctor arrived, it was blatantly evident that they could do nothing. Gordon prepared the bed, and cleaned up my dead dad as best he could, then helped the paramedics to lay him peacefully on the bed to rest. The doctor talked to my mother compassionately and assured us there would be no need for a post mortem. I was very relieved. I had read many of them in my line of work and it wasn't pleasant. It was plain for all to see, how my dad had died and as rules have it, he had been see by his G.P. recently.

When all had left, the house fell loudly silent, until my little dog Scampi scuttled in and was frantically searching for dad, whom he adored. Gordon set about cleaning the sitting room. He emptied the bucket, like disposing of dad's life once again, but it had to be done, he scrubbed the chair and the carpet, to no avail, they were soaked, and he cleaned and polished the coffee table. We threw a large hearth rug over the stained carpet temporarily, so that most of the stain was obliterated and covered the chair with a blanket. It was new and still bore the labels advising the danger of fire. As mum sat in a daze, she lamented the state of the new furniture and carpet, and contemplated how she would go about removing the stains! Shock had set in, and she was unable to function logically. I assured her we would deal with it tomorrow, and packed her an overnight bag in order to take her home with us. She was then concerned that dad would be alone all night, but I said he was peaceful and we would see him in the morning. On the way back to Sheffield, we stopped at Dora's house to break the bad news; she didn't have a telephone and knew nothing of the night's events. As I stood in the dark knocking at the door, without opening it a voice eventually spoke from inside. It was Tina telling me her mother was asleep and seemed reluctant to wake her, despite my frantic and tearful sobs. How strange, her grandfather was dead, and she didn't want to wake her mother. I couldn't fathom it, but was in no mood to try. I then banged louder and screamed at her to open the door. After informing them of our loss, they promptly went back to bed. Perhaps they couldn't take it in.

We took mum home, and as I helped her prepare for bed, for what was left of the night, she asked me to *lift* her into bed, as dad had always done. It was only then that I realised just how much my father had done for her, and just how different life was going to be from now on.

The next day, Gordon and my son-in-law Dan, drove to Derbyshire to see to dad and make some arrangements with the village undertaker, who had known all his life. My memories of sitting and listening to mum pounding away on their piano all those years before, thinking of the coffins stacked up next door, and now I was in need of one of them, yet another of life's ironies. I also asked Dora to come and sit with mum whilst we dealt with various practicalities one evening, but discovered that she had gone to the pub along with Dana, as she couldn't cope!! I'm afraid at this news, and the way I was feeling, angry, bereft, confused, I sat in the car and screamed and sobbed on Gordon's ever accommodating shoulders, until there was no emotion left. This was a time when Dora and I should have been together, to mourn our father and care for our mother. Yet here Gordon and I were, trying to hold down our jobs, look after mum, and make arrangements for her future, and Dora couldn't even be available to sit with her. My emotions at this time were, and are to this day, indescribable. Now, as Gordon already knew of course, the first line in my father's Will was 'There must be no funeral!' He was not a religious man, by any stretch of the imagination, and with all due respect, had always made jokes about undertakers having your money. "They're not bloody well having mine!" was his favourite saying. However, it is a trade, like any other, and a valuable service, at a time when grief prevents logic and despite there being no funeral, at dad's emphatic request, the final bill eventually totalled over £1,000 pounds. Dad would have been horrified!

Now I know I must have had to be a strong person, to have dealt with all that's gone before, but at this time I was a wreck. I was emotionally on my knees. My dad had been my hero and now he was gone. Not only that, but I appeared to have predicted his end in my dreams, which I still cannot explain. I am not a believer in spirits, ghosts or afterlife, so why did I foresee this terrible disaster? However, without Gordon, everything would have fallen apart. He was thirteen years old when his dad died, and must have known how it felt. He did everything. He organised for dad's body to be silently taken to the crematorium just as dad had wished. I understood and shared his sentiment on funerals; I can however understand how it gives closure for others. I, on the other hand didn't feel the need for a fuss, to dispose of his mortal remains. His memory was what was important to me, and would always remain with me. Once more, I didn't fit the 'norm' and relatives and neighbours would, I'm sure, find this quite bizarre, but my dad and I were so very much alike, and besides, it was *his* wishes we were carrying out. Whatever anyone else thought, they must draw their own conclusions. However, a couple of them made their disgust known to me, and of course must have thought it was either my lack of care, or miserliness which had been the deciding factor. To be honest, I didn't really care, I was wallowing in my own grief, but mum appeared to need a 'goodbye' and so Gordon arranged a small memorial service at the chapel for those who felt the need. I could just imagine my dad looking down, and swearing at the prospect, and I didn't want to attend. However, once more matters were taken out of my hands, mum went down with pneumonia and couldn't attend either, so we sat together in her bedroom and made decisions about the future. I think dad must have had a word with someone up there, and wanted the last laugh. The neighbours anyhow, and some people in the village had gathered together money, presumably for a wreath, but as there was no funeral, this was difficult, also my dad had been a keen gardener and loved to see flowers in their natural state, and flowers on his coffin would not have been welcome by him. I therefore decided that if dad had gone somewhere and was looking down, he would love to see something growing. I knew he wouldn't want to *be* a flower in 'God's garden.' Just as I hadn't considered years before, but a lovely weeping willow tree was what I purchased with their collection. Weeping, because of the tears we shed at losing him and a willow because they always bloom in spring, his favourite time of year – (planting.) Gordon planted it at the back of the bungalow near the Spring, so that mum could see it whenever she wanted, and the other elderly neighbours could enjoy it also as they sat there, and remembered dad.

Three weeks later, my little dog Scampi, died of kidney failure, we had loved him for ten years, a double dose of grief.

At this point I hit rock bottom. My G.P. insisted on supplying me with antidepressants which, working with the medical profession and knowing about them, I adamantly refused. She, on the other hand, insisted that if I took them for three months only, it would help me over this difficult period. Having no fight left in me I agreed, and dutifully popped one in my mouth each morning. However, I was amazed at the energy and the courage they gave me, I could have climbed Everest or even Machu Pechu without getting out of breath, (in my mind at least.) This did however, enable me, with Gordon's invaluable hard work, also, manage to sort out the many practical problems which lay ahead.

The first task was to sort out the dreadful reminder of dad's end, that of the blood- soaked chair and carpet. Gordon arranged for the chair to be removed and taken away. I organised a day to take mum, in her wheelchair around furniture stores to select a new sofa and chair, and whilst we were at it, I encouraged her to spend some of the money dad left on a new bedroom suite which I felt was much needed. We then continued on and chose a new carpet to replace the already new one which was a constant reminder, despite the huge stain being covered with rugs. Of course once this was done and we wearily returned home satisfied that we had made headway, I then needed to arrange for the carpet fitters to do their job. Of course they insisted that all furniture be removed from the room and any existing carpets to be removed also. Gordon did everything he could, but his work prevented him from being available at times. However, I decided to enlist Dora's help. I knew she wasn't perhaps able to organise but she could at least give me a hand with packing up mum's plethora of ornaments, and help moving the furniture. It took us all day to empty the room, but by tea time, all that remained was the two-toned blue carpet, bearing the large dark stain, which had soaked through to the underlay and seeped into the floorboards beneath. Dora had expressed a wish to take the good part of the carpet home and make us of it where needed. It took the Stanley knife in my hand, and as I switched the blade in readiness to cut off the stained area, Dora called to me to stop! She decided to take it as it was and cut it when she took it home. She said Dana would help her to lay it. I was slightly disturbed; here was that strange way of thinking again. I personally was eager to have this removed, destroyed and all reminders got rid of as soon as possible. Anyhow, I humoured her, and together we rolled and folded the carpet and placed it in the boot of my car.

Within a few days, the new carpet was laid, the new furniture arrived, everything was replaced and mum felt comfortable once more, minus her husband!
However, I visited Dora a couple of weeks later and was met with a sight which astonished me. Mum's carpet had been laid – in a fashion – with the stain right in the middle! Dad's 'death' lay on the floor for everyone to walk over. What was wrong with them?!

What had become of my wonderful life which began in this beautiful place, where I could see the 'world's end' everywhere I looked. This world I had discovered beyond was far from perfect.

Chapter Seventeen

Death, Life and Trauma

As with any death, life changes for someone, somewhere. Life had very definitely changed for me, my childhood hero had gone, and although as an adult I should stand alone, he had always been a source of guidance to me. Now, I would have to be *really* strong. I knew I couldn't do it without Gordon. He was my rock, my sounding board and still is to this day. My mother was going to need a great deal of care. She suffered from angina, Parkinson's and Thyroid disease and diverticulitis. She would never manage alone unless we could enlist help. The first job in hand was to find a home-help to come in each day to help her to dress and have breakfast. This was soon sorted, and one thing you learn in a small community is that everybody knows everybody else. The home-help was, believe it or not, the undertaker's wife. She was
a nice lady who was very good with mum. Every Thursday was my day off and spent cleaning the bungalow, changing the sheets and bringing them home to wash, at the same time keeping mum company whilst I did so. I would invite some of the elderly neighbours in and make them a cup of tea. Joan May and Vera were always glad of a chat and a cuppa. Working in a hospital, Gordon was often not

around at the weekends due to his shifts, and so Angeline and I would stay over, Saturday to Sunday and do whatever needed doing or take mum out in the car. Angeline, Gordon and I were still working, and Dan was too, plus studying for his degree, so we would frequently take Anna along with us, as by now she looked forward to her weekend rescue. She was very beautiful, and extremely amusing which made mum laugh. It was also very acceptable to Dana as she had by now given birth to another of her second brood, Paula, yet another little girl. Paula was Dana's fifth child, her second to Damien. Dana often spent her days in bed, and as Anna and ultimately Paula began to toddle, they too would get up in the mornings and eat whatever they could find in the cupboards. They soon learned how to turn the key in the front door and wander out onto the road with no clothes on, wearing nothing more than their mother's best stilettos and a cheeky smile. No-one would pay much attention as they clicked their heels up and down the street. At least Angeline and I could still give Anna some relief from this neglect, sadly at that time a second, younger child would have been more than we could have coped with along with everything else.

On one of our weekend visits to mum, we were about to sit down to a meal that Angeline had lovingly prepared. I helped mum into the kitchen with her walking frame and manoeuvred her into her chair in the corner, standing her walking frame beside her, and Angeline served the food. Mum had a reasonably healthy appetite and tucked in readily. After a few seconds, I realised she was not moving and looking at her face, I could see that her lips were turning blue and her eyes were bulging from her reddened face. It was evident that she was choking, but I couldn't get into the corner, and behind the chair quick enough to do an upward thrust. I'm afraid it was the next best thing. I thumped her very hard between the shoulder blades with the heel of my hand, *and* again, until the offending piece of tomato shot out across the kitchen floor. When she regained her composure, she verified how close to passing out she had become, and perhaps worse. Thank goodness we were there; thank goodness I had done my First Aid training, although this increased my concerns of what could have happened if we had *not* been there. She did have several falls, and although there was an alarm cord fitted, it was of little use unless she fell directly beneath it.

Not all was so sad though, we did have our funny moments. Cordless telephones were becoming increasingly popular, and I decided it would be useful for mum. It would remove the pressure of having to make her way into the hall, whenever the 'phone rang. We promptly had one installed and positioned next to the chair where she sat. She would usually ring me every morning, and I would ring her every evening after my return from work. During one conversation with her, I found her voice to be very faint and could barely hear what she was saying. It would appear that she could hardly hear me either. I was upstairs at the time and realised there must be a problem with one or the other of the telephones. I shouted down the receiver instructing her to 'pick up the 'phone in the hall.' "What!" Came the reply. I repeated my request, only for Gordon, who was *downstairs* to obey my instruction – and he promptly picked up the 'phone in *our* hall! I then had to tell him to put it down. What a farce, it turns out; she had the cordless receiver upside down.

Sadly my mother-in-law was now also becoming increasingly more feeble, and Gordon and I frequently found ourselves divided between them. He visiting his mother, and tending to her needs and me visiting mine. He would pop in when he was in transit from one hospital to another, just for a moment to check that she was o.k. I would call in and see how her day had been, and so life continued, but we wouldn't have had it any other way under the circumstances.

However, life still had its ups and downs, sadness and happiness bouncing around like a tennis tournament. I felt still sad at the empty space my dad left in my life and yet I couldn't help feeling there was worse to come. How right I was.

I was learning Dana's ways, was becoming more and more expert in pre-empting her next move. She would often complain 'sadly' that she had no money to buy food or nappies for the children. Men were in and out of her life like yo-yos, and she knew I would not see the children suffer. However, I was onto her little game. As soon as any old softie provided a few quid out of pity, she was off to the Off-licence for fags and booze. It was much more effective, though more effort, to buy the nappies and some cereal and chocolate etc., for the children and actually take them and make sure they went where intended.

Occasionally I would take Dora with me for the weekend to visit mum, although this didn't happen often as Dora's incessant mumblings on and on about trivia, or the latest trauma would wear us all down. Dana of course, was not happy with this little arrangement, as it meant she had no-one to wind up, and on one such occasion, no sooner had we settled down for Saturday night T.V. than Dana rang, screaming down the 'phone that she had no cigarettes and the 'brats' were getting on her nerves. This unsettled Dora, naturally and to be honest, I was concerned about the screaming children. Although I knew Dana was very manipulative, their cries were a priority and I offered to drive Dora home. What a choice, mum or the kids!

As we arrived back in Sheffield and approached the front door, the cries of the children were pitiful and could be clearly heard from outside, and as usual no-one was taking any notice at all. We entered the front door to discover Dana smoking her usual fag and pacing the floor, Tina was totally absorbed in a close relationship with the T.V. screen as usual, and raising the volume expertly with her thumb caressing the remote control button, in order to compete with the noisy infant's protestations. Poor Anna was sitting on the bare wooden floor with a bowl of some obnoxious substance, sobbing quietly as sheer exhaustion appeared to overtake her. Paula was propped up in her pram in the corner out of the way, also crying, and Leo, Tina's son, was in the kitchen, appealing with his little face upturned towards Dana, for something to eat. Each child wearing nothing but a nappy. As usual I had called at the shop on the way there, as I knew it would be the common problem.

I decided the first thing to do was to feed the children to pacify them and then get them cleaned up and comfortable. Dora decided it was more important to shout and scream about the inconvenience of having to return home. Good thing then that she didn't have to dodge the evening traffic as *I* drove all this way. After doing my best to calm the situation down, I enlisted Dora's help yet again, and instructed her to pick up Paula from her pram in the corner. All three were still being ignored by those around them, but Leo and Anna could toddle around and pester with their cries, Paula at this time, was a prisoner of her yet non-functional infant legs and her pram was like a prison cell.

I picked up Anna, as she waddled towards me with outstretched arms. Her nappy appeared to be almost touching the floor between her ankles, and then I took hold of Leo's hand. The first one I set about comforting was Anna, and armed with my newly purchased pack of nappies; I laid her on the wooden floor boards, as there was no room elsewhere, and attempted to remove the sodden, disintegrating mess between her little legs. She lay there, yielding her tired little body to me, as though she knew she would be comforted. However, more pain and trauma was to come for these little people. As I gently ripped the Velcro strips at each side of Anna's nappy, it would go no further! Although the waterproof outer layer had been almost to the floor, filled with stale urine, the inner lining of the nappy was welded to her skin with faeces which had set like a tinted concrete. It was Saturday evening, and *this* nappy had been attached to Anna from the night before, and would not be easily removed. The best course of action I thought would be to soak her in a bath of warm water and gently ease the solid faeces away, as it softened. However, this was not possible as there was no hot water. The next best thing was to boil kettles and sit her in the kitchen sink – YES! – *the sink*!

There was little alternative, and anyway I decided that in their mess, they would hardly notice the solid waste, struggling down the plughole. Anna was soon cleaned up and freshly fragranced, then given something from my shopping bag, followed by the same treatment for Paula. Both were now calm and satisfied. This just left Leo, who, being older knew what was coming, and by now was hiding in the corner, screaming that no-one should go near him. I knelt down on the floor in front of him, and took his hands. I explained to him that we were going to put nice warm water in the bath and sit him in it until he was clean. I promised him it wouldn't hurt, so I had to make absolutely certain that it didn't. He calmed down and eventually put his trust in me. I lifted him into the warm bath, after boiling endless kettles, and sat on the floor beside him splashing him gently with the soothing warm water, talking all the while about his favourite T.V. programmes. After what seemed like an age, the gentle splashing had dislodged the solid hardened mass of faeces from his little bottom, and he hadn't even noticed, there had been no pain, as I had promised. After drying and dressing him he was once more a happy chappy or as happy as he could be under the circumstances. I disposed of the melted faeces and cleaned the bath as best I could. It had never looked so sparkling.

Now, decision time again. We had left mum to deal with this most recent crisis. Now it was time to return to *her* needs. Should Dora stay with the children, and allow Dana to gloat over her achievement at getting her back home, or should she return with me as originally arranged? I took control, and decided that the children were clean and fed, a pack of nappies sat on the sideboard, they would be o.k. at least until tomorrow. Therefore I felt we could deny Dana her satisfaction for one more night and took Dora with me, back to Bradwell. Mum was delighted, as I felt she didn't think we would return, and she would have faced the evening alone, after looking forward to our company.

With Gordon's mum becoming more dependant and my mother becoming frail, we had rather hoped other distractions could take a back seat, but Dana had other ideas. She loved the limelight, being the centre of attention, and oh, how expert she was at this, but it always ended in disaster for someone else, usually the children. Anna and Paula were now more independent little people, and like most others, had their own ways of being more and more demanding. The 'fun factor' of a newborn infant had gone for Dana once more – time for another one. She had told the social worker previously when they took Andre, Leah and Adam away, that she would have three more, and so the third child, to Damien, Dana's sixth was on its way. Poor little mite, it was at this point that I had dearly wished I could have picked up a bit of knowledge from my G.P. colleagues, and sterilised her with a rusty knife and no anaesthetic, but sadly, it would have been an infringement of her human rights and no-one would let me, but what about the children's human rights, didn't they have any? I, however, didn't feel just now, that Dana *was* human. But then Angels aren't, are they?

Well, I was still working, a daily dose of drug addicts, sick and angry patients, demanding this or that doctor, swearing at us. Of course with me it just went in one ear and out the other, but there were days when it became a bit of a bore. Some of my newer colleagues didn't seem as able as me to stand their ground with verbally violent people, and would call me from the office to deal with them, but then I had had lots of practice hadn't I? Perhaps this was why I sailed through my work each day with a cheery smile, when at times my heart was not smiling. What did I really have to smile about? Let's sum up; - Dad, my hero, was dead. My mother and mother-in-law were struggling to cope alone with old-age and their respective ailments, one in Sheffield and one in Derbyshire. Dora was a wreck, Dana was a pain, children were dispersed and angry, and now there was another one on the way to worry about, I felt like I needed to divide like a human cell so there was more of me to go around. Still I tried as always to look on the bright side. At least I was no longer a Jehovah's Witness and didn't have to feel guilty because I couldn't quite squeeze in the meetings five times a week. Angeline and Dan were happy, working, studying and gradually making great improvements on the house they had bought. They were also still having Anna to stay for weekends where they could, and when they couldn't, she would stay with us. We had all wanted to maintain that weekly reprieve for her. Paula was a little scrap, whose eyes were always moist with tears, dirty, smelly and whining. If only we could have done the same for her, but this was too much to bear, at least Anna was chatty and amusing at times, and although this sounds so selfish, it gave us little light relief. I tried to think of ways we could make life easier for poor Paula. We would pass on the clothes we had bought for Anna, when she grew out of them, but it was impossible, for the following week Angeline would pick up Anna, to find *she* was still wearing them despite them being way too small for her. In any case, for reasons we didn't understand at the time, both of them would prefer to cast off everything and parade around naked. Eventually Lucas was born. He was a very sickly baby and it was obvious that something was not right. The doctors didn't expect Lucas to live very long. His little head was oddly shaped, he appeared to be unable to close his mouth, he had breathing difficulties and his arms and legs didn't kick or move in natural way for an infant at all.

I always seemed to be sitting at the computer at work, whenever unhappy calls came through for me, and this was no exception. My colleagues were very supportive and knew I had problems with family, and although I could use them as sounding boards, because the very nature of our work was confidential, I don't believe they really understood what was going on in my head. As I lifted the receiver to my ear with one hand and held the other poised above the keyboard, Dora's dulcet tones echoed through my ear and reverberated once more around my brain. It felt like the metal ball of a pinball machine, pinging from side to side of my already aching head. "We've all got a disease! You've got, I've got it, Dana's Got it, Tina's got it and Sally. Lucas is going to die; we're all going to die!" Following Dora's deluge, I replaced the receiver and somehow continued my day, doing my duty. At 6 p.m. as soon as I had seen the last patient out and locked and bolted the surgery doors, I drove like the wind to Dora's house, to try to unravel yet another tragic mystery. She wasn't in but I knew her so well and knew she would be at Dana's, so there I went. They were all sitting there, Dora with cup of tea in hand, Dana with can of obligatory lager, Damien nowhere to be seen, the kids whining, hungry and dirty.

I sat and patiently tried to encourage them to explain what the issue was. It had been evident to me that Lucas had problems, but how could this affect everyone else, I asked? After a couple of hours, and no meal, I had gathered enough information to take to work the next day. I would use my connections with the medical profession to find out more. Doctor H was the first one I approached as I knew he would give me straight no nonsense answers. I gave him what I knew; Lucas had a genetic disorder known as Myatonic Dystrophy. Doctor H asked me if I really wanted to know the details as it was not pleasant. I told him I had faced potential death before, and worse and needed to know, if, and how it might affect me if I had it. He took me to the library and pulled out a large volume from the shelf. He thumbed through the pages and stopped at a photo' of a man who had Dystrophia Myatonica (the Latin phrase.) Light bulbs started flashing in my head, as though they had been suddenly switched on simultaneously. Although this was a photograph of a man, he had the same facial features as Tina, whose learning difficulties had supposedly been attributed to deprivation of oxygen at birth. The open mouth, the droopy eyelids and the stoop. I was both amazed and relieved at the dame time, what strange emotions. As I continued to read the material I had been given, more 'light bulbs' flashed. The effects of this could range from mild to devastatingly awful. One person may have it and barely know, the next may be wheelchair bound and unable to eat or drink or walk.

How were we going to deal with this? This was something out of my control, and that's what scared me the most, like death. I had become used to problem solving, especially crisis solving, but how could I solve a faulty genetic code? I couldn't! Therefore there was no point in even trying; the task was more one of discovering the effects, and how to live with them. Of course there was the small matter of where this had originated from, mum or dad. Dad was gone, so we were unable to go down that road. Dora, Dana and Tina in their 'wisdom' had decided they were 'not going for any silly tests,' they didn't want to know, I however informed them that *I* was going to find out as much as I could as I wanted to know whether or not I had been affected. This shocked them slightly.

Genetics as you may be aware, is a very complicated subject, but I was on a quest and needed to know. I contacted the Genetics Centre in Sheffield, and they volunteered to send a nurse to 'counsel' me. I didn't feel I needed any counselling but went along with whatever it took to find out what I needed to know. The facts, when revealed were pretty grim, but I took away the information and pondered on it and worked my way through it slowly trying to unravel the situation. The symptoms were a revelation to me. tiredness, muscle stiffness, loss of function of the eyelids, cataracts, speech difficulties due to poor muscle tone of the jaw, hence the open mouth, to mention only a few. It affected anything virtually, made of muscle. I thought of all the internal muscles which could be affected also, the heart, the bowel the stomach, poor reflexes, the list was endless, and it was in some cases progressive, but the most fitting symptom was, that it also affected the thinking ability. AHA! This was the strange way of thinking I had noticed since Dora and I were young, This was the answer to the mystery. The next step then was to arrange to be tested, this also as you can imagine, affected poor Angeline, who was innocent in all of this, but had been married for about five years by now, and she and Dan were considering beginning a family of their own. However, when this bolt of lightning struck, they immediately put all thoughts of having children on hold, and decided that if Angeline had this faulty gene, she would not risk passing it on to a further generation, which was a very sensible, but heartbreaking decision to make. I would therefore have no grandchildren, which was the worst news for me, as unlike some, I longed to be a 'granny.'

The procedure began; Dora Dana and Tina discovered that if they had this 'disease' then there would be all sorts of benefits and assistance at their disposal and so they gladly went along. Dora even told me it would be good if I had it also, as I could give up work and claim benefit. She hadn't given a thought to the fact that I didn't want to give up, cave in, and be a victim of this nightmare, I wanted to fight it! However I forgave her on this occasion now that I was beginning to understand where the strange thinking came from. Individually we all visited the genetics centre for our tests. Reflexes, blood tests, urine tests, the list was endless. I would sit at home reading the material over and over and trying to work out who may have the faulty gene, chromosome number 19.

I came to a conclusion, Dana certainly had it, because she had passed it, innocently for a change on to Lucas, and who knows how many more of her children. Tina certainly had it, I only had to look at her now to see it, and Dora must have it. She had her strange little ways, her cataracts, her wobbly legs etc. Now I hadn't forgotten Sally, Dora's youngest daughter, who was living a life of her own, and whom we saw from time to time. I wasn't sure about Sally, she was different from the rest, quite intelligent and self-sufficient, motivated to try out new things. As for myself and Angeline, well I had

had my own medical problems when young, and one or two other minor things I could have attributed to the Dystrophy, but they could also be put down to other things so I kept an open mind. Genetics of course works differently to most other medical research, and this was a form of muscular dystrophy that could not skip a generation. Therefore if I didn't have it, there was no way Angeline could have it either, or be a carrier. It is also a very lengthy process and the results would be weeks or months away, which was an agonising wait for us all. However, Dora and clan had been given priority due to the birth of Lucas and their results were the first to come back. My unqualified assessment was spot on. Dora, Dana and Tina had the faulty chromosome number 19. Sally had not. Now, as you may be aware, this far into my life saga, nothing has ever gone smoothly for me and this again was no exception either. The results came back inconclusive. We have two copies of each gene, one from our mother and one from our father which makes us who we are. However, my result was inconclusive due to the fact that they could only find one copy of this chromosome. I knew I had been no immaculate conception, I knew I had a mother and a father like everybody else, so *where* had the second copy disappeared to? I was incomplete, how was I even functioning without it? It felt weird but the tests had to be repeated, they decided as they couldn't fathom it, they would conclude that the genes I *did* have were 'normal.' Once more, I had been given a reprieve.

Dora and Dana in particular were revelling in this news, that they had a 'label.' This meant that they could legitimately claim everything going via the D.S.S. Suddenly they had a *reason* why they stayed in bed 'till three in the afternoon, why they needed taxis everywhere and couldn't walk to the bus stop, why they couldn't look after the children. Blind people, those suffering from the devastating effects of the thalidomide drug, people wheelchair bound, with assistance, could care for their children, but not my family, no, this was the excuse they had been looking for and they welcomed it with open arms. Following all of this, I had *really* mixed emotions. I felt pity for them for the way they lived. I felt guilt because Dora had inherited this and I had not. Dana now had six children, and hopefully this would be the last. Now that she knew the impact of what she could pass on to them, surely she would have no more babies.

So, once more there was one of life's lulls. Dana was so tired with two young children running around, and one disabled, plus she had gained newfound wealth in the form of all the extra benefits to finance her drinking binges. As least it kept her out of my hair. I continued to visit once a week or so to see the children. I finished work early one day and decided I would drop in on my way home. As I knocked at the door, there was no answer. It was about three in the afternoon and I thought perhaps she was still in bed, and yet I couldn't hear the usual yells of children fighting. I peered through the window out of curiosity, to see Lucas sitting in his little bouncy chair two feet away from the glowing red gas fire – alone! This child could barely breath and the heat from the fire must have been causing him distress. Where was Dana? She was nowhere to be found. I went to Dora's and told her my fears. She said Dana would have gone shopping and it was easier without a baby, so she had left him there. I demanded Dora go and rescue him as she had a key. A week or two later, the health visitor called, as they were keeping a close eye on Lucas due to his condition. She too peered through the window and saw him sitting alone on yet another occasion. Following this, help was offered yet again and respite three days a week was put in place for Lucas. Once more, the child was reprieved and Dana was very satisfied, having one more screaming kid removed for a while.

Trauma was a daily occurrence, but I knew there was the input of social workers by now, as neighbours had made reports, and the intervention of this disability had brought in outside help also, therefore I thought this gave me some relief too, I could leave them safe in the knowledge that the children were being monitored. Dana had been shown at the hospital how to perform daily exercises on Lucas's legs to keep his circulation going and build his muscles. She would grasp his little cotton like ankles and push them up and out, but on one occasion she had downed a few cans of lager and had half the street in as an audience to what she had to do for her disabled son and pushed a little too hard snapping his femur in the process. The child cried in agony for three days before she gave in to Dora's plea's to take him to hospital. I was completely unaware of this at this time, and when I knew I cried at the thought of what this child must have suffered. Why wasn't someone doing something, my feelings towards Dana were changing with every week that went by. This was not the little Angel I had so dearly loved; this was a monster who put her own needs above those of her children, yet again.

Angeline was also growing more and more concerned each time she collected Anna. She brought her one day to ask my opinion of some marks she was noticing when she changed Anna's nappy. As we both unceremoniously examined Anna's nether regions, we equally came to the conclusion that these were cigarette burns. They were also perfectly round *deliberate* burns on the child's buttocks and legs. Angeline decided to challenge Dana over this only for her to be sweetly apologetic as to how she had accidentally 'caught' her whilst changing a nappy with a cigarette in her hand. Angeline didn't accept or believe this and on Monday morning, rang the social worker involved with the family, and told her, her fears. Yet again nothing was done.

All of this was praying on my mind. History was for the umpteenth time, horribly repeating itself. Three had been taken away, three more had replaced them, and the same abuse and neglect seemed to be happening.

I decided something had to be done about all this, but what? Gordon and I were still struggling with our ailing parents, so it would have been less easy for us to resolve, and in any case there were *three* children suffering, people in authority seemed to know and yet nothing was being done.

However, once more my attentions were diverted from it all. My mother had yet another fall and we had gone out late at night to sort her out, I stayed, and drove straight to work the next day. I returned again on my day off and sat and talked to mum about her situation. We had introduced every possible help we could summon to make life easier for her in her own home, but it had reached a stage where it wasn't enough. Her Parkinson's disease was so advanced that her weak legs could barely carry her to the bathroom any more. The flask of tea made each morning would soon go cold and she could no longer make her way to the kitchen to make another, and even then, how would she carry it back. I knew she had always pleaded with me not to 'put her into a rest home.' I was not about to 'put' her anywhere, and so we thought our way through several alternatives. Our house being large and built on three levels was the first option. We could convert the integral garage into a bed-sit, replace the up-and-over doors with the glazed patio type, out onto the paved area at the back, and convert the adjoining utility room into a bathroom. We could also install a chairlift up to our lounge, so that she could sit with us in the evenings, and have her meals with us. It was a perfect solution, except for one thing – she would be completely alone with only our rear garden to look at all day whilst we were at work. At least here she had the home help popping in, and neighbours passing, whom she could wave to through her window. After careful consideration, every which-way was looked at, until our final solution was nothing else but a nursing home where she would have twenty-four hour care. Mum agreed, but we were not entering into this lightly. Gordon and I explored many prospective places before reaching a decision. We took mum to visit the ones we felt had the best to offer, and found one five minutes from home and my place of work, perfect. However, we had a lengthy struggle on our hands to convince the Sheffield authorities to take the transfer from Derbyshire County

Council. Eventually though, they agreed that it would be good for mum to have us only five minutes away, but to be cared for and nursed on a daily basis. Of course I realised at the end of the day, it was all down to finances.

Mum now had those mixed emotions which had been ever so familiar to me in the past. She was relieved at the prospect of not being alone, having her needs met as and when, and us popping in more frequently. Also I had explained that I could still take her to Meadowhall Shopping Centre, yet more often. This was an activity she really enjoyed, as I loaded her wheelchair into the boot of my car, got her settled into the passenger seat and off we would go for the day. I encouraged her to spend her money and buy all the silly little things she wanted. Despite this prospect, she was naturally so terribly sad at giving up her home, and moving away from her friends and neighbours and the village where she had spent her entire life. I assured her that she didn't have to part with anything she valued. I had ample space in my loft to keep them and we could swap clothes and knick-knacks according to the season, to ring the changes. This gave her hope and she relaxed a little over the situation. A social worker became involved to help her with practical decisions regarding her affairs, and each weekend, we would spend time slowly sorting out cupboards and drawers, bit by bit, discarding old and worn out stuff, things she no longer wanted or needed, and over the next few weeks we had boxes and boxes of stuff neatly labelled and stacked. Some for the loft, some for the charity shops, loads for Dora who had quite logically let mum know what she would like. Our only decision now was what we should do with the furniture. There was of course the new sofa and chair, still bearing their labels, the new carpet, and the new bedroom furniture, but I assured mum she had everything of that nature where she was going. We took her for a visit to view her room, and although it was a little sparse, we could soon change all that. It was a modern establishment and the furniture was bright modern and clean. We chose a neutral shade of paint for the walls, as we had been granted permission to do whatever we wanted. I chose curtains that I knew mum would like, and Gordon put up her favourite pictures and mirrors on the wall. We bought little corner shelves for her ornaments, and a duvet cover for the bed. There was a hand basin in the corner of the room, and I decorated it with a little pleated curtain. We took the T.V. and lamps, bought a small C.D. player for her favourite music. It was looking more and more like home. The staff were wonderful, and mum being a very congenial sort, they became very fond of her. I had her agreement that it would be much better for her, if she moved into her new home permanently, once her room was ready, *before* we emptied the bungalow, as I felt it would be too much for her to see all her possessions being removed and furniture disposed of, and so the day arrived for her to move,. A huge upheaval this must have been for her. Some of her neighbours came to day goodbye, and assured her they would visit if, and when they were able. They sent her cards of good wishes yet sadness at her leaving. This was so hard. It was quite devastating for mum, but I too, was feeling the loss. I would miss making cups of tea for them as they sat and gossiped, the familiar room I had stayed in week after week with its little rainbow patterned pink wallpaper. The lounge where I last held my dad's lifeless and blood-soaked body in my arms, and most of all there was the tree which reminded us all of him, how it's grown these days. I've often wondered if God uses dad to cultivate His 'garden' of dead people in the place some call heaven, but if that were the case, I doubt that dad would co-operate so readily.

It had already been decided that Dora would have most of the furniture. I didn't want any of it nor needed it. Dana also had her eye on a few things and between them, they organised a removal van and driver. Mum had moved into her new dwelling and the day therefore dawned when we would complete the task in hand. I drove out to the village and waited for Dora and Dana to arrive in the van. The stuff mum wanted to keep, was by now either in her new place, or in my loft. The only items of any interest to me, were old family photo's certain trivial items which reminded me of my childhood, all of which fitted into my car. Shortly, Dora and Dana arrived and entered the house which was already cleared of all life and feeling. All that remained were the inanimate objects of daily living. Dora and Dana fussed over who would have what, and I left them to it as Gordon and I stood back and watched in disbelief as they carried out lamps, cupboards, curtains beds and when all furniture had gone, Dana single handedly took up the carpets and was not content until she had even removed the underlay, revealing the red stained floor boards where dad used to sit, and had died, which she barely noticed. This was the woman with Myatonic Dystrophy who allegedly needed assistance to do most things. When all was done and the van was full, I couldn't wait to close and lock the front door for the last time. If we really think about it, every door has its own unique sound. I can still remember the sound of that front door.

I had to think positively. A new beginning for mum, I could now visit her several times a week, take her for visits to Bradwell eventually to visit her friends and neighbours when she felt well enough and able, that was the plan. She settled in quite well, although she didn't feel too good that first week, and so no plans were made to take her anywhere, until she felt better. I would visit usually three or four times a week after work, sometimes more if Gordon was working late at the hospital. However, Dora and Dana and Tina had all day, every day, and lived walking distance now from mum. They didn't work, or have limited time, but you could guarantee, no sooner had I sat down with mum after a hard day at work, and switched on the kettle, than in they would all walk. Whatever argument they were having on the way here, would continue in mum's presence, and unsettle her. She didn't want to hear their petty squabbles, and disagreements, *or* cough and splutter on Dana's cigarette, as her never still lips gripped the filter tip, sucking in the drug, and her eyes half closed as she exhaled the disgusting fall-out without even ceasing to talk. I would demand, she either put it out or left, and after futile protest with me, she would eventually extinguish the offending butt! I never seemed to have time to be with mum in peace any more, it seemed we had exchanged one hell for another. I decided she needed both fresh air and a change of scenery after three weeks in her new home. Her health hadn't improved a great deal, but she was depressed also, no wonder. Angeline invited us to her house for tea. It wasn't far, only two minutes away, a short journey and I could take the car right up onto the front lawn, so only a few steps to the door. Between us, we managed to manoeuvre her to a comfy chair, plump up the cushions and serve her favourite for tea, salmon and cucumber sandwiches. She really enjoyed the day, watching Angeline's cats playing, and admiring what Dan had done to the house, but after a while, I could see that she was looking tired and she agreed that she was ready to leave. Angeline helped me once more to support mum to the car and into the passenger seat. We said goodbye and Angeline went inside. As I started up the engine and slid the gear stick into reverse, I heard mum give out a strange, whimpering sigh. As I looked at her, asking if she was o.k. there was no response. She had stopped breathing! I almost fell through the seat belt as I clambered out of the car and round to her side. There was no way I could perform C.P.R. in the seat, my only course of action was to drag her out onto the grass, all the while screaming for Angeline. Mum was technically 'dead.' There was no pulse and she still wasn't breathing. As I screamed once more for Angeline and she came running, I held mum under her arms and she came out of the car with a thud. I have never been so glad that she was too heavy for me, for the jolt caused her to let out a loud sigh and she opened her eyes. She was completely unaware of what had happened, this was the second time I had found it necessary to save mum's life, but this time, I couldn't help wondering whether I should have just let her go peacefully, but this thought was fleeting, it was instinct to 'put things right' and together Angeline and I lifted her back into the seat and called the doctor. He concluded that there was no evident reason for this except heart failure, I took her home and settled her into bed with the help of the nurse on duty, asking her to call me at any time if necessary.

Over the next couple of weeks mum recovered to some extent, and I insisted that Dora and Dana visit before 6 p.m. so that not only could I spend quality time with mum but that her visits would take place throughout the day, instead of all day with no-one then two hours of chaos. This of course would mean they would have to get out of their pit before tea-time. They were like vampires; it was as though daylight would dissolve them to ashes. There is really a fine line between Angels and Devils; in fact Lucifer *was* a fallen Angel, wasn't he? I suppose even he needed recruits now and then.

However, mum had now been in her new environment for five weeks and it was approaching her eightieth birthday. I had planned a visit, from us all, a cake and presents to mark the occasion, for she was still not well enough to go far, therefore I didn't arrange to take her anywhere for fear of a repeat crisis. Two days before her birthday, Gordon and I called in to see her, and take her a few treats as always. She was sitting in her chair watching T.V. and trying to eat a trifle that Dora had taken her the day before. She appeared to be having some difficulty in getting it down, so I poured her a glass of Guinness and lemonade, she enjoyed this and I felt the iron in it was good for her. I gazed into her eyes as I gave her a drink and couldn't help feeling that she looked like a different person. There was an expression in her eyes that I had never seen before. Two minutes later, in walked Dora. I suppose I couldn't fault her for her numerous visits, but although part of me wanted to stay, for the night even on the floor, I could only tolerate Dora's incessant mumblings for so long, and we chose to leave, informing the nurse on duty that I didn't like the look of my mother, and asking her to ring me if there was the slightest change. After assuring mum I would see her tomorrow, we left.

Sure enough, about 4 a.m. the 'phone rang. I knew it would be a problem because of the hour. As I answered, the duty nurse informed me that mum had been taken to hospital. She had gone to check on her to discover her on the floor, she had fallen out of bed trying to reach the bell to call for help. We raced to the hospital immediately to find she had been taken to I.C.U. A consultant was called to talk to us and took us into a small side room, just off A. & E. he explained that he thought mum had burst diverticulae (small inflamed sacs which develop on the lining of the bowel) usually these can be repaired and a full recovery made, but he explained how mum's other ailments meant it would be highly unlikely, for her to survive surgery! However, he was going to leave us to consider the options whilst they made mum comfortable. By now we had contacted Angeline and Dan, and they had joined us. Dan was a 'brick,' and drove to Dora's house to inform her of the situation. I really felt that she should be here and that we should make this decision together. However, there was no reply to his knocking, they would be fast asleep and none of them would want to be the one who had to get up and answer the door, so they ignored it as usual. Unfortunately, Angeline and Dan had Anna with them for the weekend, and couldn't rouse Dana either to return Anna home. Therefore there was no choice but to bring Anna with them to mum's bedside. Mum was attached to a drip and oxygen etc., and a bag hung from the side of the bed, with black sticky fluid draining into it from her stomach. I knew the signs, this was not good. Dan kept trying to contact Dora, and eventually managed to get her to pop her head out of the bedroom window. He was by this time, quite blunt about the fact that mum was dying. A short time later the nurse appeared to tell me that my sister was on the 'phone. I made my way to the nurse's station and picked up the receiver. Dora's question will haunt me forever. "Dan says mum's dying. Are you joking?" I could barley speak and had to hand the 'phone to the nurse to explain. Eventually Dora and Dana arrived at the I.C.U. and sat beside the bed. I was holding mum's hand, letting her know we were there, as she drifted in and out of consciousness, letting out an occasional moan. We were offered a room and a bed for the night, as by now it had been necessary for me to make the decision alone regarding mum's condition. I decided it was unfair to put her through so much more pain and suffering, which she was unlikely to survive anyhow, and agreed with the surgeon's advice not to operate. I didn't want a bed for the night. I wanted to stay with mum as long as I could and be by her side when she slid away. I arrived too late to be with dad, it wasn't going to happen again. We all sat in virtual silence, me, Gordon, Angeline and Dan, Anna and Dora. Dana decided to go home for some clothes for her and Dora to stay. Mum was dying, and I know this will sound callous, but I couldn't help thinking that the final opportunity, our last chance to find the source of the Dystrophy was fading along with mum's life. All those new generations of children needed to know whether they would be affected and how, and which side of the family should we be looking at? Who may, or may not have it? The possibilities were endless. I spoke to the consultant and asked if he could take a sample for genetics. He was quite curt and said it was not protocol. I was now distraught and told him protocol was the last thing on my mind. The welfare of future generations of children was at risk from this ignorance. My shouts and cries had an impact, and he spoke to mum despite her unconscious state (protocol) and informed her he was taking the sample. I was so relieved at that moment but was to later discover however, that it had been placed in the wrong type of container and was now useless for testing, all hope was again lost. A short while later, the nurse seeing my distress, asked me if I would like her to increase the morphine in mum's drip. I knew what she meant and readily said yes, mum was suffering longer than she should and was now completely unconscious. Dana was later to maliciously accuse me of killing my own mother.

I held mum's hand as she slid away and took her final laboured breath. This was the day before her eightieth birthday – *my birthday*!

Dana hadn't returned, and had missed what to her would have been drama. She was therefore understandably angry, and I hadn't thought to inform her, my grief had taken over. Now lay ahead of us the prospect of emptying mum's home yet again. Many of her belongings were still in my loft, and there they stayed as I couldn't bring myself to look at them let alone make decisions what to do with them, despite Dora and Dana's relentless requests for various items they *swore* were promised to them. They had forgotten I had dad's and mum's Wills, stating that Dana at least should have nothing. Gordon, once more made funeral arrangements, I couldn't function without him. He was my own personal 'Sherman Tank' forcing his strong way through everything and anything, to complete the task. Mum had said she didn't want a funeral, but I felt it was mainly to go along with dad so a small service was arranged at the crematorium to please those who needed it. I had taken mum flowers every week without fail, for her to see and enjoy. I *refused* to put them on her coffin when she couldn't see them, much to the dismay of other yet again, but it was significant to me.

It was a very short, simple affair. The absence of flowers was poignant I know, but it was important to me, although perhaps appeared desperately mean to others. My mother had had a lifetime of flowers, one way or another. Either an entire garden full on a daily basis or a bouquet full, weekly from me and Angeline and to be fair, Dora did occasionally do the same. As we made our way along the path to the funeral, I felt like the condemned man walking once more to the gallows. However, it was just too much for poor Angeline, she had been so close to her grandparents. She wasn't there when dad died and having no funeral either, she must have felt that he was here one day, gone the next, there was no closure for her. However, she had been with me at mum's side when she passed away and she just couldn't handle this goodbye. She ran off through the graveyard in floods of tears, Dan running after her to comfort her. I took control of myself and realised that everyone handles grief in their own way and decided she should be left alone, to do it her way. Myself and Angeline don't handle it very well at all.

Following the funeral, a few friends did make it back to our house for a cup of tea, including Dora, but all she could talk about was the 'reading of the Will.' I informed her that mum's Will was private and not to be read to everyone, but that on another day she was welcome to come and read it herself. She still seemed to feel that there was money somewhere. She had somehow forgotten that I had encouraged mum to spend it on furniture and whatever frivolity she wished, and that now, Dora actually owned all of the stuff bought with *that* money. She had forgotten that now two funerals had also been paid for. I gave Dora the Wills to read, but asked her not to expect me to enter into any discussion. She assured me she had a 'degree' in English. I was unaware that she had ever attended university, and asked her when she had managed this. She answered, "Well, I sat City and Guilds, well almost!"

Unfortunately, this time a post mortem could not be avoided. They needed to be 100% certain of what had killed mum. I rang her G.P. and asked him if he would go through the report with me, and because of my job he agreed. Despite being used to these, it is most unpleasant hearing the condition and weight of the heart, and the liver, the contents of the stomach, when it's your mother being discussed. I had already discovered that the sample sent for genetics had been put in the wrong container and was therefore useless. All hope gone once more. I did however discover that she also had salmonella which was quite a shock, but it was the burst diverticulum which caused her death. The most surprising and welcome news was that the pathologist had in fact taken a further tissue sample for genetics testing, relief once more.

New drama would, of course unfold. Dora and Dana accused the rest home of poisoning mum, due to the salmonella, despite no proof as to where she had contracted it. Didn't Dora and Dana take her little treats also, like Trifle? Thankfully we will never know, and it must rest with mum. We had decided to leave all shelves, curtains and fittings for anyone who may need them. However, Dana had arrived at the home armed with a screwdriver and removed everything, after hurling abuse at the staff. Gordon firmly insisted that she return, and replace it all forthwith!

Following mum's funeral and all these accusations, I received a 'phone call from Dana once more accusing me of killing mum, not to mention, *me* taking her children etc. She also called me a child predator and a Bitch! I told her, she could call *me* anything she liked as long as she put 'super' in front of it, so from then on, by Dana; I was referred to as Superbitch! Fine. By now I was pacing the floor in grief *and* anger. Gordon took the receiver from my hand and asked me why I didn't just go over there and talk face to face. The answer was simple; it knew I would have found it impossible to keep my hands off her! Hence it was sensible to keep away. It took me three days to calm down sufficiently and reach my composure before I could face Dana and sort her out. I decided to visit her the next evening, and Angeline insisted on coming to support me and keep *me* calm. As we sat down, prepared with our speeches of forthright words, making sure Dana knew exactly where we stood and what we thought, she began to waffle about a 'spirit' which had visited her, I wondered whether it was whiskey, gin, or lager, but no, it was a woman with long dark hair wearing a white flowing gown, holding out a Bible and asking for *me*! "Did I want to give her a message?" My reply was irresistible, I told her the only spirits Dana would recognise were in a bottle, and yes I had a message, it was this: - "Tell her to piss off!" was my reply. Dana immediately turned her attentions to Angeline and fired venomous accusations as to why she had run off through the cemetery at mum's funeral. Angeline could take no more and in the blink of an eye her hands were around Dana's throat. Dana was fixed to the chair as I was pulling and encouraging Angeline to let go. She was doing exactly what I, and others had wanted to do for years, but something had prevented me. Angeline later told me that it was not *me* that prevented her tightening her grip, it was a far superior power that made her let go that night. Perhaps the same power that had given me the strength to resist also. Maybe an Angel with wings? What was happening to us? This small section of my family was turning us into monsters, and I for one didn't like what I was becoming. My parents were now gone, my anchors had been removed from me. Would I now flounder? Would I allow the monster which was emerging from within me take control? I decided NOT! However I would need this strength and self-control much more in the future, than I had ever done before.

Now came the argument over mum's ashes. Dora insisted that mum had told her she wanted them scattered in the 'Moonpenny Field' which could be seen from the bungalow. A place where all of us had played as children. Mum had never mentioned this to me, and I felt she would have, but feeling the way I always did, the mortal remains were not important to me. The spirit, when the life force of a person has gone, the important things they leave behind as a legacy are the memories, all of which were permanently tattooed within my head, and so it was of little consequence to me if Dora wished to carry this out, so Gordon signed the ashes over to her, and I wished her well.

It would be two years later, before I could bring myself to go anywhere near the bungalow, but eventually plucked up courage to visit mum's old neighbours. It was then, that I discovered, that Dora and Dana had carried the ashes on the bus, and left them on the doorstep of the bungalow. The new resident, not knowing what to do, had put them in the dustbin! Now, being a practical person, I am a firm believer that the ashes in the urn probably belonged to several people who may have been cremated together, but once again, it was the significance of knowing the final destination was the dustbin!

I was devastated, though I turned my hurt to a smile as I thought what dad would have made of all this, with his atheistic beliefs. If this had been his ashes, he would have had a really good laugh.

Chapter Eighteen

What a Tangled Web!

The new task now, whilst coming to terms with my grief, was to untangle this Spider's Web. I felt like a monster, due to my thoughts, yet, also, a victim always on the edge of a sticky web, with Dana sitting silently in the centre like a huge Black Widow, waiting to ensnare her next victim, and draw them towards her in a cocoon of silk only to spit them out again. I felt the Dystrophy must have affected her the worst. Some had muscle dysfunction, couldn't walk, could barely see, but they could *feel*! Perhaps Dana's mind had been severely affected. OR, was I again trying to make excuses for her behaviour. Perhaps she was one of those fallen Angels whose wicked machinations were out of choice and God-given free will. Dana did appear to get a kick out of human distress at times. What had happened to that beautiful little girl I once knew and loved? Where had she gone?

As I mentioned, my tribulations were far from over. I tried to leave them alone, once mum and dad were gone, but I had promised I would look after Dora and so therefore I would continue to visit. Dana would be there, and so I would have to sit and be bombarded with all of their tribulations, as Dana was keeping busy with the 'next three.' Anna did her own thing, Paula whined her way through the day, always sad and unhappy. Lucas lay in his pram day after day or was positioned in his bouncy chair, feeding bottle just within sucking reach, on the end of his mother's extended arm. No cuddles, no snuggling in her arms for comfort, ho burping and rocking to sleep with a satisfied glow, just the necessary sustenance, like all the others before him. Damien was in and out of prison, but Dana was not left alone at these times, as Damien's Brother Jason, had moved in as a lodger, and was 'good' company for her during these lonely nights. Jason took up residence and the kids even called him dad. He was rather simple minded and a perfect victim for Dana, he had been drawn into the spider's web and was cocooned there in his ignorance, waiting to be spat out, when he had served his usefulness.

I tried discreetly to keep out of it all, to let them get on with it. "Life had come late to me, and I as yet hadn't had time to really enjoy it. This needed to be my time now, to relax a little. We mustn't forget Gordon's mother whose health was now failing and her needs were paramount, but Gordon and I tried to have some peace. We had a couple of holidays in Turkey with Angeline and Dan. We also later had holidays with our long-time friends J and J. However, the Angels kept busy, and as usual the next distressing call came through one day, as I sat in front of the computer at work. This time it was

Dana's social worker, Sue, asking me if I was able to pick up Anna after work. It would appear that some of the neighbours were not too enamoured with Dana either, and a gang had pushed fireworks through the letterbox. Set fire to net curtains through an open window, and thrown bricks through another window, smashing a glass table and barely missing one of the children who had ventured downstairs out of curiosity to see what was going on. There were no less than five children in the house that night, all of them in danger, any one of them could have been struck by a brick, cut by flying glass or burned along with everyone else in the house. I drove to Dana's the second I left work, to pick up Anna. Dora had been asked to take Paula home to her house, just around the corner. The house was a mess, debris everywhere and Dana pacing up and down, fag not in hand on this occasion, it was fixed permanently to her lips and wobbled up and down as she chuntered on. All the while her eyes were slit-like as a necessary protection against the endless ribbon of smoke which drifted from the cigarette precariously invading the apertures. She must have been very stressed indeed. I gathered up a few things for Anna, bundled her into the car and took her home. She was understandably distressed and didn't settle easily, but between Gordon, Angeline and me, we managed to care for her for a few days and still get to work. It wasn't easy, a lot of juggling of time was needed and a great deal of patience. After a week of this mayhem, I discovered that Dana and Jason were having a great time, having Paula with Dora, Anna with us and Lucas in respite care, they were free to party, and party they did. Although I still felt for these kids, I was totally exhausted, and had to return Anna home, these children were Dana's responsibility, and I was trying not to lose sight of my resolution to stay out of things. We also had my mother-in-law to consider, who needed more and more care, and so we continued.

At the surgery we occasionally had team-building weekends to enable us all, as you may expect, to work as a team. You may remember the previous occasion where I rather let my hair down, well yet another event was forthcoming and I couldn't wait. It was little different to the previous one in that I decided it was a safe environment in which to let off team a little, and I made sure I did! The regrets came the next day when the hangover kicked in around 6 a.m. a whole day of Archery, rock climbing and abseiling, carrying buckets of water from the stream, working out quizzes etc., was almost impossible as my head felt nearer and nearer to explosion somehow I got through the day, and set off for home around 4 p.m. I collected the dogs which had been left with Angeline on my way, so that I wouldn't have to *move* once I arrived home, but as I took their taut leads in my hand, Angeline passed me a container and very casually asked me if I could test it for her.

It was a urine sample and she just wanted to eliminate the obvious. Testing urine for pregnancy plus various other things was a part of my daily routine, and was nothing out of the ordinary for me. I prepared the test and left it to 'cook', all the while performing these tasks like a zombie. I took two paracetamol and went to bed. I had work the next day and wasn't sure if my self-inflicted condition was going to allow. However, Gordon was at work and later in the evening I came downstairs to make a cup of coffee. The paracetamol had kicked in and were beginning to work, my head was clearing a little and as I entered the kitchen my eyes fell upon the test kit. There were TWO blue lines!! Angeline was pregnant! I was going to be a granny! Cots, prams, toys Oh! My head started to spin again as I dialled Angeline's number to tell her the result. No reply, couldn't get through *all* evening and finally went to bed exhausted. The next day the minute my head lifted from my pillow, I once more dialled Angeline's number, *still* no reply. It transpired Dan had pulled the plug on the 'phone for some peace and quiet. However, I later tried one more time, or I would have had to get in the car and drive there, my excitement was uncontrollable. As I heard Angeline's voice on the line I pressed the button on the Hi-Fi to play, Cliff Richard singing 'Congratulations.' The line went dead! Angeline had realised the implication of this and the shock had been too much, she really hadn't taken it too seriously. They had been married for six years.

From now on, I was determined, my life *would* change. This grandchild would mean everything to me; it felt like I had waited forever. There were plans to be made, vital equipment to be bought. However, all this talk of test results, had put me in mind of the tests which had been carried out at mum's post mortem, and so first thing Monday morning, I rang the Genetics Centre to see if they had made progress. I felt so guilty that Angeline and I had been tested and didn't have this faulty gene, but there were others perhaps being born into the extended family that didn't know. At last we would have the answer, and could inform any relevant family members. As the consultant spoke to me, my head went hollow when he explained that, as the tissue sample was from mum, who had *died*, they had thought it was no longer any use for her to know, and had disposed of it! All hope *was* now gone forever, what could I do? This was a little known medical condition at the time, and shortly after, strangely enough, one of my G.P. colleagues, ventured into the office one morning after a busy surgery asking if anyone had ever heard of Myatonic Dystrophy. I calmly said, "Yes, I have," as I was sick of the very words by now. He was puzzled as to how I knew about a condition that even he as a doctor didn't know much about. I explained to him, and told him the whole sorry story. I also offered to lend him all the literature in my possession. He told me to consider the fact that, like any condition, it has to start somewhere, and could well have *begun* with Dora. Poor Dora, I hoped she wouldn't blame herself for unwittingly passing this on.

Oh my goodness, I could feel the need for a holiday filling my head. I had always been passionate about Egyptology and wanted to visit Egypt, but my mother had always expressed her concern at the spores which she had heard were growing inside the tombs and were making people ill. Now, of course, there was no-one to worry about me, other than Gordon, and so we decided to take a much needed break in Luxor, staying at the Winter Palace Hotel, right on the back of the Nile. It was a magnificent place, and had once been the Palace of King Farouk. The rooms were magnificent with corridors 12' wide, and double doors to each of the rooms leading off it. Outside, the double staircase leading up to the balcony was bedecked with a soft red carpet. We would sit here at 7 p.m. each evening, with a cocktail and watch the sun turn to a huge orange ball, with the image of the palm trees along the river bank silhouetted against it, as it sank slowly as though into the Nile itself. Like liquid gold. The history, the tombs and artefacts, the temples etc., were truly amazing, it was like exotic 'food' to me and I absorbed every detail. One drawback was that it was the month of July and almost unbearably hot, especially in the desert visiting the temple of Hatshepsut, and the Valley of the Kings. Tutankhamen's tomb was very quiet as few people would enter due to the 'curse' but I am not superstitious and it didn't bother me at all, I wanted to lap up all of this culture and therefore readily entered. Ten years later, I am still here. The curse has not yet touched 'Superbitch,' I have a curse of another kind, my family.

We had a wonderful time, just the two of us, but constantly my mind would wander to thoughts of Angeline and how she was, as her pregnancy was progressing and there was not long to go. One day in pensive mood floating slowly and silently along the Nile in a Felucca, I gave much thought to this grandchild and realised that she or he would need our individual attention as would Angeline. She had Grown up with all this trauma, had lived with Dana on two occasions and had been very supportive of Dana's children also. Now she and *her* child would need our support. Before we left Egypt, I bought a fluffy toy camel and named him Rashid. This would be my tool for telling my grandchild stories of Egypt, in the hope that perhaps he or she would share my passion.

A short while after our return, Angeline went into labour and was taken to hospital one Tuesday morning, ironically it was a day I normally supervised the baby clinic at work. It was about 9.15 a.m. and Dan rang to tell me it wasn't going to be long and if I wanted to, I could join him at Angeline's bedside. *If I wanted to*?! – Of course I did, I was beside myself with excitement and was there in a flash. Angeline was puffing and panting and Dan was monitoring the contractions on a machine, with his typically electronic mind. The midwife, Kay who would later become a colleague of mine, was so calm and professional, she had obviously done this a thousand time before, but I had never been a granny before, or actually watched my grandchild emerge into the world. However Kay constantly checked to see if a little head was appearing. It suddenly struck me that all the time we had been chattering on about whether it would be a boy or a girl, and hadn't given any thought to actual appearance. I had always visualised a child with our family traits of big blue eyes and blonde curly hair. My excitement grew even more as I realised this child could be like daddy, with dark skin, brown eyes and dark hair! How wonderful and different.

As poor Angeline groaned and panted with the pain of labour, my gaze was upon her nether regions as I stood at the bottom of the bed waiting, all the while Dan in his element with the machine and would announce before Angeline did that another contraction was imminent. The midwife encouraged Angeline to push and as she did so, the crown of a little head appeared. The curls were very dark and shiny. Another push and a whole head with a screwed up little face emerged, but I couldn't see the eyes as they were as yet still closed. One more push and the little body slithered out into Kay's waiting hands. It was a GIRL! Her skin was like milk chocolate, her eyes like two huge black marbles, and so *much* black curly hair! She was perfect and I knew from that moment on that she and I were going to have a very special relationship. I rushed to work and just made it in time. Baby's timing had been impeccable, it was almost as though she knew I had to go and wanted to say 'hello.' Not much work was done that afternoon, I couldn't concentrate. Immediately the surgery closed I rushed out to buy a PINK dress before my visit to the hospital. It was the beginning of august and so very very hot that summer. Poor Angeline had to stay in hospital longer than expected due to baby's feeding problems. However, all was well eventually and they came home. Life was perfect, and I remembered how overwhelmed I had felt at the birth of Angeline and this was much the same. It was decided that this child would be called Xara, and I know that it will sound biased as I am now her doting grandmother, but she was, and still is so beautiful, as everyone who sees her will testify.The following poem truly reveals my thoughts on the day she was born:-

XARA

Your skin is like creamy milk chocolate,
They call it I think Dairy Milk,
Your hair is all shiny and crinkly
Like a mix of black satin and silk.

Your eyes are like two chocolate buttons
Set in circles of ice-cream delight
And your lashes are long silky fringes
Concealing those eyes, but not quite.

Your lips are like two little cherries
Juicy, rich, ripe and plump,
Your nose is a cute little button
Just like a brown sugar lump!

Your ears are like furled chocolate fingers,
One on each side makes a pair
Though nestling and hiding discreetly,
In the soft silky curls of your hair.

Every bit of your wee little body is yummy and
scrummy and sweet.
As a doting besotted new granny,
You're thankfully *too* good to eat

!

Now with regard to Dora, and Dana, life continued much the same. The gangs were attacking the house frequently and nothing was being done. Dana rang one evening in a complete panic; I had just returned Anna after the usual weekend stay with us, as this still continued for her sake. There was incredible noise in the background. Glass shattering, shouting and swearing, children creaming. She had called the police but they were taking little notice of this abusive screaming woman. I was hardly surprised, as Dana herself called the police for the slightest thing, even to tell them she was going on holiday! So they were bound to ignore this nuisance. I decided stronger measures were called for, but knew it would only make matters worse if I drove over there, and anyway it was obviously a dangerous situation to have placed myself in, but there was the children's safety to consider. I rang the police myself and told them who I was and what my concerns were. They assured me they would respond and I put the receiver down, satisfied. However, it was several hours before they arrived, by which time the gangs had done their worst.

A week or two later Dora rang to say that Damien had returned from a holiday 'at her Majesty's pleasure' and had taken Anna <u>somewhere</u> for the weekend. The significance of this didn't hit me until she informed me that Dana had made allegations of abuse towards Damien, and regarding the children there was a court order preventing him having unsupervised contact with any of them. I was completely unaware of this and now knew that *real* action had to be taken.

I was now determined that these children would prevail in the face of adversity. 'Superbitch' to the rescue! This tarnished reputation had no effect on my determination, in fact I had occasionally been 'wicked' in my youth and enjoyed the buzz, but compared to those petty discrepancies, this was huge. However, I decided that what I was about to do would only be wicked *to* the wicked. I set off in my car and drove first to Dana's. I knocked and knocked and eventually she rose from her bed with enough energy to open the bedroom window, and out popped her dishevelled head. I called up to her, and informed her that I had had enough, and was on my way to report what was happening, to Social Services. I wanted her to be in no doubt as to whom had reported this, also someone *had* to advocate for these innocent children, no-one was doing a damn thing! Angeline had reported the cigarette burns on

Anna, I had reported how individuals were wrecking the house and children were in danger, but *nothing* was happening. As I left Dana still hanging out of the window, croaking her pleas to me, I drove to the Social Services offices and insisted upon arrival, that someone see me face to face. I had done enough on the telephone, which had been ignored, now I was going to make certain they saw a credible woman before them, who had a predicament on her hands and I needed help. I knew children were suffering in unthinkable ways, I also knew *I* had to make waves as no-one lese would, and yet this was *my* family I was incriminating. I couldn't imagine what my parents would have thought or expected me to do, therefore on my own head be it.

I sat with the female social worker who was on duty that day, as my story unfolded. I checked periodically ensuring that she had written the facts as I laid them bare, there must be no misrepresentation of truth here. I could clearly see this woman understood my firm determination that *some* action be taken, although I knew not what. This was without a doubt, the worst thing I had ever done in my life, so far.

As I left the office, my feelings and emotions were like oil and water. On the one hand I should protect the children, on the other I should respect my family and the two would not mix. However, I decided that I would not be influenced by Dana's pleas, as I knew she had a predisposition for lies, no, I must be impartial, and the children were paramount, they had to be considered above all else. I couldn't help feeling that I was about to open a Pandora's Box of aggression from all quarters, how right I was.

This was a day I have never forgotten, as I drove away, I visited Dora first, and implored her to ring Social Services herself regarding her knowledge of Damien taking Anna, she was naturally nervous and reluctant to take any active part. I was now angry, what a day this had been yet Dora was happy to ring me every time something went wrong and pass on the information to me. Expecting *me* to act upon it. However, I informed her of what I had already done, and that these were her grandchildren and that it was equally her duty to protect them.

That evening Dora rang yet again. She had plucked up enough courage to inform Social Services of the events concerning Damien. However the mayhem which ensued, I had not expected. Following my admission to Dana of what I was about to do, she had apparently visited Lucas in hospital later that day, and kidnapped him. The police raided Dana's house in an attempt to find Lucas, they then raided Dora's house but none of the children were anywhere to be found. They finally located them at the home of Damien's mother, and each child was passed through a broken window, by a police officer to a social worker, waiting outside!

This was devastating, these poor tiny children hadn't known what had hit them, I couldn't help wondering if I had done the right thing. I had taken it upon myself to rescue, and advocate for these young ones, as I had done years before with their mother, that little girl I once adored, now I had become her nemesis.

Chapter Nineteen

Hell's Not Full Yet!

Wicked, wicked, wicked, was the mildest word I could find for what was happening to these children. Even those who had rescued them had unwittingly caused far reaching emotional damage. Anna and Paula would never forget their trauma of being passed through a broken window. I myself had been the instigator in their removal from their mother, and no matter what she may have done; she was nonetheless, their mother. What kind of person am I, I wondered?

The most heartbreaking aspect of this situation was the separation of Anna and Paula. Following their traumatic removal from home, they were each taken to *separate* emergency foster carers. I do realise that this was possibly the only recourse available at the time, but was definitely not the best option; these two little girls had survived together, suffered together, and *needed* each other! Their suffering, now alone, must have been devastating for them. Despite the dynamics of their removal, and the guilt I now felt, there was only *one* person to really blame – Dana! She had been the person who could have made life better for them, made them her priority, rather than her men and herself, as we must remember,

Jason, Damien's brother was her latest. There were times when both Jason and Damien lived in the same house with Dana, and at these times Anna and Paula would have been at the bottom of the pile where attention was concerned.

It was now, of course, that the social worker paid Gordon and I a visit. Social Services had recalled that we had taken in Andre, a year or two earlier and so now this social worker had arranged a visit to ask if we would be willing to take Anna and Paula on a temporary basis until this whole sorry mess could be sorted out. My mind wandered back to the time Andre was brought overnight and stayed for two years but this time they were asking us to take on two little girls aged three and five. Now, Gordon worked odd hours at the hospital, and I worked six sometimes seven hours a day, how on earth could we manage *two* such small children, and keep our jobs? I also hadn't lost sight of the fact that my first grandchild was now my priority, she was just six weeks old, and it should have been such a happy time for us all, and yet it was tinged with sadness and guilt, not to mention that it was a time when Angeline needed our attention more than ever. Dana had robbed us of so much. We were now unable to see Anna at weekends as we had before, we didn't even know where the children were. I wasn't so close to Paula yet nor Lucas. But it was still sad not knowing where or how they were. Was *I* more wicked than Dana for being instrumental in their removal, or Dora for informing Social Services of Damien's unsupervised contact? I had to sit and think long and hard about this, but each time I tried to work out the equation, the answer was always the same. *Dana* was responsible, she had lost her first three children through her neglect and wickedness, now she had lost the three she'd had with which to replace them. Six children in all had been removed from her 'care.' How wicked was that?

As I sat gazing at my beautiful grandchild in my arms one evening, a great sadness came over me. Xara was going to be loved and nurtured, Andre hadn't known that until he moved in with us. Leah and Adam had known very little, Anna had known it each weekend, Paula and Lucas, hardly at all. The thought of these children, or any for that matter, not knowing real love, was detestable. The social worker was still calling and begging us to take them, at times almost on her knees with clasped hands. Apparently, Paula was being very verbally abusive and kicking granny on the legs, at her foster placement, and Anna was having uncontrollable tantrums. I felt that this was not only due to the trauma of being removed from home so dramatically, but also because they themselves were apart.

It was no use, Gordon and I could bear it no longer, we sat together one evening, exhausted after a day's work, and tired to work out a strategy whereby we could accommodate these little girls for however long it took to sort things out , and still continued with our respective employment.

Now Angeline was getting used to motherhood and thoroughly enjoying her new offspring, however she also needed a break, and had an interest in nails! Not the sort you hammer into walls, but the ones on the ends of fingers. She had already asked me if I would collect Xara after work and take her home, whilst she went to college in the evening, then she would collect her on the way home. It was working perfectly (as was my enjoyment of having Xara all to myself) and so we had a good system going, although it was tiring for us all, we wanted to help Angeline achieve her goal. However this gave me an idea. I asked Angeline if she would be willing to become a childminder for a couple of hours each day, in return, which would mean we could take in the girls. Angeline loved Anna as much as we did and after careful thought, agreed.

The next morning I rang the social worker and asked her if she could visit us after work. As she sat on the sofa later that day, she was more despondent than ever. Apparently the situation with Anna and Paula in their respective foster placements was falling apart. Their behaviour was so uncontrollable that the carers couldn't cope. She also announced that she would soon be leaving the Social Services, and wasn't even sure whether a new social worker would be available, plus both Dana and Damien had separately applied for custody of the children. This poor girl was on the floor, so to speak, and I was so pleased that I had good news for her. When I told her that Gordon and I had found a way to enable us to have Anna and Paula, she was ecstatic! Her mood leapt from floor to ceiling in an instant, and she rapidly left to make plans.

Of course angeling needed to be assessed and police checked etc., before she could officially care for the children, but she didn't mind that and so the wheels were set in motion. I omitted to mention when Andre moved in that we had to go through what is known as a Form F. This is an assessment of one's entire life and background in order to decide on the suitability to foster. We hadn't done this for Dana because it was a private arrangement between Dora, Gordon and myself, but with Andre we wanted the legal backing of the social services so that Dana couldn't take him back just when she wanted, but we had been made De-facto foster parents, which meant we were assessed for Andre only, at the time. Therefore we had to undergo the whole process again, but we weren't complaining, it meant we could bring these children back into the family at least, where they belonged. We were eventually allowed to see them, and visited them each in their respective foster placements, until certain paperwork had been completed. The carers would then start ringing, asking when the children could move in with us, permanently – as life was impossible for them but we also had preparations to make, mainly to decorate and rearrange the spare bedroom. We bought bunk beds as we felt they needed to share a room and to be together once more.

The day arrived for them to move in. As I answered the door, they burst through, Anna with arms extended upwards, posing for a kiss and a cuddle, Paula looking on in confused anticipation. I bent down and gave her a hug too, but there was no response from Paula, she didn't know me too well and mistrusted this offer of affection, as she stiffened coldly. I was to discover more understanding the reasons behind this, in the future. I waited for the social worker to follow through the door laden with bags and boxes containing their belongings, but alas, one carrier bag each, was all they had. These contained two changes of clothing, which were way too small anyway. They owned nothing. Just like their brother Andre.

Now in the events that follow, you the reader, must understand that Gordon, Angeline and Dan and myself, had *no* training whatsoever in caring for troubled children, neither were we ever offered any, and these experienced carers

were so very eager to part company with Anna
and Paula. We had rescued Dana out of love,
we had also rescued Andre out of love, we were
now taking Anna and Paula out of love, but
would this emotion be enough to deal with their
traumas?

However, that day we took them upstairs to see
their newly decorated bedroom, with multi-
coloured bunk beds, and duvet covers baring
every zoo creature you can think of, with
curtains to match. I recalled how very
important all this had been for Andre as he had
not even had a duvet and curtains at all. The
wardrobe stood empty in anticipation of the
clothes they would have brought, but apparently
it would remain empty, for another day or two
at least. They had no toys, no hairbrush no
sense of ownership of anything, in fact. We had
to change that, before anything else, and so a
day or two later I took them shopping for the
basic needs, and some fresh new clothes to
wear.

Life was not going to be easy with Anna and
Paula. They were very badly damaged
emotionally by whatever they had suffered at
home. We knew only the tip of the iceberg.
The running around in the nude, the lack of food
and emotional stimulation, the burns on Anna's
legs but little did we know, there were many
other traumas yet to be revealed. These tiny
children were totally confused, and many things

they said were difficult to decipher, and yet others were devastatingly adult, which no child of this age could possibly have made up. For example Anna one day hurt her finger, I asked her how she had done it, her reply? "I banged it on a rainbow, and there was a teddy in it and mummy was in it, and she flew up in the sky away from me." Was this the only way she knew how to express her separation? When things didn't go Anna's way, she would fix her gaze on an object and threaten to smash it, but I was already learning how to deal with some of these episodes therapeutically, for when she sat in the hallway one day, with her feet held in a pugilistic fashion, poised to strike at a full length mirror on the wall. She informed me she was going to smash it, at which point I realised there would be no way I could reach her from twenty feet away in order to stop her. I asked her if I could say something before she did it, and she looked right at me as I explained how the glass would shatter, she would be cut and hurt. There would be thousands of pieces of glass everywhere. I, on the other hand, was right over here and wouldn't we hurt. I had realised that Anna wanted to hurt somebody, anybody, to relieve her anger. With this she got up and calmly walked away.

Both these children were afraid of doors being closed, especially at night, therefore we had to leave them open, and lights were kept on throughout. They were constantly coming down stairs, long after bedtime, to check whether or not Gordon and I were still there. They were concerned we may 'go to the pub for a night out' and leave them alone in the house. Play, would be generally a recreation of life at home, and with a toy 'phone, Anna would 'call the coppers' which would transfix Paula to the spot with terror. When out and about, I would frequently turn around to find Paula in a stranger's arms; she would extend them upwards for anyone to pick her up. If Anna spotted a little old lady, with grey curly hair she would grasp her firmly around the knees, as this was the height she could reach, and say "Ahh!" with her head resting on their legs – and wouldn't release them until we had apologised quite profusely and literally prised her off! This I feel was borne out of unavoidably being present at my mother's death. Paula's conversation appeared to be solely in the form of questions, and seconds later could not remember what was asked of her. Anna would kick off most mornings when we finally arrived at school, and the class teacher would take her into a room, away from the other children and instruct me to leave so that they could deal with her. This type of behaviour usually preceded a contact visit with either mummy or daddy, who would usually not turn up anyway, causing further distress and rejection. The school staff were marvellous, but sadly the social worker's answer to all this was 'exclude her.' Mrs. G. would not hear of this, nor would we, and

together we fought this decision. Why should a
child be deprived of education and suffer due to
the aftermath of the traumas she had been put
through.

The decision was eventually made, to bring in a
child psychologist. I took Anna to school that
day to meet him. he was a very well built, kind
mannered black gentleman, but as he was very
calmly talking to Anna, she suddenly rose to her
feet and swiped all the books from the
bookshelves, pulled over the bookcase, ripped
pictures from the walls and literally wrecked the
classroom in seconds. We didn't have another
visit.

Bedtimes still continued to be a nightmare.
Anna would scream even when she had been
given the privilege of staying up later at
weekend. This made me start to wonder what
could have happened at bedtime, or in the
bedroom at home to make her so upset. She
would lay on the top bunk and repeatedly bang
her head on the multi-coloured metal bars of the
bed frame, to which I eventually fastened a
pillow, for fear she would split open her head
like a melon, as she bashed it so hard. Upon
discussion Anna would truly believe it was her
fault that they were taken away from their
mummy. This, I have come to realise, is a great
misconception on the part of many children
taken into care.

A typical day for me, I think looking back must have been quite different from anyone else I knew at the time, here's how it went. Monday to Friday, I would rise about 7.45 a.m. and wake up Anna and Paula. Gordon was usually at work by this time, so I knew I faced each day's battles alone. I would make the children's breakfast, which they would eat without question or fuss, it was the scene that followed which was my first task of the day. I would have laid out their clothes for them the night before, after bath time, so that it was quicker and easier for them the next morning, but they would often refuse to dress, or brush their teeth etc., all the time deliberately winding me up, and with my lack of experience, I fell so readily into their pre-meditated trap. I was tired and stressed and had a tight schedule which made me more deflated, but I knew I had to keep going, I knew I had to do whatever I could to keep these children within the family. Adam had been adopted, this was unheard of in my world, I couldn't let it happen again. First task then was to take Anna to school and endure the daily 'kick-off,' then I would take Paula to nursery which wasn't too bad, as she enjoyed this and was usually eager to go. I would then return home, with one and a half hours to do some housework, washing and prepare for work. I would collect Paula at 11.30 a.m, take her over to Angeline's for the afternoon, and arrive at work at 12 noon. After a gruelling day of drug addicts and sick people, I would leave

work about six or seven p.m. drive to
Angeline's pick up the girls, *and* Xara, take
them home, cook their tea, bath them, story, bed
screaming, arguing, Gordon home
approximately 8.30 p.m. – total exhaustion! Of
course there were also case conferences, and
reviews to attend which had to be fitted in
somewhere. This was the daily and weekly
grind, but weekends were even worse. After a
week of this, plus six or seven hours a day of
sick and agitated patients and bad-tempered
doctors, I couldn't even use the weekend to
recoup my energy, as I would have Anna and
Paula, 24/7. Poor Angeline, she had also gone
suddenly from nought to three children within a
matter of weeks, but coped reasonably well
under the circumstances.

These two little girls were so badly damaged, in
many ways. As time trudged on and they began
to trust us, and to see that we carried through on
promises and wanted nothing but good
behaviour in return, further revelations
unfolded. Saturday mornings were *slightly*
more relaxed now, we all knew that there would
be no rushing around and getting to school. The
girls would come downstairs whenever they
were hungry and have their breakfast. When
finished they would then ask me if they could
'talk about mummy.' I would invite them to
come and sit beside me on the sofa and have a
hug, which surprisingly they readily did, and
then the story unfolded. They would spend an

hour or two describing to me the things they had witnessed, and I fear, been involved in, events which I *cannot* write about in this book! They would also proceed to physically demonstrate together in front of me to obviously give me a clearer understanding of what they were saying. I found this so difficult but tried hard to keep my composure, and to keep silent so as not to stop them or shut them up. This emotional and physical horror obviously *needed* to come out. This became a regular Saturday a.m occurrence, these were events which no three or five year old could make up, these things must have been *experienced*, and although no-one had mentioned writing daily logs to me, I felt instinctively I had to record this somehow, I had already made notes of behaviours and delays in development, purely for my own benefit in order to observe when problems had been rectified, and so, as soon as they had got it off their chests, and toddled off to play, out would come my shorthand spiral notebook and I would jot down all their comments and demonstrations. I was not kept informed of what was happening with regard to the girls, nor was I asked for anything, or instructed to *do* anything. I truly believe I was looked upon as purely a relative who had stepped in, but it just seemed logical to me that when things were written down, a pattern would usually emerge, and that was all I was doing.

However, I decided that some action was called for. Matters had to improve if we were going to survive this, I would need to be *resilient*, I would need to be *resistant* to Dana's onslaughts, which still continued throughout, and most of all I needed to be *unyielding*! Once I had made these resolutions, I had to also find practical ways of changing the children's behaviour. I must no longer put up with being attacked and throttled from behind when I was driving, it was downright dangerous. No! It had to stop. We had a book which travelled from home to school every day, carrying vital information regarding Anna's behaviour, we would now work as a better team and give stickers for positive behaviour, a Star Chart was my next creation. Together with the girls, we created a beautiful chart. We marked out the days of the week, and at the end of the lines we cut out pictures from catalogues and magazines of toys they wanted, and each day, if they could try to modify certain behaviours, a coloured sticky star would be attached to that day's slot. When they had achieved a full row of stars, they would receive whatever was on their picture. This worked wonderfully; Anna particularly responded to this and enjoyed her reward at the end. School began to see an improvement in her behaviour. Paula had a stuffed spotty doll called 'Bill' and Bill would take the blame for many an accident. Of course, behaviour didn't change over night, and there were still times when it was extreme, and therefore more extreme measures were called for. So I introduced, rightly or wrongly, a 'time out' step. This was one particular 'stair' which I selected, it was half way up and half way down. In other words right in the middle of the staircase with nothing to look at but the walls on either side. Two or three minutes on here was usually enough, although Anna began to challenge this and started to slide down each stair declaring she was not going to stay. I soon realised that the secret to success was in keeping one step ahead, so to speak. I therefore told her that every time she moved from the 'time out' step, another minute would be added! I'll give her ten out of ten for tenacity though, for we did get up to ten minutes before she realised that *she* was the one suffering for her disobedience.

The new boundaries were working well, most of the time, but these children still had fears firmly attached due to the trauma of their early life. Having been passed, that fateful night, through a broken window, left them terrified of the slightest crack in *any* window. They were terrified someone was going to smash our windows, only time would help with that one. They also had the terrors whenever they saw anyone in uniform. I overcame this by taking them to the local shopping mall, and introducing them to one of the security guards called Jim. Week after week, when shopping we would stop and have a brief chat with Jim, who was willing to engage in the 'game.' However, I did of course need to explain that they only spoke to *anyone* when with an adult they knew.

Now we have had many pets over the years, rabbits, gerbils, goldfish etc., and several cats and dogs. There was Mitzy a grey tabby who was flattened by the milkman's cart, there was Whiskas who disappeared. Then came Dingle who was a blue point Siamese cat whose pedigree name was Marowden Changroc Ramases the 3rd, but it took much too long to call that name up the garden path and so she somehow ended up with Dingle. Then came Sapphire Ming, a beautiful Siamese Seal point Queen, who was unceremoniously christened 'Pussmog.' We then decided to have our first dog, a Yorkshire terrier called Samson, who lived a good ten years followed by Scampi, another Yorkshire terrier. Ultimately, after Scampi's demise we decided to call it a day where pets were concerned. It was just too painful when they died. However, this didn't last long as we missed the scurrying of little paws around the place and the wet noses that greeted us on our return from anywhere. Therefore at the time Anna and Paula were with us we had two dogs, Oscar a white poodle and Bruno, a blonde Cairn terrier. Both these animals loved children and were as soft as putty. We were driving to visit Dora, and Anna and Paula were sitting in the back of the car, when I heard very strange noises and asked them what it was. As I looked in my rear view mirror I could see only two little angel faces with blonde hair and blue eyes bearing huge smiles, replying "Nothing!" As the noise continued I stopped at a red light, pulled on the handbrake and turned round to explore the source of this queer noise, to find Oscar sitting bolt upright, facing front on Anna's lap, eyes bulging and croaking as Anna twisted her fingers round and round his collar. He was literally being choked to death and he was almost silently allowing her to continue! Poor Oscar, he was, and still is, just *too* obliging.

Behaviour however, was definitely improving, although there were occasions when we despaired. We bought the girls dolls and prams, amongst other things, all little girls like a doll and pram, but in order to reach the rear garden, they had to go through the garage, where their prams were kept, a few basic tools and at one side Gordon's pride and joy, his latest motorbike, a classic Moto Guzzi Nevada. I had taken every precaution to ensure what I considered dangerous articles were removed from reach as much as possible and informed them *very* strongly that they must touch nothing other than their prams. Our house is built on three levels and as they played in the garden, I would occasionally pop my head out of the bedroom window, three floors up if I was upstairs, to check that they were o.k. I was cleaning the bathroom when I heard it, the loud clanging noise of metal on metal. After the second time of hearing this, I decided I should check it out. After wearily struggling down two flights of stairs, through the garage to the garden, I enquired what the noise had been, as they strutted about with their handbags, wearing my high heels, and carrying toy 'phones, calling the 'coppers' and pushing their prams. Their innocent little upturned faces informed me that they had no idea what I was talking about, but as I turned to continued scrubbing the bathroom, I noticed that their little prams were not conveying their dollies, no, they contained screwdrivers, chisels, files and hammers. I was horrified at the danger of these tools, and would not have forgiven myself had they been hurt, despite the fact that they had raided Gordon's tool box. I chastised them for touching what was not theirs, explained the danger and moved the toolbox elsewhere. Yet another lesson I have learned, never trust sweet innocent 'angelic' faces! It was about a week later however, when Gordon decided to give his pride and joy a bit of a polish, that he discovered exactly what the clanging of metal upon metal had achieved. The chrome mudguards on his motorbike had been filed. The shiny tank had been hammered and chiselled, he was in total disbelief!

There was a time when Paula spat on all the mirrors and rubbed it in, and the morning she decided she was not getting dressed for nursery. I'd had enough that day, and pointed to the clock in order for her to understand the situation fully. I told her that when the big hand was on nine, we would be leaving – and whatever she was wearing is what she would be going in. Defiant to the end, she watched the hands of the clock slowly turn, and I watched her stay cross-legged, unmoving. Therefore I had to be equally if not more resolved than she, remember, one step ahead at all times, I picked up her shoes from the hallway, I then picked up Paula, who was by now spitting on everything and everyone in sight, but mainly me, full back-of-the-throat type projectile saliva, everywhere, and bundled her under one arm. I offered her her shoes as we stepped through the front door, but she flung them into the rose bushes. As I fastened Anna and Paula into their seatbelts, I was still being bombarded with saliva, as she made a very concerted effort to secrete the maximum with each shot. As we arrived at nursery, I carried her in, still unceremoniously under my arm and plonked her by the sand pit, all the while the nursery teacher staring open-mouthed. With dishevelled hair, and covered in 'spit,' I adjusted my jacket and calmly informed the teacher that Paula would be unable to play out at play time as she wanted to stay in her P.J's and had thrown her shoes away, then promptly left. What a wicked witch am I? How I now cringe at my actions and wouldn't dream of doing such a thing nowadays, though I have to tell you that Paula never dallied in the mornings again, we now had an unspoken understanding of one another.

It was hardly surprising that their behaviour was such, they were both so confused. Contact was an impossible minefield, as Dana would bring along half the street to witness her 'dreadful' situation, and would ague with everything the social workers said in front of her devoted audience. She told them strongly that she *should* be able to smack her own children as often as she liked. Damien demanded that he have contact of his own, but then didn't turn up, more rejection for these little mites. The results were devastating, Paula would turn to any stranger, would pull her lip constantly. Anna was always 'touching' herself, would be aggressive with teachers at school or bite the headmistress. Much therapy was needed.

Christmas was almost upon us, and I was going to make sure these children experienced what it was all about. It wasn't about mum and dad getting plastered out of their skulls, and the kids being sent to bed, it was a time to be together, for fun and toys and being happy. We hadn't celebrated Christmas for years, being Jehovah's Witnesses, so I was a little out of practice but in between everything else I did my best. I bought toys, sweets, decorations, even a Christmas tree and all the trimmings for a good Christmas dinner. I took Anna and Paula to visit Santa at the shopping mall and had their photos taken, something I had noticed they were not too comfortable with, it was almost as though they had a fear, as if something about having pictures taken was unpleasant. I wondered what, and my imagination was beginning to run away with me.

However, Christmas Eve I told the children they must be in bed early so that Santa could deliver their toys. They were so excited, as I had created anticipation in their little heads. Dora had made quite an effort, and had bought several black sacks full of presents, all neatly wrapped for them. At 9.30 p.m. Dana rang to ask if she could speak to the children and wish them happy Christmas. I told her they were by now in bed, but that she could ring them tomorrow, Christmas day. She had sent nothing for them, but now, at 9.30 p.m. on Christmas Eve she was asking me to go out and buy them something, from *her*, and she would give me a fiver. I think you may imagine my reaction, yes, I told her where to shove it! She rapidly accused me of not understanding, and that I had plenty of money. I told her that one item bought from the 'pound shop' given to them, by her, would have meant the world to them. She didn't seem to realise that our money paid the bills, fed and clothed her children and met their needs. I was a relative so the social services paid a pittance once more.

Christmas came and went, Anna and Paula were ecstatic with the new gifts and toys they now had, and life returned to its hectic 'normality.' I was also trying desperately to give any time I could to Xara and Angeline, looking after Xara when I wasn't working so that Angeline could continue at college, also whenever Gordon was available to baby sit, I would be used as a 'model' for Angeline to practice on, then Angeline would baby sit whilst I attended meetings with Gordon for a new venture he had begun, and so between us we juggled our lives and cared for each other. Dora by now was complaining that she didn't see her grandchildren, and although spare time was no-existent, I did feel sorry for Dora, she had done nothing wrong, and yet she had six grandchildren which she hardly saw, one was adopted possibly never to be seen again. Therefore, Angeline came to the rescue and offered her home as a venue once a week for Dora to visit the children whilst she had them after school, yet another commitment all in the name of family loyalty. Dana on the other hand was committed to making life as hellish as she could, for everybody. She even resorted to frightening threats, and on return from a shopping trip one afternoon, Angeline switched on her answer machine to pick up her messages, only to hear Dana's cider induced drawl, telling her to beware when she got into her car, her brakes may not work, and to 'keep and eye on her little black bastard, her little liquorice allsort' referring to Xara, 'or she may have an accident.' How silly of Dana, she was usually much more cunning and clever than this, but this time she had made a grave error, this time she had left us her evidence in this recorded message. I am 'Superbitch' and she was attacking my daughter, and my beautiful grandchild. Of course I took this evidence to the police, and she was given a verbal caution. Not much of a consequence I know, but being one who likes to turn the negatives into positives, I thought about my 'sweet' poem about Xara, and thought *yes*! What an interesting allegory, she *is* a delicious little liquorice allsort, and once more turned Dana's efforts inside out and upside down. Naturally she didn't give up or desist, she would have solicitor's letters sent to us, accusing Gordon and I of teaching the children to swear, smacking them and that they were unhappy etc. I suppose the solicitors were clever enough to realise they could make money, despite the futile stupidity of it all.

Following one 'normal' hectic day, school, nursery, Angeline's work, Angeline's, home, bath, tea etc., I hurried to change in order to attend college once more as Angeline's model. Gordon walked in the door from work, the girls were playing up, I walked out and set off in my car for college. I was panicking slightly, trying not to be late, when I stupidly took a wrong turn. Normally in this sort of situation I would curse to myself then turn around and find my way back, but this night something strange happened. It is a vague recollection, but I suddenly couldn't see too well, and bright lights were coming towards me, and coloured lights were flashing before my eyes, then I remember very little until I came to, in the fog, on the moors! I later discovered that the bright lights were car head lights, as I was going the wrong way around a roundabout in town. The coloured lights, were the traffic lights, the sequence of which had meant nothing to me. When I had recovered, in a ditch on the moors, it later occurred to me that I perhaps subconsciously was heading for 'home,' for Derbyshire.

This was horrendous. It now hit me also that I was not the superwoman I had tried to be, I was fragile, flawed, human, but more to the point I realised I was very overstretched, stressed and worn out. My colleagues at work had expressed a concern about my usually smart appearance not being what it once was, but I couldn't see it, perhaps didn't want to, but one thing I did know, was that I had a duty to myself as well as everyone else around me and I *had* to pull myself together. If I didn't look after myself then how could I care for others?

Worse was yet to come however. Due to these disclosures of abuse from Anna and Paula, the case had to go to court, and I was asked to do, what in my opinion, was the most damaging thing I have ever had to do in my life. Yet little did I know at the time, I would have to do it yet again in the future. I was asked to take two very young children for an intimate forensic examination at the hospital. This was a nightmare! To me it felt like they were being abused all over again. It was not conclusive *who* had abused them or where, and so quite useless really, so why put them through such a horrific ordeal. Anna in particular never forgot it, and I can't help feeling that, as it was not dealt with at the time, for these children were offered no further counselling or therapy of any kind in order to help them come to terms with all that had happened to them, it will come back and haunt them in the future when they are much older. One thing I did know which would never be proved, was that Dana played some part in this somewhere. She had a propensity for evil, and would destroy a lie detector if she was ever asked to challenge one; no machine would be able to cope with her volume of lies.

Strange how the word 'evil' spelt backwards gives us the word 'live', and yet Dana was incapable of understanding the phrase, live and let live.

I have spoken much about 'Angels,' those with wings, those with horns, and sometimes it's so very hard to differentiate between the two, as they can be so deceptive you see, and falsehood breeds distrust. However, there is a place for the horned ones, where they all could gather, and there's plenty of space left for those who qualify. Hell, Is not full, yet!

Chapter Twenty

Fragmentation

It was another day in this fitful existence, but there were occasionally little chinks of light, through the gloomy window of my mind, and on this particular day my emotional sun was shining. Angeline had passed her exams and received her diploma; she was now a fully qualified Nail Technician and Manicurist. I was so proud of her not only for her efforts in this regard, but also for this achievement despite the complications we were all trying to overcome. This euphoria was, however short lived, for the next 'phone call that came in as I sat, once more at my desk, was to result in my emotional sunshine becoming a total eclipse and I was plunged once more into a lonely darkness. It was the social worker on the other end of the line, and as soon as I heard her voice I instinctively knew that another shovel full of earth was about to be flung out of this ever gaping deep hole our family was sinking into. I was not wrong, they had once more been to court, unknown to me, and it had been decided that these two little girls, part of my family, flesh and blood, were going to be adopted. I had failed! My dreams or nightmares as they had now become, of them returning to their mummy were not going to be realised. My brain was like a roller coaster, up and down with good thoughts, bad thoughts. Was it good that they were not to return to this monster that Dana had become, or not? After all she *was* their mother. They would leave the bosom of the family and never return, would we ever see them again once they were gone? How could I tell them and what would be their reaction, *how* were they going to deal with this. As for me, I had grown to love them, despite their problems, how would I deal with it?

In the days and weeks that followed there was much to be done, and done under a heavy black cloud. This may sound strange, but this situation felt like yet another bereavement, like a death sentence, waiting for the fateful day. Not only this, but *I* felt like the executioner, I was the one who was instrumental in their removal from 'home,' I had been their confidant, privy to their innermost dark secrets, I was the 'Witch' who took them to the hospital to be examined and now, I was asked to be the one to tell them that they were to see mummy for the *last time*!

All these months I had hoped their suffering would be eased but this felt like the harshest punishment for them and me. I would *not* miss the screaming and shouting, being throttled and sworn at, nor would Oscar I'm sure, but I would miss the big blue eyes, the smiling faces when they were happy and their endless chatter. However I had to be realistic, of course they could not return to Dana, for their degraded little lives to continue, they deserved the chance of a better life. Gordon and I *were* asked, and for a fleeting moment did consider whether or not we could keep them long-term, but there was still the big Bluebottle in the proverbial ointment – Dana! Just as she had continued her onslaughts with me, I knew she would certainly not leave us, or them alone, their lives would continue to be hell from a distance, also how much longer could I continue with the daily stresses of their behaviour, and work too! It wouldn't have been fair, I had to let them go, I also had to spare a thought for poor Dora, for she was to lose yet again, more of her grandchildren. Being now, a grandmother myself, I know how precious these little people are to us, they are a legacy to be cherished by us, but poor Dora was denied this unique endowment. I am sure that those of you who are grandparents will understand a little of how we were feeling, just imagine this happening to your own grandchild.

On the subject of losing once more even our sleep was disturbed by yet another 'phone call. It was from the nursing home that Gordon's mother now lived in, quite happily. As Gordon got out of bed and fumbled for his clothes and shoes he hurriedly relayed the message that his mother had taken a turn for the worst and they wanted him to go there immediately. I so much wanted to go with him, and help as he had done with me. *But*, Anna and Paula were fast asleep in the next room, and it was not a situation which they should be part of. Therefore I had to stay. When Gordon returned that night, he calmly told me that his mother was dead! She had actually been dead for some time when he arrived at the home, but perhaps they didn't quite know how to tell him on the 'phone. Little did they know that Gordon had worked in a mortuary and knew the signs of rigor mortis. So once again we went through the whole grieving process, yet carried on caring for the children.

There was much to do in the following weeks, lots of preparation was needed before these children were to go anywhere. There seemed to be endless case conferences, reviews etc., in order to make decisions. One decision which gave me hope and spurred me on was that the court had decided that due to our positive influence and input, Gordon, Angeline, Dan and I were granted continued contact with the girls, I was elated. This not only selfishly meant that we would still see them occasionally, but also more importantly that they would grow up knowing *some* of their birth family cared a great deal for them, that they were not just abandoned and that they had been loved. The first task was to tell the girls of their impending move, to find an explanation as to why, and that it would be forever! Little did I know in my naivety that this should have been the job of the social worker, but strangely no-one enlightened me. However, I sat them down one evening, one either side of me on the sofa and gave them a hug. I cannot now remember the words I chose to inform them of their fate/future, whatever it would be, but I *do* remember their reaction. They screamed, they howled, they banged their heads and hid behind the furniture, then cried and sobbed late into the evening. How strange it is, that despite the cruelty and neglect they had suffered, the invisible bond between mother and child is so strong that even being torn from this abusive life was unbearable for them – I wondered if Dana felt the same, I hoped so!

A final contact was arranged for them to see Dana. It must have felt like the condemned man's last meal for these little mites, and yet in the weeks that followed I was amazed at how much calmer they had become, almost as though a burden had been lifted. I don't profess to understand the psychology of it all at this point but I think the pressure of enduring the difficult contacts had been lifted and they felt relieved in some way, although I wondered whether they truly understood what lay ahead.

When the trauma had settled and work began, to locate suitable adoptive parents, I was asked to write a profile on each child, along with a photograph to be placed in the adoption magazine. It was awful, like placing an ad' for 'puppies for sale,' but I decided I had to be truthful, *these* 'puppies' could bite! This may sound as though I was hoping to delay the inevitable, but not at all, I simply wanted to be sure that whoever took them was completely prepared for what they may have to deal with, perhaps way into the future. I wrote the profiles as fairly, factually and positively as I could and offered my favourite photo of the two of them together, on the promise that it would be returned to me, it never was.

These two little girls were so beautiful and angelic in their picture that it wasn't long before prospective adopters began making enquiries. Our task was then to welcome them into our home to discuss Anna and Paula. Once more we tried to be diplomatic, but truthful. The first through our front door were a lovely young couple, he a solicitor and she a manager in education. We were informed that they lived in a large house and the girls would want for nothing. This was confirmed when they arrived in their beautiful Mercedes. They were indeed a lovely young couple and asked many questions regarding the girl's behaviour, habits and especially education. The most important question being, did I think they would ever catch up to an acceptable level academically? In all honesty my answer was that I had no idea. Who was I to anticipate whether the traumas in their lives would allow for normality? After they left, I reflected on how I could envisage their lives together. I could imagine this lovely upper class pair, inviting guests to dinner to meet their newly acquired offspring, only for them to be entertained by Paula telling Anna 'not to pick her nose and eat it!' As nice as they were, I felt it would be a disaster and was greatly relieved when they declined.

However, eventually someone read my files and took them at face value. She apparently said 'they sound like something out of the Exorcist.' This felt much more positive, a more down to earth approach. She was single, her name was Margaret and she shared a house with her cousin Mary. Margaret appeared to be quite a serious person and did not present herself to us at least, as the jovial sort, although very capable and determined, Mary had been widowed and also lost a daughter and was subsequently and understandably quite compassionate, I thought. They visited us on several occasions to spend time with the girls to get to know them. Unfortunately, I had been preparing them for moving in with a 'new' mummy and daddy. I now had to modify this to a new mummy only. However, they appeared to like her and Mary, and so the process began. I put together a 'Life Story Book' for them, this is something we do for foster children when moving on, it helps to fill the gaps, to complete the jigsaw if you like, of their lives. When all the little pieces fit, the picture is then complete. However, I wrote pages of information regarding their birth, life and family, quaint little sayings and phrases they had. I was in a better position than most to do this, being part of their family, I had information no social workers could ever have. They each insisted on leaving a toy here, 'for when they visit' I still have them to this day, waiting for their return. I also saved their favourite T shirts as mementos. Anna's is a blue one with a printed portrait of the Spice Girls across the front, Paula loved 'Dennis be Dennis' (Dennis the Menace) and hers is black with the mischievous monster emblazoned in full Technicolor down the front. We made use of our twenty foot long lounge and spread a roll of old wallpaper, plain side up from on end to the other on the floor. We drew a picture of our house at one end, complete with Oscar and Bruno in the garden, and their 'forever' house at the other end, because they would be a long way apart, but adjoining the two, was the yellow brick road, along which we would travel when we visited. We rolled it up and tied it with ribbon to keep it safe.

We chose a day to take them all the way to their new home, we checked out their bedroom, the garden and where the school was, they loved it and I felt more positive about their future. We then had another visit to deliver the enormous amount of toys, books and clothes that they had accumulated in the two years they had spent with us. The bicycles, prams and dolls, little Hoovers, and ironing boards, the seesaw, the list was endless and the vehicle was full.

The day finally arrived for Margaret and Mary to collect Anna and Paula to take them to their new home, forever. It was so swift, as they came to the door, loaded up the car and were gone in the blink of a very tear –filled eye. I tried so hard to be positive and happy for them but failed yet again as I sobbed when the car drove away, and their little tear-stained faces grew ever smaller into the distance. I strolled back into the house, and once again experienced the loudest noise *ever*! That of silence. The chatter was just an echo, and their beautiful little faces were a blur.

I was so pleased I had taken the day off work as I would not have functioned well. I madly put my *all* into rearranging the house, stripping off their animal printed duvet covers, dismantling the multi-coloured bunks and removing the pillow I had strapped to it to prevent Anna from cracking her head when she bashed it repeatedly in anger and frustration. I felt an overwhelming need to wipe out anything that even reminded me that they had been here, almost as though it would remove the pain, both emotional and physical, but it didn't.

I had done this! I was the devil's advocate who had reported the abuse, which in turn led to their being removed from home, which then ultimately led to them being removed permanently from within our's and their own family. Then, this was my irrational way of thinking in my grief, for this was yet *another* bereavement, my self-punishment for my sins, and yet, would I really have wanted them to return to such abuse and neglect? Of course this was the case with the 'first three', Andre, Leah and Adam, and here we were with the 'three more' that Dana so readily had, and history was well and truly repeating itself. I eventually felt that perhaps rather than their lives being disrupted further, they would now actually be spared many more years of abuse, although I still fear for their emotional future, as many of these issues were not resolved and may well rear their ugly heads many years from now. Of course we mustn't forget poor helpless little Lucas, for he had been fostered, and the great news was that despite all his difficulties, his wonderful foster carers had decided to adopt him too.

We had prepared Anna and Paula extremely well for their move to their new adoptive family and although sad, they had left with a positive outlook. I hoped that they were settling, but had little information to begin with. I couldn't just forget them, they had not only dominated two years of our lives in our home, they were also part of my family and meant a great deal to me.

Following their move, I heard nothing from anyone, not the social worker, the department of social services in general, no thanks for helping them out of an impossible situation, no mention of whether *I* may need any help to get over my loss, nothing.

However, we gave them time to settle but not enough for them to feel they had been forgotten and eventually, several months later, started negotiations with Margaret, to pay them a visit, but although we knew where they lived, we *had* moved them in after all, we felt the first visit should be on neutral ground, so that Anna and Paula would not feel under threat or wonder if they were moving again. I had assured them that it was their 'forever' house and they would only come back here (as they kept asking) maybe in the future, to visit. We arranged to meet at a stately home for the afternoon. It had been almost a year since they left us and I wondered with great anticipation what they would look like and how they might have grown. We had bought them gifts each and as Gordon and I, Angeline and Dan, waited we saw the vehicle pull into the car park. Anna ran straight into my arms as I picked her up and swung her around. Paula seemed much more withdrawn, and reluctant, as always, and slightly confused. However, we had a lovely day and were sad to see them go once more. But felt much more hopeful for the future and had some lovely memories and photos to keep me going until the next visit. In the meantime I wrote to them just on Birthdays and Christmas and sent cards. Another year went by and I had contacted Margaret to arrange a visit. I didn't feel that two visits in two years were excessive and I *had* told the girls we would always love them and always think of them. The visit was arranged for a day or two before we were to fly to the Greek Islands for a holiday, and unfortunately it was right in the middle of the fuel crisis. We therefore had to evaluate our fuel allowance, could we travel all the way to see Anna and Paula *and* have enough fuel for the airport the same week? If not I knew which was most important to me and it was not the holiday. We did make it to see them at home as before, they were literally all over us. They cuddled us, they played with us and Anna wanted desperately to look at my car. I assured her it was the same old car, but she also wanted to know *when* they could come and see Bruno and Oscar, I told her, one day perhaps, but not yet. Margaret, I could sense was understandably not happy with their obvious display of affection towards us, but when we were ready to leave, as Gordon put the key in the car door, Anna dragged it open, scrambled into the back seat and refused to come out. We assured her that everything was fine, we would visit again sometime, and most of all we still loved them both. Eventually, she emerged reluctantly; we said our goodbyes and were on our way home.

It was about a week or so later that I received the letter from Margaret. I opened it with eager anticipation that it would have more news of the girls and how much they appeared to enjoy our visit, but alas it was quite the opposite. Margaret was telling us in no uncertain terms that Anna and Paula were *her* daughters now and *her* daughters did not wish to see us anymore, as they were afraid they may have to come back and live with us! There was only one way to interpret the content of this letter as I felt and saw it at the time – sour grapes! I could fully understand her fear and possible envy at their display of affection, she must have felt somewhat insecure in her new role, but she and I knew she had nothing to fear. I had prepared them exceptionally well for their move, and I felt that they had experienced only nostalgia which in my mind was inevitable and understandable, and perhaps now, two years on a visit to see Bruno and Oscar may have been beneficial and put their minds at rest. However Margaret also instructed us to communicate *only* via social services letterbox system.

This is a system set up by the social services, for fostered and adopted children, when there is no face to face contact with family for whatever reason. The letters or cards are sent to a central address at the social services department, read and checked before forwarding on to the recipient. This I felt was quite unnecessary in this case, as we knew their address and could have written directly to Margaret to read and to pass on. It seems that even once a year was too much of a threat for Margaret. Nonetheless neither our welfare not hers were paramount here, only that of the children was of the utmost importance. I am unsure, but in view of the court's recommendation, we could possibly have made a fuss, and I could have maybe been granted a continuance of the occasional rare visit. The downside to this course of action was, that I didn't know for sure what effect this may have had of the girls, and there would therefore be no winners. I felt it best in the long run for all, to let sleeping dogs lie. However, this was also not without its flaws, Anna and Paula would now believe that we had disappeared, not kept our word, that we had also not considered them worthy or lovable enough to continue our efforts to see them. If only they knew how heartbreaking it all was. I did reply to Margaret's letter and politely expressed my fears of how the girls may feel in the future if they ever discovered that they had been denied our visits. Also I was honest in pointing out to her that they may be curious, remember us, and search for us one day, maybe years from now.

I will *never* give up on them, never stop thinking about them, they are never out of my thoughts. I have placed their photos in the best room ever, in the house – the toilet! I visit several times a day and as I sit there, alone, I look at their pictures and think of the happy times we had, and the sad ones too. It's sometimes the only room in the whole house that I can retreat to, purely on my own, and reflect. However, I have begun a journal, of life within our family, good and bad, so that one day, if they should ever come searching for us I can hand it over to them and it will hopefully serve two purposes. One, to fill in all the pieces of their 'missing' years like a completed jigsaw, and two, they will hopefully realise that they were and still are loved, and important people to us. Once each year I write to them and send photos and a cheque. I *never* forget, and each time I receive confirmation that they have been received and forwarded, I keep all such letters, as this will prove my determination to keep their memory alive, in the hopefully unlikely event that my correspondence was not passed on to them. On a couple of occasions nothing was received in return, but I pursued this and fortunately Mary, Margaret's cousin *is* a compassionate woman and I feel she understands how important it is for all concerned, and very kindly responds to my yearly letters with a note and a few pictures. It's wonderful, but at the same time scary to see the changes in them year after year. Thank you, Mary!

As I reflect now, once more on the day they left, it was as though they had died. I felt like I was in mourning and cried at the slightest thing, though it was worse because I knew they were out there, and wondered how they were. I think this would have been normal for anyone parting with a long-term foster child, but these two were also part of *my* family, I had cared about them from birth. I wondered if mothers felt like this when they had been responsible for similar preceding events, though it was within their power to put it right- yet didn't. Just like Dana.

However, the house felt empty, how I loved looking after Xara as her gurglings and laughter made the house come alive again. At least I could now give her all my undivided attention. I cared for her almost daily after work, so that Angeline could pursue her career, and savoured every second. I felt it strange whenever I met grandparents who resented having their grandchildren and couldn't wait to give them back, but Xara was such a delightful child from day one. She was very engaging and cheery and filled my heart with love, which left less space for my grief. There were times when we enjoyed the peace and quiet, getting on with our lives, and taking holidays with friends. We had bought a Timeshare apartment in a beautiful fifteenth century Manor House near Lancaster. Not only were we able to enjoy wonderful exchange holidays abroad, but we could also use our time at the Manor House on occasional weekends. It was superb five star accommodation and was very relaxing. We would sometimes take friends or Dan and Angeline. Xara's first holiday abroad was in a beautiful location in Spain, although her first ever passport didn't arrive on time and she and daddy had to join us for the second week only once sorted. It could only happen to us. At least *our* little section of the family was not fragmenting as the rest had done, there were bits of us all over the place. Let's see, Andre and Leah were struggling on with Dad and Ronda, all the while growing up and continuing to be confused by Dana's relentless barrage. Adam was goodness knows where, Anna and Paula were out of sight, but not out of mind, and Lucas was now to be finally adopted by his foster carers. All six of them appeared to be stable, but I had not yet been allowed to sterilise Dana with a rusty knife and no anaesthetic, and true to form she was now expecting baby number seven, but this time the daddy was Damien's brother, Jason. *WHEN* was this going to end? I felt as though I was on a roundabout.

Yet more fragmentation was around the corner. Leah was not settling well with her dad and Ronda. She was, as I had foreseen when she was a baby, quite wilful and as she moved into her teenage years was feeling her feet and stamping them firmly. She and Pete did not see eye to eye, therefore it wasn't long before Pete could take no more and asked Leah to leave. Naturally she gravitated toward Dana, she was her mother after all, and moved in with her. This of course was a recipe for disaster. Dana wanted benefit payments for her and control, naturally. Control she took, for just as Leah was made spuriously to feel as though she was welcome, and therefore relaxed, Dana woke her in the middle of the night and threw her out into the street. Leah was fourteen years old. Inevitably she was then taken in by Dora, who had taken pity on her granddaughter, but couldn't control her. Of course I was not going to be allowed to escape this trauma as Dora would ring me every night on my return from work whining about Leah's behaviour and her abusive lack of respect. Dora hadn't a clue how to control Leah, but in all fairness, respect is a mutual negotiation and Dora hardly spoke with due respect either. There came a time inevitably when Dora also could take no more and asked Leah to leave. Dad, mum, grandma, none had given thought as to where Leah would go or what support she would have. Obviously, we couldn't allow this situation to continued and once more invited Leah to stay a while with us, just as she had wanted to years before.

We had almost two years of peace and quiet and life had slipped back once again to the norm with the added benefit of Xara's presence. Now it was about to 'hot up' again. Leah had not been attending school; she was defiant and running wild. This would need careful handling. We could hardly use a 'time out' step for a fourteen year old.

I decided that giving Leah what she was lacking most in her life was worth a try – respect! I sat and talked to her about her future, asked her what plans she had. Between us, we drew up a written agreement, a contract. She would wash up the dishes once a day, after our evening meal, and keep her room tidy, and I would cook for her, clean her room etc., in return. I also negotiated an agreement on school. If she attended every day I would give her reasonable pocket money at the end of the week. I created a Star Chart, as I would have done for a toddler, but it actually worked with Leah too. For each day that she respected others and did her chores, she was given a star for which money was saved for her for special occasions. On the whole it all worked quite well. We spoke to her politely and she in return to us. Showing an interest in her education was all that was required to encourage her to attend school, most of the time.

Leah made great progress, with encouragement. We knew of course, that she was smoking, though she denied this, but the odour on her clothes when she came home gave the game away. I would give her money each day for school lunch, but discovered that she was not eating, yet had money each day for cigarettes. Always being one step ahead, meant great effort had to be put into thinking of ways to achieve this. Therefore I would give her a cheque every Monday morning, to cover the whole week's lunches, she then had no choice but to eat and not smoke. Showing so much interest in her education also meant attending school parent's evenings, an event which had never been experienced by Leah, with her mum. Also liaison with the school's learning mentor was paramount, as young people like Leah, often get in scrapes at school and need someone to talk to. Having decent 'cool' clothing to wear is very important also in order to be accepted by one's peers, rather than stuff from the charity shop, not that there's anything wrong with this if by choice, but teenagers should experience being bought and wearing the latest trend now and then, and there's nothing quite so therapeutic as unwrapping, and removing the price tag from that brand new pair of jeans. I also began to negotiate some communication with dad and Ronda, as they had once more reached a stale mate and nothing was happening between them and Leah.

Life was in danger of becoming very difficult once again, as it had done with Anna and Paula. There were endless arrangements to be made, as I still had to organise life around my job. Gordon was equally willing to help Leah but he also had his job to consider at the hospital. However, we got a good system going. Dora lived only minutes from Leah's school and this was handy, as between us we agreed that Leah could retreat to Dora's after school and have her tea there. This was also useful because it meant that they could spend time together without the pressure of responsibility, and I would collect Leah a couple of hours later as I left work. I would pay Dora for Leah's food, and this system worked well.

The 'Bluebottle' was frequently in the ointment here, as Dana would visit Dora more often, in order to see Leah. If only her visits had been borne out of love for Leah and a desperate need to see her, we could have been onto a winner, relationship wise. Of course this was not the case at all; Dana's only motive was to wind up and upset as many members of her gullible family as she could possibly manage in a day. She would tell Tina she was not caring for Leo adequately and that she would have to inform social services. Poor Tina, with her learning difficulties would sadly believe her, and little Leo would be terrified he would be removed from his mummy like all his cousins. She would then remind Dora that she would lose yet another grandchild, the one that lived with her, day to day and so Dora would disintegrate into tears of yet more desperation. Mission accomplished! Dana would by this time be sitting triumphantly in the armchair, grinning from ear to ear. She couldn't always obtain drugs. This was her fix, her 'high' and she breathed in this negative emotion, like the rest of us breathe oxygen. Of course there was Leah to come home from school yet, another top up of Dana's fix. As Leah walked in the door one evening, Dana immediately took her by the shoulders, and guiding her backwards to a chair said she had something to tell her. Apparently

Leah was quite smug and compliant, expecting her mother to tell her that another baby was on the way. However, Dana had decided more shocking tactics would be more entertaining, and proceeded to explain to Leah that her father had cancer and was going to die. I walked in the door that night, following a particularly gruelling day at the surgery. A poor patient had actually died of a heart attack in the waiting room, this had been a sad day and I was not feeling at my best. To overhear Dana's 'kind and loving' revelations to her daughter was like a haze of the deepest red in my mind that day. I had left weeping relatives, after work, and had walked into yet another room full of weeping relatives of my own. Poor Leah was beside herself, and helpless, as her dad was not yet talking to her and Dana knew this, therefore there was no way she could know how her dad was feeling. What Dana did not know, was that I had been in contact with Pete only the previous evening and knew there was no truth in any of this! Dana was feeding like a vampire on their grief, especially that of young Leah. How cruel! How could she? I asked myself as I instinctively hurled myself across the room at her. Once again, as my right hand grasped her throat and my left hand was pointed at her with jerking finger extended, an invisible force held me back and I released her in a nanosecond. Dana was actually enjoying my end of tether anger, as her face was inches from mine, her sarcastic grin beckoning me to 'do it.' I knew that something divine had intervened yet again. What couldn't be altered was that Dana was the *only* human being I had ever hated or wanted to attack. Her hateful actions towards children were just too much and call it what you like, but I believe it was a protective instinct which took over me. I have since learned a great deal from analysing my feelings toward Dana, to the point where I have no feelings left, and now literally feel neither love nor hatred towards her. All Feeling of any kind becomes extinct when in her presence. Of course I have also since learned that calmness can over come most, if not all aggressive situations. Perhaps Dana had her uses after all.

However, work was now needed to assure Leah that her dad was *not* dying, he did not have cancer. It was necessary for me to talk intimately with Pete to establish the problem, which was quite intrusive for him. He had in fact been diagnosed with a much less serious problem and was not dying.

Before moving in with us, Leah had been invited on a trip to Blackpool for the day, Dora was taking her and Leo. However, Dana was also going, and so I asked Leah if she felt she could manage this. She assured me that she would be o.k. and had in fact been looking forward to it. Dora asked if Leah could stay overnight as they were leaving early the next morning, and this was met by everyone's agreement. I must admit I was on pins all day at work the next day, wondering whether Leah was managing to cope with her mother. Dana's mother-in-law, May was also going, along with her fifteen year old daughter Stacey. I felt this would be good for Leah, having someone of a similar age to spend the day with.

I should have known! No sooner had I put my key in the front door that evening, than the 'phone was ringing. They had returned from Blackpool, however, Dora's voice was incoherent as she screamed and mumbled down the line that 'someone was arrested and taken away,' this was all I could understand. I knew instinctively that I should just drive over there to untangle yet another web. Unbelievably this incident did *not* appear to involve Dana. May, the mother-in-law was an alcoholic also, had got drunk and decided for whatever reason to attack Leah, a hammer being the nearest weapon to hand. As she was lurching forward, hammer in raised hand, Leah's head was apparently the target. There was a very timely assault by Stacey – May's daughter, who flung herself at her mother and pushed her away in the nick of time, the hammer thankfully caught Leah's upper arm, resulting in a large bruise, but at least her head was still on her shoulders, and still containing brain! Phew! When Gordon and I arrived at the scene to remove Leah from the apparent danger, the police were just leaving and May had been arrested for drunken behaviour and grievous bodily harm. Everyone was shocked and shaken, everyone was crying and screaming, all except Stacey. Stacey was sitting on a stool staring into space. Her mother had just been arrested and taken away, Stacy had 'saved' Leah, and Dora was screaming that she didn't know what to do with her; the police had just left Stacey sitting there.

We had never met Stacey before, or May for that matter. Gordon and I later discussed this issue and discovered that we had *both* been standing there, looking at this unknown young girl staring unseeing into thin air, and thought simultaneously, we had to do something, I kneeled on the floor, in front of Stacey and asked her gently if she would like to come home with us to spend the weekend with Leah, until she knew what would be happening to her mother. She immediately snapped out of her catatonic state and jumped to her feet saying emphatically, 'Yes.' Six months later, she was still with us.

It was a tough time for Stacey, she had no social work input at all, therefore we had no backup, support or funding when we needed to get anything done for her so the first action required was to obtain the services of a social worker, which wasn't easy. Stacey apparently had hardly been in school and averaged perhaps two days a week, sometimes none. This had to change; we talked to her about her future and her wishes and took an interest in her education and progress, just as we had done with Leah. She never missed a day over the next six months; she went from strength to strength and flourished. We did however, have some concerns. Leah was occupying one of our spare rooms. The other was equipped as an office, so we put a folding bed in Leah's room for Stacey, time being, as at this stage we had no idea how long she would be here. Believe it or not, Leah objected to this arrangement, she had finally made it to our house, like all the others and she wasn't about to be sharing her room with anyone. We therefore hit a compromise. We had a room on the lower ground floor, with little in it, but with a bit of carpet on the floor, curtains to the window and a camp bed and set of drawers, hey presto, a makeshift bedroom. We even put a portable T.V. in there, and it was, at times difficult to get Stacey out of it. I think possibly it was the first time Stacey had had any privacy and a room to call her own, despite its temporary set up. Leah then settled down and felt, I'm sure, that she had satisfactorily been given priority over the bedroom. She and Stacey were after all, related by marriage and similar in age and therefore became good friends, living together, going to school, etc. they also went out in the evenings together, we're not sure where, and never did find out, but more often than not they came home smelling of tobacco – worse – but when challenged, their replies were the same, "We've been with friends who smoke." O.K. what could we do?

Many obstacles were put in their way, and many things they had seen had an adverse effect on these two girls as it had on those before them. I already knew that her mum May, had divorced Stacey's dad and remarried, unfortunately the poor man, (husband number two) had fallen down the stairs and died. However, during one of my chats with Stacey, when she was opening up and felt she could trust us, she revealed to me that she had actually seen her mother push him from top to bottom of the stairs. Wow! Truth or the vengeful ramblings of a troubled teenager? As this was so long ago there was no proof, only the word of a young girl, and I know from experience that no-one listens to young children in such circumstances.

As you may understand by now, there were many times when I cursed the invention of Alexander Graham Bell, and wished the telephone had never been invented. There was rarely ever good news which travelled through the cables and air waves to our ears, and sure enough, yes you've guessed – we received a 'phone call, this time from Stacey's brother Jason, telling us that he and Dana were going to be married. She had divorced Pete, the father of 'the first three,' married Damien the father of 'the three more,' divorced him and was about to marry *his brother* who would be the potential father of baby number seven, which was well and truly on its weary way. I tell you, sterilisation is the only answer. Well, perhaps there was another one, but not legal and I wouldn't have been capable of it.

Anyhow, more calls were to follow, many of them negotiating with me as to whether Leah and Stacey were to attend the wedding. I informed Dana and Jason that I couldn't stop them attending, but it wouldn't be with my blessing. During one such conversation, Jason was extolling Dana's virtues to me, which fell on deaf ears, as I could hear her intoxicated drawl in the background guiding him like a puppet. I implored him not to marry her, he seemed harmless enough but didn't seem to have the intelligence to see beyond the obvious. He once more relayed the message that Dana 'wanted to bury the hatchet.' I assured him that I agreed, I would also like to bury it, which he relayed to her. I continued to clarify that out of choice I would prefer to bury it in her head, which he also relayed.

What a foolish move on my part. The next thing I knew, I received a solicitor's letter, saying Dana was suing me for the nightmares she was having of me 'coming at her with a hatchet!' Hatchets had played a repeating role in my life.

Happily, I will tell you, the girls did not attend wedding number three. They decided all on their own it was the wisest decision, and I had to agree. Also I managed to convince the solicitor in question, that it was utterly ridiculous to pursue the hatchet thing.

Stacey was eventually encouraged by her social worker to visit dad and we took her on a couple of occasions. She seemed reluctant to go alone, and did not appear at all happy when the social worker decided she should move in with dad as he had indicated that he would like her to live with him. I can understand Stacey's reluctance, as she disclosed things which didn't sound too savoury but declined when I suggested that together we talk to her social worker or anyone else about it, hence she was returned to her father. There's no smoke without fire as they say but I truly believe that had I even mentioned anything she had told me that she would have instantly denied it. She didn't want the furore that would follow a disclosure just now, and I had to respect that, after all she had seen fit to put her trust in me, she was sixteen, and to have broken that trust would have done more harm than good.

Leah also, was not far behind, living with us for a few months had given her and her dad some respite, time to reflect on the situation and plan how they could move forward from here and so eventually she moved back in with him and Ronda.

Shortly afterwards, baby number seven, John, was born to Dana but thankfully for him, he was adopted a few hours after birth. The social services had by now realised they were making no headway with Dana and a procedure had been set in place whereby as soon as they discovered she was pregnant, they had a plan and informed her of what was going to happen. Dana's answer to all this? "I'll stop eating so the baby will die, then no-one can have it!" She was even prepared to use her unborn child as a sort of 'currency,' yet another fragment of our family was disappearing.

It wasn't long, perhaps six months or so, before Pete could take no more, and once again asked Leah to move out. She was fifteen years old now, and of course she yet again moved in with Dora. I think she felt she couldn't approach us a second time, it must have felt like failure to her. I kept an eye on Leah from a distance, visited two or three times a week to see how they were coping, which was not very well at all. Leah suspected that she might be pregnant and no-one wanted *that* responsibility. Would this be yet another little fragment? And so once more Gordon and I relented and took in Leah yet again.

Chapter Twenty One

Forget Retirement

Only six years to go – to retirement that is. Yet how could I even consider it, when children were suffering left right and centre and we were constantly trying to see that they were happy, yet ultimately failing miserably one way or another. I now started to wonder what path our lives would take from here, with Leah possibly pregnant, meaning yet another young life to consider, not to mention what was going to happen to Leah herself. Also, what did *I* want to do with what was left of my life, which direction did I want it to take from here? Gordon and I had many discussions on this subject and whilst we were deciding, Dana conceived baby number eight. – to third husband Jason, brother of second husband Damien. Are you keeping up?

It was just after Christmas, and Gordon and I were feeling restless. After Leah had left us the first time, we had realised that we actually missed the satisfaction of putting right the wrongs, and giving these children what they needed, love, security and freedom from fear, all the things we had as children. We had become wedged in a rut like a truck in the mud, and the more we tried to rev the engine of our lives the deeper we became entrenched in frustration and boredom. I knew it was time for a change. There had been a time when I had looked forward with happy anticipation to the peace and quiet of retirement, the freedom to do what I want, but as this prospect loomed ever nearer, thoughts of boredom and sedentary old age clouded my horizon. Between us we decided to actually *do* something about our future prospects. Gordon was also tired of the regular day to day routine at work and we quickly realised that this was never the case when troubled children were around, there was always some crisis or other to sort out, or consoling to do.

After lengthy negotiation with each other regarding our future path we made a bold decision. We wanted to open a children's home! A 'Home' with a difference, and great ideas flowed. We could have retired craftsmen and women approved to show the young people their skills. The children could design and help decorate their own rooms to encourage them to take a pride in their efforts. We wanted to be 'hands on' as it were, involved in the running the home on a daily basis, parenting these kids the best way we could.

We visited and viewed several properties which may be suitable, we even considered staying put and buying the house next door when it came up for sale to knock through and double the size of our existing home.

However, we knew there must be rules and regulations involved and therefore contacted the social services first, for advice. The managing Director came personally to visit us to suss out our intentions and to advise. It was an exciting prospect which filled our minds with hope and anticipation. However when he left our home that day, our hopes were dashed. We knew there would be certain procedures to follow of course, but we were not prepared for the miles of red tape and the volumes of paperwork he left us to read. I won't bore you with all the details, but, in a nutshell, we would need a manager to run the place, one who had a certain 'qualification.'

This was *not* what we had in mind, our idea was not to buy a place and install someone to run it, to sit back and reap the profits. Our desire was to be an active part of it, to plough profits paid by Local Authorities, back into the place to constantly improve it. Of course we were informed that another option would be for one of us to attend university in order to obtain this particular qualification, which would take about three to four years! I ask you, at our age!! Had I been younger, I would certainly have done it, but time for us was short.

We were beginning to realise more and more, that there were too many obstacles in our way for us to consider proceeding with our plans, perhaps we had been a little *too* ambitious.

As I sat at the computer one day at work, a thought occurred to me. Why didn't I just give up my job and become a full time foster carer? It made sense; I had had years of experience – the hard way, having relatives virtually dumped on me one way or another. What more experience would I need? Once more, I contacted some names I knew in social services and a social worker was sent out to visit us to give us the low down. It soon occurred to me, when given the basic information that if I gave up my job, we would find it difficult to survive on the pittance which would be paid by social services. This would not have helped the children at all, to be struggling. How inconceivably stupid it is that it costs thousands of pounds a week to keep a child in a care home, and yet they pay so little to the people who are at the rough end. If only they put more care, effort and support into the carers, there would be more of them around. However as the social worker was telling us of all the assessments we would have to undergo, she asked us if we had checked out any of the private agencies. Private agencies? We had never heard of such a thing. She continued to explain how they paid a very substantial sum, but that they had higher expectations of us as carers. I certainly didn't mind higher expectations, or harder work. If it meant I had an income in order to pay the bills, and keep the wolves at bay. I checked out one of these Fostering Agencies and gave them a call. I was informed of what was required, the assessment I would have to undergo and the sum I would be paid per child per week once I had passed through the panel, been accepted and undergone some basic training.

Now I had undergone a great deal of training in the years I had worked at the surgery, and before that in other avenues, but when it came to looking after children, training was alien to me. I had always been thrown in at the deep end and was forced to handle behaviours and problems alone. *I* learned the hard way. However, Gordon and I went through the in's and out's with a fine tooth comb. It would mean leaving the secure job I had enjoyed for the past fifteen years, my N.H.S. pension, and retirement of course. But I decided it was what I really wanted to do. We had cared for troubled kids of all ages over the years, with little or not help, just how hard could it be to do it professionally and *with* support. We requested that someone from this agency, come out and see us, which they did. We were not pressured at all and felt that they had been explicit and truthful in their explanation. We decided to go ahead, take a leap in the dark, and the assessment began. The Agency covering Yorkshire and Lincolnshire, informed us that the assessment could take approximately six months, and Leah had of course, jut moved in. I therefore informed Social Services that they had the six months to sort out accommodation for Leah, as hopefully by then, I would be working with the Agency. Her social worker advised me that they would be pursuing independent living accommodation for Leah as she was almost sixteen now, this is a type of accommodation which is an option for young people post sixteen, when there are no other options available, whereby they live independently but at the same time, still have the support of the social services.

Good news came shortly after this, Leah was *not* pregnant! What a relief, no more unwanted, damaged children entering the world. Despite this, Leah's behaviour could be somewhat erratic at times. She would often not come home on time as requested, causing great concern for Gordon and me. She would skip school, as before, and would prefer to visit and argue with her mother instead. It was often a case of damned if you do, damned if you don't, because, as before, I was giving her a cheque each Monday for lunches, this was to ensure she didn't spend lunch money on cigarettes or drugs, but they were never eaten, she would rather skip school and obtain cigarettes from her mother.

This was no good for Leah. I tired to think of ways to encourage her to change her self-

destructive ways. The first step was to draw up
a contract between Leah and myself as before.
She wrote down all the things she expected of
me as her carere, and I wrote down all the
things I would expect of her. It was a mutual
agreement. On my contract there were such
things as:-

Keep your room tidy
Come home on time
No smoking in the house
Attend school
Less contact time with mum to avoid rows
To wash dishes once a day etc.

On Leah's contract she had written that she would:-

Like me to take care of her
Help her with school work
Advise her re her independence
Give her pocket money (of course) etc.

I also created a star chart for her. Usually kept
for much younger children I know, but given
Leah's background it seemed to work. For each
time she came home, washed up, tidied her
room or obeyed any specific house rule she was
given a star, and as before, for a week's full row
of stars she was awarded a set amount of money
which was saved for her until she had enough to

buy something she wanted. It worked *most* of the time.

There were, however occasions when she blatantly flouted the rules. She had been asked to stay away from her dad's house, but appeared to know when he was not there one night, whilst Andre was home on army leave, and decided to break the rule and visit the house. She didn't come home at the usual time. I started ringing around, Mum. Gran, friends and finally as a last resort, rang Andre, and he truthfully told me she had been there but had left some time ago. Now I was worried. I once more rang Dana and Dora and requested they inform me if Leah turned up, and surprise surprise she was there, at Dana's house, but Dan was gushing down the phone something about Leah being attacked and the police were there. Here we go again. I thought. Such drama unfolding. It was about eleven p.m. when Gordon and I drove over to Dana's house and arrived as the police were leaving. I managed to speak to one of the officers before they left, who informed me that he wasn't sure he quite believed her story. We entered the house to find Leah sitting on Dana's sofa, crying and holding her left arm, bearing a large and lengthy scratch along the inside of her forearm. I asked her calmly to explain what had happened. Her story unfolded as to how she had been leaving Andre, at about ten thirty p.m., when she could hear footsteps behind her in the dark. Suddenly she was knocked to the ground and wrestled with the man, who was tall and black and wearing blue trousers and dark top. Her arm was cut in the struggle and her ribs were apparently bruised. She did surprisingly manage to take out of her pocket, a rubber ball I had bought her that day and apparently threw it at the man and he ran away.

After sitting beside her, nodding at her dreadful tale, I then pointed out, that, first of all ten thirty was late, had she been home an hour earlier, it may not have happened, also, to say she had been knocked to the ground, her *white* track-suit was remarkably clean. How did she see his skin colour in the dark, when attacked from behind? And if she had thrown the rubber ball at him how did it get back in her pocket, where it now was? I was also particularly determined to show her how the scratch on her arm fitted perfectly with the ring on her right hand which I had given her, as though it had been drawn along it.

Leah was not pleased that her lies had been uncovered, Dana was angry that she had fallen for these lies and Gordon and I were angry at Leah's lack of consideration. We gave her the opportunity to come back home with us that night and we could try to resolve any issues troubling her, but she refused and stayed with Dana. However the next day she was back.

Dana and Jason of course were now married and sure enough, baby number eight was well on its way. How long would this continue? As the pregnancy progressed, it became clear that there were complications and yet another caesarean section was performed. There was one advantage however, as this meant that Dana would have to be sterilised this time, meaning *NO MORE BABIES*! I wanted to rejoice, to throw a party! The poor little mite was adopted a few hours after birth, just like the last one.

As I have said before, this was such irony. I had cousins who had adopted children because they couldn't conceive their own, and here we were, having children adopted *out* of our family, being spread around the country like cattle being sold. This was a ludicrous situation. Six, of these eight children were now adopted.

Was life always to be this way? One crisis following the other, even the pleasant occasions were to be blighted by trauma. Pete and Ronda had finally decided to get married, after years of being together and their best attempts at raising Andre and Leah, the wedding plans were made, but sadly did not include Leah, Pete's own daughter. Don't misunderstand me here, I completely and utterly understand Pete and Ronda's feelings, they had been terribly hurt by Leah, more than once. They didn't want their special day ruined by any unfolding drama and I didn't blame them. They were also concerned that Dana may turn up and embarrass them. I assured them they shouldn't worry about Dana; I had my little way of making sure Dana would think twice about doing *anything*. I was Superbitch wasn't I? Andre had obtained leave from his army duties and was coming over from Germany to give away the bride and would be wearing his regimental uniform. Gordon and I had been invited, and I so wanted to see my handsome, now grown, great-nephew in his uniform, the symbol of the goal he had so wanted to achieve, and yet I would feel disloyal to Leah. I was so used to being between a rock and a hard place by now, and had to contemplate some sort of compromise. I talked to Leah and explained how hurt her dad and Ronda were and how difficult it must be for them also. I knew she would want to see how they all looked that day and reasoned with her that if *we* attended the wedding, then at least we could take photos of everyone for her album. And so we did. We took pictures of Ronda in her beautiful wedding gown, Ronda and Pete together. Wonderful pictures of her handsome brother, also grandma, cousins aunties etc. Leah, although sad at not being there was delighted with the produce of our trusty camera, and together we created an album of her own with which to reminisce.

There were more sad days to come in the months that followed. Leah did a fair bit of running off and not coming home. Dora wasn't well and was admitted to hospital for a pacemaker to be fitted. Gordon was concerned that it may be a bit too fast for her! All the while, our assessment with The Agency was ongoing on a weekly basis. Our lives were poked and prodded down to the most intimate detail. Our childhoods were unpicked stitch by memorable stitch and rewound like a ball of wool. Our youth was dissected with the finest tweezers. Had we been in trouble with the law? Even a parking fine could be uncovered, and we remembered that Gordon had been fined for having a faulty handbrake, even though it was a car he had borrowed for the day. Police checks had to be carried out, even our Cairn Terrier Bruno and our poodle Oscar had to be checked for any doggy criminal record. Safety checks on the house had to be carried out. The electricity and wiring was checked, cupboards bolted to the wall, any glass must be to British Standards. Stair rails must be so many inches apart, no more, unnecessary knives and scissors should be put away, and any alcohol must be kept under lock and key. Smoke and carbon monoxide alarms were a *must*, a fire-drill had to be sorted out, and our safe-caring policy written out for anyone to see. Our lives would be turned upside down, yet it was what we wanted to do.

During this time, we were also attending reviews and meetings to plan Leah's move to independence, but at the same time have a watchful eye kept on her progress.

It was now the fourth of July, and we were preparing to go to panel later in the day. I decided to contact Leah's social worker in order to be prepared with an update on the progress they were making as to her move, just in case we were asked as to what would be happening, by the panel. The social worker was on leave, this explained why I hadn't heard anything from her, because Kath was one of the better ones, and was usually up to date with everything. However, when I pursued the question of Leah, no-one seemed to know anything at all regarding her situation. Nothing, in fact had been done over the previous six months to locate somewhere for her to live,

Despite my avid suggestions at the beginning that we would need her placed *before* we went to panel. I was speechless, furious, and fearful for Leah, what would we do, we couldn't just throw her out?

I had to put all thoughts and feelings out of my head in order to face this panel of social workers, police officers, doctors and other professionals before me. I cleared my mind of all this emotional debris, before I entered the room that day, with Gordon alongside, me. We sat at the end of a very long table, our Agency link worker, Sarah, dutifully accompanied us, offering physical and moral support. I felt as though I was seated before a hanging judge, my heart pounding as we were asked questions. "Why do you want to foster?" was the first one. Why indeed? However, after these smiling polite people had made their enquiries, we were asked to wait outside whilst they consulted each other and reached their decision about our suitability. I guess looking back it was no worse than any interview might be, except for the six months gruelling assessment preceding it. Standing by the water fountain in the corner, we waited, me with trembling legs, for what seemed like forever, to hear the outcome. Our future direction depended upon the feelings and observations of these few people. Eventually the door opened and we were beckoned to return to the room. We sat tentatively down on the same two chairs, and searched their faces for clues as to the decision they had reached. The first person to speak was Andrew, a reviewing officer we had encountered several times before when sorting out the lives of children. His words were very precious to me. He said: - "I have known Sandy and Gordon a long time and there is nothing more to say on their suitability to become professional Foster Carers, welcome to the Agency!"

It didn't sink in. Did this mean we had been accepted? We soon had our answer, as Sarah our link worker turned to me and said, "Have you given your notice in at the surgery yet?"

"No." I answered. "I wanted to be sure."
"Well," said Sarah, "Do it tomorrow, we have three Local Authorities fighting over you already." Wow!

There was however, a small matter to be dealt with first. That of Leah! As soon as I arrived home, I reached for the 'phone and began making calls. Some of the people I spoke to, I had encountered before on the telephone, and had altercations with. This didn't deter me though from executing my anger at the lack of action for Leah. I was her advocate, who else was there to fight for her when bureaucracy had failed her? I lost count of how many people I spoke to that day, but my anger knew no bounds. Perhaps the relief of Panel being over released the restraints of my wrath, who knows? Poor Leah however, didn't know how to handle this. The fear she must have felt at her future prospects which were fading with every call I made. She couldn't take any more and ran off yet again. Fight or Flight, she chose them both, but my deepest fear struck when I discovered where she had flown to. Damien! She had discovered he was living not far from us, with his new girlfriend and two children in a two bed flat, and now Leah had joined them. I couldn't believe it! Life was so full of ironies and here was yet another. The very man who was the reason, Andre, Leah and Adam had been removed from their home lives, was now being allowed to have Leah live with him, *ten years on*! Social services were giving him money and a bed to 'take care' of her, how contradictory. On the other hand, with hindsight, perhaps they had realised that at least they knew where she was and could track her down. Unlikely had she disappeared into oblivion.

However, the social services then decided in their wisdom that *we* had wanted to manoeuvre Leah into staying so that she could be placed through The Agency. How wrong they were, we had wanted Leah to be properly settled *before* we embarked on our new career in fostering. Surely they didn't want us to disown her, throw her out? They had completely misunderstood our feelings, or were we just being made scapegoats for their incompetence's? This was the first occasion where The Agency would come to our rescue. They had informed us that Leah could stay, alongside any placement from them until such time as she wanted to leave. They also helped put together a very polite and professional letter to social services outlining exactly what the position was. Despite all of this, Leah refused to return, refused even to talk to us. I was devastated and hoped for everyone's sake, nothing happened to her whilst in the care of Damien. Fortunately, shortly afterwards, she left Damien's flat and moved in with friends.

Well, the next major step was to inform my colleagues at the surgery that I would be leaving. It wasn't going to be easy after fifteen years working there, and my private N.H.S. Pension scheme would end. I would miss my workmates, even some of the patients too, whom I had grown to know well. Their response when I told them what direction I was taking was one of utter disbelief. To some extent they had travelled this bumpy road of fostering, so far, with me. They had been there to listen to my woes, to send me home early when there was a crisis, but because it had been so traumatic at times, they rally *couldn't* understand why I would now wish to pursue it out of choice, and with a very few short years to retirement, it seemed incredulous to them. But I had a very different view, I was still alive and had done so many things on this borrowed time, why stop now?

I was ready, I was full of anticipation, and couldn't wait to begin. The Agency had given us some induction training, and I was already beginning to see the differences between their professional approach, and the untrained hands-on, get-on-with-it sort of methods I had become used to.

My month's notice had to be worked, and it seemed to pass very slowly indeed, the last two weeks of which were spent also with our very first placement. Somehow I knew this could be no worse than what I'd had to do in the past. I was eager to begin.

Chapter Twenty Two

A Professional Approach

Naomi was a fourteen year old girl. We had been asked to take her, on respite whilst her carers went away for two weeks. She arrived on the Saturday looking very anxious; her first concern was whether she could visit the toilet in the night. Apparently somewhere in her past she had been denied this and whenever she went anywhere new it was a worry to her. I told her, that her room was right next door to the loo, and she could go any time she liked. She was also concerned that she wouldn't be allowed a bath each morning and evening, and one again I had to allay her fears and she then appeared to relax considerably.

We are hopefully given as much information as possible or necessary regarding each placement, which is most valuable to us as carers. We can for instance, exercise caution where appropriate. Now, Naomi had, shall we say, problems with younger children, and could not be left alone with them. This proved to be quite a challenge, and also meant that for the two weeks of her stay, Xara could not visit. Therefore Gordon and I worked out a rota system whereby, one evening I would visit Xara and Angeline after work for half an hour and the next night I would go home and allow Gordon to visit. Whatever happened, we could not neglect our own family, they were part of the fostering process too.

Despite these issues, which I agree some may find difficult to deal with, I actually like this girl, and we got on well. Naomi thought she was quite ugly and would never get a boyfriend, so I spent time telling her what a lovely colour her hair was, and her eyes etc., and that I couldn't see any reason why she wouldn't find a boyfriend at the right time. However, these two long weeks were not to be easy. Gordon decided to do some washing one day, but sadly it all came out grey. Therefore I had to take Naomi shopping for certain items of clothing which were no longer presentable. As I was cooking in the kitchen one day, I heard my little white poodle, Oscar, shriek and wimp, and as I ran into the sitting room, he was limping away from Naomi. This was little Oscar, who had sat and allowed a young child to throttle him, he'd had his doggy police checks, and wouldn't hurt a fly! Well actually, that was all he did hurt. He just hated the damn things, hated the buzzing, so he would catch and eat them. I always knew that saying was a myth. However it was plainly obvious that Naomi had done something deliberately to hurt Oscar, she flew upstairs, flung herself on the bed and sobbed. She knew what I was going to say, she had teased the dogs constantly, blowing in their faces, withholding their toys and doggy chews. We had asked her repeatedly to leave them alone and she had ignored us. I decided that a telling off wouldn't really solve the problem long term, so I decided a different approach was called for. When she had calmed down, I asked her to come and sit with me. I explained what lovely creatures Oscar and Bruno were, and how, if they were teased so much they *may* eventually bite, they are like any living thing, they have limits, and then they would have to leave us and everyone would be sad. Thankfully this had the desired effect. It gave her food for thought and she could see further forward to the long term consequences.

It was my last day at the surgery and a lunch out had been arranged. I always imagined I was going to cry and be very upset when I left here, but strangely I was quite composed. I knew my colleagues were not far away and I would keep in touch and the exciting anticipation that I had found my niche and was beginning a career I really wanted, was far more powerful.

I was given leaving gifts, and cards which I will always treasure, and the doctors made speeches as to how they would miss the clatter of my three inch heels around the place, and my perfume wafting behind me as I charged about, the laughter at my faux pars and wardrobe malfunctions when my skirt got stuck in my pants, or my blouse was undone exposing my red lace lingerie, (yes, I still wear it.) The girls,

I suppose would miss my constant chatter and joking as this was the only way I could get myself through the day at times. And so I said farewell to Peter, Simon, Debbie Linda and Jill, Alison, Carol and Sarah, Karen Maryann and Janet and the many others I had spent my days with and left for home.

It was a strange feeling, I must admit, knowing I wouldn't be going back, wouldn't be sitting at the computer waiting for the telephone to ring with the next trauma unfolding. These mixed feelings and thoughts were still going through my head as I put the key in the lock to open my front door. Before I stepped inside, Angeline pulled up in her car. The devastation had *not* ended. After ten years of marriage, she and Dan decided to part. It was Angeline's decision and Dan was devastated. He was a workaholic, he thrived on it, and Angeline had been telling him since the birth of Xara, that he needed to spend more time with his family, but poor Dan couldn't really see it. It was almost as though he had gone into overdrive and must provide *more* for his family. Poor Angeline didn't want more, she just wanted a family life, but she appeared to be doing more and more as a 'single' parent. Parties, weddings, days out, she and Xara were always alone, Dan was working. Eventually Angeline felt she could take no more and left with Xara. It struck Dan hard, he really hadn't realised just how hard he was working and how little time he spent with his family, but it was too late. I was also devastated, it was yet another bereavement, the end of a family. I had come to love Dan like a son and would miss him being around, as little as it may have been. But I did understand Angeline's feelings and knew how much time she spent alone. There were difficult times ahead for all, trying to come to terms with this, not least of all, Xara, she couldn't understand the situation and it struck her hard too. However, a house across the road from us became available and Gordon got on well with the owner, Richard, and negotiated for Angeline and Xara to rent temporarily, and so they moved in.

Once again, life's anxieties were encroaching on what should have been a more peaceful time. Negotiations had been ongoing for our second placement, but our first long-term one with The Agency. We had been given information on this child and now my attention had to be focussed two ways, on Angeline and Xara and of course this new and unknown young person joining our family.

On the Saturday morning Naomi was collected by her carers, refreshed from their holiday and we waved goodbye. A mixture of satisfaction at a job well done, despite the recent events, and relief that we could relax a little and Xara could now visit again.

By four p.m. that day, Rosie arrived with all her worldly good. She had been told that she would be spending two weeks respite with us, and this would also be our way of assessing whether she would be a good match to stay long-term.

Rosie was the feisty sort. Eleven years old, very thin and pale with dark circles under her eyes. As she pushed open the garden gate and made her way down the path, she announced her first observation of her new surroundings. "There's a lot of Asians around here!" She had been influenced by her father and was very racially prejudiced. I informed Rosie that we lived in a very ethnic community in the city and we had neighbours of many different nationalities around us. Perhaps it was not going to be easy for her to integrate, and I must point out at this stage, we do well to remember that *all* of these children that we take have had traumatic lives one way or another, before they come to us. It's up to us to help them untangle some of that emotional or physical mess, to enable them to move forward and become happy and motivated adults. However we began by taking Rosie to McDonalds as a treat and to help her feel at home, followed by a lovely walk by Ladybower Reseviour, thereby giving her a little space.

The next morning Rosie emerged from her bed and descended for breakfast. We needed to get to know Rosie and her likes and dislikes. I offered her the choice of a variety of cereals or toast etc., her eyes skimmed passed the choices on offer and she then made her decision. "I'll just have some chocolate and a packet of crisps!" I don't think so! This explained the dark circles under her eyes and the pallor of her skin. I took control and poured some cereal into a bowl. Added some milk and asked her to try it. She enjoyed it to the last cornflake.

She had been given the usual basic information about us, her new prospective carers. Unfortunately they told her our age and her reaction to this was "I can't live with them, they're so fucking old they're practically dead!" How we laughed at this later, she would soon discover that despite the age, I am very unconventional, and love anything and everything modern and colourful. My orange, pink and red swirly wallpaper and lime green furniture would have been quite a shock I think.

I knew it was to be a long road ahead with Rosie. She was quite argumentative and it was to be a seven year project – until she was eighteen. Now Rosie could be very controlling over the most trivial things. She was one of nine siblings, and I guess under such circumstances, one has to establish one's place in the pecking order, and Rosie wanted to be at the top. There was an older brother living with grandparents, three sisters individually placed within the local authority, Rosie with us and two siblings adopted, plus two more would follow. Surprisingly, she did get along most of the time, with Xara despite her brown skin dark eyes and almost black curly hair, not to mention Rosie's racist views. There was lots of contact with family for Rosie. Now normally, I am all for it, when it's positive for the child, but in my opinion there was too much. There would be a weekly session with mum and sisters, then grandparents, and older brother, and finally dad and the dog, although he would rarely turn up. This was, at times very confusing for the children and very frustrating when repeated knock backs were felt when this happened. In the beginning the local authority social worker wanted Rosie to be placed alone, we advised him that it was our long-term plan to care for two foster children but we would agree to give her three months on her own to see how she settled. In fact one of Rosie's gripes was to be that it was 'boring with us because there are no other kids here' but we kept to our word.

It took Rosie a while to settle, although we were later to discover that she would never settle anywhere, but her uneasiness manifested itself in the beginning in her sleepwalking. There were several occasions when she would be active in the middle of the night. She could make her way downstairs, switch on all the lights, trailing her duvet behind her, or swipe all the contents of her dressing table onto the floor.

This did however, cease once she felt more comfortable.

It was her first day in her new school. We had bought the complete uniform, and she looked very smart as she finally put on her shoes to leave that morning. Rosie, however, had other ideas, she was not happy and decided that her trousers were too 'gay,' she wouldn't be seen dead in the skirt, and wanted nothing for lunch when I gave her the choice of school dinner or packed lunch. She also decided she didn't much care for the area we live in and wanted to move as she 'could get killed or somethin' around 'ere/' I remembered my faithful old Star Charts. It didn't matter that she was eleven years old, and so I sat her down and explained the principle of the Star Chart system. She quite liked this idea and her behaviour began to improve.

When Rosie moved in with us, she had come from a carer in another city and so far as we knew, was a complete stranger. Although as her background was emerging it all sounded very familiar to me and pretty soon I realised why. The whole family didn't live far away and they had actually been patients at the surgery. Everything fell into place and I realised the situation. This actually turned out to be an advantage as I saw it. It was rather like my family and knowledge of the family assisted my understanding.

As I said before, contact was chaotic for this family with people not turning up, an older sister encouraging Rosie to 'run.' This was in the early days and I now realise how significant this would become. Eventually we were able to convince the social worker that contact had to be tailored to benefit the family rather than becoming a forum with which to destroy them further. Rosie was up and down, good then defiant, she *must* be in control at all times. It was my mission to ensure that she would discover that the *adults* were in control, that there were boundaries and there were certain things to which she must conform. Life was a constant roller coaster of desperate measures with Rosie. I would buy her new clothes, which she would choose, only for her to complain that they were rubbish and that she had none. She still insisted on sweets for supper or breakfast – although to no avail. Anything to be in *control*. We would have her sisters over to stay, to give her more contact with them in a controlled environment but even then, there were refusals to comply. Her favourite trick was to suddenly walk away when in the middle of talking to her, and on one of these occasions, Gordon caught her coat sleeve to encourage her to wait. Rosie told him she would 'get him done,' a dangerous entity indeed. This is where carers tread a fine line when dealing with such a streetwise kid. There would be many more threats over trivial matters. She gave us a really bad time one Sunday afternoon when we took her along with her sister to the local garden centre. It had snowed that morning and we had all wrapped up warm in coats scarves and gloves.

Rosie and her sister were standing in the little square under Gordon's watchful eye, whilst I was browsing in on the craft shops. The Sunday shoppers were sedately walking on the surrounding pathway, when my peaceful browsing was disturbed by shouts and screams from outside. Everyone was turning or emerging from their interests to see. The voice I could hear was very familiar, and knowing Rosie by now I was sure it would be one of her dramas. As I emerged from the pottery, I had to push my way through the standing crowd, to be met by the sight of Rosie playing to her unsuspecting audience. She was screaming that Gordon had hit her, and she couldn't wait 'till Monday morning to ring her solicitor and have him prosecuted! Apparently what had really happened was that Rosie had sat down on the ground in her new white coat, and after asking her to stand up, Gordon was trying to remove the snow and grit which was now adorning the back of it. This was all it needed for Rosie to turn it around to suit her needs, to take control. However, once more I decided that *I* must turn it around yet again. I calmly walked up to Rosie, with the crowd still watching the unfolding drama and offered her my mobile phone, I suggested that she ring now and let's sort it out in front of these good people, as my gaze took a half circle turn, to look at them, their faces moving as I did so, as though they were not even paying any attention to us. She declined and it was never mentioned again. One more huge drama calmly sorted.

Although now almost twelve years old, Rosie loved dolls and prams, but had never had them, so we decided it was never too late to get something out of your system, we bought her a doll and pram and she was able to play out in the rear garden without being disturbed or ridiculed by her peers. Despite this, she would still threaten when she couldn't have her way. She'd wag school, refuse to do P.E., use bad language knowing we disliked it, yet she could be so polite and lovable, until she got what she wanted and then in an instant would turn nasty. Now I know there may be some of you who will scratch your heads at my next statement, but despite all this, there was something within Rosie that I was strangely attached to, and this was what kept me going. It would have been so easy to say 'take her away.' there was also that part of me that wanted to keep going in order to achieve what I set out to do, and that was to change negative behaviour, to find the good human being who stood a chance in the world, in society, to make something of her life. We could also see an amusing side to some of the behaviours. Our friends J and J worked and lived at Chatsworth House, and this gave us the wonderful privilege of being able to visit the House and Estate free of charge. I took Rosie one day, and arranged to meet 'J' in the Stables Restaurant for lunch. As we were nibbling on tea and scones, in walked the Duchess of Devonshire and 'J' discreetly pointed her out to Rosie, thinking this would be quite exciting for her. In a flash, Rosie was up on her feet and heading in the direction of the Duchess yelling – "I'm just gonna ask her if she's posh!"

However, as time wore heavily on, we did feel a certain pride when people who knew Rosie, commented on how different and well she looked. I had taken her for a brand new hairdo, and her lank straight brown hair was cut into a bob and dyed blue on the ends, her choice, but it looked strangely becoming. The dark circles beneath her eyes had disappeared, no more 'choccy' breakfasts and suppers, and her once pallid skin, now had a certain glow. Not to mention of course, her more polite approach and more calm behaviour. We were making headway, the decent human being was beginning to emerge and Rosie felt so much happier. At home of course, there were still occasions when the rebellion struck through like a sword, usually whenever she was asked to do *anything*! Once more I had to try something, anything to change this and sometimes I took a deep breath and did something reckless. For instance, Rosie was doing one of her 'victim' displays which comprised of, rolling around on the spacious floor of our living room, pulling her hair, thumping her face and legs and wailing like a baby, with her legs in the air. Drastic, reckless action was called for, and either it would work, or it wouldn't. Without further ado, I dropped to my knees. I wailed and pulled and tugged at my hair – carefully, it's precious at my age – then fell to the floor and rolled and thumped and wailed some more. Rosie immediately sprang to her feet like a gazelle, stood back aghast and said "What on earth are you doing?" my reply was short and simple. "I just thought I'd join you, see how it feels." "You look ridiculous "she responded. "I know" said I, "I've watched you, so I know how ridiculous it looks." But I continued until she burst into uncontrollable laughter. I must admit, when I had a mental picture in my head as to how I must have looked I couldn't help chuckling with her. She never did it again.

In the beginning, Rosie wasn't the cleanest of kids. She didn't appear to want to actually get wet when having a shower. This was evident when she was in the bathroom one evening 'showering,' and I was seated on the toilet next door. I could hear her humming happily to herself; she thought she was in control. I sat unceremoniously longer than usual and as I heard the lock on the bathroom door open, I opened mine too, and we emerged together, face to face, Rosie in her P.J's with towel around her head. I gently tugged at the towel, which slowly unwound revealing dry, unwashed hair, and touched her arm with the back of my hand, and said: - "Now would you like to go back in and actually get *in* the shower?" How did I know? We have squeaky floorboards and Rosie had stood for a good ten minutes in front of the mirror, which is nowhere near the shower, before emerging. As I sat in the toilet next door, I could hear the floorboards by the mirror, squeak to and fro. She thought I could see through walls, and I had been called a witch before, but this was miraculous. Never fix your squeaky floorboards.

There would be many rocky times. She would accuse Gordon of kicking her, and on these occasions I would ask her if she would be willing to sign a statement as to what happened. She would usually refuse, because she knew there was no truth in it.

The day after I had a lovely beige carpet fitted in the sitting room, Rosie asked me if I had a sharp knife, as she sat making sculptures in the deep pile with her fingers. I asked her what she would want a knife for, and her reply was that she wanted to slit her wrists. I replied "In that case, no, I don't want blood stains on my new carpet!" She was shocked; I knew she had done this before. However, I must stress that one has to know the child well, in order to understand their reasoning, and in this case I knew it was simply to shock and gain attention.

Rosie continued to make progress, with occasional setbacks. She would always suffer regression when her social worker visited. It was usually because the poor man was the bearer of bad news, but he would allow her to swear at him to be verbally abusive and not say a word. I couldn't allow this, and although most carers may have felt they shouldn't say anything in the presence of the social worker I could not allow it to continue, and shocked Rosie by informing her she would be sent to her room immediately if it continued. However, we conversely would support her if we felt wrong decisions were being made regarding her future.

There was always food available, and fruit in the fruit bowl in the kitchen, and yet more than once, cherries had dropped from her T shirt having been 'stolen' and hidden.

The first review we had for Rosie was held here in our home. We thought it would be more comfortable for her and less stressful. We were wrong, Rosie saw it as a forum to trot around the house and do what she wanted, and therefore subsequent reviews were held at the office, sitting round a table where she had no choice but to focus on the task in hand.

It was three months into Rosie's arrival, that we began negotiation for a new placement to join her. Her social worker was still insisting that she should be placed alone – permanently, we'd decide otherwise and were not changing our minds. The Agency began to sift through the list of children waiting for placements to find a match with Rosie. The matching process is of paramount importance. To study backgrounds, behaviours, hobbies and personalities etc., to try to ensure the youngsters who live together, get along together. Mostly we get it right, sometimes we get it wrong. Now during the period of waiting for a match, we would do respite care for other carers, or day care, in order to give these carers a break particularly if they had a difficult child, or were having problems, and so we did a week's respite for an eight year old boy called James. Now James was a very handsome little chap and quite a character. He was duel-ethnicity, being half Asian and half Irish, he'd had eighteen placements in a period of two years and unfortunately, none of them had worked out well. He had a lot to be angry about and made sure he displayed his anger frequently
He had a tendency to explode, throw things and usually wreck his room, but thankfully for the one week with us, he refrained from doing this and we returned him to his carers. However, the first time we had met James, the first words he spoke to us were. "You do know I'm not full English don't you?" I replied "Yes, I can see

that" and when he met Xara of course, he and she looked like brother and sister. They had the same hair colour and eyes, and the same creamy milk chocolate skin tone. He immediately relaxed and smiled, he felt accepted. However he did constantly become somewhat agitated because someone or other was 'staring at him.' so, driving him to school one day, I asked him if he knew why people stared at him, and said I thought I knew why. (It's wonderful talking about sensitive subjects when driving, no eye contact) I said, "If I were out there and looked at you, I would *have* to take a second look, because you are *such* a handsome young man." I couldn't look at James, couldn't take my eyes from the road ahead, but I could feel him become taller in his seat, his stature was growing with his confidence. Now a few weeks later we were asked once more if we could have James for the day, just to give his carers a break as things were not going well. Being used to him by now we readily agreed and decided we would go to the park as there had been a light covering of snow and snowballs were calling. As we were due to leave to pick up James, we received a 'phone call from his carers saying that they literally had a fight and James had shut himself in his bedroom. This was after he had thrown his dinner on the floor and his carer had cleaned it all up and given him some more. You see, this is where I differ. The dinner would have stayed on the floor, at least until I had finished mine, because the idea here is to spoil my meal and ensure it would go cold. No way! And then of course, there wouldn't be any more until the next meal. However, we asked if we could still go over there and talk to him. When we arrived we were shocked to see the carer with cuts and scratches, James was still in his room therefore Gordon and I ventured upstairs and knocked on the door which was firmly shut against the world. A little voice from inside said 'come in.' Gordon and I entered together and immediately set eyes on this small boy sitting on the floor with a book in his hand poised to hurl it at us. As his arm reached backwards for maximum leverage, Gordon raised his flat hand in the air and said, "Ah Ah, we don't want that do we?" Straight away James put the missile down and lowered his head. We sat on the floor with him and asked him if he would still like to come out, to which he responded by grabbing his shoes and saying "Yes!" We drove to a large country park, fed the ducks and swans and played in the snow. It was nearing home time, when my mobile rang. I walked away from everyone for privacy, it was the Agency saying 'don't' take him back, it's been decided his carers had reached the end of their tether,' this fight had been the final straw. We were asked if we could take him home with us until alternative arrangements could be made.

Now you may be thinking, this was an ideal situation. We were looking for a second placement; James now needed one, why don't we keep him? I can hear you saying. Well, the answer was simple, matching! Rosie and James didn't always see eye to eye. They didn't fight, but argued a fair bit, until I put up my hands and said 'enough!' They then knew it was time to shut up. Although we were ticking over quite nicely, it would never have worked long term. James stayed with us for three months, slightly longer than a day, and during this time new foster carers were identified for him in another town. We arranged several visits, prior to his move, to make the transition smoother and easier for him. It's never easy when a child moves on whatever the circumstances, and at this point, just as we thought arrangements were going well he announced, "I wish I could live here forever. I like it here" I cannot describe the thoughts that go through one's head at a time like that. However, eventually James left us and moved in with his new, hopefully long-term foster carers. I put together a small photo album for him, pictures of days out, events etc., and little messages from us all. A fellow carer said to me recently, 'You can't do anything with a child on a short-term placement.' I had to disagree strongly. If you have a child for a *day* you can make it memorable, that day can be a small part of the jigsaw of their life, without it there would be a piece missing and the whole picture would be permanently incomplete. This was actually proved, two years after James left us. We received a 'phone call one day, a small, timid little voice on the end of the line. "It's James" were the words spoken. "James?" I replied back into the receiver. Yes, he had taken out his little album form time to time to look through it, to remember that bit of the jigsaw, when there were happy times. Unfortunately, his foster placement didn't work out long-term as hoped, didn't last long like all the others. He was now placed in a unit, perhaps the only place which could contain him, yet still he remembered us, and it was important enough to him to check out whether we were still 'there' for him, that he hadn't been forgotten.

It was sad to see him go, but he took with him his little book of happy memories, and we also had happy and amusing memories which we held in our hearts. None of us will ever forget the day that the social workers and resource workers were all piling into our living room in an attempt to get James settled and the paperwork sorted out. The three children, Rosie, James and Xara were all painting at the dining room table, Bruno, our dog was nervously scuttling around everyone's feet, and I was to and fro' the kitchen trying to calm everyone with cups of tea. As I entered the living room with a tray full of steaming beverages, trying to remember who had what, and how many sugars, concentrating on *not* making a complete fool of myself and dropping the tray, but as I walked towards the waiting visitors sitting on the sofa, with strangely open mouths, there was silence and an air of astonishment. It would appear that Xara had learned a new word from the kids at nursery, and had decided to practice this word – 'F---' *that* day, at *that* precise moment in the presence of these people and to top It all, poor Bruno, feeling anxious at all the comings and goings had poohed at their feet! I wanted the pooh stained carpet to open like a hungry mouth and swallow me whole! Despite all this, we always laugh when we remember this day.

However, after James left, Rosie continued as usual, the same old threats, refusals to go to school etc. She disliked James and was glad he was gone. I hoped her behaviour and threats would now calm down, as I was beginning to think that the social worker's decision for her to be placed alone was right and we were wrong, but no, her bad behaviour soon escalated even more. She began accusing us of not looking after her properly, of not taking her to school and of course asking me for a knife with which to cut her throat. Naturally, following all this, she would then throw her arms around me and say she was sorry. This of course was because the weekend was approaching and she wanted to stay with her sister, as *her* carer gave them much more freedom that we felt safe, but I assured her that the sanction still stood, and she was not going on this occasion. Contact often didn't go well for Rosie, especially with dad.

He would lie about mum, usually saying she had been hurt or burnt, or kicked or beaten. This was to worry the children and upset them, he was the male equivalent of Dana, he gained some sort of 'kick' out of people's distress. I decided that contact arrangements for these kids were horrendously chaotic and benefiting no-one. Rosie would always attempt to take control and on one occasion, this resulted in her baby sister's head being bashed on a wall, because no-one else was taking control. This is another lesson I have learned and one I would advocate strongly to other carers and that is, if you feel something's not right, and of no benefit to the children in your care, then advocate for them, disagree with whomsoever you have to, and fight for things to change. Young people often cannot do this for themselves, and don't know how, sometimes don't even recognise where the problem lies, it's our responsibility. Things *did* change however; contact was broken down into smaller gatherings and supervised. It was, however, lovely to know that the family, mum and grandparents at least, had noticed a vast improvement in Rosie's appearance and behaviour, despite her still being very difficult to live with at times. She is constantly threatening to run off, and telling Gordon and I, she is going to see her solicitor to get us 'done.' *We* are not quite sure however, what the accusation is.

Despite this ongoing onslaught from Rosie, we felt it was time for a second placement to live alongside her. We felt that part of her problem may be because she felt isolated here; after all she had come from a large family of nine siblings to a home where there were no other children. Therefore The Agency began the search for a suitable match. This, I thought, was not going to be easy. But, true to form, the Agency had found a child needing a placement and felt she may be right for us. Our Agency worker, Sarah, paid us a visit with all the information regarding this child for us to mull over. As is my habit, I read it over and over again, digesting every word, every poignant incident, or relevant situation in her life, in order to see a clear emotional picture of this child in my head. It was very traumatic and sad reading indeed. As I have mentioned before, there is nothing to be served in detailing these young people's traumatic backgrounds, the fact that they find themselves in these situations, is testimony enough to their need for love and security. This was an eleven year old girl called Charlotte, who was currently residing in a children's home and had been for about three years, along with her sister Tara. Her background and family history were frighteningly similar to those in my own family. A great deal of alcoholism, violence and neglect, and Charlotte had suffered a lot of bereavement in her short life. I immediately felt an empathy with this little girl, and yet I had reservations. Why was she in a children's home, was it because she was extremely badly behaved and no-one could cope with her, or were there other reasons why she was there? We didn't know what to think, but after careful consideration and talks with Sarah, we felt, like every other child, Charlotte deserved a chance at least, and so we made an arrangement to visit the unit and get to know her a little better. We didn't tell Rosie at this point, we didn't want to excite her only to then disappoint her. We arrived at the unit just after lunch, and as we pulled up outside, kids were scurrying around like little monkeys, hanging from the fire escape, climbing through the serving hatch and making a great deal of noise into the bargain. We began to wonder what we had let ourselves in for. However, someone was busy trying to locate Charlotte, who was nowhere to be seen, but all the staff seemed amazingly calm. Apparently, she had shot upstairs, as nerves took over and we were to discover that she was in fact, a very shy child. Minutes later we were led up the stairs to Charlotte's room which she shared with another girl. There was plain wood-chip paper on the walls, no pictures, although the place was tidy and clean. Charlotte was sitting, cross-legged on the bed, head down as we entered the room, and she didn't look up at all or give any eye contact. She was feeling just as nervous as we were. We decided the best course of action would be to sit on the floor beside her, so we were lower than she was and not towering above her, the last thing we wanted to do was to intimidate her. We slowly introduced ourselves and began to tell her about our family, about Xara and Oscar and Bruno. She relaxed a little, spoke now and then, and soon began asking questions. We stayed about half an hour, we didn't want to overwhelm, or bore her even. Charlotte of course, had been told a bit about us prior to our visit, and on hearing our age, her response was similar to that of Rosie, although much more dignified. Before we had arrived, she had announced "I'm not living there, it'll be an old granny house." However she was persuaded to meet us before making a judgement, and fortunately, despite my age, I was wearing the latest 'skinny' jeans that day. After we left, my blue denim jeans, long hair and three inch heels had obviously dispelled some of her initial fears, and we were one step further, she agreed to visit us at home. I liked Charlotte from the beginning, there was something about her which reminded me of myself at her age and I felt we would get along very well. We now had to decide whether she and Rosie would 'click,' though we did agree that her first visit to us should take place when Rosie wasn't there.

One week later, we collected Charlotte mid-morning and brought her home for the rest of the day. She couldn't wait to see the room that would be hers and so we ran up the stairs together, before we did anything else to check it out. You must realise that Charlotte had never had a room that was all her own. She loved it, she loved the wallpaper and the furniture in red and yellow, it wasn't 'grannified' at all as she so delicately put it. At the end of a lovely day together, we took her back to the unit. As we got out of the vehicle, Charlotte shot up the path and inside to her room. I was later to discover the reason for this was, that she had liked it so much at our house, she wanted to move in straight away and knew there was a procedure ahead, it was very difficult for her to handle.

Rosie's behaviour meanwhile, was up and down as usual, but by now we had explained that we had visited Charlotte and that she may be moving in. We told her as much as was appropriate about Charlotte and the things they may have in common. Rosie was also now having some therapy which seemed to be helping, although we had a constant battle with regard to mobile 'phones and belly button piercing. Mobile 'phones for looked after children, can be a positive curse. Anyone, can contact them at any time, not always a good idea, and dad of course would use this as a form of control from afar, would contact Tara in the middle of the night, encouraging her to leave or run away. We were not about to allow him to do the same here, and so we compromised and told Rosie we'd re-consider after her next birthday, a year away, this seemed to keep her happy, for a while at least. The belly-button, well that continued to be a bone of contention. Rosie even secretly plotted with her friend's uncle to do it, but thankfully we uncovered their little secret in the nick of time.

Charlotte visited again, however, and this time met Rosie. They appeared to get along reasonably well, and the day went quite smoothly. Rosie still tried to control every situation and if I didn't respond to her requests as she expected, she would tell me I 'wasn't fit to foster and shouldn't be looking after children,' she would be horrible to her sisters on the 'phone, yet she appeared calm and helpful when Charlotte visited. Perhaps this was what Rosie needed, and Charlotte seemed o.k. when with her too.

It was April Fool's day, and our wedding anniversary. We had decided to have a party, which I had arranged at a suitable venue for over one hundred guests, and although we had been having contact with Charlotte, we didn't invite her to the party as our application for approval to foster her, hadn't yet been to Panel, and if they refused, it would have been unfair to have integrated her into our family too much, to then be saying goodbye. However, a couple of days later, Charlotte had her first overnight stay, and the next morning we spent the day together at Nostell Priory, a beautiful peaceful place. Charlotte, however, managed to keep a healthy independence from Rosie, I think she had quickly picked up on Rosie's controlling behaviour, and was having none of it. This was good, it meant they were going to understand one another, and Charlotte was not going to be controlled by her.

Following a couple more overnight stays, Charlotte had left some small items in 'her' room. This was a silent suggestion on her part that she was determined to be moving in. There was just one obstacle to overcome, Panel, would they agree or would they take notice of Rosie's social worker and say no? No, would have been devastating for Charlotte. Needless to say, the answer was thankfully, yes! Someone, somewhere, had listened to us and Charlotte was to move in for six months trial and then Panel again if it were to become permanent. We decided it would be better and easier for Charlotte to settle in if she didn't have Rosie's excitement and controlling nature to deal with and so arrangements were made for Rosie to stay with her sister overnight. We picked up Charlotte approximately eleven thirty a.m. *and* all her belongings. I had never seen so much stuff from a child in my life. It took two journeys filling our people carrier twice. It turned out however, that most of it was rubbish, quite literally. Charlotte was a sort of rubbish kleptomaniac, endless empty crisp packets, neatly folded and stored, and carrier bags, much the same. It was lunchtime when we arrived back home, Charlotte's *new* home, and so we thought it would be good to have fish and chips. As Charlotte sat to the table and I unfolded the steaming greasy paper from the chips, she began to cry, it had all been just too much for her but it was a case of 'finally – I'm here!' I gave her a hug and assured her she would feel better after a few days.

We sorted and sifted through her stuff together. Most went into her room, the crisp packets and carrier bags went into the bin and stuff she wished to keep but didn't use, went in the loft to be saved. Pretty soon she was feeling like she belonged and her spirits lifted. She was still a very shy child and spoke very little. She would talk to the kids outside, but only from *inside* the garden gate and wouldn't venture beyond. As we sorted her things we collected up the numerous school certificates she had for Punctuality etc. and carefully placed them in a folder, they were precious, and would be more so in the future. She showed me the crumpled photos of her family, some she didn't see any more, some deceased; she shared with me a very private book about her dad, who passed away in tragic circumstances. This told me she trusted me already. Over the next few weeks we made agreements on issues like pocket money etc.

Now strangely, Rosie and Charlotte's relationship together was quite good. Although Rosie 'upped the anti' somewhat and decided she didn't want to live here any more, everyone in this household hated her, and 'others treated her better.' Charlotte however, was more than happy to be here. She would ring the unit now and then to speak to staff and catch up on all the other kids, and her key worker.

So life continued with daily ups and downs, which was by now normal, for us. One exciting event though was that the house next door to us was becoming empty. The owner rented it out to various people who were not always desirable, but this time Gordon, as usual stepped in and negotiated with the owner whom he had naturally befriended, and asked if Angeline and Xara could move in. They had lived over the road for six months which was great, but now they were moving in right next door, fantastic, we were going to be neighbours! We all helped them to move, even the kids enjoyed joining in and soon we had the place ship-shape.

Rosie still continued her attempts at control. She returned home late one day from a walk with a friend's dog and told us such a tale, it put me in mind of Leah. *Apparently*, she had been approached by a gang of black youths who had stolen her school report and thrown her sister's mobile 'phone, which Rosie was carrying, into the bushes, which she retrieved of course. They then threatened her with a knife. Oh my goodness! How would we continue without her report, I asked myself? There were, however, to be many other stories from Rosie regarding attacks and being followed when she needed an excuse for being late. I therefore decided it was time to tell her the tale of Matilda, who cried 'Fire Fire' from her bedroom window so many Times that people eventually ignored her, until one day the house actually *was* on fire and guess what, no-one believed her and the house burned down, with Matilda in it. This revelation however, did little to change Rosie's lies and so she continued with her wondrous tales. Charlotte, on the other hand, was a very truthful girl, perhaps *too* truthful at times. Her many Sundays at church had obviously paid off in the honesty stakes, therefore she was only too ready to tell what Rosie had been up to, or what she may have neglected to do. She hadn't turned the shower off properly, left the soap in the basin, not put the milk back in the fridge etc. In the early days it was hard to tell whether Charlotte just had a compulsion for truth and honesty or whether she had something to invest in being the 'good girl' of the two, for she never swore, never stole and her bedroom was immaculately kept. On the other hand Rosie's immediate reaction to anything she didn't like or was asked to do was along the lines of 'shit' or 'fucking hell.' She thought it was extremely amusing, when playing Blind Man's Bluff, one day, to place the laundry basket in front of Charlotte who was innocently wearing the blindfold, only for her to inevitably fall flat on her face.

We tried our level best to keep up any contact necessary for these kids, and therefore took Charlotte back to the unit a couple of times for a visit until the desire to do so dwindled away. Mum would ring Charlotte, usually when she was inebriated and within minutes Charlotte would dissolve into tears at whatever was being relayed to her. These calls were a condition of the placement negotiated between mum and social services. However, I considered them to be destructive to this child and this reached a climax one day, when Charlotte was smiling and happily took a call from mum. It is our policy to hover around when young people are on the 'phone, not for the purpose of listening in to their conversation gratuitously, but for reasons of making sure they are safe and that no-one is misleading or encouraging them to sabotage their placement in any way, and on this occasion within minutes of the call, Charlotte silently dissolved into tears. I glanced her way, discreetly, as there was a strange silence only to see the floods of silent tears trickling down Charlotte's flushed cheeks, her excited smile at taking the call from her mum had disappeared and her hand was gripping the receiver so tightly, her knuckles were white. I instinctively prised her fingers, one by one from the receiver and lifted it to my ear, only to be met by the rasping sound of this woman drunkenly piling the guilt of all that had happened within the family, firmly upon

Charlotte's eleven year old shoulders. I politely but frostily informed her that I was ending the call and not allowing Charlotte to be upset any further. Her response to this was to hurl abuse and *demand* that I put Charlotte back on the line as she *was* allowed to speak to her. I informed her not so politely, that it was my 'phone and I wasn't allowing the call to continue, neither would I allow such abuse to enter my home, however it was delivered. As I have said before, we must advocate for these children at such times, and I really felt these calls were not helpful for Charlotte, although I knew I was battling against an agreement set up with social services. However, I battled on until the agreement was changed, whereby no incoming calls would be accepted, but Charlotte could call mum herself, on her own terms. This worked perfectly, for despite regular reminders, Charlotte never decided to ring mum. This reinforced to me that we had made the right decision.

Contact for Rosie was equally strained. Dad was always complaining he didn't see his girls enough and didn't know how they lived, despite the fact that he didn't show up for arranged contacts. I decided we needed to remove this ammunition from him and came to an agreement with the social worker that he could visit Rosie, here at home. This was to be a 'one off' visit so that he could see where and how she lived, and stop his complaints. We normally don't have contact at home. This is a child's place of safety, refuge, if that becomes violated where do they run for comfort and security? We would, however have Rosie's siblings, Susan and Abby regularly to stay; they were in the care of Local Authority carers. Now Abby was just a year or so older than Rosie and although it was plain to see, there was a great bond between them, though they didn't always get along when in each other's company. However Rosie would often stay over at Abby's carer's house, and was cared for by Janet. Janet would often ring me and tell me how well behaved Rosie and Abby had been the previous day; therefore she had given the two of them some money to go shopping. I found this rather curious, given Rosie's usual behaviour and wondered what magic Janet used, to obtain such a compliant attitude, because the minute Rosie returned home she was back to her old self. However, it didn't take me long to realise that Rosie was getting her own way, the freedom to travel to town, with money, something I would have been reluctant to trust her with. We soon discovered that my fears were well founded, Rosie and Abby had *not* been going shopping at all, as I had suspected, but had been visiting dad, which was not allowed. He'd had great fun, plying them with drink, and I suspect, possibly drugs.

Now as I said previously, Charlotte had suffered a fair bit of bereavement in her young life. Not only had her dad passed away in tragic circumstances, but her young cousin aged three, had died in a house fire, and her favourite teacher had died suddenly of a heart attack. Also her two younger siblings had been adopted which is yet another form of bereavement, as I can personally testify. This was not the end for poor Charlotte. Don, her social work rang to tell us that her Nan, Hilda had passed away, and we needed to find an appropriate time to tell Charlotte. She was understandably upset, even though she hadn't been particularly close to this Nan; it was yet another loss that was the upsetting thing, as the members of her family were deserting her one by one. However, Charlotte found it very difficult to communicate when upset. She would write down her feelings on a scrap of paper and push it under my bedroom door. Almost as though she needed to share these feelings but didn't know any other way to communicate them.

Now the Agency would organise a holiday each year during the summer, for carers to take the children away. That first year it was Skipsea, in a caravan. Charlotte asked me if we had to go by aeroplane as she didn't think she would like flying. I assured her that we would manage to get there by car, bless her. How she and Rosie enjoyed that week, and Xara came too, as the Agency does not discriminate between birth children and those looked after. We did so much, the beach, the karaoke etc. We visited a stately home and Charlotte got lost in the maze. How she panicked, poor love. She was still as yet struggling to gain her self-confidence, and finding herself alone amongst the privet hedges was overwhelming. Gordon ventured through the maze to find her whilst I calmed her from beyond her leafy prison as she screamed and fought the thorny barrier between us.

It was almost Christmas, and we had not yet been informed whether Charlotte would be allowed to stay with us long-term. We arranged yet another holiday for the children, this time to Center Parcs in the beautiful setting of Sherwood Forest. We had planned to be there the week before Christmas, when the trees are bare and there's a chill in the air, but when darkness fell the illuminated reindeer could be seen amongst the bushes, and Santa was beckoning all the children into his ice cave, to discover their hopes and wishes for Christmas Day. As we walked home to our villa after a good meal, we would put a log on the fire and drink hot chocolate before bedtime. A couple of things however, would mar our pleasure. Charlotte's social worker had called us a few days before to give us a date for the Panel, at which Charlotte's fate would be decided, it was to be right in the middle of the holiday. The social worker wanted to cancel and rearrange, but we decided it was best to go ahead or it could be another six months, therefore we agreed to travel home for the meeting, although we didn't tell Charlotte, she was such a worrier and it would have spoilt her happiness, the first proper holiday she had ever had as a family.

We had agreed to take Rosie's sister Abby, with us though her carer Janet had liked the idea, and booked a villa the same week for herself and her two boys, so that we could all spend time together. Now, Janet had recently split with her husband and was trying to enjoy a new life with a family friend she had known for some years. The night before we were due to embark on our holiday, the kids had gone to bed early and I was finishing the packing, when the 'phone rang, that dreaded 'phone. It was Janet, in great distress, the kind I had heard many times from Dora, and my blood ran cold as I knew it meant trouble of some kind. She was very incoherent, something about –'Daniel may die!' and could I go immediately? I left Gordon with the sleeping children, and sped off the five miles or so to Janet's house. The police were just leaving as I arrived and as I peered around the door, I could see the kitchen floor awash with blood, Daniel's blood. It would appear her jealous ex-husband had dived through a lounge window as they sat watching T.V. Daniel, being a bouncer, had wrestled him to the floor as he attacked but Janet felt sorry for her estranged spouse, and asked Daniel to let him go. Now Daniel was a very tall, but gentle natured man and did, immediately release his assailant. However, this attacker did not return the favour, and promptly hit Daniel over the head with a five foot long wrought iron candlestick, felling him to the floor in one blow, leaving him unconscious with blood pouring from his head wound. They were both taken away, Daniel to hospital, his assailant to the police cells.

Janet was beside herself, there were three children in the house, including her own two boys. It was not known at this point whether Daniel was going to live or die from his injuries. Added to that, Janet's husband, the father of her children could then be put on a murder charge. He was already now in custody for attempted murder. Poor Janet just didn't know which way to turn. However, I suggested it would be best if I took Abby home with me, and Janet and the boys went home with her mother. Naturally this meant she would not be going on holiday the next morning. These poor children, not only had they just witnessed their dad, whom they loved being violent and led away in handcuffs by the police, a man they respected taken to hospital, and their mum distraught, they also would not be having the holiday they had so looked forward to. There wasn't much we could do about dad, or Daniel, but perhaps Gordon and I could take the boys away whilst it was all sorted out. So the very next morning we set off with Rosie, Charlotte, Xara Abby and the boys. We had obtained the key of Janet's villa from her, and the arrangement we came up with was that I would stay with the girls and Gordon would look after the two boys. Somehow, they all enjoyed the holiday.

For us of course, there was still the small matter of the Panel on Wednesday. By this time Janet had joined us and took over the care of her sons. Daniel had regained consciousness and was going to be o.k. We asked her if she could manage the girls for the afternoon, the day of the Panel. However, despite Janet being a fully qualified carer, Xara refused to stay with someone she hardly knew, and so we had to take her with us. We made our excuses to the girls and drove back to Sheffield for the all important 'Panel.' As we gave our names and reason for visit to the receptionist, our support from the Agency, Paul, was there waiting for us. Two hours we waited, they were running late, but eventually our names were called.
Excitedly we jumped from our seats and walked nervously down the corridor toward the open door. Xara however, was tired and promptly tripped over the carpet and fell flat on her face as we entered the room. What a good start. Gordon swooped her up and comforted her, whilst a rather official looking lady reached for a plate in the centre of the mile-long shiny oak table they were all sitting round, and offering up the plate said. "Oh darling, would you like a biscuit?" in response to Xara's tears. "No thanks, not just now." Replied *Gordon*! No, not now, this was no time for jokes I thought, as my eyes scanned the faces of the seated officials.

To my horror, half of them were people I had slated over the 'phone regarding Leah that day. We were doomed. None of these were going to do *me* the favour of allowing Charlotte to stay. All they would see was the face of the horrible ranting woman they had encountered previously. Thankfully, they were true professionals, they knew that I'd had Leah's best interests at heart, and didn't hold it against me. Our bums had barely touched the seats before one of them announced their decision for Charlotte to stay with us until she was eighteen. We broke the news to Charlotte on our return, only to be met by anger from her that they had chosen to do it during her holiday. This of course was her way of concealing the immense joy and relief she felt, at her immediate future being secure, but she was not about to let her true feelings be known, for fear of revealing too much of herself.

Despite the traumas preceding it, the holiday went well and we returned home in time for Christmas. 'Life' picked up more or less where it had left off. Rosie was back on form, swearing, ranting and accusing us of all sorts. It usually meant something was on her mind and sure enough, a day or two later she began to tell me how her uncle kindly informed her that she was mental and 'should be in a Nut House.' He had said she was horrible and nobody liked her. Now I know from my description of Rosie, you may be thinking, perhaps he was right, but I can assure you he wasn't. These children are very troubled and it shows itself in many ways, but if you dig deep enough, there is always something likeable, even lovable within them, and there were lots of things about Rosie I liked. So we had a long conversation about the differences between liking someone, but not necessarily liking the things that they do. This was how I felt about Rosie, she did some horrible things sometimes, but where was it coming from? The situation started to pick up for a while, she settled down and we felt we were beginning to live a 'normal' life, as much as it could be. By the time the following summer arrived we felt we needed a break and used our respite allowance to take a holiday to Tunisia with J and J. Through the Agency, carers are given three weeks respite yearly, whereby they arrange for the children to stay with other carers in order for us to recharge our batteries. I can tell you that at times it is more than welcome.

The holiday was wonderful and we returned home rejuvenated. However, Rosie was once more becoming aggressive and demanding. Her good behaviour had been short lived, and she was doing anything and everything to annoy us. I was called upstairs one day, when Rosie and Charlotte were listening to music in Rosie's room. They had found it quite amusing that there was a 'caterpillar' crawling across the bedroom floor. I thought this sounded strange and felt it wise to investigate. As I plodded across the bright red carpet, scanning every inch of it for this offending grub, my eyes fell upon a tiny, white, creature, hurriedly attempting to make its way across the floor towards the bed, Maggots! I thought, not caterpillars, this was a whole different story. I explained the difference to the giggling girls, and advised that there must be rotting food somewhere, something to which neither of them would admit, as I didn't allow food in bedrooms for this very reason. Sure enough as we searched, we soon uncovered Charlotte's little forgotten stash under the bed. Bags of rotting sandwiches, the remnants of a picnic that she couldn't be bothered to dispose of. We also discovered a secret stash of Rosie's but of a very different kind. Letters, that she had so delicately penned, and signed with *my* name, excusing her from P.E. lessons. How disappointing!

Rosie's behaviour started to take a nose dive. She flitted from euphoria to despair at lightening speed, and flew into frightening rages. She increased every negative move one could imagine. She constantly wanted her mother to die. She verbally trashed everything and anything Charlotte did or had which was now naturally beginning to affect Charlotte's mood. The situation regarding Rosie and Abby's illicit rendezvous with dad was also becoming more serious. He was encouraging Rosie to subversively have her 'belly-button' pierced, in order for him to then sue the social services, because she didn't have his written permission. Rosie was frequently late home, almost every day, with some excuse or another. Daily, there would be negative comments regarding my hair or makeup, or the clothes I was wearing. I realise I am an adult, professional, but my energies both physical and emotional were flagging, Rosie was doing a good demolition job.

School were also suffering, she would often tell her teacher she won't listen because she is a 'Packi.' A very racist and derogatory remark which was totally unacceptable. She was also attempting to pull Charlotte into her world. Encouraging her to lock herself in the bathroom with her, or climb into Charlotte's bed and shut the door, knowing this was against our house rules. I tried every approach know to man and womankind, to help; her. I even encouraged her to punch her pillow when she felt angry at anyone as it wouldn't hurt, but she could get some of the anger out. To write angry thoughts down on paper and give them to me to dispose of, effectively disposing of the anger. This worked, momentarily, and then she was back to wedging me in the door with her foot behind it, blocking my way from room to room and throwing things at me. I often found letters written to me containing death threats that she was going to kill me or get her dad to kill me. One even had a coffin bearing the letters, R.I.P. Sandy, drawn on the front, after which I removed her Hi-Fi system for a couple of days, to no avail. The school learning mentor was now becoming involved due to homework not being completed and 'bunking' off school. Even the contact workers were refusing to supervise these girls, and in particular Rosie, but I *still* didn't want to give up on her.

I decided something was perhaps needed in order to cheer everyone up. A re-vamp of bedrooms was what I came up with. We decided to tackle Rosie's first and set about stripping off the old wallpaper one Saturday morning. Rosie began with great enthusiasm, but within ten minutes she decided she was cold and put on her dressing gown over her clothing. Then she was hot, tired and needed to lie down. Charlotte, Gordon and I were all pitching in to help, but the minute Rosie decided she couldn't make the effort, I advised everyone to down tools and leave it. This stunned her, she was totally shocked. By the afternoon, when it finally dawned on her that we had given up, she suddenly set to, with scraper in hand, and, give her her due, she didn't stop until every tiny scrap of paper was in a heap on the floor. It was almost midnight but we had left her to it.

I later promised, and arranged a helicopter flight for Rosie and Charlotte, if they could keep up more positive behaviour. Every effort was put into promoting a positive attitude. Then Rosie dropped her latest bombshell! Apparently, on one of her escapades with Abby, she had had sex in a field, with Abby's encouragement. I wasn't sure whether this was true or just a ploy for attention. Nonetheless, we did a pregnancy test which thankfully proved negative.

The pressure was building, and we needed a break. Occasionally Gordon and I attended Induction courses for new carers, to give advice and be available for them to ask questions. It also gave us a chance for a change of scenery and a little adult conversation, and although it was work of a kind, it was a refreshing change and somewhat of an escape. Also during this difficult time, the Agency helped us with extra support where possible, and sent us a beautiful bouquet of flowers as encouragement, which was very much appreciated.

Rosie's birthday was forthcoming and she had given me a list of requests for her special day. However, sadly there was nothing from her family which understandably upset her. I just knew we would be in for a bad time. True to form, Rosie increased the number of occasions when she would venture out to school in the morning, but the pull was just too strong, and rather than turn right at the end of the road, to school, she would turn left, and off to dad'.' The police were now frequent visitors to our home. We were regularly giving statements, photographs etc., until it reached a point where I was on first name terms with half of South

Yorkshire Police Force. It became so frequent, that they would eventually take details over the 'phone. We desperately needed help, Rosie was taking over, it was affecting us all, and a couple of times I had burst into tears of sheer despair and frustration, I was losing the plot. The Agency came up with a hopeful answer and invited us to attend a course on Attachment Theories. It was decided that Rosie had severe attachment difficulties, and training for us on this subject may help.

Though I am no expert on *anything*, perhaps I should explain briefly, the theory of Attachment. When a baby is born, the neurons in the brain which allow us to form relationships, or attachments to others, or to care givers, are feeling their way, and growing. However, if there is no affection, no bonding with an infant, or the cycle of needs are not met correctly, then these neurons simply die, as they are of no further use. This may then result in the young person growing to adulthood, lacking the ability to form suitable secure attachments. This is a brief explanation, in a nutshell, it is in actual fact, far more complex than this. Therefore you may understand why we would need this vital training and information, which hopefully would help us to understand Rosie, to look beyond the obvious behaviour, to the underlying cause. If we can then tackle the root cause, it may result in better success. For example, we observed bad behaviour when

Rosie received nothing for her birthday from her family, but to understand her hurt and let her know that she had every right to be upset, to show empathy may reach the core of the issue, rather than condemning her for the resulting behaviour. If only we had been able to understand this before now, but then, would it have made any difference? Would it make a difference now? It was like light bulbs flashing. We began putting what we were learning into practice immediately, and the result, for ourselves, was amazing. We felt calmer, and much more in control again. The understanding alone of what we were dealing with helped tremendously.

Sadly, it appeared to be too late for Rosie. No matter what we did, she fought against us. We discovered that on one of her jaunts, when missing, she and Abby had been visiting the flat of some asylum seekers they had met in town. It was felt necessary to consult the sexual exploitation team, to unravel these tenuous threads. The police raided the flat in question, to find a young girl locked in the bedroom. Even this didn't deter Rosie, she was on a mission of self-destruct, and seemed more determined than ever to pull Charlotte into her web of lies and degradation. Charlotte was becoming more and more withdrawn and Xara was telling me even at her young age, to send Rosie away.

The months and seasons were dragging on and summer was upon us yet again. We organised a holiday in the Scottish Highlands for the children, in a bungalow in a small village. Charlotte and Xara were excited and looking forward to this, but Rosie was up and down like a see-saw, one minute she was coming, the next, she wasn't going to 'that crappy place.' This indecision went on for a number of weeks and was really wearing thin. One day, she was feeling particularly annoyed with her dad for some reason and began pacing the floor, then ran upstairs, growling like a wild animal and gritting her teeth and spreading her extended fingers like a wildcat unsheathing its claws. The sounds emanating from our house were pitiful and we were concerned as to what the neighbours may make of the snarls and growls. I opened the front door and stood in the open doorway for our own safety, and Gordon sat on the bottom of the stairs in order to try to prevent Rosie from leaving. We feared for her safety should she run off in this condition, all the while she was kicking Gordon in the back, pulling the handrail from its brackets on the wall, and relishing every second she screamed, that I was 'a fucking liar.' When calm, and 'rational', following these episodes, Rosie would tell us how she could see little men with blonde hair telling her to kill herself. I feared that either she was under the influence of drugs, or on the verge of schizophrenia, though again; I had no qualifications to diagnose such things, just my intuition and gut instinct.

Another evening, Rosie was in a foul mood because I felt it inappropriate for her to stay over at Abby's. She shut herself in her room and we could hear a great deal of crashing and banging, but despite this we left her to it. The toilet was next to Rosie's room and upon hearing me open the door, she opened hers simultaneously. There are five doors along our landing and each one had been decorated, by Rosie, with a large sheet of paper attached with Bluetac, bearing various statements such as: - 'Sandy is a Bitch.' 'Sandy is a f----ing liar.' 'Sandy is a mother-f---ing whore,' and so forth, plus an emotional letter I had written for Rosie, was torn to shreds and scattered around my door. I calmly took them down and gently rolled them up in my hands, and thanked her for sharing this information with me. Upon doing this, she lurched forward and screamed her request 'Take me to hospital, I've eaten the soap.' All the time spitting on me as I descended the stairs. I stopped and looked up at her, Rosie's ejected saliva trickling down my face and hair, and told her not to worry, it would be out the other end by morning! Eventually she calmed down and went to bed. This was too much. The next morning she went into town and walked into the office of 'her' solicitor, to accuse me of sitting on her and forcing a bar of soap down her throat, that Gordon had put her on the floor and pushed her face into a mirror. Either she had a very vivid imagination or someone was putting the ideas in her head.

The solicitor rang us regarding these allegations and the social worker had to contact the police, Rosie was asked to make a written statement in respect of her accusations several times but each time she refused.

We decided there was no way we could tolerate taking Rosie to Scotland. It wouldn't be fair to Xara and Charlotte, they had behaved so well. I contacted the Agency and was offered several alternatives, all of which I declined. I simply did not want to take her! She had always accused us of not listening to her, but this time we did, and when she again said she might not go, we informed her that we *had* listened – and she wasn't going! She covered her face with her hands and couldn't actually believe that we would not take her. She was transported to carers in the middle of nowhere, for her respite, miles from civilisation, nowhere to run.

On our return from Scotland, Rosie came back to us, only to run off the next day. Abby kindly informed us that she had left Rosie with a known drug dealer but wouldn't tell us where. She was gone for a week and no-one knew where, or what was happening to her. This was intolerable.

It was Bonfire Night, fifth of November, and Rosie was still missing. That evening, following a few fireworks and sparklers for Charlotte and Xara, we were about to go to bed, when the dreaded 'phone rang, seven times in fifteen minutes, with each call the voice was threatening to kill us, to push fireworks through our letterbox etc. I couldn't sleep that night and admit to placing a bucket full of water behind the front door.

However, eventually she turned up with Abby, at Janet's house. I drove over there only to find Rosie ranting and raving as usual, but I was used to it by now. Janet though, had never seen her behave this way before and was obviously upset by it, but Rosie continued, accusing our Link worker and her social worker of having an affair. Due to Rosie's state of mind, secure transport had to be arranged, whereby she could be physically manhandled by those qualified to do so, we were not.

I'm afraid this was the final straw. We had done our best for Rosie, and there was of course, Charlotte *an*d Xara to consider. They had, in essence been somewhat neglected in all honesty. Rosie had commanded *all* the attention for too long.

Charlotte particularly had been confused and frightened by some events. Rosie had told her that, if she herself left, then Charlotte also would have to leave. This naturally frightened Charlotte as she didn't want to leave. Rosie had also told her she would get Gordon and I 'done' for 'not feeding her, and dad would do this house in!' She demanded tea served in her room, etc., etc.

We had meetings with all involved and it was mutually decided that Rosie should go, should actually be moved out of the city, away from dad's destructive influence. The Agency therapist, Karen was wonderful, and gave us lots of uplifting advice and help.

There was a mixture of feelings following Rosie's departure. The house was calm quiet and peaceful and yet I couldn't help feeling we had failed her in some way, and missed her lively chatter, though not the traumas which ensued. However, Charlotte began to gain confidence once more and was much less withdrawn.

Almost a whole year had gone by, it was near to Christmas again, and it had been a year of Hell! We had tried to cling on to Rosie, to no avail, where did we go from here. We had wanted to give both she and Charlotte, a long-term home, but our plans were in shreds. We decided we needed time for another appropriate placement to be selected, and in the mean time we did some day-care and respite.

Now Jake was a particularly obstinate young man, aged about ten years old. His carers had regularly felt much the same way that we had with Rosie and needed an occasional break. We were asked to have Jake for the day, and decided to take him out to Castleton, a small and select village in the Peak District of Derbyshire, famous for its cave networks and home of the Blue John Stone, and not far from my place of birth. It wasn't easy, but Rosie had been a good initiation for us if nothing else. I was feeling a sense of loss, losing Rosie, and needed a new challenge. Jake was certainly that! He would enter the sedate country shops and announce loudly, to the sedate country shopkeepers, that what they were selling 'was absolute crap.' I loudly announced that in that case he wouldn't want to buy anything, and suggested he go outside. Near to lunchtime, we decided to take everyone for fish and chips. It was winter, cold, and the normally babbling brook had become a raging torrent due to the thaw from the surrounding hills. Jake decided to climb onto the wall and hover back and forth on his stomach, hanging over the river, mistakenly thinking that this would prevent us all having lunch, *but*, he had never met anyone like Gordon and me. I suggested that Gordon continue with the children, for their food. Jake knew I was unable to leave him there alone in such a dangerous situation. As Gordon and the children walked away into the distance, I folded my arms and leaned on the wall beside Jake. I pointed out to him that I couldn't swim, therefore if he were to fall in, *I* would not be going after him. I also made him understand that I wasn't hungry and was prepared to stand there until the others had eaten, but it was his choice, either we could stay there for an hour, or go and join the others, either way, I was o.k. Guess what? He chose to go eat!

The next through our door was such a refreshing change. His name was Seamus, once again half Caribbean origin and half Irish. The difference with Seamus was, he was only six weeks old, but had the same creamy mild chocolate skin, and big brown eyes as Xara. He had such a mop of thick black crinkly hair which was a delightful distraction from the sad wrinkled expression permanently fixed to his little face. On returning from school that day, Xara fell in love with him immediately and asked, "What language does he speak?" He was such a tiny little mite, with very slender little arms and legs, and he cried all the time. His mother was from London and had no family or friends here in the north. She had been taken into hospital with pancreatitis and possibly Hepatitis C; it was also considered that Seamus may have succumbed to the Hepatitis.

I have never witnessed the attachment issue in a child so young before. Seamus would become quiescent following a feed, bath and nappy change, but there was no smile, no eye contact or kicking of his legs, and still this deep frown on his little face. We had been due to attend a conference for two days in Harrogate but due to this latest emergency, we decided that Gordon would have to go alone, and I would stay here and look after Seamus. How he loved the lights twinkling on the Christmas tree, and the fluffy snowman on the mantelpiece which played Away in a Manger. When he was feeding, I would hold him in one arm and 'pat' his nappy gently, his eyelids would droop, lulled by the rhythmic sucking sound as he gripped the teat of the bottle with his rosebud lips. He fought sleep, as all babies do, but after three days with us, his eyes sought mine when I gazed and smiled at him. He eventually returned the smile and kicked his legs in excitement and anticipation of the 'tickle' on his tummy that would follow. After a full bottle and a bit of winding, I would put on some music and dance slowly round the room until he could fight the battle with sleep no longer. My little dog, Oscar *loves* babies, loves their smell, and is certainly very protective towards them. He would take up position beside the cot and lay there, unmoving until Seamus stirred, then he was alerted to the soft whimpering sounds he could hear from the cot as the baby was slowly emerging from his deep sleep, and dutifully come to find me, to alert me to the need to attend. The change in this child was so dramatic in such a short space of time. It was part of my duty to take Seamus to visit his mother in hospital *every* day. After a period of ten days we had to hand Seamus back to his mum, it was sad, but I insisted he was checked and weighed. He had gained two pounds and was very content; the frown had disappeared from his brow, for now. I wondered if it would return.

Now, despite our traumas with Rosie, she still rang us frequently, was very apologetic and wanted to come back, but I knew I had to stick to my guns as hard as it was, to say no. We did return her calls however, and because it had been leading up to Christmas, we had obviously bought all her presents, including a portable T.V. for her room. We decided that she should still have them, after all they were bought for her so we arranged to visit her, the day before Christmas Eve in her temporary home, in the middle of nowhere. We took her for a walk and she was happily reminiscing over the good times we'd had, and turned to me and said, with a grin on her face: - "Do you remember when I swallowed the soap Sandy?" I replied, "Yes, but I found it when I packed your stuff!" (Because I knew it hadn't really been swallowed.) Her face was a picture of disbelief, and I truly think that at that moment, Rosie could not believe that despite us knowing what she had put us through, we were still fond of her. A sense of humour is essential, and amongst her gifts I had wrapped a lovely soap in the shape of a piece of cheesecake with cherries on top, and inside I had written a note which read, 'It's soap, Rosie, please don't swallow it!'

However, the day came to an end and we had to say goodbye. Naturally Rosie was very tearful but we assured her we would keep in touch. As we were about to head for home, Gordon's mobile rang. It was the Agency asking us if we could take a thirteen year old girl called Ruth for an unknown period, arriving the day after Boxing Day. We were then asked what time we would be home that day so that they could bring her to meet us. As we pulled up outside our home, two hours later, they were waiting for us. Ruth was not pleased about any of it. Apparently she wanted to stay at her dad's and so they had allowed her to, for a couple of days only, but her previous placement had broken down, hence her need to stay with us. At least we thought we had Christmas Eve, and Boxing Day to recoup. However, as usual things rarely work out perfectly, and sure enough as we were about to have a peaceful evening meal, *on* Boxing Day, the police knocked at our door, with Ruth. Her dad had hit her and plied her with beer, followed by abusive 'phone calls to the police.

It was not an easy few weeks with Ruth. She was a strange, although very damaged girl, and had enormous issues with her mother, who, by the way, turned up on our doorstep the next day, demanding to see her daughter. Social services had given her our address. Gordon and I stood side by side in the doorway and insisted with great resolve, that we do not conduct contact sessions in our home and therefore she must contact her social worker. There were many issues with Ruth; she wasn't a very sociable girl, quite 'boyish' in her manner and dress. She seemed to want to spend much of her time in her room, therefore we temporarily installed a spare portable T.V. in there, so that at least she had some form of entertainment. Unfortunately the signal wasn't good and it was only possible to use the combined V.C.R. and so she would venture downstairs in silence, select a video cassette and return to her room until she had watched it.

Kids always seem to feel they are much cleverer than adults, I suppose I was the same, despite the lack of experience and years, and sure enough, Ruth was no exception, as I awoke one morning at two a.m. and was aware that Ruth was watching T.V. Our bedroom doors have a small glass pane above each one and I could see the light flickering from the screen. I knocked quietly so not to wake Charlotte, asleep in the next room, and asked Ruth to switch off the T.V. "Yeah" came her reply, yet nothing happened. I knocked again and entered the room to find Ruth still laid on the bed, fully dressed, remote in hand but refusing to switch it off. She said she should be able to do what she wanted in her room. I agreed, but not at two in the morning, and always being one step ahead, I ejected the cassette and removed it, to her protestation, asking when she will get it back. She then refused to switch out the light. At this, without further ado, I stood on the end of the bed and removed the light bulb! One step ahead at all times.

Ruth was by now beginning to realise who was in control, and it wasn't her. She asked one day if she could go for a walk, Gordon asked her not to be long as lunch would be ready in about an hour. We had my niece Sally and her partner, who by the way were both police officers, visiting for lunch, and when Ruth had not returned by four thirty p.m. I began to feel concerned. The only number I had was for her mother, it was still Bank Holiday and the office was closed. I didn't want to alert the out-of-hours team until I felt it essential. Shortly afterwards, Ruth's mother rang back, very angry and upset. She didn't actually live far from us and had discovered that Ruth had visited a known paedophile on the road below us and got herself abused. Was this an odd method of self-harm, I asked myself? Had Ruth visited, knowing that this might happen to her? Whatever the reason, this man had abused a child and it *must* be reported. Two police women arrived and informed me that we needed to attend the hospital with Ruth, for forensic examination but they were trying to locate the police surgeon. It was about eleven p.m. by the time he arrived, before which Ruth had been tearing around the hospital through the wards, waking the sleeping and sick children, and chatting to the nurses whom she obviously knew. It would appear she had stayed here several times before, due to overdose of paracetamol. When I finally caught up with her and persuaded her to come back down, we then had the battle of persuading her to go through with this awful examination. Poor girl, I really felt for her despite the escapades we had just had. I had been in this position before and it was not a happy or comfortable place to be. If I'd had my way I would probably have just taken her home, not put her through this, but I knew this man had to be stopped. After many objections, I took Ruth to one side and explained how I felt for her, I understood, but it would be her bravery that would put him away, prevent him from doing this again. With that, she jumped up, ran into the room and said, "O.K. let's get it over with." When it was all over, I was thankful that I could take Ruth home, let her have a hot bath and straight to bed. I was wrong! It was three a.m., and the police had taken her clothes and shoes for forensic evidence. Eventually the doctor appeared and handed Ruth a box of paracetamol. This was a child who was known to overdose! I was annoyed and angry, but Ruth was now full of glee, and stuffed the box of pills into the pocket of the fresh trousers I had thankfully thought to bring along. I asked her to hand them over but she refused, saying "No, let's go!" Remember, one step ahead, take control. I folded my arms, much as I had done with Jake that day, and slid down the wall, sitting cross-legged on the floor. Ruth looked perplexed and asked me what I was doing. I replied that we were not moving until she handed the pills over. She laughed, but *there*, I was determined to stay. It was about another half an hour of arguments from her, before Ruth finally remembered my determination, that *I* was the grown-up, the one in control, and reluctantly she gave me the pills. The next day we spent at the police station, Ruth's testimony to be videoed.

It had been an ordeal of a different kind caring for Ruth; it was difficult for the authorities to know what best to do for her future and asked us if we could keep her longer. I was not sorry that a few days later, we were going away on holiday, and had to decline, though I was so sad for poor Ruth, therefore I enquired about her situation on my return.

Chapter Twenty Three

Old Friends – New Beginnings

We were tidying up the garden ready for winter, when the 'phone rang from inside. It was mid-October and feeling rather chilly. The call was from Australia but it wasn't our old friends, Lionel and Trish, it was their daughter, Karen. My heart always skips a beat when it's a relative of friends on the line, it's usually bad news. Thankfully this time it was not. Quite the opposite in fact, and just what we needed. Karen was calling to tell us it was her parent's thirtieth wedding anniversary in January and she was planning a big surprise party for them, and she had been wondering if we would be able to attend! It must have been a long shot for her, twelve thousand miles away, and the other side of the word to attend a party?! However, this was not out of the question for us, Lionel and Trish were very dear friends of ours, dear to our hearts, and it would be our great pleasure and privilege to join them on such a special occasion. Of course we didn't know quite *how* we would manage it, but we were determined we would. For a start it was going to cost a fortune, and second, what would we do with the children? This would be the third time I had travelled to Australia, the second for Gordon, so the distance didn't really faze me at all. Also of course, it wasn't going to be easy to arrange. If Lional and Trish didn't know we were going, we would have to ensure every tiny detail was perfectly organised in order to keep the secret. We began making the arrangements and checked with the travel agent for flights. We mustn't arrive *too* soon or they would discover us, but mustn't arrive late and miss the party. We finally found a flight which would only have one stopover, in Dubai, and deliver us to Perth W.A. by five p.m. the day *before* the party, it was perfect.

Angeline was now our respite carer and arrangements were made for Charlotte to stay with her and Xara, for the two weeks or so we would be away. Yes I know, it's such a long way to go for such a short time, but we were well aware that it wasn't good for children to be left for too long, to feel insecure, therefore we had to settle for what we knew was right.

However, by now Seamus had been and gone and the lovely Ruth bless her, had also gone, but this didn't mean we had any sort of reprieve. Negotiations had already begun for a teenage girl, whose placement had broken down. Her name was Maryan and she was almost sixteen years old, and as soon as Christmas was out of the way, we managed to fit in a visit with her before we flew off into the sunset. It was agreed she would move in on our return.

We said our goodbyes to Angeline, Xara and Charlotte and set off for W.A. After a long though very comfortable flight with Royal Arab Emirates, we landed at Perth airport in good time. Karen and her husband Mark, and children Montana and Cameron were waiting there to meet us. The sun was shining high in the clear blue sky, though we were wearing woolly jackets and jumpers. It was January back in England after all. Following the short drive to Karen's house, and exchanging a few pleasantries and updates about our families, they kindly allowed us to retreat to our room and slumber.

I looked at my watch in the half light, it was three a.m. Where was I? As I lifted my head from the pillow in an attempt to collect my thoughts, the pain at the back of my eyes forced me to lie back down. I remembered that I was in the Antipodes, where everything was the other way round and my head felt like it was too. I knew I couldn't wake the whole household, and tried to lie perfectly still so as not to feel the pain when I moved. Fatigue must have eventually caught up with me some time later. I could hear the faint sounds of people chatting, and as I looked to my right, Gordon was not there, so I decided I must get up and find out what was going on, the pain had not subsided. As I staggered into the living room,

Karen was bubbling with excitement and everyone was preparing for the forthcoming party at five p.m. It was now three thirty and I hadn't even unpacked! There was no *way* I was going to this party, I felt like *death*! All this way and all I wanted to do was curl up and die. It was decided by Karen's friend that it was jet lag, which she announced as she calmly waved two tiny bottles back and forth in her hand, and in her lovely Aussie twang, she guided me back to the bedroom and ordered me to strip off and lie face down on the bed. I couldn't be bothered to argue and meekly obeyed. She sat beside me and dripped the liquid from the two bottles onto my neck and with a cheery dialogue, massaged it in. Eventually, with a little tap on my shoulders she brightly said "Up you get!"

A miracle had occurred. As I sat up, my headache had gone; the fatigue of the jet lag was replaced with a renewed energy. What a wonderful woman! I had about thirty minutes to shower, put on my slap and find my dress. Karen worked her magic on my hair and I felt quite human and raring to go.

The party was wonderful. It was held at a winery not far away, a beautiful venue. Everything had been so carefully thought out. Everyone was instructed to form an arch when Lionel and Trish arrived, and the children were to blow bubbles. *We,* however, were to stand at the end of the arch, to face them both as they came through. They had been told they were just going to a surprise location for a meal with Karen and Mark. The car drew up outside and out stepped Lionel and Trish, blindfolded and guided by Karen. As the blindfolds came off, and the bubbles drifted skywards, they smiled as they were pleasantly surprised by the presence of all their friends, and dutifully bowed as they linked hands to walk through the arch of people. Gordon and I were waiting and were overwhelmed to be here, seeing our friends face to face after so many years. They, were equally overcome when they realised we were actually *there*, in the flesh. Many tears of joy were shed that night.

It was a wonderful two weeks. We spent as much time as we could with our wonderful friends, and travelled around Perth and Fremantle. The day came all too soon for us to leave for home. To return to the U.K. in the middle of the worst month of the year – February!

We didn't have time to be depressed and miserable, Maryan was moving in, and there was such a lot to do. She had never had a room decorated to her liking and I was determined that she should. She chose bright pink.

My youngest niece Sally, came to visit. I haven't mentioned much about Sally; suffice to

say she is Dora's youngest daughter. Sally is
the one who is free of the Dystrophy.

She married and divorced after having her
daughter Lola, and now had a new partner, and
seemed happy. Sally had always tried to make
something of herself, primarily with no
support from anyone; her dream had always
been to join the Mounted Police Force. I was so
proud of her, and the effort she had made. On
the evening of her Attestation, it was *me* she
asked to be there. I felt so honoured and was so
very proud of her as she took her oath in her
smart officer's uniform. What an achievement
for
Sally, everything she had done, was under her
own steam with no help or encouragement at
all. She would visit her family frequently. But
she also tried to
support her mum, although all she usually got
for her trouble was condemnation of
some sort, not one word of praise from Dora.

Speaking of Dora, things had been pretty tame
for a while plus I had been so busy settling in
Maryan etc. Now, Dora had made a couple of
calls to me regarding Leo. They were
unsurprisingly having problems with his
attitude, and the trouble he was getting into. It
was a quiet evening when their next call came
through, Dora was beside herself as her voice
reached a shrill crescendo. I asked her to put
Leo on the line so that I could talk to him, he

usually listened to me, but he had shot upstairs and refused to talk to anyone. I considered it easier to pop over in the car and have a chat with him. I tapped on the front door and pushed my way in past the pile of clothing which had slowly built up behind it, goodness knows why. Anyhow, Leo was still upstairs when I arrived and was talking to no-one! I struggled up the bare wooden stairs, strewn with various precariously placed objects, and at the top found myself before three doors. I pushed open the first door only to find that this was the bathroom, although I use the term loosely. Very little bathing had obviously taken place, as the bath itself was overflowing with bulging black bin bags, the wash basin was also full, of empty beer cans – how did they wash? The next room I pushed my way into had just a single bed in the centre of the room, piled high with everything imaginable, handbags, clothes, shoes and boxes and an obsolete sewing machine. Leo couldn't be in here. The third room was dark and dingy, the curtains festooned across the window allowed a chink of day light to penetrate but I could see that if any attempt were made to open them they would collapse. As my eyes adjusted to the semi-light, I could just about make out two single divan beds side by side. One appeared to be divest of any bedding; the other had a duvet sitting in a heap in the middle. Leo must be under here I thought. As I clambered over the debris on the floor, I caught sight of movement at the corner of my eye. As my eyes shot sideways, there was Leo, under a thin, dirty duvet; he was laid on a pile of yet more *very* full bin bags which covered half the floor – holding the cat! I talked to him and promised we would sort out his room and make it good for a boy his age to be in. When I challenged Dora and Tina about Leo sleeping on the bags, their indignant response was, "I'll have you know everything in those bags is clean!"

A week or two later Gordon and I gathered together what was necessary and tackled Leo's room, putting up curtain rails and curtains, new duvet and bedding, and sorting out all the rubbish. He was so proud of it when we'd done, despite saying to me that he wished he was in care.

I tried to involve someone from school, which Leo hadn't attended for months, a mentor perhaps who could give him some encouragement. Two women eventually called at the house, unknown to me, to offer some sort of help if possible, though it was unclear to me exactly where they were from. Unfortunately, Dana had stayed over the previous night and was still intoxicated – and naked – laid out on the only available space on the living room floor. When they entered, Dana rose to her feet, in her full, 'natural' glory and proceeded to pour out a barrage of abuse at the two, regarding their dress, hair and demeanour, followed by a heavy backhander when Leo tried to intervene, which hurled him straight over the back of the sofa, leaving him with a very bruised face. The two made their apologies and quickly left. *Nothing* was done, Dana had yet again got away, almost, with murder. If only I could have been present that day, at that moment, I would have had her arrested in the blink of an eye. I was understandably concerned regarding Leo but there was the small matter of Maryan moving in and all energies for the moment, had to be put in here at home.

Maryan was, first and foremost, definitely *not* a morning girl. She was a moody teenager at the best of times, but 'a.m.' was not her favourite time of day. In the brief synopsis we were given to familiarise ourselves with Maryan, we had been informed that she was a very bright girl, 'University material' in fact, she just needed a little encouragement to make the effort. We could undoubtedly offer that, along with the usual boundaries and guidance. However, we were also under the distinct impression that Maryan considered all adults to be stupid. Oh, how that would have to change! There were also other little alterations and modifications to be put in place. Her boyfriend apparently was prone to climbing in through the bedroom window at her previous placement. This would not be happening here. He had been in and out of prison and was obviously a negative influence on Maryan. However, we were well aware that, had we tried to stop her seeing him, or spoken negatively about him, then we would send her careering in the opposite direction. She was atypical teenager. Alternative tactics were necessary. We sat down with Maryan and told her we felt it best to establish our 'House Rules' from the outset, in order for us all to understand each other. First and foremost we did not encourage boyfriends to visit as and when they saw fit. The house was everyone's sanctuary, a place of safety and relaxation. Therefore, others would be unable to relax if strangers were coming and going. Second, mobile 'phones *must* be placed in the kitchen after nine p.m. There should be no put-downs or derogatory remarks to each other, and no bullying. Maryan managed to fulfil a couple of these, however she was very clever at the put-downs, constantly telling Charlotte she had 'chinky' eyes, 'like a Chinaman', or she on one occasion held Xara face down in the paddling pool, and yanked Charlotte's legs from beneath her when sitting on the floor. I sincerely believe that Maryan really had no malicious intent or desire to truly physically hurt when she did these things. In her mind she was having fun, joking. Despite my thoughts, the taunts regarding her eyes became just too much for Charlotte, she took it to heart. So the next time Maryan pursued this in my hearing, I turned to both of them and said, "Actually Charlotte, in a way Maryan is right, you do have the most beautiful almond shaped eyes, and when you're older you will be the envy of many other girls." Charlotte was uplifted, Maryan got the message. She would then taunt Xara about her 'brown hands.' I reminded Xara that Maryan was like the rest of us, and would have to 'bake' in the sun for hours for such a tan, which was not good; Xara's 'tan' was natural, and permanent. Amazingly, Maryan did get her comeuppance for this. It was a few weeks later that Gordon and I were to attend an award ceremony for more than twenty five years in fostering. The children were also invited to this, and this was therefore a good excuse for new outfits. *I* dragged a lacy dress from the back of the wardrobe, Charlotte was content with her favourite top and skirt, but not Maryan. Maryan wanted a new dress, and on a visit to the shopping centre, she spotted a black chiffon number, with deep, plunge neckline and the sort of tiny pleats which rippled along the short 'flippy' skirt. She practically begged us to buy it for the occasion, despite our attempts to point out its many failings and that it was totally inappropriate. She has to learn, we thought, so we bought it on the proviso that she paid us back from her pocket money each week. Now Maryan was not the most well endowed young lady shall we say? In my opinion, beautifully slim and well proportioned. Therefore the plunging neckline didn't really know where to begin and end! The dress also revealed a fair amount of flesh – fair being the operative word here, as Maryan's complexion was very much, the pale English rose. Her next plan of action was a request for fake tan. Here is where Angeline's expertise came in. I had found in the back of the cupboard, a spray bottle of a well known tanning fluid, which I had never found the time or occasion to use, and offered this to Maryan. Angeline instructed her to put on shorts and an old vest, and she would do the trick. Standing in the kitchen with Angeline paying attention to every inch of visible pale skin, Maryan was sprayed, proud, and waiting for the product to develop in excited anticipation, bless her. I'm sure she was thinking she would emerge tomorrow morning with a tan that would put Xara's in the shade. Early the next morning, I woke to the sound of desperate, heartfelt sobbing. As I made my way to the bathroom, there was Maryan face in arms, over the washbasin. I thought at the very least she must have received bad news, or hurt herself. As I approached her to offer comfort, she turned to face me with abject misery on her face – along with an 'orange' glow! The fake tan had developed well, too well; she appeared to have been 'Tangoed' from head to foot. Oh dear! She never teased Xara again though.

It took a while for Maryan to learn that adults were *not* stupid. She would try to intimidate *me* even, and had been heard to say 'I'm not afraid of little people, I'll smack her' referring to myself. She would stand directly behind me when I was paying for goods, in order that I would bump into her when I turned around to walk away, when she would then look down at me with a smirk on her face. Time for action! One day as I paid for the groceries and thanked the checkout assistant for her help, I was acutely aware of her, so *very* close. I spun round on my heels, looked up at her smirking face and said, very loudly, 'back off! It aint working.' She was shocked. Her moods would swing faster than a pendulum. One minute she would bring me flowers, the next she would scream that I was 'a cocky sod, and treated her like shit.' On these occasions, Charlotte bless her, would spring to my defence with some reminders of the more positive things I may have done. Sometimes Maryan would decide she wasn't speaking to me, and she was very accomplished at it. After three days of complete silence from her, I announced: - "It's no good, it won't work, I'm going to answer you, whether you speak to me or not!" (Think about it for a moment.) That gave her food for thought also.

She was an incredibly untidy young lady and would go off out and leave stuff all over her room. Dirty washing on the floor, school books everywhere. I decided what the answer was, and contacted her social worker to discuss her agreement for what I was about to implement. All carers know that we should never put children's belongings into black bin bags, like rubbish. I therefore found a pretty silver mesh basket, and informed Maryan that everything which was not put away, would be collected up and placed in the basket each day, and twenty pence per item would be deducted from her

pocket money at the end of the week. She was slightly surprised at this but nevertheless, I carried through, and each morning I would give the duvet a little shake – only to find that items had been stuffed under here in order that I wouldn't notice. I would therefore carefully place each item in the basket, count how many there were and leave her a little note on her bed with a calculation of the day's 'losses' then take the basket into the garage, two floors down. In the evening, when Maryan came home from college, she would begin the ritual of preparation to meet her boyfriend. Sadly she would realise that her mascara was not where she left it, under the duvet, but in the silver basket, so she would trudge down and retrieve it. Then she would find her hairbrush was not in its usual place and would repeat her trip to the garage, and back up again. After her third trip, I commented that, for a very intelligent young woman, it seemed rather futile going up and down two staircases for each item, when it was much more sensible to take the basket up once, and put everything away where they belonged. "Oh! And by the way, every item that is left in the basket the next day will be charged all over again!" It worked, from then on. Most of the time Maryan put her stuff away. However in the process, there had been some weeks where she had hardly any pocket money at all. You may be thinking I would have been better off financially for this, not having to pay pocket money, well think again. I began a savings book, and every little 'debit' note I left in Maryan's room, I also dated and on that date I wrote the amount in the book and saved it. She accumulated a tidy sum by the time her lesson was learnt.

Despite the difficult personality of Maryan, there were many times I felt 'hurt' on her behalf. We had to visit the social services offices for her first review since moving in and her previous carers were leaving with their current placement as we were arriving. They completely ignored Maryan and turned away from her. How desolate and let down she must have felt at this rebuff. Yes, she gave them hell, but as carers we've all been there. These young people have been dreadfully hurt and let down in many ways, and we should maintain the old adage, regarding the differences between liking them but *not* what they do. It did however, bring home to me that not *all* professional carers, are *truly* professional.

Life however, could still be very confusing at times. There was Maryan often not speaking, Charlotte being kind and thoughtful, I would always receive gifts and flowers on Mother's Day from Charlotte, not so her own mother. It has to be said though, that Maryan could be very generous and giving when in the righ mood. Then we would hear from Rosie from time to time. Most recently, she had managed to convince a taxi driver in the town where she now lived with her new carers, that she needed to get home, approximately one hundred miles away and arrived several hours later on her Mother' doorstep, the driver demanding a sixty pounds fare. Mum then rang *me* for advice!

Charlotte had obviously, as had so many others, been previously in trouble for making a mess. She had been petrified on the occasion, in the middle of the night, she had eaten too much kebab and chips and woke with projectile vomit. Up the walls, down the door, and covering a fair patch of the floor. I ventured into her room and on pushing open the door, spread the chippy, kebaby, vomit further into the carpet. Her face was one of horror and fear at the 'obvious' telling off she thought she was about to receive. She was perplexed when I calmly told her to go into the bathroom and
shower and change, whilst I changed the bedding and cleaned up the room. It was much the same when she accidentally knocked over a curry flavoured Pot-Noodle, onto the beige living room carpet. She froze in fear of what would follow. Over time, she had found the confidence to realise that the 'repercussions' from such accidents are easily dealt with.

Now Charlotte was becoming a very different young lady, from the one who wouldn't venture through the garden gate. She was gaining confidence, and doing extremely well at school. She loved school and never missed. Her attendance was always one hundred percent. I feel one day Charlotte is going to be a real credit to both social services and the Agency, not to mention to herself. A rare commodity in the looked after system. She had just had her thirteenth birthday and wanted to make the trip to the shopping mall – alone! This was a huge act of courage and bravery for Charlotte. So, I gave her the bus fare, lunch money, directions and bus numbers etc., and waved goodbye as she left the garden gate. There couldn't have been more preparation and goodbyes had she been embarking on an expedition to the North Pole. We expected not to hear much from her for a while, given the time needed to get there, and back and a little time to spend her pocket money, which in Charlotte's case could take all day. However, two hours later we received a call from her, saying, "I'm lost, come and get me please!" Poor love, she hadn't even made it to the Mall. One day, she'll make it.

Maryan also began making some progress. Gordon managed with his charm, to secure her a job at the private hospital where he used to work. Though it was only a cleaning job, the pay was excellent and it would give her extra cash whilst she studied. She had decided to study Law. As she so delicately put it, "I want to be a divorce lawyer, 'cos I'll never be out of work." Perhaps rather cynical, nevertheless possibly true. Surprisingly, she stuck at this job, perhaps due to the financial reward, though her room continued to be a disaster zone. She had now taken to stuffing things into her wardrobe, until it was literally bulging and the doors were becoming strained with items of clothing wedged in the space created where the doors used to meet. The 'cabin' bed which was also brand new was slowly falling apart. Maryan valued little, even her washing wasn't done when required and her wash bin would be over-flowing. When she ran out of clean pants, she resorted to bikini bottoms. Effort is a rude word to Maryan. It is so difficult for me as I love to *give*, to be involved and help, yet I know it's much harder for Maryan to receive. She finds it so very difficult to accept anything given or bought for her. Perhaps there was not a lot of giving in her family, which is a raw subject, although she is beginning to talk about her parents now, albeit in a derogatory fashion.

The time had come once more for the annual Agency holiday to Center Parcs. This was now to be Maryan's first proper holiday and she was quite excited. There are various sporting activities here, plus lots of swimming in the Sub-Tropical dome, but when evening falls, there's not much for the teenagers to do. However, the posh French restaurant in the village square, put on a Murder Mystery evening set around the evening meal, and so I felt this might be fun for Charlotte and Maryan and they seemed eager to go. We dressed up, and were soon approaching the bar for a drink. Maryan was adamant she should be allowed a glass of wine with her meal and was arguing the point as I had said definitely not. Ultimately I felt it necessary to remind her that although I was the small person, *I* was actually the grown-up and the grown-up was saying NO! She wanted her meal therefore she had little choice but to shut up and accept Cola. We were each given a character to play and shown the 'body' with a brief description of the setting, which was a 'plane journey to Sydney, Australia. I was Mary Bell, the stewardess, and Maryan was a rich playgirl called – wait for it – Tanya Legs! Well! My mind drifted back to the disastrous spray tan Maryan had been covered in, I couldn't contain myself, it was almost as if it had been especially chosen for her. Thankfully Maryan saw the funny side to this and we had a wonderful, happy evening of fun.

Sadly, as with all these things, the holiday ended and we returned once more to the daily grind. Occasionally though, there were small punctuations of something different. I was contacted by professors M.B. and G.S. from a well know university, asking if I would be willing to take part in a discussion group for a book being written on Attachment. I was delighted at the opportunity of a diversion from day to day routine, also Attachment was a subject which I found fascinating, how exciting it would be to become involved in something like this. Of course there was a fair bit of travelling involved, to London and back, and staying in hotels, but it was very very interesting, though slightly daunting at first, as all others around the table were social workers, health visitors, therapists and other professionals, and as I was the only foster carer, I wondered if I would find myself out of my league. However, I did put in my two penneth, put forward my observations as a professional carer. Before my next trip to London however, I'd had an accident and hurt my leg. As I travelled by train, I was a little nervous about being able to board the trains without assistance, although I was able to hobble around. I enquired as to whether it would be acceptable for Gordon to travel with me for physical support which was agreed. The idea was, that he would help me to the venue, and then have a stroll around London until the meeting was over. However, when we arrived 'M' invited him to stay and join in, he had equal knowledge of Attachment as I did and they would welcome a man's point of view. We were then asked if we would be prepared to take part in the D.V.D. which was to accompany the book. The film crew arrived one day and 'rearranged' our lounge. Gordon and I sat side by side on the sofa and cleared our throats ready to begin. I had made a mental note that I would keep my hands firmly clasped on my lap, as I am rather expressive when I talk and my hands make quite a lot of gestures, for which I am often chastised by my daughter. I have even been known, when my hands are not free, to use my feet! Anyhow, I began my first sentence, when the cameraman called 'cut.' My poodle Oscar had discreetly climbed onto my lap and white fluff could be seen at the bottom of the screen, it was Oscar's woolly top-knot bobbing up and down. The whole day proceeded much the same, stomachs rumbled, words stumbled, but eventually they appeared happy with what they had achieved, and left. The book and D.V.D. were eventually published as a training tool for social workers and therapists. I have not yet watched the D.V.D. all the way through. I cringe when my episodes appear, but I feel it was a privilege to have been part of it all.

The girls were quite proud of Gordon and I, fame at last, and we were *their* carers. However, we must continue the task in hand and not allow 'fame' to distort our thinking. Mayan needed a computer for her college work. The government says, that every looked after child should have access to a computer. However Maryan's Local Authority were deciding differently and telling us that funds were not available. Gordon kept on reassuring Maryan that he *would* obtain a computer for her, to which she replied, "Don't 'old yer breath."

In her strong dialect. He re-iterated once more that he would get it. He fought and fought, even informed the Local Authority he would take it further if necessary. At this point we received a call to say the social worker would visit on Monday, with a cheque for the computer. Maryan was gob smacked as she would put it. Obviously, nothing like this had ever been achieved for her. The next issue was a passport, which was tirelessly met with "Don't 'old yer breath." I *will* get it I told her. She knew how difficult this might be due to the fact that permission would be needed from her parents and the Local Authority, and they would need to deal with it. Needless to say, she got it!

Charlotte was up and down, sometimes Maryan would deflate her confidence in one sentence. Charlotte came home one day, at the age of fourteen, with a baby's feeding bottle and began to walk around drinking from it instead of a cup. We never said a word! This was either to shock us for some sort of attention, or perhaps slight regression, maybe she didn't have proper nurturing as a young child and needed to get it out of her system, she also encouraged Xara to have one, and the two of them would giggle as they sucked away at their orange squash. Gordon and I decided to buy one each and sit down one evening together on the sofa and suck away at our feeding bottles, and be a whole family of 'suckers'.

Our house was full, and there was no space for any other children to stay here, however, we were occasionally asked to do day-care for some children, when other carers had training etc. We had a few over time. There was Gareth, who was quite a character, and then there was Amelia, a young baby with special needs. Amelia had many physical impairments, and was profoundly deaf, but a child with more guts and determination I have yet to meet. Despite her problems, I feel Amelia will one day go far, and with the aid of the two excellent carers she is now with J. and L. I am sure she will achieve a great deal in her life.

One young lady we will never forget is Emily. Emily was fifteen years old, almost sixteen. She was what is known as accommodated. This means she had been placed voluntarily into care by her father as he could no longer cope with her behaviour. Emily was a very pretty and appealing young lady, with her naturally blonde hair and brown eyes, an unusual combination. She had a neat figure and the softest little voice, the voice of an Angel! Though believe it or not she could be a very truculent young lady at times and her longest time spent with most carers was twenty eight days, the standard length of notice to be given when a placement is not working out as desired. Emily was sent from one placement to another, and another due to behavioural problems they couldn't manage, each lasting the statutory twenty eight days.

Needless to say, the most current one had broken down in traumatic circumstances and the Agency needed somewhere else for her to go – NOW! 'L' was now manager of the branch office in Emily's home town, and rang us in desperation, knowing that we couldn't accommodate Emily or anyone for that matter, but she had come up with a brilliant idea. Perhaps Angeline could have her in placement, after all, she had two empty bedrooms, and we could care for her during the day when Angeline was at work, day-care. What a clever idea, Angeline was up for it, and so we agreed and Emily was brought and introduced to us. Gordon, especially, immediately, felt empathy towards her, she was so very sad when she spoke, especially about her mother's death which occurred when Emily was approximately three or four years old. I had every sympathy, empathy even with Emily, but oh how she used her motherless state to gain these very emotions, and then she would meekly and desolately tell you, she needed a 'fag' (cigarette.)

Emily was always needing a 'fag' but rarely had any. She was all out of luck with Gordon and I, we were both adamant non-smokers. I did try to help her though; I contacted the surgery I used to work in and had a chat with on of my Practise Nurse friends Linda, for advice regarding obtaining some nicotine patches for Emily. I was advised that she would have to be over eighteen to be put on the programme and receive the recommended dosage, but I was also advised that I could buy them over the counter. I spoke to Emily about this and those concerned, and she agreed, she desperately wanted to give up smoking. I bought her a pack of the recommended patches, and together we read the leaflet and discussed how we would go about it. I explained to Emily that these were a substitute for the nicotine in the 'fags' she was smoking and that slowly she would be able to give up. However, I eventually discovered that she was dutifully applying her patch each morning – and smoking as well! She would beg, borrow or steal, although begging here fell upon deaf ears.

The 'fag' situation caused Emily many problems and not all of these acquainted with her health. She would frequently fly into a strop, but we were used to that. As I sat calmly one evening intently watching my favourite programme on T.V. The front door flew open and rebounded off the wall, as Emily frantically ran into the room screaming, "Ring the police, now!" I didn't take my eyes off the T.V. screen, or move a muscle, but blindly pointed to the telephone and said, "999 is the number." (For I just knew it would be yet another drama) She was stunned. "Aren't you going to do anything?" She screeched, her angelic voice transformed into that of a cartoon witch. The story began to unfold, she had apparently been borrowing 'fags' and money from a young girl down the road, one who is not to be messed with, and had been unable or unwilling to pay it back. The girl, in turn had 'removed' Emily's precious mobile 'phone from her hand whilst her dexterous thumbs had been clicking out the latest text message. Emily, like most teens could not be parted from her mobile, and this was, to her, the crime of the century. After an appropriate length of time, and of course when my T.V. programme had finished, I offered to visit the girl and her mum regarding the 'phone. I knocked at the door, and the offender herself answered. I was eventually invited in by her mother and after a lengthy discussion, I could see the girl's point of view. She was owed, and the 'phone was substitute payment. However, we did come to an agreement. I compromised that, if she gave me the 'phone I would not allow Emily to have it until she had repaid all that was owed. Amazingly the girl trusted me to do this and handed over the object of nuisance. After approximately half an hour, in walked Emily once more, grinning like the proverbial Cheshire cat. "You've got my 'phone back, haven't you?" She said, through clenched grinning teeth. "Yes" I replied, "Well can I have it?"! She asked. "Yes, as soon as you have paid your debts from your pocket money, then you can have it." "But I'll have messages!" She protested. "I'm sure you will." I agreed. "The battery'll be dead." "Oh yes, it most certainly will." I again agreed, but I was unrelenting.

It took ten days for Emily to retrieve her 'phone, despite pushing Xara to go and look in our bedroom, where it wouldn't have been found anyway. I paid back her debts, but then her behaviour was so horrendous, I kept the 'phone for another couple of days. Emily didn't seem to realise that had I not agreed to these negotiations, she may never have had her 'phone returned at all. Amazingly she stayed, she didn't demand, and threaten to run off as she had with previous carers, perhaps these firm boundaries were what she really needed. Angeline was just as unrelenting too, and yet still no threats to leave. She would however, request a tea bag when she ran out of 'fags', and roll it up and smoke it, Yuk!

Now I have never had much time, as you can imagine to pursue some of the hobbies I would have enjoyed, but I did indulge myself, in buying a two-seater speedy sports car, a Toyota M.R.2. It was bright red when I bought it, along with instructions on how to purchase and apply a kit which would transform it into a 'Ferrari' for it was similar in shape. I though, had other different ideas. I had it re-sprayed in 'flip' colours. For those of you unfamiliar, this is a sort of two-tone colour which changes with the angle of light, the colour I chose was called, Magenta-Gold Rage Extreme Illusion. It is predominantly a sort of metallic purple, changing to deep pink to gold, to green as the light catches it. It certainly received some attention, and it's such fun watching people's reaction, some have been seen to walk into lampposts etc., due to paying more attention to the car than where they were going. However, Emily like most young people, thought it was the 'bees-knees' and pestered me to take her out in it. I told her if she behaved, and stopped demanding like a spoiled brat, then I would do so. Following a reasonable week, with no strops I agreed she deserved a trip out and decided to take her Christmas shopping at some of my favourite haunts in Derbyshire. She climbed into the passenger seat and placed her little white handbag on her lap with a look of sheer glee on her face. We set off, and I was secretly amused as Emily gave eye contact to every passer-by, as if to say, 'look at me, in this car.'

Within fifteen minutes we were driving over the Derbyshire moors. It was a lovely crisp day, the sun was low in the sky, outlining the hills as we approached the 'world's end', when Emily sharply demanded that she *needed* a 'fag.' I couldn't believe it. I looked more intently out of the windscreen of the car and said "I don't see any shops!" Bearing in mind we were in the middle of the moors, and the only visible living creatures were the thick-coated sheep, grazing here and there. She followed my cue and looked out, expecting to see a shop. "I've been known to hit people when I don't have a 'fag."

She said coldly. This I was very well aware of. "Is that supposed to scare me?" I asked, followed by, "I'll give you two good reasons why it's not such a good idea right now. One, I'm driving and we would most certainly crash, and two, even if you hit me, when I get up you *still* don't get your 'fag.' "Anyway" I said. "If you behave, there'll be a treat for you when you get home." "Really!" she said with growing anticipation. "Yes" I said. "I'll ask Gordon if you can have a special Earl Grey tea bag to roll up!" She was speechless, but the day progressed with a subdued obedience.

It was New Year, and I thought perhaps we all needed cheering up, so I booked a holiday to Turkey, it would be our ninth visit to various parts of Turkey, but I felt it better to go somewhere familiar as it would be Charlotte and Maryan's first tip abroad. They were overjoyed. Angeline and her partner and Xara agreed to come along too which would make it extra special. I was hoping things would pick up a bit, New Year – new start. Rosie began to visit regularly to spend time with Charlotte. She was now permanently back home with mum and didn't live far away. We arranged that she could visit each Thursday, after school, have tea and spend the evening with Charlotte. It was good to see her again, despite her *still* not being truly happy. That dreaded 'phone rang once more with bad news. Charlotte's other grandmother had died. She had been particularly close to this one and it hit her hard. *Another* loss for Charlotte to absorb and she was devastated, she spoke of killing herself as it should have been her instead of Nan. It was the grief talking of course, but it had a negative effect on Charlotte, she would stay out late and not tell us where she was, influenced of course by Rosie, it was almost as if she was taking out her anger on those closest to her – ourselves. Emily naturally, was a little peeved at Charlotte 'stealing' the limelight in the grief stakes. This just confirmed my earlier suspicions that Emily actually enjoyed the sympathy of others.

It was the day of the funeral, and I picked up Charlotte from school. We had agreed the procedure beforehand, that we would visit the church and attend the service then come home. Charlotte chose to sit with her mum at the front of the church and I allowed them this sad family time together, and made myself invisible at the back of the church. It was quite a grand affair. Gran had been the landlady of a pub, and there were at least two hundred people in attendance. The coffin arrived in a glass carriage, pulled by a team of four beautiful black horses, with black feathered plumes in their manes. However, after the service Charlotte desperately felt the need to accompany the rest of the family to the crematorium and so I agreed to take her, after which they were all gathering at the pub in which Gran had lived, where I dutifully sat on a stool in the middle of the large room surrounded by *so many* people, each with a 'fag' in one hand and a pint in the other. I managed to sit there for a whole hour until the smoke was so thick, my eyes were streaming and I could hardly see. I then encouraged Charlotte that it was time to go. She was understandably grief stricken, so when we arrived home I advised her to lie down and lent her one of my classical C.D's to help her relax.

I was both amazed and touched by how protective and sensitive Maryan was towards Charlotte at this difficult time, and even more so on an occasion when Gordon and I went shopping and asked Angeline if the girls could stay with her for an hour. We hadn't been gone too long when I received a call on my mobile from Angeline, to say that Emily was bullying Charlotte mercifully and she had discovered that Emily had Charlotte on the floor and was sitting on her face. By the time we arrived home, Maryan was in from work and was also very angry towards Emily. We had to separate the girls and sent charlotte and Maryan home with Gordon, whilst I had a heart to heart with Emily. She did rather well, considering her twenty eight day stints everywhere else, she had now managed to stay with us for nine weeks, though it hadn't been easy. However, she eventually had itchy feet, plus Maryan had told her that if she left now she'd turned sixteen, she would be given a £1,000 grant from social services. This of course wasn't true, but maybe

Maryan had a method in her madness, because it worked, and Emily made life much more difficult, in order to encourage us to throw her out, which of course we didn't, so she therefore found it necessary to engineer a row in order to leave. Poor Emily, she ended up in bed and breakfast accommodation, as a permanent placement still couldn't be found for her, and of course the £1,000 wasn't forthcoming.
One week later, she rang on some pretext of what to do with her nails, and said that Gordon had been right, she should have listened. How sad.

This 'New' year was becoming a roller coaster of misery and grief. Charlotte's grief was affecting her school work and I felt I needed to access some professional help for her, which isn't always easy due to protocol. I took Charlotte to our G.P. for a referral to the N.S.P.C.C. therapy services, and also contacted CRUSE myself to obtain bereavement counselling for her. It wasn't truly helpful, Charlotte didn't like the counsellor much, and refused to engage most of the time, but it gave me a little insight into what was going on in Charlotte's mind, as she refused to go in without me.

Our training is of course ongoing, and coming up was a much needed course on Stress Management. However, there were no major revelations, no magic answers. The instructor advised us that a nice warm bath with aromatic oils and scented candles was the best way of relaxing. However, my mental pictures were not so euphoric. If I relaxed in the bath, I am so short my feet don't touch the other end, therefore if I lay back I would drown, and as you can imagine, the oil would speed me on my way. No, a bath for me was a quick affair purely for the purposes of getting clean.

Maryan was also up and down, she had a new boyfriend called Asif. There were constant disagreements and we tried to tell her that it may always be difficult due to the cultural differences. His parents weren't allowed to know the Maryan existed; this must have been extremely hurtful for her. She would sometimes come home in tears and fly up to her room. I soon learned that, as she sobbed, if the bedroom door was closed, she couldn't talk about it, if the door was wide open as she lay on her bed crying, then she wanted advice and comfort.

Maryan would still find it difficult to make much effort at college. She was always ready and off to work but not so for her exams, though we tried hard to encourage her to study. She was so lazy at times she wouldn't even bother to reach for the light switch when going up and down stairs despite our reminders on safety. This resulted in her slipping from top to bottom one night, in the darkness. Gordon constantly encouraged her to save, in fact begged her, so that on her return from Turkey, as she turned seventeen, she would be able to afford driving lessons, which would have been a real asset to her. He managed to wheedle out of her £319.00 but due to her constant whining and winging that he 'was taking all her money' I felt it prudent to give her all her savings and let her make her own mistakes with it as a lesson in life, that some people *do* care, and do their best for her. Of course she squandered it all in a very short space of time. Despite all this she was nominated for a Young Achievers Award, and managed to obtain ten 'A' levels, which is excellent, but for a 'looked after' young person it is *quite* an achievement.

Mother's Day was lovely for me, not only had I the attention of my only daughter Angeline, my beautiful granddaughter Xara, but Charlotte would buy flowers and cards, and so would Maryan. I also received a 'mug' from Charlotte and a card bearing the words: - 'You have been like a Mother to me.' The mug was filled with folded pieces of paper with little anecdotes of fondness on them and the following will always be very precious to me and I will never forget the feeling of love which came with it:-

The Queen of My Heart

Sandy is the queen of my heart,
Rules in my sky like a moon,
Pulling the tides of my feelings,
Lighting the paths of my dreams

She is there for me whenever I need her,
She will never turn her back against me,
She will be there for me in times of sorrow,
And there for me to share nice memories.

The doors of the past will not open,
And the doors of the future will be wide open.

By charlotte

There are no words which can describe the feeling of satisfaction, sense of a job well done when you receive this type of gift from a child, not to mention the success of helping them to learn to love.

There were many words of gratitude from Charlotte over the years. Each year carers have to have an Annual Review, to be re-instated, to keep a constant eye on our methods of practice. I usually ask the children in our care if they wish to contribute by letting the Local Authority or the Agency know how they feel, whether everything is going o.k. for them. For some, this is an ideal opportunity to complain if they have a mind, but I feel it is important that their feelings should be heard. The following statement is the most recent one that Charlotte wrote to the Agency, conveying her thoughts and feelings:-

'I have been living with Sandy and Gordon over five years now, it feels like
I have been with them forever because often I forget about what happened
When I was living at home because of where I live now it is so much better.
I feel part of their family. I get on with their family members really well.
They feed me at meal times, and feed me with food that I like and that is
healthy for you. They both buy me clothes when ever I need them. They
buy me presents when it is my birthday and when it is Christmas.

They support me and care about me a lot. They help me with any problems
That I have. They understand and listen to me whenever I need their advice
And support. When I am upset they understand and try to help me wherever
possible. They make me feel good about myself by giving compliments about work and myself.

Over the past five years I have made a dramatic improvement with my
school work and with my life. When I first moved in I could barely spell

and put two words together. Now I am
proud of myself and Sandy and
Gordon for helping me reach my potential.
I would not have been where I am now
without Sandy and Gordon there to help
me. I have become more Confident and
independent in myself. I trust them both.

Sandy and Gordon make me feel better
and less worried about my future plans. I
have a really nice bedroom which was
done to the liking that I wanted. It gets
cleaned on a regular basis. The house is
clean and there are no danger hazards
within the home. At home I feel as though
I am in a safe Loving and caring
environment. The house overall is really
nice and I am happy with the way it looks
and I feel that it is a nice place to be in.

Sandy and Gordon treat me with respect
and I treat them with respect. I am polite
to them and they are polite to me.
We use manners when we are talking
to each other. I have a set bedtime
So that i don't go to bed tired. They teach
me to do my own washing and ironing so
that in the future I am able to do simple
things for myself.

<u>Sandy</u> - Sandy is an extremely positive
woman. She has always got

something nice to say to someone. When
Sandy says she will do something
Or sort something out for me she will do it
whatever the problem is. Sandy
will take me out shopping and we will
have a good time together.

<u>Gordon</u> – Gordon is a positive person. He
is always up in a morning when I
Am going to school. He buys me sweets.
Whenever I need something sorting out I
know that Gordon will be able to help
whatever the situation.
Gordon takes me to places if I need to go
somewhere.

They both have a lot of knowledge and
understanding about things and
therefore they help me when I need it.
Overall Sandy and Gordon are the
best people and carers I know. They are
truly amazing fantastic foster
carers and I am so glad that I was placed
with them.'

Charlotte.

For all those people out there who always say "I don't know why you do it." Well the above is why, and it is worth every minute, just to receive something like this. Sadly though, these children rarely want to send such thoughts to their own parents.

Now, a bit of good news for a change, my niece, Sally, Dora's youngest daughter, has decided to marry her partner Kevin. They are planning something different and are going to Gretna Green in Scotland. Sally has not had assistance with anything in her life and this wedding was no exception. In fact she was not about to invite her own mother or sisters, Dana and Tina. I couldn't blame her of course, but it's sad nonetheless. She also asked for my help in selecting her dress etc., and her daughter Lola, and Xara were to be bridesmaids. This was a great honour and I was touched that she had asked for my help.

Whilst these plans were whirring around in my head, life continued. Charlotte had a contact with her brother Sam. Now Sam is a lovable rogue, a rather flamboyant 'out' Gay Guy, and a lovely young person with a good heart. We decided to take them to Hardwick Hall, the stately home of Elizabeth Shrewsbury, otherwise know as Bess of Hardwick. As we were strolling around the lawns, surrounded by rather poised ladies in their best Sunday hats, Sam thought he might shock me, and them, and loudly informed me that he had a new boyfriend. "Have you?" I asked, "And how are you getting on?" "Well I haven't f---ed him yet!" Yelled Sam as I turned around to face him, walking backwards as I went. "Why haven't you f---ed him yet?" I asked, equally as loud.

All the nice old ladies were scurrying in opposite directions as we spoke, their walking sticks clicking with the speed at which they moved. Sam knew from that day on, he could not shock *me*!

Our holiday to Turkey soon arrived, everyone was excited. Charlotte and Maryan had never flown before, and Xara only once, so even the flight itself was to be an education for them. We stayed in a hotel in Hisaronou, a lovely place, and did many things whilst there. Charlotte even had a go at scuba diving with Gordon and brought home a photo of her feeding the fish under water. We saw many historic and biblical sights which fascinated the children. All too soon it was time to go home. Charlotte cried all the way, Maryan was indifferent and had, as usual done her best to be awkward whilst there. When we arrived back home, everything returned to normal. Maryan's room was an ever growing mess. I had now increased the 'fine' of each item to fifty pence if not put away. One morning, as I attempted to make her room look and smell reasonable, I felt a pang of anger as I saw coat sleeves and belts bulging through the wardrobe doors. I sighed in exasperation as I pulled them open in order to get them to meet, when out fell a video case. I picked it up to place it in the pretty mesh basket, when I caught sight of the very pornographic nature of the graphics on the cover. It was called 'Triple X' and it *wasn't* the well known version. I challenged Maryan regarding this; her excuse was that her boyfriend Asif, had asked her to look after it, so his parents wouldn't find it. I was so angry that, if true, he hadn't given a thought to what would happen to Maryan if *we* found it. There had to be a sanction for this, and when there *has* to be punishment, I like it to fit the 'crime.' I therefore had her T.V. disconnected for a few days. It still sat there in full view, but she couldn't use it. Despite all this negativity, Maryan had a good heart when she had a mind to. I decided that she shouldn't take all the flack for this, and the next time Asif came to the door, I answered and said we had something belonging to him. When I held up the offending video, his face was unbelievably flushed and he apologised when I said we needed to see what his parents thought of it. Of course we were not serious about this, as it could have caused him more trouble than it was worth.

This was all followed by a happy visit from Andre, who now had a son of his own. He brought James and his partner Alison with him. It was so lovely to see them. We then decided on a last minute break to the island of Rhodes, just Gordon and I.

It was a lovely peaceful week, just the two of us, and we came back feeling refreshed and ready to meet any new challenge, though we were quite unprepared for the news that followed. It was a call from Charlotte's social worker to tell us that granddad was seriously ill and she would like to take Charlotte to visit him. Inevitably he died the next day. Poor, poor Charlotte. Her family were leaving her, left, right and centre, she'd had much more loss than anyone should, but certainly too much for someone so young.

This meant that there was now another funeral to attend. I talked to Charlotte and came to a similar arrangement as with Grandma's. We attended the service, at the same church, and agreed we would go home afterwards. Once more I allowed Charlotte to be with her birth family at such a sad time. It seemed so little time ago since we were last here. When the service was over, the wake was to be held at Granddad's favourite pub, which was not in the most desirable part of town. I, once again, made myself invisible and waited until all the family had filed forlornly outside, to find Charlotte sitting in one of the funeral cars with Sam and Tara, and just about to drive off with the cortege. I couldn't believe it. I mimed through the car window as it drove away, for her to ring me.

It was twelve thirty, midday and I had just watched my responsibility wave as she was driven away to goodness knows where. By six p.m. I had heard nothing from Charlotte, not a word. By seven forty five p.m., still no word, I was beginning to worry. I managed to obtain a relative's mobile number and discovered that Tara and Sam had arrived home long ago, and the last time they saw Charlotte she was still in the pub. Now by this time I had eaten my evening meal and enjoyed the proverbial glass of wine which always accompanies such, and therefore would not drive, just as Gordon arrived home and I therefore asked him to quickly drive me to the pub to pick up Charlotte. We pulled up outside and Gordon sat in the vehicle whilst I 'popped' in briefly to find her. It had also been necessary for Maryan to come along as we couldn't leave her alone in the house. I walked into the bar and looked around, until I spotted Charlotte sitting in a corner, a family member on either side of her. I made my way over to Charlotte and leaned in to tell her, above the noise, that Gordon was waiting for us outside, and beckoned her to follow me. To my amazement, she shook her head and refused to come with me. As I spoke I felt four sharp prods in my back and without turning around, I raised my flat hand and said "One minute please!" as I wasn't pleased at the intrusion. However the prods became more penetrating, and as I swung round, displeasure written all over my face, four of the most burley men I have looked *up* at, were three inches away from me. Threats were coming thick fast and furious. 'Mum' was sitting to my right, basically because she couldn't stand due to intoxication, screaming at her family allies not to let me out of there. Auntie Joan, a large lady took a full knuckle punch at me but thankfully having also consumed way too much alcohol, could see three of me, went for the wrong one, and fell promptly onto the floor. I decided it would be prudent to leave at this point, with or without Charlotte. More people were advancing towards me from all four corners of the room. It was like 'The Day of the Zombies.' However, before leaving, I very adamantly sympathised with their loss, but pointed out that they really didn't need this neither did I, but if Charlotte didn't come with me then I *must* inform social services and the police. With that, I walked very quickly-didn't run- towards the door. Gordon was in the vehicle, blissfully unaware of the fearful drama unfolding inside. As I pushed my way out the door, half of the relatives in the room promptly followed me onto the pavement outside. One of them hurled herself at me with the challenge that she would tell the police I had left Charlotte in a pub, I returned the favour by informing her that *I* had left her in a funeral car at lunchtime, *she* had the dubious honour of keeping her in the pub, another shouted that I shouldn't be driving because I had mentioned on the 'phone earlier that I'd had a glass of wine, and had asked them to put Charlotte in a taxi. I said, "I'm not driving, *he* is, pointing to Gordon sitting in the car with poor Maryan in the back witnessing all of this. With no further ado. I opened the car door to go home, when the tallest of the group, lurched forward and kicked the car door leaving a large mark in the paintwork. I stepped back out and surveyed the damage, telling this young man "that this was not a clever thing to do." I decided to just go home and make some 'phone calls, and climbed into the car to drive away, when he lurched forward once more, and called me a 'fucking bitch!' I opened the window and replied, "That's *Miss* Bitch to you, and don't you forget it!"

The police finally located Charlotte and brought her home around one thirty a.m. She refused to look at us or talk to us, so we asked her to go to bed and we would talk in the morning. For the next few days, Charlotte was more difficult than she had *ever* been. We have no idea why, other than the grief is so overwhelming she can't handle reality.

The load of recent events was lifted to some degree as Sally and Kevin's wedding was approaching at the weekend, and we were packing, preparing to travel up to Gretna Green. I was relating to Sally that we'd had a few problems recently and that Charlotte was not doing so well. Sally, bless her, informed me that one of Kevin's relatives was unable to attend and Charlotte was welcome to go. Not only this, but she offered to make Charlotte honorary 'Flower Girl' handing out little cones of rose petals for guests to scatter over the happy couple following their vows over the

Anvil. Charlotte was elated at this. She had never even been to a decent wedding, let alone officiated in any way. The plans were set, a new outfit was put together for Charlotte and, come the weekend we were on our way.

It was a lovely wedding. Kevin, and Gordon, who was giving the Bride away in the absence of her father, were dressed in full Scottish regalia. They looked so smart and handsome in their Tartan Kilts with complete accessories. Everything was so well organised and Sally looked divine, in her beautiful bridal gown. Something which had been denied her at her first wedding due to circumstances. This time she was determined to experience everything a young bride should on her wedding day. She and Gordon arrived at the Old Blacksmith's Shop, in a horse-drawn carriage. For those who are not aware of the history of Gretna Green, it really is an old Blacksmith's shop on the borders of Scotland and England. In days gone by, when young lovers wanted to wed and were not granted the permission from parents, they would elope to Gretna Green where parental consent was not required, and in an unconventional ceremony over the anvil, and the use of a hammer comes into it somewhere, the couple could exchange their vows to each other and become man and wife. These days, it's used for weddings, with more of a romantic notion, but unusual and different it is. The day went well. Sally's daughter Lola, and Xara were bridesmaids, dressed in the pales baby pink and Charlotte happily and confidently did *her* duty that day as Flower Girl, with all the pride and professionalism one would expect. We spent three days in Scotland and enjoyed every moment of sharing this special occasion. It was slightly tinged with sadness at Sally's dad not attending and her mother and sister being kept out of the equation caused anguish for me on Dora's behalf. Though I fully understood Sally's feelings. If only Dora had been more positive for Sally, more supportive, she could have been an important part of this day, but the dystrophy had robbed her of so much, including her sense of pride and affection at her daughter's happiness.

However, the reprieve was over all too soon and we had to return to 'normality.' We would occasionally, and still do, attend induction courses for newly selected carers, who are about to go before Panel. We would be on hand to answer questions, advise and generally reassure them, prior to them attending the Panel which may choose to appoint them as fully fledged foster carers. This *did* give us an occasional change from 'kiddie' chatter, and an opportunity to mingle with our potential peers, and it was light relief to return from Scotland to such a session.

It was also around now that I received a call asking if I would be willing to stay a couple of nights in a neighbouring town, at another carer's home, to assess and monitor a mother and child placement. Lewis was three years old and had been showered in hot oil, the contents of a possibly unattended chip pan. The poor little mite had 90% burns to his head and almost his entire body. He had been in hospital for three months, but had pulled through. Unfortunately, he also contracted the super bug, M.R.S.A. during this time, had to wear a full body compression garment and a mask to support his face. Some of his little fingers were fused together and he had difficulty talking and eating. But like to many little people who suffer dreadful traumas, he was *so* resilient, and tremendously courageous. How difficult it was, *not* to 'spoil' such a child and yet, I knew how important it would be for the normal boundaries to be kept in place, even for Lewis.

Christmas came and went, and yet another New Year began. We started receiving calls from Rosie, at times in a suicidal state, wanting to move back in. How sad, I felt that we were not in a position to do this, but at least I could talk with her on the 'phone and felt glad that she saw fit to ring at these unhappy times. At the end of our conversations she usually felt better and cheered up, to battle yet another day.

It was now that I decided that we needed a new bathroom fitting. It was becoming a bit jaded, and so we set about redesigning it. I planned to have a 'spa' bath installed, my little treat to myself. I recalled how I had to explain at the 'Stress' training, how I couldn't lie down for fear of drowning, and felt elated at the thought of this oval-shaped bath, with a seat, and how I *could* lie down in this one, switch on the bubble jets – and *relax*! I had a natty little wine glass holder fixed to the tiles, Angeline bought me a pink wine glass with a lovely twisted stem, and after a particularly stressful day, when the children were all in bed, I could unwind with a glass of wine, some aromatic crystals, and tickly bubbles. I was rejuvenated! Until tomorrow at least.

It didn't last long however, news came that our lovely friend Rita, who returned from Australia, had died. She was in her nineties and would be sadly missed indeed.

Maryan, meanwhile descended from being untidy to becoming downright smelly and dirty. She always *appeared* reasonably smart and well groomed in actual fact, but we knew the days when she hadn't showered, the clothes that hadn't been washed, but recycled for another day. We were quite concerned for her, as she seemed unable to see how this might affect her. I made it the girls' responsibility to change their own bedding; in order to encourage self-care skills, but Maryan would leave hers a month, until I would strip off the sheets and covers and leave the bed bereft of any comfort, which enforced the application of clean linen before bedtime.

We now also had to begin making plans for Maryan's eighteenth birthday, at which time she would also be leaving us, to become an adult, independent. There was a lot of work to be done and much planning not to mention the search for somewhere for Maryan to live. We were rather concerned about her life skills, her budgeting left much to be desired, her self-care skills were not the best either. This was all the sadder, as she was most certainly capable, but wasn't big on effort. Now, Maryan could also cook very well when she put her mind to it, the problem was, this also required effort, and as I have mentioned, *effort* was not her forte. But despite all this, she had her moments, when she could be caring and protective, just as she was with Charlotte when in grief.

Meanwhile back at the 'Old Homestead,' it's announced that Leah had given birth to a bouncing baby boy. I didn't know whether to feel joy, or sadness at this news. Joy at a new life entering the world, or sadness at what the future may hold for this next generation. One thing I do know, I will not become too intently involved. Though I did notice Maryan's generous nature here. She went out and chose and bought lovely gifts to take on a visit to this child, despite not being acquainted with Leah at all. This will set Maryan well for the future, in the relationship stakes, I hope.

Life became very hit and miss, and very uncertain indeed. Dora was taken into hospital with breathing difficulties. She spent three weeks there, undergoing every test known to mankind, and nothing could they find wrong. My guess was, it was all due to the stress of the continuing conflicts within her immediate family. The constant bickering, and shouting at each other, seemed to be the norm to them, but it was obviously taking its toll. Therefore I felt it prudent to mention this home situation to the medical staff, in order for them to offer the appropriate help. Dana insisted on visiting and would be sitting at the bedside each time I arrived, having made various arrangements for the care of the children before I was even able to be there, though I felt that Dana had been attached to her chair from the moment visitors were allowed to enter, and would remain there until she was virtually thrown out. She didn't want to miss anything, and occupied her time there, by instructing the doctors and nurses of their duty, and demanding an answer to her mother's ailments. She was equipped with renewed confidence as she strutted about in her new finery of faux fur coat, mini skirt and white stilettos with matching genuine P.V.C. handbag, the newest accessory being her new 'boyfriend,' thirty years her senior, but then he wa providing these latest 'catwalk' creations.

There *were* intermittent burst of blue on the horizon. Our Sundays were somewhat more relaxing, which were usually spent with our good friends J and J. Either we would visit them in their home in the Derbyshire countryside, or they would drive to the city to visit us. We would sit and plan our next holiday, and this time we had chosen Portugal. All four of us felt much happier once a destination had been chosen, and bookings had been made. This also meant respite for us from the children, and it was usually very welcome. Charlotte was doing well; she had a busy social life. Dancing class, trampolining and drama. Maryan was busy buying knick-knacks for her forthcoming accommodation which we had managed to locate for her in secure surroundings. We had received and invitation to a 'Dinner' where we along with others, were to be presented with a Silver Pin in recognition of being with the Agency for over five years. Strangely, this fell on the very day we were to depart for Portugal. However, given the timing, we were able to plan to attend the presentation and travel straight to the airport from the hotel. I wore a little used pair of my three inch heels for the presentation, but took with me a pair of sandals to wear on the journey that followed all this in the name of vanity versus comfort. However, in my haste, I discovered half way to Portugal, that although they *were* similar, I was wearing 'odd' shoes!

The week in Portugal was calm and relaxing, though J and J did not appear to be their usual selves, I have to say. There was some animosity towards each other, and they appeared to be quite distant with us. We couldn't think of any reason for this, other than perhaps they were going through a rough patch with each other, it happens to the best of us at times. We just muddled through the week in the optimistic hope that whatever it was would pass, after the holiday. We travelled home, to the U.K. in an odd sort of silence. We drove the one hour or so journey from the airport to take J and J home; I hugged J and said we would be in touch soon. It was over a week before we contacted them, due to settling the kids back home etc. Gordon emailed the holiday photos to them. No response. I wrote secretively regarding Gordon's surprise birthday arrangements. The response to this was, that 'All outings are off! J is acting strangely and she J had even asked their own daughter to 'keep our of it' she also said, 'I am not as strong as you.' I wrote my reply, and told J, she was *much* stronger than me, because I would not put up, and shut up! This was most odd. Gordon and I didn't understand any of it, and we were quite concerned. We had all known each other for almost forty years. As soon as Sunday arrived, we took ourselves off to see them in person. Anything could be wrong. When we arrived outside their house, both theirs and their daughter's cars were parked outside. We walked through the garden gate and up the path to the door. They had three little poodles, who barked profusely whenever Gordon teased them by knocking. There was silence, and odd silence, and then we heard a muffled little bark, followed by 'Shh!' from inside. We could hardly believe it, but J and J *and* their daughter, were hiding from us, and not answering the door. How childish and cowardly we thought at the time. What had we done? Whatever it was, we couldn't fathom. Whatever it was, it should have been possible for four old friends, to sort it out. We travelled home in silence. The feeling was one I cannot describe, other than to say it felt like yet another loss, bereavement. We had been, and still were, so fond of J and J, and this was such a mystery to us.

The next day, an e-mail came through. "Our friendship is over! We are sick of the 'tricks' you played on us on holiday, etc." *What* was this all about? We couldn't believe it. As I am a complete technophobe, I wrote a letter in response. I expressed our disappointment, the perplexity of it all, but more importantly, I left them with the clear message that they would always be welcome in our home, therefore, J and J if you ever read this, I sincerely hope that one day you will be able to make contact with us once more. Our door is always open to you.

Life was now, yet again, a roller coaster of ups and downs. There were problems for Charlotte at school. Some of her so-called friends were bullying her. The school's intake is predominantly Asian or Somalian and these girls saw fit to make racist remarks to Charlotte as she was in the minority, calling her a 'white bitch,' along with a little bit of tapping and pushing. It happened to such an extent that Charlotte eventually walked out of the classroom, she could take no more. She was given detention for this though the problem was; *I* refused to allow her to carry this through. I didn't feel she deserved it and asked the Deputy Head, 'where, when and what time' as *I* would be doing it on Charlotte's behalf! Her reply was "I take your point." These girls had also taken pictures of charlotte and placed them on the internet on very dubiously titled websites. This of course is illegal; therefore I found it necessary for the Local Authority Legal Team to be alerted, and for them to deal with the matter.

Now, at long last the book which we had been involved with, dealing with Attachment was to be launched in London. We were invited along with two fellow carers, who had been interviewed for the D.V.D. We arrived the previous evening, settled into our hotel, and arranged to meet up with Linda and Sam for dinner and drinks, and reserved a table for our evening meal. It was a very relaxing evening as we sat together, enjoying our steaks, and a glass of wine. Sam was chatting on, about something or other, when Linda stopped, and was rigid, holding her knife and fork firmly in her hands. I thought for a moment, she was perhaps annoyed with Sam for twittering on bless him, and I looked at her with a wry smile. As I looked into her silent eyes, I felt them imploring me to *do* something, but what? I thought back to the day my mother had choked on a piece of tomato and couldn't speak, and immediately realised that something similar was wrong. I instinctively got up out of my seat, ran behind Linda, Sam still chattering away, and thumped her firmly between her shoulder blades, by which time Gordon also realised something wasn't right, in fact the whole restaurant must have believed I was trying to murder poor Linda, everything fell silent, when a large piece of steak shot across the restaurant, through the air. Linda coughed and wheezed and drank some water as she revived herself. She later told me she had been seconds from passing away!

On our return from London, we began negotiations for another child to move in, after Maryan had moved out. It sounds rather odd I know, almost like a conveyer belt, but the sad fact is that there are always children out there, ready and waiting for someone to offer them a loving and secure home. Plus once we feel we have gone as far as we can with a young person, and brought them to adulthood, we are always eager to get started again. Having said this, we hopefully try to keep in touch with those who leave us, no matter what the circumstances, and encourage them to come and visit.

Nevertheless, we were approached about a ten year old girl, by the name of Susannah. We were given a great deal of written information about Susannah and it didn't exactly sound appealing in itself, but we believe every child deserves a chance, and although Susannah would tell you of her own admission that she could at times be violent and aggressive, we felt that the 'matching' looked good. As I have mentioned before, when placing a child, the matching process is of paramount importance, particularly if they are to be placed alongside other children. Charlotte was an easy child to match with, for anyone. She was calm, and much wiser than anyone gave her credit for. Therefore when we read that Susannah loved art, liked going out, liked animals etc., we realised that she had 99% of the same interests as Charlotte. Also some of her background was similar which made us feel that this was a reasonable match. When I thought back to how very different Rosie and Charlotte were and yet they got along well, this seemed almost perfect.

We now knew a busy time lay ahead. Not only were we to begin what turned out to be lengthy introductions with Susannah, but we were also nearing the end of the moving process for

Maryan. Her eighteenth birthday was upon us, and Maryan was determined to sabotage the day from the moment she came down to breakfast. This is a classic attachment issue for some young people. They are so afraid of disappointment and rejection that they tend to 'get in their first,' to be upset and angry from the outset, to soften the blow that they are always expecting.

Anyhow, we had arranged a surprise helicopter flight for Maryan, on the day, a meal, and I had also bought her one or two pieces of gold and gemstone jewellery. After all, it was a special birthday. We arrived at the pub which was the launch site late morning. It was a lovely sunny day so we sat out in the sunshine for a while before lunch. Charlotte noticed the check-in desk for the flights, and pointed out that they were 'doing helicopter flights, just like the one me and Rosie did.' We gave Maryan her presents and cards as we sat there, along with the envelope holding the flight ticket, and waited in anticipation as she opened it, waiting for her face to crease into a smile and excitement to follow as we could now hear the low drone of the engines, and the 'phut phut' of the rotor blades as the helicopter approached and landed in the adjacent field. Not from Maryan! She stood and looked at the ticket for a few tense seconds, before announcing "Anyway, I don't like flying." To my eternal shame, I replied "Tough s--t! Now get yourself over there and check in!" Not only was this a rare opportunity for Maryan, but I had paid a considerable amount extra for her to be seated in the front with the Pilot – as Co-Pilot, in fact in full electrical communication with him during the whole flight! However, from then on the day picked up, as Maryan realised she was not going to get the better of me *or* even match me. I offered her whatever she liked to drink as she was now eighteen. She chose a glass of red wine, great as I also had likewise. As she sat down she took one sip of the wine and predictably screwed up her face and said "Oh! That's awful." "Never mind" I interjected, as I picked up her glass and tipped the contents into mine, by now the double quantity was more than welcome, I needed it. Maryan was a little shocked at this, but then realised her usual negative attitude had denied her what she really wanted, yet again. Eventually however, she began to laugh along with us and joined in our conversation, I believe she actually enjoyed the day.

We had located a place for Maryan which took interest in young people leaving care. They would offer them a small but pleasant bed-sit in a very secure building, manned twenty four hours a day. They had free access and could come and go as they pleased, but they were required to attend, at their convenience, training and supervision of their 'life-skills.' Cooking, budgeting, washing and ironing etc., to ensure they could look after themselves. When they had shown that they could manage these necessary skills, they would then be allocated a flat or house of their own. We felt, despite being eighteen, Maryan needed *more* encouragement in these areas than even we had given her and thought this would be ideal. We took Maryan along and everything was explained to her before she agreed to give it a try. The day came ever nearer for Maryan to move out. Nothing ever prepares you for this, no matter what the circumstances. I was extremely proud of Maryan for continuing to stay with us beyond her eighteenth birthday. I had always felt that she would, and could have taken off at any moment, when our boundaries didn't suit her, but she stuck it out. Therefore I hoped she would make something of her life, she certainly had the intelligence and the potential to succeed. However, although we were all in happy mood for Maryan, that we had found her somewhere to live as an adult, it was nevertheless sad and emotional the day she was moving out. I was very hopeful that she would visit and not be too far away. Maryan was also quite emotional despite trying in her usual manner to conceal her sadness. Me too!

A leaving party was arranged for her by the Agency, after all she had been in their care for about nine years, and ours for two and a half years. We had also been through a lot of heartache with Maryan's emotions, her boyfriends, jobs, college, not to mention the many differences of opinion she and I had had. I wrote Maryan a poem, when she reached eighteen, here it is:-

You're eighteen today, that's very grown up,
I suppose you'll be wondering how much wine you can sup.
How many bottles, soon we will see,
Whatever it is, you can't keep up with me
Two and a half years you've shared our home,
We cannot believe how quickly it's flown.
Though it has to be noticed when all's said and done,
That at times you have been quite a difficult one.
But beyond all that drama, when you have a mind,
I've noticed that you can be helpful and kind.
You settled in well, hardly ever been late.
You even learned how to communicate.
When you're sitting relaxing and having a 'fag'
Please do remember how I used to nag!
"Washing must be done, at least twice a week,
Wednesdays and Sundays, don't give me no cheek!"
Pick up your stuff, and tidy your room,
But it wasn't really, all doom and gloom.
Good guidance is what we were trying to give
Advice for the future by which you can live.
We wish you the best Maryan, 'n time will tell
Whether or not we have taught you well.

> So take with you our love, and leave with a smile,
> And remember us all, who you lived with awhile!

We still see Maryan now and then, invite her for Christmas, and ring her on her birthday etc; I hope she stays in touch.

Negotiations for Susannah's move were nearing an end. The process had taken longer than most due to her turbulent background, but a process of introduction had now been set in place and we were to visit her every day for the next two weeks, in order to introduce ourselves gently. This wasn't easy, as she lived in a unit twenty miles or so away, so timing was of the essence as we had Charlotte to consider and must make sure everything was done in the day, before school's end. It was exhausting, travelling back and forth, getting to know this child, yet another with a difficult past. However, Susannah was a pretty ten year old with pale blue-grey eyes and a charming smile, when she tried. Some times we would stay with her at the unit; sometimes we would take her out, over the two week period. Each day we saw her, we liked her more and more and felt she would fit in with our family, she loved art and craft and we discussed all her interests, likes and dislikes, then we began to tell her a little about Charlotte, whom she would be sharing a home with, and of course, Xara whom she would see quite frequently. Everything seemed to be going extremely well. Susannah needed people who had experience in attachment, someone, with very firm boundaries, but nurturing too. That's us!

We began to prepare the room for Susannah to move into. It had to be gutted when Maryan left. Though intelligent, Maryan was rather careless with her belongings, the bed though new, was now falling to bits, the wardrobe of course, was strained, the carpet stained, and paper peeling from the wall. In sharp contrast Susannah was a *very* punctilious child. *Everything* in its place almost regimented.

The day arrived for her to move in. The bedroom had been completely refurbished. New furniture, floor and walls etc. All her stuff was placed perfectly where required, the duvet fluffed and smoothed, she was happy. Xara had gone off to Spain with her dad, which gave Susannah and Charlotte time to get to know one another. A day or two later we took Susannah shopping for items she didn't have, and Charlotte was extremely helpful and kind, as is her nature, matching tops to trousers, skirts to blouses, and showing Susannah how she could put them together. Halfway around the store, I met up with some friends I hadn't seen for a while and stood for a chat for about ten minutes. All the while, Susannah was getting edgy.

Eventually she took off at full speed around the store, of course I had to follow out of safety, it was a big store, and she was new to me. I soon caught up with her, after we had dodged a few shelves and rails along the way. We sat down on a vacant seat, I had no idea why this had happened and she wasn't about to enlighten me. I simply said "Look, there are two ways we can do this. Either we can walk out of here right now, with nothing, and I'll be a lot richer, or we can wait in the till queue, and go home with your new stuff. You choose!" She chose to wait – of course.

Those first weeks were quite difficult with Susannah, as she had been used to being both physically and verbally violent, therefore it was also hard for Xara and Charlotte. Charlotte was on the receiving end of a great deal of verbal bullying and tapping on the head, that sort of thing. She pushed Xara into the shed one day, and locked her in, traumatising poor Xara. She was so shocked and frightened that she vomited. This way of 'being' was so entrenched in Susannah, that afterwards she couldn't understand why other children would then not want to play with her. Because of this kind of behaviour, Susannah had been excluded from every school she'd attended. In her first week back at school, she unfastened the taxi driver's seat belt and then threatened to hit him with her school bag, when he chastised her for doing so. The verbal aggression would be to tell people they were ugly or fat or have 'elf ears' etc. She would storm upstairs and *slam* the door until the whole house shook. The first time *this* happened, I made it very clear that if that happens in this house, we leave you to calm down, and then we would talk about it, as the object of the exercise was for someone to follow and ask what was wrong, therefore engaging in one-to-one attention. After several occasions of door slamming, Susannah soon realised that we did indeed leave her alone until she came back down – calmer.

However, despite all of the above, the Headmaster of the school rang after the first two weeks back, following Susannah moving in with us, to say he couldn't believe the change in her. She was a pleasure to teach, *and* she was in full-time! We were quite pleased with Susannah, and ourselves. We must be doing *something* right. Despite this encouragement, we knew there was a long way to go. The unit she had lived in for the past twelve months had done a lot of work with Susannah and therefore there had been some improvement for us to work on. The 'splitting' was a much more subtle issue. It's a classic tool for a child with attachment difficulties and Susannah was very good at it. The idea is to 'split' people and divide their loyalties to each other. For example, the first time Susannah tried this with us was during her first week at school. She told the teacher she had a hole in her tights, which indeed she did, but she wanted the teacher to ring home to tell us before she arrived here, because she would 'get into terrible trouble for it.' Of course it is possible that she may have been in trouble when at home for something like this, or maybe she was just testing out the relationship we may, or may not have with her teacher. We had an explicit talk with Susannah and explained she would not be in trouble for that sort of thing, and she didn't need to ask anyone to ring, but to talk to us herself when she came home.

There were other ways that Susannah would attempt to covet all the attention. It was Charlotte's birthday, and she had chosen to have a meal at a local Indian Restaurant and so a table was reserved, for all the family, Charlotte didn't wish to invite anyone else. We arrived at the restaurant in good time and were shown to our table, after which everyone selected their chosen dish. As we waited for the food to be served, Susannah asked if I could take her to the toilet, as she felt sick. She then turned on the tears and said she wanted to go home, she felt ill. After many years of dealing with children, I knew from experience that Susannah was not ill, she was not sick, but she *did* know that had she needed to be taken home, then we would all have to go, as we had all travelled together in the M.P.V. Ultimately, Charlotte's birthday would have been ruined. I told Susannah we couldn't go home, but I would stay here, in the toilet with her, until she had been sick, and I wouldn't leave her. She struggled. She didn't know how to make herself sick, therefore the vomit must have gone in a different direction as it didn't come out of her mouth. I did however, very nurturingly, say that she mustn't eat the Indian food that night, as it would make it worse, perhaps some cereal later. Chicken Korma was her favourite, but it sat on the table in front of her. Well, she wouldn't want it, would she?

The good behaviour at school didn't last long. The next call we received from the Headmaster, was to ask us to collect Susannah immediately as she had run off around the school, *after* hitting the dinner lady, pushing her to the floor and standing over her.

This time the teacher wasn't so tolerant, Susannah was now to be permanently excluded for this violent outburst. I honestly couldn't blame him, there had been other acts of violence previously and they had to be cautious. On arriving home we felt we must sit Susannah down and ask her what went wrong, try to understand her need for aggression with everyone. Her reply was to tell me that, "It hasn't happened here, yet." *My* reply was, that I hoped it wouldn't but if it did, we would handle it!

This was a tough time for everyone, including Susannah, everything was new to her, she didn't see any of her family and understandably had much to be angry about, but we had to channel that anger in a controlled fashion. There had been promises from the Local Authority that there would be therapeutic input, specific to attachment of course, but as yet it had not been forthcoming. However, we enlisted the help of the Agency's therapist, Peter, who was extremely helpful and gave us insight into what may be going on in Susannah's head. No matter how long you do this job, or how much experience you have, there is always the chance that something new will come through your door, if so, I had learned to enlist help, there's always room for learning. However, we put into practice some of Peter's suggestions, or took on board his explanations which proved to be very useful indeed.

We now had a situation whereby Susannah was at home *every* day. This was an awful time for Gordon and me. We have a routine that everything we need to do, or meetings we attend, must be done in school time, so that when the kids walk through the door at home time, we are done, and can give them our full attention. Now, we had Susannah to consider in everything we did. This was made more difficult due to the fact that I desperately wanted to ensure that during the hours of school time, we kept Susannah busy with school work, therefore also ensuring that she was not under the impression that she could 'do her own thing' all day. This ultimately had a strange advantage which would change the course of Susannah's life quite dramatically. As I helped her or watched her struggling with her schoolwork, due to non-attendance and exclusions in the early days, I began to feel that her learning difficulties were not entirely due to lack of education, or bad behaviour. There were strange ways in which she wrote words etc. that made me wonder if she was dyslexic. Now once again, I am no expert by any stretch of the imagination, but it was a hunch, a gut instinct. I began to mention my feelings and observations to professionals, we must advocate for these children. There were one or two murmurings of 'oh possibly,' until one day someone actually listened, and somewhere along the line she was tested and proved to be suffering from dyslexia. Susannah was initially upset, naturally. She didn't understand what dyslexia was. Gordon sat down with her, and explained the best he could, what it was all about, and how it may affect the way she sees things. He told her of many famous people who were also dyslexic, but above all he explained to Susannah, that this was just a different way of seeing things, therefore there was a different way of teaching her, but most of all, he instilled in her that this was predominantly responsible for her educational delay, and *not* because she was thick, or stupid, as she had been led to believe all her life. I knew after the first week she came her, that Susannah was not stupid. She is in fac a very intuitive child, bright and with great potential, in the right environment. This revelation, naturally had worked wonders for her self-esteem, from that moment on, she progressed educationally in leaps and bounds.

Frustratingly, the anger took a little longer to alter. Susannah would always speak very negatively of Xara and Charlotte whenever anyone came to the house. She would have aggressive moods, refuse to answer when spoken to, of course that didn't work with me. She would frequently throw pens, pencils etc., around the room. On one occasion, she had Xara and Charlotte as an audience and for no reason at all, threw a tin full of pencils in the air and was charging in a rage, with arms extended, straight towards a glass display cabinet. Gordon grabbed her gently but firmly around the wrists, to prevent her hurting herself, and held on to her in silence, until she collapsed in tears and exhaustion against his chest, and said, "You're stronger than me aren't you?" He replied, "That's right, and don't you forget that." There was another occasion when I was in the hallway at the foot of the stairs, in a crouching position as I was searching in a drawer. I was suddenly aware of Susannah charging down the stairs like a steamroller, intent on crushing all in her path, and the only thing in her path was me. I had literally seconds to raise myself to my feet, and brace myself against the approaching force, and force it was. Susannah had such strength for a ten year old, *that*, I can vouch for. As she ploughed her way through me to reach the front door, the force of her attack sent me reeling sideways, twisting my back in the process, which was in the very least, painful, though had I not braced myself, I would undoubtedly have ended up on the kitchen floor. The week which followed was spent in acute pain. I know I should have been upset and angry, but I was acutely aware that Susannah had received some bad news that day regarding her family, and had every good reason to feel angry. I understood, and tried desperately to play it down, keep the attack low-key. However, try as I may I could not conceal the pain I was suffering, for each time I moved, stood, sat , or turned, I would uncontrollably wince in agony. It was bonfire Night, fifth of November, a few days after and the children were looking forward to a Bonfire and Firework display we had been invited to. I wasn't sure whether I could attend and stand in the cold, and dark, in such pain, and no-one was prepared to take Susannah due to her attitude and behaviour. I decided that this could be used as an appropriate sanction for her unbridled aggression. Firstly, I couldn't bear the thought of any child missing the fireworks, after all it only took place once a year, despite everyone around me advising that she should not be allowed to go. I therefore compromised. I told

Susannah we would take her to the display but as soon as it was over, despite the others staying, we would have to come home due to the pain I was in. Someone kindly gave me a chair, and I sat through the colourful and noisy display, and would have loved to have joined everyone at the party which followed, but the minute the fireworks were over, we left for home, driving away in the car to the sounds of laughter as everyone was enjoying the occasion. Susannah was only too well aware that, she had been fortunate to see the fireworks at all, and had she controlled her anger and aggression, she would also have stayed to the party.

The days continued to be difficult with Susannah at home all the time. She wanted to draw me into her world at every opportunity. The fact that housework needed to be done and meals prepared was irrelevant to her, she fully expected me to sit with her all day, and give her one-to-one tuition. I am not a teacher; I had the practical matters to attend to. Telephone calls were virtually impossible particularly ones of a confidential nature, as she was always around. On a particularly pleasant Sunday morning, Angeline suggested that Gordon and I have an afternoon out on our own in my car. She offered to have Susannah for an hour or two and take her to lunch. As late a.m. approached, I suggested Susannah gather anything she would like to take with her, put on her shoes and pop round to Angeline's, next door. Gordon decided on a last trip to the bathroom before we left for our drive. As he came down the stairs he asked me if I'd had an accident with the picture frame. Strange I know, but I have a lovely quirky frame in my bathroom, containing pictures of my family and the children we have fostered. Each photo sits behind a clear Perspex bubble. It was obvious that Susannah had done this, immediately before she went next door. Neither Charlotte, nor Xara were here, Gordon certainly hadn't done it, and I naturally hadn't a process of elimination. I was, however, only glad that it was *my* photo and no-one else's. I am the 'wicked witch' figure. The one taking the female or 'mother' role. These youngsters want all the good things we do for them, things they may have never had, but it's not us whom they want to carry them out, it's their own mothers, hence the resentment. This is why we don't take these negative actions personally, there's much more behind this than meets the eye. I challenged Susannah about this incident. She swore 'on her mother's life' she hadn't done it. Little did she realise that I would know that this was a sure admission that she had. Later she broke down and confessed to Angeline.

Gradually, Susannah was allocated a place in the local junior school. She began attending only half days, and gradually another and another, then full days with a view to slowly building up to full time eventually. We had a book which travelled daily between school and home, recording the day's events of any significance. This enabled ourselves and school to work together as a team, and keep on top of any issues that might arise with behaviour.

Susannah's behaviour left much to be desired at school. She would frequently swear at teachers and accuse them of lying. She would upturn tables and throw chairs, walk out of class and be generally abusive to all around her. It has to be said, the school were exceptionally tolerant, and continued to support her and us. Others would notice the strange way she would look at me with utter contempt. There was continued bullying toward Xara and she would have nightmares involving Susannah drowning her and pushing her under the water in the swimming pool. Even Charlotte was on the receiving end of 'silent' bullying, the use of body language to shun, ignore. Understandably Xara and Charlotte began to silently distance themselves from her, although Susannah would then accuse them of being unfriendly, and I found this more difficult to deal with than full on arguing.

I was, at this point becoming increasingly concerned at Dora's living conditions. It was *dire*! You thought I'd forgotten Dora, didn't you? The house was becoming dirtier and smellier than ever. I was at a loss as to what to do, where to go for help, but help, they needed.

I contacted various agencies, in an attempt to secure some regular cleaning, but each agency that visited refused to return due to health and safety issues.

I have to admit that I could see their point. The front door would not fully open due to the build up of rubbish behind it. The staircase was a dangerous obstacle course, as was the 'sitting' room. I use the term 'sitting' loosely as there was rarely a vacant seat available, these were occupied by clothing in piles, some to be washed, others washed and awaiting the application of an iron. The trash cans were overflowing with empty lager cans and the cigarette ash of visitors to the house, usually Dana, who would stay the night, and doss down either on the sofa, or failing this, if it were *too* full of clothes, the sitting room floor. The stained and greasy carpet being her mattress for the night. The curtains often could not be opened, or closed, as they were fixed on a wire across the window. The smell was overpowering. It was almost like a wall which smacked you in the face the second the front door was opened. This was largely due to the three beautiful yet housebound cats, urinating and defecating, along with kittens being born. I did manage to acquire *some help*, in the form of a mobility scooter for Dora to enable her to escape her incarcerated lifestyle, to get out into the fresh air, and the community. I contacted the Royal Society for the Blind, as Dora could barely see due to early cataracts on her eyes, a legacy of the Dystrophy. They visited and offered various gadgets to assist in pouring tea, writing her signature etc. A section dealing with the deaf, visited and offered devices to help her hear the T.V. a little easier, and meals on wheels solved some of the nutritional issues which bothered me; at least they ate one good meal a day. The help for Leo appeared to have reached a dead end after he was attacked in front of the two 'helpers' from the education department. No-one appeared to care, I couldn't seem to tie things together or convince anyone, that we needed these services amalgamating, for continuity of care, and consistency of assessment.

It was time for more serious and determined action. I drew on past experience. How many times had I helped patients at the surgery, pointed them in the right direction for help or re-housing? That *was* what Dora and Tina needed, re-housing, a fresh start. What they needed was a social worker. I took Dora off to see her G.P. to explain to him her plight, her ailments and how they affected her life. I doubted there would be much he could do to improve her thinking ability, but *anything* would be a start.

Dora and I had never seen eye to eye on most things, but I hated seeing her ripped off by workmen or even relative due to her soft and inadequate nature, and I hated seeing her health and life decline as it was, before my eyes. I had to do something. She was my sister, and when it came to anyone actually taking some action, it appeared I was all she had.

When I had put their case before the doctor, he agreed that the situation was far from good and suggested we begin with an assessment by the district nurses. I offered my 'phone number as a contact and he agreed they would call me for further information. It would be a slow process. A week or two later, the district nurse contacted me to meet her at Dora's. The assessment was carried out and it was eventually agreed that what they needed was a social worker, to co-ordinate their needs – Result! At last, I was making progress. Dora however, was deteriorating before my eyes.

My number was given to various contacts. I began receiving calls with suggestions of help. Many weeks later, I was contacted by a lady called Elaine. A very softly spoken person with a rather refined voice. She was a social worker; at long last we were getting somewhere. I was beginning to feel calmer, listened to, and as though I was actually achieving something. I agreed a date on which to meet Elaine at Dora's house to discuss her needs.

On this particular Monday morning, I decided to arrive half an hour or so before Elaine, to go through some of the areas which needed priority attention. We discussed the cats, first and foremost and as heart rending as it was, Dora agreed they needed re-homing. This would solve some of the odour problems in the house. We decided that the carpets should be disposed of, as they were stained with cat urine, and 'spilled' food and drink which hadn't been cleaned. As I made my list and jotted down all the action that needed implementing, I asked Dora and Tina if *they* had any ideas of how they could be helped. Dora's main concern was the spiders in the toilet! The toilet was situated through the kitchen and in a small porch at the back. "We can't use the toilet," she said. "We're both afraid of a spider, that's why we use the commode!!" I really wished I hadn't asked. Tina led me into the kitchen, an area I had managed to avoid until this point. As the kitchen door opened, I was met with sights that will haunt me forever. The commode was sitting to the right of the kitchen door as it was opened. *All*, of my senses kicked in as I entered my eyes fell upon the obvious contents of this receptacle, my nose recognised the source of the stench that had eluded me until now. As I looked around, I consciously avoided touching anything that surrounded me.

Elaine was due any minute, and I was now deeply concerned about her reaction to what *I* was now seeing – and smelling. I endeavoured to explain to Dora and Tina, the dangers at every turn, in their kitchen alone. I explained, graphically, and in detail, how the flies buzzing around the room were settling on the contents of the commode, then they would visit the sugar, butter, jam and bread which were uncovered and available. It was obviously the most popular 'fly supermarket' in the whole area! I couldn't understand why the cable from the freezer was trailed across the front of two drawers, and plugged in above the work surface with full access to the water within the nearby kettle. The plug was so greasy, I couldn't get a grip on it in order to remove it from the danger it could pose. As I surveyed the freezer, trying to come up with a solution to the 'cable' problem, I queried the green mass on the top of it. I had at first thought it to be a large piece of broccoli, but on closer inspection, it turned out to be an old, very old, lump of 'something?' which had turned dark green with mould! Tina extolled her virtues as a cleaner, as she pointed out that she had recently washed the floor, but omitted to realise that the cat faeces was so solidified, she had simply 'mopped' over it.

I was astonished, and devastated, now realising that this all seemed insurmountable. Just as my eyes fell on the snails crawling up and down the window, my nightmare was momentarily interrupted by the shrill, discordant sound of the doorbell, playing 'There's no Place Like Home.' As this tune reverberated around the house, I once more turned negative into positive, my coping mechanism, and my mind drifted on a higher plain, with thoughts of Dorothy Gale, and her desperate quest to return home to Kansas. If only I could now click my three inch heels, and wake up elsewhere, anywhere! A voice jolted me back to reality. I wondered if it had all been a dream, like Dorothy's, but no, this was a nightmare – a living nightmare. The voice was Elaine's! *How* was I going to explain all this, it was unbelievable.

Tina answered the door, as it struggled once more to allow entry to its most recent visitor. Elaine introduced herself and tenuously shook my hand, as she peered at her surroundings. She was a petite, black lady of slender and delicate build, with beautifully quaffed hair, and fine gold-rimmed spectacles. Her tweed two-piece suit was not at home in this environment, and neither was she. I now faced the daunting task of offering a guided tour of Dora's uncomfortable abode, and explaining the occupancy of spiders, flies and snails!

Once Elaine recovered from the sights she saw, and overcame her newly acquired breathing difficulties, she began making notes. She admonished Dora and Tina for the absence of 'proper' toilet facilities and recognised their fear of spiders in the toilet, situated through the door. Less than five feet away from the offending commode, and then it came! The question I had been oblivious to, the answer to which I *really* didn't want. Elaine spoke slowly, with a puzzled expression on her face, and asked in her quiet, soft voice, "Dora, if you are so afraid of the spiders, that you don't use the toilet, then *where*, do you empty the commode??? Ahhhhh! The very nano-second this question was asked, I knew only too well what the answer was going to be, but perhaps my subconscious had obliterated all thoughts of it previously

It seemed like forever before Dora answered Elaine's poignant question. "Well, down the sink of course!!".

Chapter Twenty Four

A New Life? Or the Final Solution

The snails have now finished their 'eggy' meal on the window pane. Even the rainbow coloured ribbons they have left behind them cannot brighten my thoughts and feelings as they leave Dora's window resembling 'stained glass.' Where were my positives now? They eluded me.

Elaine couldn't speak for a few silent second; she appeared to be searching for answers. Her first response was to inform Dora and Tina that the Health and Safety department would have to be called in to flush out and clean the waste pipes, as she was very concerned at the health hazard now posed by the open drain below the kitchen window, outside. The snails didn't appear to mind. She then sat and very patiently talked to them about how they really *must* make the effort to sort out and tidy the mounting rubbish around the house, (something I have requested, many times, I thought.) I was beginning to feel by now, that events were just going round in circles. This wasn't sounding 'new' and therefore not very positive to me. What progress were we going to make? While all changes do not lead to improvement, all improvement requires change. If anything I felt disillusioned and defeated in all honesty, as I took stock of the amount of work required to make life even resemble normality for them. Leo was barely at home, the poor lad obviously spent as much of his time as he could elsewhere, in order to escape reality. I was truly amazed that he hadn't got himself in trouble in some way, but that was yet to come.

However, once more I continued the struggles with Susannah, though she *was* showing much improvement. She no longer displayed violent behaviour, at home at least. She was now, respectful to Gordon and I, had a very good routine and was very helpful and obedient. Those 'higher up' wondered what we had done. My only answer was that our calmness, but firmness, respect and consistency towards her, was now being reciprocated. She also knows what the boundaries are, and knows life is good if you keep to the rules. If we could just achieve similar results in school, we would have an *almost* perfect child! Mind you, that, we would never expect, such a thing doesn't exist. It wasn't easy for Susannah, she'd had a particularly difficult beginning in life, like so many others, and had no comparisons as a yardstick for assessing how life should 'be.' Susannah is still with us, and although she struggles daily, she is determined to catch up to be where she should for her age, level with her peers, and I truly believe she has enough intelligence, determination and resilience, to reach her goal one day.

Charlotte, however, is gaining confidence, in leaps and bounds. She goes from strength to strength and I feel she may *never* leave us, at least not for quite a while. She tells me she is going to care for me in my old age, along with Xara, and make me cups of tea, and that the two of them will always be there for me. Nothing fills me with greater pleasure, than the thought of spending my days in their company. Charlotte is determined to succeed to the best of her ability, and will slog away at her education until she reaches her goal. She has just had her sixteenth birthday, and like all young teenagers was completely wrapped up in it all, enjoying every second of the celebration of this milestone. Yet there is one difference with Charlotte, she actually does appreciate everything done for her, this is what sets her apart from so many and is so rewarding. Despite her early traumas in life, Charlotte has remained steadfast in her determination, not to let her family associations let her down, or keep her down. She has seen events in my family, and realises that one can break free. We are not all tarred with the same brush.

The following is a letter charlotte gave to Gordon and me, following her sixteenth birthday, it reads:-

Dear Sandy and Gordon,

Thank you so much for making my sixteenth birthday, the very best I could have wished for.

It was the best birthday I have ever had and each birthday I spend with you gets even better.

I feel as though you both love me more than my parents do. You make sure I have everything I need.

I thank you from the whole of my heart for giving me the best birthday ever, and for being there for me forever and always. I got more than I expected from you for my birthday.

Love you, Charlotte.

This is what makes it all worthwhile. This is what makes the hard work and suffering pay off in the end. If we only make this much difference to one child, then our efforts in fostering have not been wasted. This, is our reward.

Little does Charlotte yet realise, but she had been nominated as this year's recipient of a very special award, at an achievement ceremony for Looked After Children, in recognition of her steadfast efforts, and achievements, against all the odds. No-one deserves it more.

It was about six weeks later that I received a call from Elaine. She had, in the interim, set several wheels in motion and was achieving a certain success in bringing services on board for Dora and Tina. Great stuff Elaine! But better than that, for this call was to tell me that a house had been identified for them. It was available and appeared to meet Dora's needs. The only reservation Elaine and I had, was that the house was in a different area of town, quite a distance from where they presently lived. I couldn't help thinking that this may be beneficial, a fresh start, but I wondered if Dora and Tina would see it that way. I was pleasantly surprised however when they showed enthusiasm, and couldn't wait to see the house, so Elaine arranged a visit. The house was much more spacious than their present 'shoe box!' Amazingly there was an actual 'lift' in the corner of the sitting room, which when operated, ascended through a trap door in the ceiling and arrived in the corner of the bedroom above. This meant Dora wouldn't have to struggle up and down the stairs, and therefore eliminated the risk of falling, which she had frequently done in the past. There were no steps to the front door, which would enable her to come and go on her mobility scooter with much more ease. It was perfect, and they loved it. Dora gave notice on her present home without delay, and made arrangements for the removals. Unfortunately, the date she chose was during a spell I was away in Portugal, maybe this was not a bad thing though, as had I been around, I would most certainly have become embroiled in it all, though I had been in telephone contact to discover how the move had gone and how they were settling. They were thrilled with their new surroundings and even more thrilled with the many avenues of help Elaine now made available to them. I would be eternally grateful to Elaine for her hard work and dedication, and no doubt it would be an experience that Elaine would never forget. Well done Elaine!

Leo was also quite 'chuffed' with his new sizable bedroom, a new area and new friends. This was the fresh start they all needed, a completely new beginning, in a new place.

It was three weeks later, before I was able to visit Dora in her new home. Gordon was quite sceptical the day I chose to visit. "New house, new tip, new shit!" was his very pessimistic view. He was *absolutely* right, as always! As I approached the garden gate, my first impression was slight disappointment at the outside appearance, although they had been promised that new windows and doors were due to be fitted within the year. Despite my initial feelings, I was quite hopeful as I approached the door and knocked. Remember, negatives into positives, the inside may be what they had been concentrating their efforts on. After a few seconds struggle, Tina opened the reluctant front door, about six inches, for this was the furthest it would go, nothing new here, I thought. I entered the sitting room, and *was* pleasantly surprised to notice that the 'wall' of odour had gone, it didn't growl and jump out and hit me by the time I made my way through, but I couldn't help slight disappointment at the amount of rubbish scattered around, furniture in disarray. There was a distinct lack of the 'Feng Shui' factor, but I should be thankful for the small mercies so far. As I was given a guided tour, I omitted to see the sink and cooker, as they were covered in dirty dishes and unpacked shopping bags were strewn about the floor. As we proceeded to the upper level, I was perplexed to see Dora climbing the stairs, as the 'lift' was already up there, meaning she must have *descended* via the stairs earlier. As I was shown into the first bedroom, I understood why. The lift was full of clothing and was now being used as a convenient linen bin, clean or dirty, who knows? Only one third of the room was actually visible as clutter ascended in a semi-circle from wall to wall, and ended in a 'pyramid,' its apex at the corner of the ceiling. The staircase was the old familiar obstacle course, which I had hoped they had left behind. Their only excuse for all this was that they hadn't yet got around to unpacking.

And so the saga continued for Dora, Tina and Leo, living together in their unique abode. The only change, apart from the area, was that the rooms of this house offered more space for the endless clutter, and the odours were mostly gone due to proper toilet facilities being used, and no 'captive' cats urinating daily on the carpets. I feel there is nothing more I can do for them now. This *was* the final solution, *and* the fresh start as far as I was concerned. Sadly now, I must leave them to their own devices. Its so disheartening, to exert such effort, especially at my age, again and again to no avail. My duties lie elsewhere, where hopefully, I *am* making a difference.

A year or so down the line, I made one of my *occasional* visits to Dora, to find they now have a dog! The cream coloured carpet they chose for the sitting room, is now 'patterned' with yellow and brown patches and the overpowering odour is worse than it has ever been.

Sally visits rarely, and who can blame her? Lola is yet another grandchild, Dora is deprived of seeing regularly, but this is due to her own inadequacies, and Dana bless her, cannot be blamed for this one.

Andre is safe in Germany with his partner and a young son of his own, though on the occasions he visits England I am glad to say he still visits Gordon and me, and I am, always eternally grateful to see him, though sadly for Dana, he still refuses to take her grandson to see her. I for one, hope he keeps it that way. Oh, the irony of it all. What goes around comes around as they say. Dora has been deprived of eight of her ten grandchildren due to the actions of Dana, now years later, Dana is suffering the same fate, and denied hers.

Leah falls in and out of friendship with her mother and grandmother, but has been known to leave her young son with Dana. An action I fear she will live to regret in the future.

Anna and Paula? Well as far as I am aware, are still successfully living with their adopted mother. I *still* insist on the letterbox contact, and each year, dutifully write, send photos and money to them. I will *never* forget, and will *never* forget them or give up on the two of them. In a couple of years, Anna will turn eighteen. Perhaps one day she will be curious regarding her birth family. My only hope is that she seeks *us* out, before she seeks out Dana, or she would never want to know the rest of her family or her history, a great deal of which I can give her.

Now, as for Dana, well, I haven't seen her in a long time, and whenever I do, it is purely by accident. I would never see fit to seek her out. At least these days she leaves me well alone. A while ago, Dora told me how upset Dana was, that she had no pictures of her dad, Vince. I had one or two, and sent her copies of what I had. Despite my long-term, crossed-swords with

Dana, I felt for anybody who had no record of
the dead father they could barely remember, and
a few copies were small offering, but I feel that
it is since this act, which to her must have been
totally unexpected, that she has bowed out of
my life to my great comfort, though let's not
forget that she was once my 'Angel', and I once
loved her. However, not much can be said for
poor Jason, Dana's third and last husband. I
had predicted to him, many years ago, and prior
to his wedding that he was mad if he married
Dana. My words came sadly true when he was
admitted to a hospital for the mentally ill, and
apparently is completely and utterly 'gone.'
Dana's most current ' beau,' is thirty years her
senior, a sugar daddy, and she's enjoying her
foreign holidays, and fake fur coats, yet
eternally denied the love of her children.

Now, poor Leo has just turned sixteen. From
the day he was born he knew nothing of his
father, not even what he looked like, until a man
turned up at the door only a few months ago,
and announced:- "Hi, I'm your dad!" No
explanation, no mediation, and no chance for
Leo to come to terms with this. I told Dora
then, it will end in tears, and it will not benefit
Leo. Now, Leo is about to become a dad
himself. He had got a young member of his
dad's family pregnant, but her parents are
allowing her to have the baby – lovely – for
them! A whole new generation is being born.

Will it all begin again? I have great great nephews to consider, but sad as it may sound, I have to let it go, I must stay virtually anonymous to them for my own sanity. I will not be around when they are grown up, someone else, will have to take over life's journey from here. Oh! By the way, who do you think was responsible for Leo's dad turning up? Remember Carla, yes, the other 'Angel' in my life, she had informed him of their whereabouts, with not a care in the world for the consequences which would follow.

Where, and when will it end? Dora believes that 'spirits' can steal your money! "Only the ones you buy in a bottle" I told her. Dana occasionally sees aliens, but then looking through the bottom of a bottle can distort the vision, can't it? Perhaps that's what this had all been, an Alien experience, not real. Beam me up Scotty!

There have been times along life's journey when I have often asked, "Am I the 'normal' one?" For frequently I have wondered whether this *has* been my life, or could I have been lucky enough for it all to have been a dream. If so, when will I wake up?

Angeline and Xara, still live right next door, for the time being, I feel extremely fortunate in this respect. At least I have had them close for a while longer. I am extremely proud of my daughter, Angeline. She had made her own way in the world, and I know there have been times when she has had to share my time with others, but I hope she realises that she was always my priority, and at times I did my duty to others but was always mindful of her needs. I also think that she has become a stronger person because of it. She owns her own home, and now also owns her own beauty salon, which I'm sure will be a great success. She had always laughed at the fact that, despite having two crazy parents, and a mother with 'individual' quirks.' She didn't turn out too badly. My nails would not have survived the ravages of the keyboard, in writing this book, without her expertise.

Angeline and I have been more than mother and daughter. We were friends when she was young, when her dad was always at work, she and I went everywhere together. When she was a teenager, and had no friends amongst the Witnesses, who wouldn't go out, I accompanied her on her nights out, as a 'scatty' friend as well as a mum. I hope we will remain such friends, forever.

Xara! She and I have a very special relationship, which goes deeper that I can explain. I believe we have a spiritual connection, one that cannot be broken, I hope I am right, I hope we will always be in each other's lives, and that she and Charlotte will be true to their word. Looking after me in my dotage means they will always be around, selfish, I know, but what a lovely thought. However, Xara is now the most beautiful ten year old, and still my little 'milk chocolate bunny' with liquorice hair, and 'chocolate drop' freckles adorning her little rosy cheeks and right across her button nose. She is going to grow up into a most attractive adult. I can see her mother now, trying to keep the boys at bay.

As for Gordon, well he has been trying to wake me from my dream for many years, though even a 'princely' kiss through his prickly beard, didn't do the trick. He had figuratively 'shaken' me, telling me to stop, to leave them all alone, and it has taken many, many years for me to 'wake up' and see that he *was* right, things would never change. Gordon has been my rock throughout it all, he has assisted where necessary, though at times, reluctantly. He has always been a total support in whatever I have had to deal with, to the extent that he agreed, even decided, that we take in these damaged members of my family. Helped my parents beyond all normal son-in-law duties, and these days goes above and beyond in his duty to the children we now care for. I could not have done any of it without him as my right-hand man. None, of it could I have done alone. He is now also, Foster Carer Representative, for our area and supports other carers with advice and practical help where possible.

As for myself, I have asked the question many times, "I wonder when it will all end?" Well, it's rather like the repetitive disasters in the movie 'Jaws.' Just when I think it's safe, when I'm swimming and not sinking, the 'shark' rears its ugly head and bites me yet again, and Dana hasn't disappointed me. She has again recently turned to the spirit world, (the ethereal kind) *along* with those in a bottle, and has been apparently informed – by my mother, that she is angry with me for trying to kill her! Why, I ask myself, did my mother's spirit, speak to Dana, whom she loathed, rather than me?

However, life is pleasantly peaceful at present, though it is autumn and I have heard nothing at all from Anna and Paula.

As the weeks pass and Christmas approaches once more, I receive a 'phone call from CARLA! Out of the blue this *definitely* came. She continues to bombard me with how disappointed *she* is in her own daughter. That she has turned to drink and drugs! What goes around, comes around, I thought to myself. This passes over my head like a wave, though I must be careful, there are more 'sharks' lurking beneath.

However, we have a trip to India approaching in the New Year, and I am relishing the thought of relaxing in the sum, on a white sandy beach, perhaps writing some poetry, inspired by the beautiful surroundings. Despite this, I still feel sadness at hearing nothing at all from Anna and Paula. It constantly pervades my thoughts still, and I promise to pursue it again when I return.

Charlotte accompanied me to India, as a reward for all her hard work and effort in being who she wants to be. It *was* a wonderful couple of weeks, despite almost drowning in the sea. We had arranged a trip on the ocean to see the Bottlenose Dolphins leaping to greet us from the sparkly, sequinned waters as the sun played on the little white crests of waves. I had however, expected a *large* boat, with tables and decks and *toilets*! Needless to say, it was no bigger than a fishing boat, meaning the water was just 6" below the boat's edge. Every wave that rolled, was out to get *me*! we were given little wooden boards wrapped with twine and a hook on the end, along with a little heap of dead shrimps for bait, and instructed to chuck the hook over the side of the boat (which I did without looking) I was amazed at how quickly my 'shipmates' began catching the most wondrous creatures. Ones I had only seen on nature programmes on T.V. There were Parrot fish, Blue Mammas, Sea Snakes, Tiger Barbs and even a Puffer fish. However, after approximately an hour and a half at sea, coping with the undulating waves, I needed the loo! The anti-malaria tablets were doing me not favours. We were anchored in a tiny cove in the middle of nowhere, but the lads in charge of the boat, could not understand why I couldn't just swim to the tiny beach. Once I had assured them in no uncertain terms that I couldn't swim, and was actually terrified of the water, they very kindly pulled and manoeuvred the boat backwards by its anchor rope, as close to the shore as they possibly could. Carefully avoiding the craggy volcanic rocks. One of the boys was by now, up to his chest in the water and suggested I could jump in, and walk from here. *JUMP IN* ?! If it was up to *his* chest, you can rest assured it would have been above my head. In the nick of time, my future son-in-law Neil saved the day. He jumped in before me and instructed me to hold on to his shoulders as he led me to the shore – fully clothed I might add. Whereupon I found a big rock, and had the longest pee in history! Poor Neil, I strangled him, and scratched him, as I endeavoured to cling on for dear life, as the strong current continually hurled us back to the shore. I couldn't get a grip on Neil's sun-oil drenched shoulders and kept slipping off, plunging into the swirling waters, which were all of four feet deep. As we were about to reach the boat, the tide (thinking it was perhaps doing us a favour) kindly brought the boat towards us. However, the propellers of the two outboard motors were heading for each of our faces. Neil very calmly pushed them away with his hand, and the tide obliged by returning the boat towards the sea as we scrambled aboard. I had forgotten, when I jumped into that water, that I was wearing my favourite Versace sunglasses, the real thing, yet despite the struggle, they were still firmly attached to my face.

The following week, we decided on a relaxing day on the river – crocodile hunting! *Why*, do I put myself through it? I ask. Perhaps I needed a different and new challenge with something other than children. Needless to say, I did not get on that boat until I'd had a pee! I was not jumping into any more water, particularly with a pack of Mugger crocs,'

Anyhow, following an otherwise wonderful trip, we set out on the journey to the airport for our return to England, but nothing I do, is without trauma or drama. We could not return that morning as an eagle had been sucked into one of the engines of the aeroplane on landing. "It could be a day or two" was the announcement. You see, there's British time, and there's Goan time. Charlotte was distraught, but I told her not to worry, we may have an extra day or two in India. This however proved to be the worst twenty four hours of my life (apart from my near-death experience in the sea) We were parted from Neil Angeline and Xara and were not reunited with them again until we arrived at the airport for our second attempt to return home.

All in all, it was a wonderful experience for us all, but particularly for Xara and Charlotte. It gave us all renewed vigour to face the coming year, and whatever it may throw at us.

Chapter Twenty Five

The Icing on the Cake!

This book, as I thought in its entirety was completed last autumn. I contacted my publisher to discuss the layout etc, but due to the intervention of Christmas and arrangements for our trip to India, publication was delayed. Perhaps there was a reason.

Two things I had promised myself for the New Year were, firstly to chase up my correspondence with Anna and Paula, and to finally, have the book published. I couldn't allow two years work to drip down the drain. Also despite my resolutions, I am beginning to feel I will never hear from the girls ever again. There is still no reply, no word from them.

Dana however, is reaping what she has sown all her life. She has just discovered that her latest sugar daddy has previously spent two and a half years of a prison sentence for paedophile activities. Yet despite this, she is staying with him. Shortly after *this* news was broken, other news was unfolding. Leo's baby was being born, he was about to become a dad, at the tender age of just sixteen. Sadly, Leo's son didn't make it into this world alive, he was stillborn.

However, it is nine years and one month to the day since Anna and Paula walked out of my life. I sit down to write a letter to the social services, in a last ditch attempt to make some contact. Alas, I don't have a stamp; therefore the letter sits in the hallway, waiting to be posted. At 4 p.m. this afternoon the 'phone rings, yet again, and as I listen to the lady on the end of the line introducing herself as Elizabeth, calling from the Post Adoption Team, my mind semi-switches off. Is it another charity begging me for money? My mind was jolted back to reality when she uttered the words: - Anna and Paula!! I pricked up my ears spontaneously. "What was that?" I asked. She repeated what she had said a second time, but now I was listening acutely to every word. Apparently, Anna has been having problems and is asking about her birth family, and understandably she is wanting some contact. Her desire has become so strong that eventually her frustrations are turning to anger, and for several hours today, Anna has screamed and shouted, and kicked off. Margaret therefore, had little choice but to call Elizabeth for advice. Hence the call today. There was no way I wanted Anna or Paula to locate Dana – with a paedophile? Wow! There was no way I could allow this. Shocked at this news I was then asked whether they could bring Anna here. My reply was, "I would give my right arm to see Anna and Paula again."

There were some drawbacks to this of course. I had a house full of children and no spare room for Anna to stay in. Also, because those I had, were looked-after young people, I needed the permission of the relevant Local Authorities to bring another young person into the house. The first task was to ring each of them, and the Agency, because I knew they may need to call me back, and time was running out. It was now 4.30 p.m. and most offices would be closed by 5 p.m. I then needed to speak to Angeline, as she had a spare room. She was simultaneously upset and overjoyed when I told her and readily agreed. After all it was just next door, and therefore we could care for Anna jointly.

Before I could receive the answers I needed, Elizabeth was calling me back, asking if I had managed anything, as Anna was in a dreadful state at home. I assured Elizabeth that as soon as people had returned my calls I would ring her immediately.

I am so relieved to say, that everyone concerned agreed to my request, and within the hour, Margaret was on her way with Anna. I felt quite sorry for Margaret in a way. Perhaps the realisation of the errors of the past nine years, in not allowing some contact with the girls, was just too much. I had always known this would happen one day, for I knew these girls better than anyone. After all, I'd had involvement with each of them from the day they were born.

I had seen their little personalities being shaped. At a time like this, any normal human being, I'm sure would feel like saying 'I told you so' and I *am* human. Margaret is also human, and I'm sure, did everything she thought was in the girls' best interests. However, this would not have benefited anyone, we all make mistakes. Apparently, Paula had also had similar episodes some time earlier but had received some help, yet Anna was a very different personality and much more work would be required.

However, within two or three hours they arrived at my door. As they entered, the first thing I did was to give both Anna and Paula a big hug, one which covered the nine years since they left. The next thing, which made me smile, was Anna's observation of my perfume. I hadn't realised, but she had. It was my favourite, and the perfume I always wore when they were here. This served to reinforce what I had always felt. That sights, sounds and smells are significant to children. They are signatures of events – good or bad – which will stick with them forever. I silently asked myself how many times I had bought a teddy bear for a child who was leaving us, and sprayed it with my perfume in order to keep a link between us.

Sadly, I was to discover that all the cards, photos and letters I had sent over the years had not been given to Anna and Paula, as it was thought they didn't want them. When we were asked not to visit them anymore, my greatest fear had been that *they* would feel they had been dumped and forgotten. Today that fear had been well founded. If only the 'link' had been maintained, perhaps the children would not be feeling this way so many years later. A lesson for all of us.

However, Anna stayed with us for seven weeks all told. She shared Easter with us and was the calmest girl I could have wished for, and Paula also came for a visit. Despite this, there was another observation. Anna regressed during her time spent with us. In many ways she was the five year old who left, all that while ago. She even sucked a dummy, which we gave her, to replace her shrivelled over-sucked fingers. It was very strange seeing a tall, fifteen year old girl, and a very beautiful one I might add, sucking a dummy and watching children's programmes on T.V. Perhaps she needed to do this to move on. Fine by me!

During her stay with us, Anna expressed that she didn't want to go back home, that she hated everyone there. Much work was needed to help her to see that it was the best place for her. That despite her longing to see us, she was well cared for and loved by her new family, that she could now have the best of both worlds, if she behaved appropriately. I put together a Family History book for them both, and a family tree. I need to be careful. I have no wish to upset anyone, but I feel that if the girls have the 'jigsaw' pieces of their past completed they will recover their sense of identity. This does not detract in any way from Margaret's parenting skills, or decrease the love they have for each other. I have no wish to battle, I would love to work *with* Margaret, have contact even if only once or twice a year perhaps. To be able to send cards on their birthdays, and perhaps a 'phone call now and then, as I have asked Anna to make me a promise, that when she is angry and feels like running away, she will ring me instead, and maybe we can talk about the problems.

I desperately wanted Dora to see the children. She also loved them and never harmed any of them. However, I knew that in her excitement she would 'blab' to Dana that the girls were here. Therefore, subversive I know, but careful handling was required. We arranged the day that Anna would be returning home, and simultaneously I asked Dora to visit *me* for a change. What a nice surprise it would be, and of course by the time Dora left, the girls would be on their way home. This way, if Dana used her usual venom, it wouldn't harm Anna and Paula. *I* could cope with Dana!

As Dora seated herself on my sofa that day, in walked Anna. "Don't I know you?" asked Dora, as she peered at Anna's familiar smiling face. "I'm Anna" she said.

Immediately Dora showed both recognition and disbelief. Her eyes filled with tears as the enormity of it sunk in. They reminisced and hugged each other until Paula arrived with Margaret, the reunion complete.

This – was the icing on the cake, so to speak! The culmination of years of heartache and devastating loss. It would have been so easy, and tempting to have encouraged Anna to stay. Had I done that, I feel it wouldn't have been long before Paula followed. Besides, it was just not the right thing to do. Not what they needed at all, it wouldn't have been right for anyone. *They* then would have suffered the loss of the new family they had made. Margaret has been a good mother to them and they are well cared for where they are. It *is* the right place for them to be.

I have discussed the way forward for the future with all concerned, and have realised that I know the whereabouts of six of the eight siblings. Perhaps in the future when they are all older, we could have a reunion of some kind.

Meanwhile, I hope to work along with Margaret to secure stability for the children, and calm and settled future at home with their new family. Safe in the knowledge that we can communicate now and then, that the link has been restored. What a unique and wonderful alliance. Adoptive parent and birth family member, working together to give a contented and successful future to previously damaged children.

There is a lesson in here for all of us. Foster Carers and Adopters alike, to understand a child's inner feeling and *listen* to them. To question the outward behaviour, as to what lies beneath. To work *together* to bring out the best in everyone.

A miracle – perhaps *other* kinds of Angels had a hand in it somewhere!

However, I realise that retirement is just around the corner, and knocking at my door. But the thought of doing nothing, and not being involved with people, would be like giving up on life itself. There is life in the old girl yet, and I feel I still have much to give. Gordon and I have just received an award from the Local Authority, linked with the school we liaise well with, for the Celebration of Success Awards, for significant enhancement of children's experiences by a foster carer. This is a powerful recognition of the commitment we have shown to children over the years and it is very much appreciated.

Though for now at least, I gain most pleasure from my occasional meetings with Sue, Sharon and Estelle, as we become 'Ladies-wot-do-lunch' when we gather at the local shopping centre for a 'natter,' some retail therapy, and a cappuccino now and then. Many a trauma has been put to rights between us!

However, I'm sure there will come a day when I will feel the need to retire and relax, to do something for myself in life, and when I do, I hope there will be the many children we have known and cared for, coming to visit for a cuppa, and most of all, that I will still have Gordon, Angeline and Xara as a focus in my life.

Noah spent forty years of his life, laboriously building an ark on dry land, in an attempt to persuade the people to join him, when the rains came, and be saved. I feel as though I have done pretty much the same for more than forty years to no avail also,
with my family, but you know what? I have reached a conclusion. From now on, let them build their own Bloody Ark!

Ten Top Tips

For Successful Parenting

Whether we are parents, grandparents or foster parents, we all have issues to overcome in caring for children. Parenting is not an easy task, whatever our relationship, and No-one is born a fully –fledged, perfect role mode, it has to be worked at!

Here are some tips I have learned along the way, the hard way, which I have found invaluable in finding success in building relationships with young people, along with a few coping strategies for ourselves. Sometimes, however, we will get it wrong. Perfectionism is for Snowflakes! We are not Snowflakes, so don't beat yourself up about it, if a strategy doesn't work. Failure is a learning curve. However, when you find yourself doing something right, praise yourself.

1. NEVER LIE.

As you have read in this book, it never pays to lie to young people. It will come back and 'hit' you. always be as truthful as you possible can, and *never* make promises you're not sure you can keep, otherwise the trust you are trying to build up, will be broken down.

2. STAY CALM

NEVER shout! sometimes it may be necessary to raise the level of your voice slightly in order to emphasize what you are saying, but this is different from shouting orders at young people, or using a tone of voice which can be very frightening to a child who may have left a household where this way of communicating was an every day occurrence. Engage brain, before putting mouth in gear. Get the 'butterflies' flying in formation – calmly. Walk away!

My favourite method of course, is to walk away, into another room, and pace the floor as the tension flows out, all the while repeating my least favourite four letter work, under my breath! This I find has a remarkably calming effect, yours may be quite different. Whenever I use the particular word I have in mind (which I might add is extremely rare) others usually laugh as it is so out of character. Perhaps that's why it calms me, my wicked side kicks in.

3. FIRM BOUNDARIES

This sometimes seems a little harsh, as it is often so easy to 'give in' or pander to every whim of a child or young person when they enter our homes. Believe me, when I say my mother's favourite phrase, 'Start as you mean to go on!' is essential. I cannot emphasize this enough. Children will almost always try to rebel against your boundaries or 'house rules' as sure as snowflakes are perfect, but children *really* do want, and need the basic rules at least. It makes them feel safe, and in some cases loved even. To feel that you care about their safety when you ask them to be home by an agreed time, or ask their whereabouts. Draw up a contract between you if necessary.

Always stay firm because rest assured, despite these young people trying to *take* control, what they really want, and may not realise, is someone *else* to take control, to be responsible for them. In some cases to even just acknowledge their very existence. However, moderation has to be used, allow them *some* control where appropriate, it's a juggling act, and every child's needs must be judged on their own merits, but *never* allow them to intimidate you, without your consent! Remember – *we* train people how to treat us.

4. BE CONSISTENT

Don't waver in agreements you have made. For instance if you have said, 'mobile 'phones must be downstairs by 9 p.m.' – stick to it. If you say 'no food upstairs' this means *ever*, not even a piece of chewing gum. If you are not consistent and resolved, then the light will shine through the 'chink' in your armour, like a beacon in a storm. Always, carry through.

5. GIVE CHOICES

Wherever possible, always give a young person at least two choices when you have a dispute over something. However, *one* of the choices has to be virtually impossible for them to make, in order to encourage them to choose wisely. A prime example was the incident with Jake. If you remember, he was wobbling to and fro' on top of the wall over the river. I gave him the choice of 'wobbling' for another hour, whilst I stayed with him (although I also refused to follow him If he fell into the river, as I can't swim) OR going for fish and chips along with everyone else. What boy wouldn't want fish and chips on a crisp, cold winter's day? Therefore it was obvious what his choice was going to be – the *right* one – not to mention, the one we wanted! The difference as you can see is, that, had I ordered Jake to get down from the wall, or demanded that he go with us, he most certainly would have refused and we would have had a battle on our hands. Giving these 'impossible' choices helps us to choose our battles, and win them without confrontation, therefore remaining in control, though the young person will feel that they did have a choice. One word of warning, though, you *must* be prepared to keep your word, whatever their decision.

Look at it this way, a child is like a coiled spring in our hand. If we keep it tightly squeezed, the second it is released it will expand quickly and sharply away from us and be lost. If we release it slowly and gently, bit by bit, we will manage to hold onto it, safely in our hand, and not lose it.

6. A THERAPEUTIC APPROACH

We are much more likely to build up a rapport with a child if we can empathise with their thoughts and feelings, rather than dismiss them without a second thought. Here is a prime example of how to say No, appropriately!

Child: - "*I*, want a horse, my friend's got one!"

Adult: - "O.K. that would be nice. Let's see now what colour would he be?"

Child: - "Ooh! A brown one with white spots.
Adult: - "O.k. where shall we keep him? Perhaps we could put him on the decking,
      down the garden!"

Child: - "Mmm, he wouldn't fit.

Adult: - "Mmm, perhaps his hooves would get stuck in the grooves! O.k., where would he sleep and what would he eat?"

Child: - Well, I don't know where he'd sleep but we could buy him some hay to eat!"

Adult: - "Yes we could, but who's going to buy it? I know, you could buy it from your pocket money, 'cos it would be your horse! Also we would need to get a shovel, because you would need to clean him out every day, after school. I think you'd better save up first. Think about all the stuff you're going to need, a saddle, and a brush to groom him with, a *big* bucket and shovel and hay to feed him with, and a FIELD!

I think you may find in the end, they'll settle for a hamster!

Another approach is to make sure you 'match the mood.' For example, if someone says 'I'm feeling a bit sad today.' The last response they want to hear is, "Oh snap out of it!" Empathise! Try saying, "Really, why is that, do you want to talk about it! If appropriate, agree that they have every right to feel sad, angry etc., and perhaps offer if possible, some sort of help or at least comfort. Try to replace the negative feeling with something positive or hopeful. Remember, our feelings are controlled by our thoughts.

7. DON'T TAKE IT PERSONALLY

When we are sworn at or ridiculed, it is human nature to retaliate. Though it is so very difficult at times to hold back from verbally reciprocating the abuse, it is essential *not* to take this personally. It's highly likely that the anger is not aimed at you but internally it may be someone else the child wants or needs to lash out at emotionally, but unfortunately, we are the ones in the immediate firing line, and *we* are going to 'get it!' Particularly the one taking the female or 'mother' role. *We* fit into the Wicked Witch of the West syndrome! Some of these children do often realise that they need and want all the lovely things we do for them, but they would much prefer their own mother to have done them. Therefore this makes us 'wicked' for taking her place, so to speak. However, we need, with professional help, to develop the skills of looking beyond this behaviour, to ignore to some degree, the verbal abuse and name-calling, and endeavour to find out what the thoughts and feelings are which have caused the child to be hurt or angry and where possible, to deal with that, rather than the immediate behaviour we see before us. This is where training is essential. Listening and learning is crucial to our ability to carry out these difficult tasks. It isn't easy, but then anything worthwhile rarely is. Tell yourself: - 'It'll be difficult, but that's o.k., because I'm good at difficult things!'

8. TEAM WORK

One habit I found very difficult to change, when I joined the Agency, was 'not to do it alone!' many times when I had been caring for my relatives, I was seen as exactly that – a relative, and left largely by social services to just get on with it. I now realise with hindsight that many of the problems were dealt with by me, rather than the social workers. In essence, much of the time I did their jobs for them, yet was left 'out of the loop' where information was concerned more often than not. Naturally with the Agency, it was very different. Help and advice was at there end of the 'phone twenty four hours a day. Remember, help is out there, work as a team in order to create the best life for these children. Ask for help, sometimes it is necessary to *demand* help, (politely of course) but always advocate for the child. Remember, you have the right to say no, appropriately! Build your confidence, confidence is a D.I.Y. job.

9. KEEP ONE STEP AHEAD

Learn from experience; be prepared with certain sanctions which can be imposed for negative behaviours. Try, where possible to make the 'punishment fit the crime.' For example, if a young person repeatedly switches on their T.V. late at night after lights out time, an appropriate sanction might be to disconnect the T.V. for a day or two, depending on the severity, and it is 'fitting.' It would be of little consequence stopping sweets for a week for example, as they may still use the T.V. inappropriately.

Don't fix squeaky floorboards! I have many, and each one has its own unique sound. I know *exactly* where anyone is in the house, by each 'unique squeak!' Being one step ahead also means letting the child know you are aware. For example, if after bedtime (our time, when we sit down to finally relax and discuss private stuff) I hear the 'Stair' squeak, this means they are ear wigging, I will call out "You're out of bed, do you want something?" I then hear the 'squeak' once more as they scurry back to their bedroom, struggling to understand *how* on earth I knew they were there! *You*, are in control, *You*, are the adult!

10. A SENSE OF HUMOUR

Whenever it is appropriate, (remember mood matching) be light-hearted and use your sense of humour. Making a young person laugh is much more satisfying than seeing them cry. Use life experiences, especially if a young person is feeling down, or had a sense of failure. I never hold back from relating how many times I have walked into meetings or posh do's with my skirt tucked in my knickers! Or how I slipped in the snow, landing on my butt, to be unceremoniously hauled to my feet by two small boys with a ferret! This type of thing not only makes them laugh at the mental pictures which form, but they also see that this 'perfect' foster carer they see before them can be just as fallible in some ways.

Some children may be ashamed of their families (though they will put them on the highest pedestal) I can't tell you how many 'barriers' I have broken down by telling them the funnier tales about *my own* family. Laugh *with* them not *at* them. Remember the serious incident in the pub that night with Charlotte and her family? It could have been much worse of course. However, some time afterwards, the issue arose in a conversation about drinking alcohol. I looked at charlotte, who was in a good frame of mind, and said "Of course there are sometimes favourable exceptions to the demon drink, if your auntie had been sober that night, she wouldn't have seen three of me and wound up hitting the wrong one!" Charlotte was hysterical – with laughter! Tell them, they can be who they choose to be, *if* they want to!

These tips are a guide only, based on situations I have encountered. Please be flexible and I hope you will gain as much satisfaction as I have, in diffusing difficult moments.

EPILOGUE

The writing of this book seems to have taken forever, and yet has been a relatively easy achievement in as much as I have had no need of great imagination, in order to reveal my story. I have simply needed to draw on life's experiences and tell it 'like it is.' It has been both amusing, and at times devastating, remembering past events, almost like reliving my life all over again. Though strangely enough, it has been therapeutic in many ways too.

I have also learned many lessons along life's road, the hard way. Remember the tale of Snowy the cat, whom, I was told, had fallen into the 'babbling brook' and drowned, then returned home days later? Well, this taught me never to lie to children, they will 'suss' you out in a heartbeat. My very own life has taught me that, not all children in care have come from troubled backgrounds. Dora had a loving family, and a great deal of affection in her young life, but it has to start somewhere. Treat all children with equality. There should be no difference between what we offer our own, and others in our care. This includes love, affection, and inclusion. Children must always come first, and foremost, they must take priority in all things. I have also learned from my family's errors that alcohol doesn't work to change anything. The problem with still be there when one sobers up. Also, loss can take many forms, bereavement, absence of loved ones whom we may never see again, for any reason, be it death, adoption or merely geographical location etc. Never give up on adopted children. Persevere through thick and thin, ultimately to let them know you will *never* forget them, and will always love them. We should never judge people, especially children, totally by their behaviour. There is a distinction between liking them, but perhaps not what they do. Look for positives in a young person; they are there somewhere if we dig deep enough. Above all else, take care of yourself, if you neglect your own well being, you are not in a position to look after others. Operate 'safe-caring' when looking after children, protect yourself from allegations. A good policy is, 'hands off' even clothing, at all times, and walk away. This will help ensure that allegations are scarce – stay safe!

If you have a faith, cling on to it. My many connections with various religions did me no real favours, but that is one thing I can thank Jehovah's Witnesses for, they gave me a true belief in God, and although I am no longer a member of any organised religion, I do still believe that God exists. These days though, I prefer to honour Him in my own way, in the hope that he will judge me on my way of life, or on my deeds, when the time comes.

I hope my life has not only served the children I have known, but that it will now serve any of you out there, who have ever considered fostering *or* adopting. It's truly hard work! But I have yet to try anything which could bring me more reward and satisfaction than this. Happy fostering!

So, beware, when you listen to secrets
and lies,
Please don't be fooled by family
blood ties.
The 'Angels' you love, who are
closest to you,
Will secretly despise, in my
cynical view.
Their subversive desires, their hate
and their scorn,
Will eat at your heart, leave you unsure
and torn.
Don't give of your time, in their trouble
and strife.
It will suck out your energy, you're wasting
your life.
It's hard to distinguish, the day they
are born
If they'll have wings, or sharp
nasty horns.
They're deceitful, and crafty, you really
can't tell,
If they flew down from Heaven,
or rose up from Hell!

One day at a time
This is enough

Do not look back and grieve over the past
For it is gone.

And do not be troubled about the future
For it has not yet come.

Live in the present!
And make it so beautiful it will be worth
remembering!

© Copyright 2008
held by author Sandy Brown
All rights reserved

ALSO AUTHOR Of, A GLASS BOUQUET
and   ICE COLD REVENGE.

Printed in Great Britain
by Amazon